IMPERIAL POLICING

IMPERIAL POLICING

WEAPONIZED DATA IN CARCERAL CHICAGO

The Policing in Chicago Research Group

Andy Clarno, Enrique Alvear Moreno,
Janaé Bonsu-Love, Lydia Dana,
Michael De Anda Muñiz,
Ilā Ravichandran,
and Haley Volpintesta

UNIVERSITY OF MINNESOTA PRESS
Minneapolis
London

Published by the University of Minnesota Press
111 Third Avenue South, Suite 290
Minneapolis, MN 55401-2520
http://www.upress.umn.edu

ISBN 978-1-5179-1770-8 (hc)
ISBN 978-1-5179-1771-5 (pb)

A Cataloging-in-Publication record for this book is available from the Library of Congress.

Printed in the United States of America on acid-free paper

The University of Minnesota is an equal-opportunity educator and employer.

UMP BmB 2024

We dedicate this book to everyone we've lost and to everyone whose love, labor, and joy are leading us to another world.

For Marquise, Devell, Jaquan, Derrick, Taivon, Mike, and Deshawn. You are not forgotten.

En memoria de Celene y para Wilmer. Con la esperanza de que estas páginas contribuyan a hacer justicia.

إلى رسمية. حتى التحرير والعودة

For Rasmea. Until liberation and return.

Contents

Preface

The Policing in Chicago Research Group

The Policing in Chicago Research Group (PCRG) is an activist research collective composed primarily of current and former graduate students at the University of Illinois at Chicago (UIC) whose work is committed to supporting abolitionist movements, transformative justice organizations, and targeted communities. In dialogue with organizations on the front lines of struggles against police repression in Black, Latinx, and Arab/Muslim communities, we conduct research that assists their ongoing campaigns. Taking direction from organizers, we study high-tech surveillance, massive databases, predictive analytics, and data-sharing mechanisms that facilitate coordination between local police, federal immigration authorities, national security agencies, and close allies of the U.S. empire around the world.

Using a combination of interviews, archives, Freedom of Information Act requests, quantitative data analysis, and participatory action research projects with young people at grassroots organizations, we examine the technologies, policies, and practices that policing agencies use to target Black, Latinx, and Arab/Muslim communities. Then, we share our findings with organizers and community members through meetings, teach-ins, and public reports. Our partners draw on this research as they develop and implement campaigns against criminalization, deportation, and surveillance. Overall, our research lays bare the structures of racialized surveillance and provides resources for movements challenging imperial policing. But how did we find each other and create this space? We offer a brief history to contextualize how the PCRG came together and the labor that led to this book.

The idea for the PCRG began with Andy Clarno's aspiration to leverage his institutional position as a tenured professor to build a research collective that would carry out projects in solidarity with social movements. Andy invited Michael De Anda Muñiz, a sociology doctoral candidate at the time, to help train a cohort of graduate students to conduct collaborative and ethical research with grassroots organizations mobilizing for radical change. Andy and Michael had worked together previously and shared a commitment to community-engaged political research.

In fall 2016, we began meeting with three Chicago-based organizations engaged in struggles against police violence and racialized surveillance: Black Youth Project 100 (BYP100), Organized Communities Against Deportations (OCAD), and the Arab American Action Network (AAAN). We chose to start with these organizations because they shared a commitment to abolition and a history of collaborating on campaigns and joint actions. In addition, PCRG members already had connections with these organizations, had worked with them, or were engaged in shared activist networks.

In our initial communications, we shared a short proposal for a research team that would deploy the resources of the university to support social movement campaigns. We asked about their research priorities, their experiences with academics, and their suggestions for how to ensure accountability. The three organizations had similar responses: they were interested in working together but did not want to host a student or facilitate a study of the movement. As one organizer pointed out, "every week, we receive at least one request from an MA student who wants to study our organization." We clarified that we were not interested in studying movements; instead, we wanted to work with movements to study the state. This principle would become the foundation of our countersurveillant abolitionist methodology. Organizers discussed the issues that were most pressing in their communities and agreed to take our proposal back to their membership. After further consultation, all three organizations agreed to work with the PCRG.

In January 2017, we launched the PCRG by organizing a public teach-in on policing in Chicago. Representatives from BYP100, OCAD, and the AAAN shared knowledge about existing police strategies, possibilities for resistance, and new threats represented by the Trump regime. They emphasized connections between the strategies used by local and federal agencies to police communities of color and called for solidarity in the struggle against racist policing. The teach-in launched a dialogue between the research team and our partners. We soon agreed to focus on two projects. With BYP100 and OCAD, the PCRG would examine the ways that *gang databases and predictive algorithms* are used by the Chicago Police Department (CPD) and Immigration and Customs Enforcement (ICE) as pipelines to prison and deportation. With the AAAN, we would research the role of *fusion centers and suspicious activity reports* as mechanisms for the surveillance of Arab and Muslim communities by the CPD and the Federal Bureau of Investigation (FBI). These projects fundamentally shaped the arguments we present in this book.

In spring and fall 2017, a two-semester graduate seminar in UIC's sociology department served as a home for the PCRG. The seminars attracted students interested in producing activist research in dialogue with community-based partners. This provided a space to train students in research methods and ethics; develop research projects; collect data; and prepare research articles, public reports, and teach-ins. The students who brought their experiences, skills, and knowledge to these seminars shaped the foundation of the PCRG. Throughout the year, we met with organizers to discuss emerging findings and determine future directions.

In November 2017, the research team shared our initial findings at three public events. First, BYP100 and OCAD teamed up with Critical Resistance to organize a teach-in on the gang database. The PCRG presented our findings and shared a draft of our first report, later published as *Tracked and Targeted: Early Findings on Chicago's Gang Database.* Second, we shared our research about fusion centers with the Youth Organizing Program of the AAAN. A few weeks later, the youth organized a town hall meeting where they presented these findings to a broader public. Finally, we were invited to discuss our findings on the gang database at Circles & Ciphers, a youth-led organization that uses transformative justice and hip-hop arts and culture to engage young people directly impacted by criminalization. During a community circle, we discussed our research on data-based policing while the young people shared their experiences with surveillance, harassment, and police violence.

In January 2018, the PCRG transitioned from a formal research practicum to a more dispersed research collective. This allowed us to continue growing in scope and impact. Research and reporting on gang databases became a key focus because of the rapid progress of political organizing by BYP100, OCAD, and their partners in the Chicago Campaign to Erase the Database (#EraseTheDatabase). In addition, young people involved with Circles & Ciphers and the Youth Organizing Project at the AAAN invited the PCRG to support their respective youth-led participatory action research projects. We provided training in research methods and guidance as the youth developed projects to explore strategies used by local and federal law enforcement agencies to surveil people of color in the Chicago area. As our work develops in new directions, the PCRG remains a dynamic collective. A core of active and committed members is involved in multiple projects that are relatively dispersed while remaining focused on policing in Chicago. We have collectively nurtured the PCRG into something that exceeds what any one team member could have imagined.

While producing research for our partners, PCRG members also began sharing our work at academic conferences, panels, and colloquiums around the United States. We had the privilege to meet community members, activists, and scholars who found our work useful, wanted to know more, were passionate about movement-aligned research, and shared many of the values at the foundation of the PCRG. In summer 2018, Andy proposed that we collectively write a book so that our work could reach a larger audience. Since then, the PCRG has met regularly to produce this book as we continue our research with community partners. In our meetings, we workshopped and discussed writing, theory, research findings, authorship, and organization. Writing a book is already a difficult endeavor, but the Covid-19 pandemic, graduations, new jobs, and relocations made it even more challenging. Yet we remained committed to this book and the impact we hope it will have.

Imperial Policing is a collectively authored project of the Policing in Chicago Research Group. It documents the analysis of data-based policing, criminalization, and surveillance that we have developed alongside our movement partners. The book highlights the codification of criminal archetypes, the maintenance of permanent records, and the role of data

sharing in facilitating interagency collaboration. It also addresses abolitionist efforts to counteract criminalizing surveillance. Since 2017, many
individuals have contributed to research projects, data collection and
analysis, and team discussions that indelibly impacted the PCRG and
this book. We are profoundly grateful for all of their work.

Introduction

Imperial Policing in Carceral Chicago

Listening to news stories or politicians talking about Chicago is a dizzying experience. On one hand, local elites and city boosters celebrate Chicago as a "global city," one of the most important hubs of commercial and financial activity in the globalizing world of the early twenty-first century.[1] They highlight the many corporate headquarters located in the city, the high-end shopping along the Magnificent Mile, the beautiful lakefront, the sports teams and museums, the cultural diversity, and the endless amenities for upscale urban living. On the other hand, Chicago has a notorious reputation as a violent, chaotic, crime-ridden "hellhole" where no one is safe from gunshots and gang wars.[2] For many politicians and people across the country, Chicago represents the failures of "soft-on-crime" and "sanctuary city" policies.

What these seemingly incompatible narratives obscure are the *connections* between the glittery global aspirations of the elite and the daily lives and struggles of the Black, Indigenous, immigrant, diasporic, and working-class communities that call Chicago home. Our book focuses on one of the most important connections: the role of local law enforcement, federal immigration authorities, and national security agencies in upholding a highly unequal social order. Chicago is certainly not "soft" on crime. On the contrary, policing in Chicago is expansive and aggressive. With extreme inequality and concentrations of racialized poverty, Chicago relies on an extensive network of repressive agencies to police the poor, enforce order, and suppress struggles for social justice. Rather than a purely local affair, however, policing in Chicago is part of a multiscalar project that stretches across the country and around the world. We define this project as *imperial policing*.

1

In summer 2016, local organizers cast a bright, abolitionist light on imperial policing when the #LetUsBreathe Collective launched Freedom Square, a forty-one-day protest camp outside of the Chicago Police Department's (CPD) secretive Homan Square facility on Chicago's West Side. For Black residents, Homan Square had a long-standing reputation for police torture. But the 2012 North Atlantic Treaty Organization Summit in Chicago helped expose the CPD's use of "black site" tactics similar to those of the Central Intelligence Agency (CIA) when several white protesters were taken to Homan Square, shackled for hours, and denied access to lawyers while CPD officials claimed no record of their arrest.[3]

The #LetUsBreathe Collective, a Black-led alliance of artists and organizers, initiated the Freedom Square encampment to demand the closure of Homan Square and the redirection of resources from police to communities. Highlighting the connections between policing, war, and empire, organizers drew attention to tanks and other military equipment coming in and out of Homan Square as well as the presence of the Federal Bureau of Investigation (FBI) and other national agencies. They began referring to police as a "domestic military."[4] As part of the protest against imperial policing, the encampment also provided resources that actually keep communities safe, including housing, food, books, clothing, health care, and education. With support and affirmation from comrades throughout the city and around the world, Freedom Square actively rehearsed living in a world without police.

Taking inspiration from their brilliance, *Imperial Policing* analyzes the structures and practices of imperial policing in Chicago today, with a focus on carceral webs and the weaponization of data. In this introduction, we provide a genealogy of imperial policing and discuss the impacts of neoliberal restructuring on Chicago. Next, we develop the concept of imperial policing by describing the three police wars—on crime, terror, and immigrants—that are pillars of imperial policing in Chicago today. Each of these police wars is grounded in a particular racial archetype, involves a localized combination of carceral agencies, and is part of a broader carceral web that spans the globe. As we explain in the next chapter, the rise of big data provides a key weapon of imperial policing in the twenty-first century. The rest of *Imperial Policing* explores the dynamics of each

FIGURE 1. Freedom Square was a forty-one-day "community laboratory for police abolition" built on reciprocity, restorative justice, and community care and love (https://www.letusbreathecollective.com/). Photograph by and courtesy of Sarah Jane Rhee (@loveandstrugglephotos).

police war, with attention to the role of data and technology, to excavate the ties that connect local networks to a global web of imperial policing.

FOUNDATIONS OF POLICING IN CHICAGO

We begin our exploration of imperial policing in twenty-first-century Chicago with a brief history to demonstrate that contemporary policing has deep roots. While big databases, surveillance technology, and military weaponry stand out as the latest advances in policing, they largely reinforce two dynamics that are central to our analysis and can be traced back to the early history of Chicago. First, systems of policing were developed to support settler colonialism, racial capitalism, white supremacy, and empire. Second, policing was never just the work of the local police.

Settler colonialism refers to processes through which a settler population establishes and institutionalizes its domination over Indigenous land and people through dispossession, elimination, and subjugation.[5] *Racial capitalism* is a term we use to emphasize that capital accumulation operates through racialized forms of dispossession, exploitation, and exclusion. In other words, capitalism cannot be understood without attention to processes of racial formation that define categories of difference on the basis of phenotype, religion, culture, and nationality; assign differential value to human lives and labor; and create unequal vulnerability to premature death.[6] *White supremacy* is the dominant racial project behind modern racial formations, including efforts to exploit, assimilate, exclude, and eliminate Black people, Indigenous people, and other people of color.[7] And *empire* refers to transnational political formations that exercise power over racially devalued populations through territorial conquest, political domination, cultural imposition, labor exploitation, and resource extraction.[8] These forms of power are deeply intertwined, and they all operate through heteronormative patriarchal gender and sexual relations.[9] These are the foundations of policing in Chicago.

Built on the traditional unceded homelands of the Council of Three Fires, the colony that became Chicago developed around Fort Dearborn, a U.S. Army base established in 1803 to secure the mouth of the Chicago River and its environs for white merchants and settlers. As the first police force in what became Chicago, the U.S. Army enabled the growth of the colonial settlement by policing and displacing Indigenous populations. Operating from Fort Dearborn and other outposts, the army compelled the Ojibwe, Odawa, Potawatomi, Miami, Ho-Chunk, Menominee, Sac, and Fox nations to give up their lands and move west of the Mississippi River. In 1832, the army massacred the last remaining band of Sac and Fox rebels—led by Black Hawk—who refused to cede their lands near what are today the Quad Cities.[10] A year later, the Treaty of Chicago sanctioned the final removal of all Indigenous peoples from the region. After securing white domination, the settlers around Fort Dearborn incorporated the City of Chicago in 1837.[11] The land that was violently taken from Native Americans soon became the private property of white settlers, demonstrating the intimacy between settler colonialism, racial capitalism, and imperial expansion.

By the 1850s, Chicago had become a hub of commerce and industry. A small class of Anglo-Saxon industrialists dominated business and politics, whereas the rapidly growing working class was composed primarily of German and Irish immigrants. Although legally recognized as white, and therefore eligible for citizenship, German and Irish immigrants—especially Catholics and Jews—were popularly considered racially inferior. Because immigrant workers formed the core of Chicago's vibrant nineteenth-century socialist and anarchist movements, efforts to suppress working-class radicalism were linked from the start with xenophobia.[12] The Pinkerton Detective Agency was established in Chicago in 1850 to provide business owners with a private-sector armed force to investigate property crimes and break strikes.[13] Three years later, local elites created the CPD to protect private property, suppress worker militancy, and discipline immigrant (especially Irish) neighborhoods that they considered "disorderly."[14] In 1886, after a bomb exploded during a worker rally at Haymarket Square, the CPD repressed immigrant-led anarchist movements in a crackdown that historian Sam Mitrani describes as the "first red squad in American history."[15] Impressed with the ability of Chicago's police to protect their interests, local elites paid for increases in the police budget. As the police force grew, it became a pathway to assimilation and upward mobility for German, Irish, and other European immigrant workers.[16] But the Chicago police retained its focus on suppressing radicalism among working-class immigrants.

The Great Migration, which brought nearly five hundred thousand Black Americans to Chicago, provided a new target for police action and enabled European immigrants to assert their whiteness by embracing and enforcing anti-Black racism.[17] Recently emancipated Black residents and their descendants faced employment discrimination, housing segregation, mob violence, and a combination of abuse and neglect by the Chicago police. Politicians, police, and the Mafia conspired to concentrate illicit drugs, alcohol, and sex in segregated Black neighborhoods on Chicago's South Side. Chicago police also aggressively targeted spaces of interracial mixing and subjected Black residents to disproportionate arrests, abuse, and death.[18] The systemic anti-Blackness of the Chicago police became clear during the 1919 riots, when police refused to arrest the white man who murdered a Black teenager on the 29th Street beach, failed to protect Black residents from white mobs, and arrested twice as many Black people as white people even though twice as many Black people were injured and killed. As historian Simon Balto documents, "black communities increasingly became both overpatrolled and underprotected, and faced harassment, violence, and neglect from the police department that their taxes helped fund."[19]

Along with the criminalization of Blackness and the regulation of immigrant workers, the suppression of struggles against racism, capitalism, colonialism, and empire has remained a priority of the CPD, along with state and federal law enforcement agencies. Among the more notorious examples of political repression are the CPD assault on antiwar activists during the 1968 Democratic National Convention and the joint FBI–CPD assassination of Black Panther Party chairman Fred Hampton in 1969. Indeed, Black political communities have been a primary target of police repression due to their historical involvement with civil rights, Black Power, and Communist movements and support for liberation struggles around the world. And the CPD and FBI have consistently targeted Chicago's diasporic communities—from Puerto Rico, Palestine, and beyond—for linking struggles for social justice in Chicago with demands for an end to imperialism, colonialism, and capitalism in their homelands. Police repression has most aggressively targeted efforts to build multiracial coalitions, transnational connections, or links between political movements and disenfranchised youth in Chicago.

Importantly, policing in Chicago has never been the work only of the local police department. Despite menacing threats by Donald Trump to "send in the feds," federal agencies have operated in the city since Chicago was a small colonial outpost. After the Haymarket uprising, wealthy residents purchased land in the northern suburbs so the U.S. Army could build a base—Fort Sheridan—for rapid deployment during future urban rebellions. Eight years later, the army sent troops from Fort Sheridan to occupy Chicago during the Pullman strike.[20] On New Year's Day 1920, Chicago police arrested 150 suspected radicals as part of the nationwide Palmer Raids led by the U.S. Department of Justice. In the 1930s, U.S. Treasury Department agents led by Eliot Ness worked with Chicago police to take down Al Capone. In 1954, the U.S. Immigration and Naturalization Service (INS) carried out a mass expulsion of Mexican immigrants living in Chicago as part of a nationwide sweep called Operation Wetback.[21] During the 1960s and 1970s, FBI COINTELPRO agents worked with the CPD Red Squad to disrupt Black, Puerto Rican, Palestinian, Indigenous, Communist, anti-imperialist, and antiwar movements.[22] In the 1970s and 1980s, CPD commander Jon Burge brought interrogation techniques to Chicago that he learned as a soldier with the U.S. Army in Vietnam. He and his "midnight crew" used these techniques to torture hundreds of Black Chicago residents into false confessions.[23] And throughout the twentieth century, the federal government actively used immigration agencies to target political radicals for deportation.

Moreover, private-sector forces played a role in policing Chicago. As described, the Pinkertons preceded the CPD. In the 1920s, Chicago elites created the Chicago Crime Commission to promote punitive, tough-on-crime policies—a role it still plays today.[24] Starting in the 1980s, the Chicago Alliance for Neighborhood Safety laid the foundations for both computerized crime mapping and community policing.[25] And, as we discuss throughout the book, private corporations, such as Oracle, ShotSpotter, LexisNexis, and Geofeedia, profit from police technology while academics, philanthropists, professionals, nonprofits, and residents participate in the carceral webs of empire.

Policing in Chicago today remains grounded in the logics of settler colonialism, racial capitalism, white supremacy, and empire. And it still operates through combinations of local, federal, and private-sector agencies that operate at a range of scales, from the local to the global. But two processes have come together to reshape imperial policing in the early twenty-first century: (1) neoliberal restructuring has generated vast inequality and racialized poverty, along with a proliferation of carceral agencies that carry out joint projects designed to protect the powerful by policing the racialized poor, and (2) the rapid expansion and weaponization of surveillance technology, databases, data analysis, and data sharing has facilitated coordination between agencies. We focus on the first process in this chapter and on the second in the next.

NEOLIBERAL APARTHEID CITY

Chicago has an almost equal distribution of white (33 percent), Black (29 percent), and Latinx (28.8 percent) residents, along with rapidly growing Asian American and Arab American populations and the third largest urban Native American population in the United States.[26] Despite demographic diversity, Chicago remains a highly segregated city, with stark disparities between wealthy white communities concentrated on the North Side lakefront and working-class Black and Latinx communities located primarily on the South and West Sides.[27] Long-standing racialized class divisions have been amplified by neoliberal restructuring.

In the New Deal era, labor unions and government policies created opportunities for working-class communities in Chicago. While industrial unions fought for better pay and working conditions, the state supported the working class through investments in employment, housing, transportation, education, health care, and recreation. Yet these policies did not benefit all working people equally. White supremacy ensured that the benefits were unevenly distributed along racial lines. Skilled trade unions excluded Black workers; federal legislation prevented domestic and agricultural workers from unionizing; red lining, restrictive covenants, and white mob violence contained Black and Latinx residents in strictly segregated ghettos. Black workers benefited from public employment, public housing, public transportation, and public education but were systematically excluded from other opportunities. Federal subsidies for higher education and home loans, for instance, helped Italian, Jewish, Polish, Russian, and other European immigrants move from blue-collar to white-collar work and from ethnic enclaves to middle-class suburbs,[28] but Black Americans faced educational and occupational barriers, segregated neighborhoods, and other exclusionary policies that limited their residential mobility, professional advancement, and share of government investments.

By the 1960s, automation and deindustrialization were wreaking havoc on Chicago's Black and Latinx working class, as well as on Native Americans, who began returning to Chicago after the U.S. government decided to terminate Indigenous sovereignty and disperse reservation communities.[29] Meanwhile, suburbanization and reactionary white politics gutted the city's budget and initiated a sustained process of disinvestment from public housing and public education. Despite efforts to "professionalize" the CPD during the 1960s, Chicago police continued to treat working-class Black neighborhoods as "occupied territory."[30]

In response, Black, Indigenous, diasporic, and working-class communities across Chicago launched waves of resistance, including the 1963 public school boycotts; Dr. Martin Luther King Jr.'s movement for housing justice; the Puerto Rican–led Division Street uprising in Humboldt Park and West Town; a rebellion on the West Side after King's assassination; revolutionary mobilizations by the Black Panther Party, the Brown Berets, and the Young Lords; American Indian land occupations near Wrigley Field and Belmont Harbor; mass mobilizations against U.S. imperial warfare in Vietnam; and struggles against colonial domination in Puerto Rico and Palestine.

Chicago's political and economic elites responded to these rebellions with a two-pronged strategy. In the short term, the CPD brutally repressed movements for liberation. National audiences were shocked by the violence that the CPD used against antiwar protesters during the 1968 Democratic National Convention, but this paled in comparison to the deadly violence unleashed against Black residents during the West Side rebellion earlier that year, when mayor Richard J. Daley issued a shoot-to-kill order for people suspected of starting fires and a shoot-to-maim order for people suspected of looting.[31] The Chicago chapter of the Black Panther Party became a primary target of police repression in the late 1960s and early 1970s because they mobilized Black residents through free breakfast programs, health clinics, and educational initiatives; built a revolutionary Rainbow Coalition with Puerto Rican and white youth; deepened ties with street gangs, such as the Blackstone Rangers, in the hope of politicizing marginalized Black youth; and embraced an internationalist critique of imperialism and racial capitalism.[32] This repression culminated in a conspiracy between the FBI, the CPD, and the Cook County state's attorney to assassinate Fred Hampton.[33]

At the same time, elites began developing long-term plans to restructure Chicago's economy to attract corporate investment while "reclaiming" the city for white professionals, along with wealthy immigrants and the nascent Black and Latinx middle class.[34] Embracing a vision of Chicago as a "global city," an alliance of economic and political elites transformed downtown into a hub of corporate, finance, and real estate capital. Business-friendly neoliberal policies that combine subsidies for corporations and elites with austerity for the working class have transformed Chicago into a deeply divided and unequal *neoliberal apartheid city* marked by extreme inequality, racialized poverty, and militarized policing.[35] Celebratory narratives by city boosters obscure the racialized exploitation and dispossession that generate the city's wealth and power. The neoliberalization of racial capitalism has concentrated wealth in the hands of billionaire capitalists while exposing the racialized poor to intense forms of exploitation, abandonment, and death.

Chicago-based multinational corporations rely on the political, economic, and military might of the U.S. empire to maintain their position as global leaders in military (Boeing), agriculture (Archer Daniels Midland, Conagra), food (McDonald's, Mondelez, Kraft Heinz), pharmaceutical (Abbott Laboratories), technology (Motorola), transportation (United Airlines), and other (Caterpillar, Allstate, Sears, etc.) sectors.[36] Chicago has experienced a real estate boom, extensive gentrification, and the development of privatized commercial and leisure spaces for tourists and professionals. The city relies on highly speculative forms of debt financing to support the real estate boom and the development of amenities for the elite, including notorious tax increment financing districts that have transferred billions of dollars from schools, libraries, and public services to corporate capitalists and real estate magnates.[37]

Chicago elites like to portray neoliberal restructuring as a "colorblind" project that leaves behind the history of racial exclusion in the city. They highlight the emergence of Black, Latinx, and immigrant elites and professionals. While creating openings for some members of historically oppressed populations to claim middle-class respectability, neoliberalism has intensified the vulnerability of the racialized poor in Chicago and beyond.[38] The elimination of stable jobs, union wages, public housing, public education, mental health care, and other social services has deepened the crises facing Chicago's Black, Latinx, and diasporic working-class communities. At the same time, neoliberal restructuring and U.S. imperial interventions abroad have displaced millions of people, bringing new diasporic communities to Chicago from across the Global South.[39] Yet the state uses the expansion of Black, Latinx, Indigenous, and immigrant middle classes to claim that race no longer matters and that poor and working-class communities are now responsible for their own marginalization.

Chicago has witnessed an evisceration of blue-collar jobs and a decline of real wages and union membership due to outsourcing, automation, and deindustrialization.[40] Service work has largely replaced industrial employment, and many of the remaining factories now use temp agencies. As a result, working-class jobs in Chicago are increasingly low wage, temporary, and nonunionized. The dynamics of exploitation and disposability are heavily racialized, with Latinx immigrants (especially the undocumented) targeted for contingent, low-wage jobs and Black workers increasingly abandoned by employers.[41] Many families rely on a constant, creative hustle that requires multiple formal and informal sector jobs to survive. Indeed, the informal economy has become a refuge for tens of thousands of people—especially in Black and Latinx communities—cut off from formal economic opportunities in neoliberal Chicago.[42]

Along with the Loop, the North Side lakefront became an early target for gentrification. But pockets of poverty and multiracial working-class communities still exist on the North Side, in places like Rogers Park, Uptown, and Albany Park. Over time, the frontiers of gentrification have moved west and south, with upscale housing, high-end shopping districts, and privatized leisure activities displacing working-class communities and people of color from Wicker Park, Logan Square, the South Loop, Bronzeville, Pilsen, Hyde Park, Humboldt Park, and other neighborhoods.[43] Like elsewhere, gentrification in Chicago is driven by demands for capital accumulation and the racialized desire to "reclaim" parts of the city that white residents and investors had previously abandoned.[44] The last twenty years have witnessed the systematic elimination of public housing from Chicago. The city allowed its public housing stock to deteriorate for decades, creating dangerous conditions for residents who nevertheless built communities and networks of support. Disinvestment and deterioration laid the groundwork for the neoliberal Plan for Transformation, a $1.6 billion project to replace concentrations of public housing with mixed-income projects developed by the private sector. Since the late 1990s, the city has demolished tens of thousands of public housing units, built thousands of market-rate condos and townhouses, and distributed a small number of Section 8 housing vouchers.[45] The Plan for Transformation has eliminated affordable housing, displaced working-class residents, destroyed communities, disrupted support networks, and intensified vulnerabilities for those forced to relocate, while accelerating gentrification and redistributing amenities to affluent residents.

Much like public housing, the Chicago public school system has suffered decades of neglect and disinvestment. Deterioration set the stage for Renaissance 2010, a neoliberal plan to close public schools and replace them with charter, magnet, and selective-enrollment schools. Driven by the neoliberal embrace of "school choice" and demands from wealthy families, Renaissance 2010 has increased the vulnerability of children forced to attend schools in other neighborhoods while intensifying apartheid divisions between neighborhood schools and selective-enrollment schools, public schools and private or charter schools, and urban and suburban school districts.[46] Along with school closures and privatization, neoliberal education in Chicago has led to an increased emphasis on standardized tests, school accountability, and police surveillance. As Pauline Lipman explains, the overall goal is to produce dispositions required by the shift from a manufacturing to a service economy.[47]

In addition, neoliberal restructuring has generated deep cuts to welfare and social services. The 1996 Personal Responsibility and Work Opportunity Reconciliation Act, better known as welfare reform, placed strict limitations on eligibility for welfare, including time limits, work requirements, and a lifetime ban for people convicted of drug offenses.[48] All of these provisions were designed to force working-class people, especially women of color, to rely on low-wage work to survive. Other cuts, such as mayor Rahm Emanuel's decision to close half of the mental health clinics and scores of public schools in Chicago, are justified as cost-cutting measures in a context of austerity.

At the same time, neoliberal restructuring imposed on countries across the world has devastated poor and working-class communities, especially in the Global South. With their livelihoods destroyed, millions of people have sought opportunities in the megacities of the Global South, borderland industrial zones, or advanced capitalist countries in Europe and North America.[49] These migrants are accompanied by millions of people forcibly displaced by imperial warfare, climate catastrophes, resource wars, and land grabs driven by corporate greed. Together, they form the diasporas of empire that confront border walls, cages, surveillance, and policing.[50] The U.S. immigration system is bifurcated, providing visas and pathways to citizenship for elites and professionals but not for working-class people (with the partial exception of asylum seekers and refugees). As a result, most working-class migrants live under the constant threat of deportation—even in cities, like Chicago, that claim to provide "sanctuary" for the undocumented. These diasporic communities make up a growing percentage of Chicago's working class.

In short, neoliberalism, white supremacy, and U.S. imperialism have generated vast wealth for elites while intensifying the suffering of Black and brown working-class and diasporic communities in Chicago. This has generated deep crises for the racialized, working-class populations whose lives have been devalued by white supremacy, upended by austerity, and rendered disposable by automation and outsourcing.

Chicago's multiracial working class has boldly resisted neoliberal apartheid, working to reduce material harm to communities while raising fundamental questions about the oppressive, unjust, and unsustainable social order. Antigentrification and tenants' rights organizers won moratoriums on evictions and demolitions, curtailing the power of slumlords and developers to displace unhoused people or those vulnerable to gentrification. Mutual aid groups organized neighborhoods and redistributed food and clothing to members of their communities. Parents and teachers held successful sit-ins and hunger strikes to protect libraries, prevent school closures, and even open new schools in low-income neighborhoods. Indigenous and Black people reclaimed plots of land for housing, food, and self-sovereign developments. Latinx, Indigenous, and Black youth removed a toxic coal plant on the Southwest Side and a statue of Christopher Columbus from Grant Park. Queer and trans BIPOC people organized safe spaces and trained community members as emergency street medics. The Chicago Teachers Union has stood on the front lines of local and national struggles over quality public education by bargaining for the common good. And a growing number of socialist and progressive city councillors and representatives are challenging the Democratic establishment on behalf of working-class communities and grassroots movements.

All neoliberal apartheid regimes rely on policing and surveillance to contain crises and struggles.[51] While cutting funds for social services, these regimes expand funding for prisons and police, border security and immigration enforcement, homeland security, and imperial warfare. As Stephen Dillon demonstrates, neoliberal economists and law-and-order politicians recognized that the "free market" required the heavy hand of state repression to enforce wage discipline, suppress resistance, and redistribute resources from the working class to the elite.[52] In the words of Ruth Wilson Gilmore, "what holds together the possibility of mass incarceration in the richest country in the history of the world is a combination of *organized abandonment,* which is to say austerity, and *organized violence,* which is to say criminalization, policing, prisons, detention, deportation."[53]

Chicago is no different. Neoliberal restructuring has intensified the crises facing Chicago's Black, Indigenous, immigrant, diasporic, and working-class communities and led to a surge of struggles demanding fundamental social transformation. To contain these crises and struggles, Chicago has expanded its carceral apparatuses. This is key to understanding policing in twenty-first-century Chicago. With an ever-growing budget ($1.9 billion, or 40 percent of the city's budget in 2022), the CPD employs more than thirteen thousand police officers and adopts the latest technology and equipment. The local police work with state and federal agencies, as well as private-sector corporations and community organizations, to police imperial Chicago.

WEBS OF IMPERIAL POLICING

Dozens of law enforcement agencies operate in Chicago today: the CPD, the Cook County Sheriff's Office, the Illinois State Police, the FBI, and the U.S. Department of Homeland Security (DHS), to name just a few. These agencies have similar yet distinct missions and overlapping jurisdictions. In addition, a wide range of public- and private-sector organizations participate in policing and punishing people in Chicago. Critics of the carceral state have drawn attention to these criminalizing webs, which extend beyond the police to include schools, social workers, mental health professionals, probation officers, private security companies, child welfare agencies, and even violence-prevention programs.[54]

In describing these structures as *webs of imperial policing*, we are emphasizing four points about carceral power. First, we are suggesting that to understand policing in Chicago, it is necessary to recognize that the United States is an empire state.[55] The use of violence to police Black, Indigenous, diasporic, and working-class communities is inseparable from the long history of slavery, conquest, and warfare through which the United States became a settler-colonial, racial capitalist empire state. Understanding the United States as an empire state helps draw attention to the links between police and military operations targeting racialized communities in U.S. cities, borderlands, colonies, and the furthest reaches of empire. Whereas some carceral agencies have a primarily local focus, others operate on a state, regional, federal, or global scale. These agencies deploy distinct but related strategies to rule different populations and territories.[56] In Chicago, law enforcement agencies operate differently, depending on the race and class composition of the neighborhoods and the legal status of the populations they police. In what follows, we describe three distinct yet interconnected strategies that we call *police wars*.

Second, we are pointing to the global reach of criminalizing webs. The federal agencies that operate in Chicago—such as the FBI, the DHS, and the State Department—also operate worldwide to uphold U.S. corporate interests and imperial power. And these agencies work closely with military, intelligence, and police forces of other countries, especially those that embrace (or have been compelled into) alignment with the U.S. empire.

Personnel, knowledge, technology, and discourses circulate through these webs, linking carceral projects across time and space.[57]

Third, policing in Chicago is organized to address not only the effects of neoliberal racial capitalism in the city itself but also the role of the U.S. empire in upholding repressive regimes and enforcing an exploitative and socially, economically, and environmentally destructive racial capitalist system around the world. Indeed, the primary targets of policing in Chicago today are Black and diasporic working-class communities devastated and displaced by neoliberal racial capitalism, many of whom are invested in liberation struggles that link Chicago to the rest of the world.[58]

Finally, the language of empire serves as a reminder that policing is both a state project and a racial capitalist accumulation strategy. Corporations involved with the prison– and military–industrial complexes, as well as the homeland security and private security markets, reap billions of dollars in profits each year from surveillance and securitization, incarceration and deportation, policing and warfare.[59] More broadly, carceral efforts to repress and discipline the populations that W. E. B. Du Bois called the "dark proletariat" are foundational strategies of capital accumulation throughout the world.[60]

The carceral structure of the U.S. empire state is unified but differentiated; it is composed of a vast array of repressive and disciplinary agencies articulated together as a complex unity.[61] The complex formations constituted by these links are what we call the *webs of imperial policing*. State and private-sector agencies are linked together in concrete local formations that take the form of hierarchically structured networks. Whereas some agencies have an exclusively local jurisdiction, others have a global reach. The local networks, therefore, are constitutive segments of carceral webs that encircle the globe.

To be sure, coordination within these webs is not always easy. The networks are hierarchically organized, creating struggles over power, recognition, and information. Different agencies claim primary jurisdiction over issues like street crime or immigration violations but cannot always convince or compel other agencies to provide support. Although federal agencies expect local police to share intelligence and provide backup, they do not necessarily reciprocate. Similarly, U.S. agencies operate in a highly unequal global system, requiring partners to cooperate but only selectively providing support in return. In addition, the priorities and policies of carceral agencies do not always align. And there are recurrent tensions between those calling for centralization and others demanding decentralization of decision-making power. As a result, imperial policing is riven with hierarchies, contradictions, tensions, and possibilities for rupture that social movements can exploit.

Throughout the twentieth century, the U.S. empire state experimented with strategies to overcome these tensions. During the height of the Cold War, the Office of Public Safety—part of the U.S. Agency for International Development—provided funding and counterinsurgency training to police departments around the world in an effort to coordinate campaigns against communism.[62] In the 1970s, Richard Nixon established the Cabinet Committee to Combat Terrorism, which encouraged coordination between the FBI, INS, the CIA, and the State Department to target Arab students in the United States and movements supporting Palestine liberation.[63] Interagency task forces are perhaps the most common model of coordination. In the 1980s, the FBI began partnering with local police departments to create Joint Terrorism Task Forces, whose first targets were political leftists and antiwar militants, such as the Weather Underground.[64]

Over the last twenty years, a new approach to coordination has risen to prominence. It involves a proliferation of carceral agents linked together in decentralized but coordinated networks. We use the term *dif/fusion* to describe this model of articulation; it is the dominant model of imperial policing in the early twenty-first century. The term highlights the proliferation of carceral agencies (diffusion) as well as the mechanisms that enable coordination (fusion). Data sharing—also known as data fusion—has become a particularly important mechanism for coordination within the decentralized networks. Indeed, the weaponization of data is key to understanding imperial policing today.[65] We explore the weaponization of data in chapter 1 and develop the concept of dif/fusion in chapter 4.

Networks of state and private security agencies crisscross the globe and congeal in context-specific formations at a range of geographic scales. They operate locally through multiple police wars that are grounded in racialized archetypes, incorporate a range of overtly violent and carceral liberal strategies, and increasingly rely on data as both weapons of war and mechanisms of coordination. The result is a swarm of carceral agencies and an expanding spiral of surveillance.

Three Police Wars

The agencies that police Chicago wage simultaneous and interconnected police wars designed to protect the powerful by containing the racialized poor and suppressing struggles for justice. We focus on three police wars, each of which is a pillar of imperial policing in twenty-first-century Chicago: the War on Crime, the War on Terror, and the War on Immigrants.[66] Distinct combinations of agencies carry out each war, generating context-specific formations focused on crime, terror, and immigration. Yet there is also considerable similarity and deep connections between these formations. The similarity is grounded in overlapping missions, training, equipment, and discourses. The connections are vast. Many agencies— including the CPD, the FBI, and the DHS—participate in multiple wars. Some have deep connections with people and institutions at the hyperlocal level; some have a global reach and ties to agencies in other countries.

The density of carceral webs is highly uneven. Each police war targets particular people and neighborhoods with more intensity. Some neighborhoods are densely surveilled as part of one war, others as part of another war, others as part of multiple wars. As a result, the carceral webs are layered and overlapping.

As the primary police war in Chicago, the *War on Crime*[67] has by far the thickest carceral webs—with coordinated deployments by local police, federal agencies, community organizations, and active residents, all supported by an arsenal of high-tech surveillance equipment. Nationally, the War on Crime has expanded criminalization and punishment by extending the definition of "illegality" to activities not previously considered criminal (such as loitering, panhandling, and street art) and intensifying the punishment of minor offenses (such as sex work, drug possession, and street vending). Life outside of white, middle-class normativity has also been criminalized, including working-class queer and trans BIPOC people as well as heterosexual working-class people of color whose lives do not meet idealized standards of monogamous, heteropatriarchal, nuclear families.[68] Certain behaviors or styles are also rendered deviant by the

FIGURE 2. On October 9, 2016, a multiracial coalition of organizers disrupted the beginning of the Illinois Tactical Officer's Association Conference in Chicago. Photograph by and courtesy of Sarah Jane Rhee (@loveandstrugglephotos).

War on Crime, such as the clothes, speech, and bodily comportment of young Black and brown people.[69]

In Chicago, the front line of the War on Crime is the *War on Gangs*. The War on Gangs is a strategy deployed to criminalize and contain a racialized surplus population—particularly young Black men, but also Latinx men as well as women, girls, and femmes of color—living in neighborhoods shaped by decades of racialized disinvestment and confronting a lifetime of unemployment, economic insecurity, and dehumanization due to white supremacy and neoliberal racial capitalism. Rather than addressing the root causes of community violence, the state relies on policing to contain and punish the racialized poor. Almost every police strategy, tactic, and operation in Chicago is justified in the name of combating gang violence, including stop-and-frisk, electronic surveillance, beatdowns, false confessions, torture, and murder.

While the CPD takes the lead in the War on Gangs, federal agencies, such as the FBI, the Drug Enforcement Agency, the Bureau of Alcohol, Tobacco, Firearms and Explosives (ATF), and U.S. Immigration and Customs Enforcement (ICE), also target alleged gang members in the city. Federal agencies approach the War on Gangs as a transnational project that includes militarizing the border, deporting alleged gang members, and working with partners in the Global South to confront cartels, destroy crops, and surveil alleged gang members who have been deported from the United States.[70] In Chicago, local and federal agencies rely on an ever-expanding arsenal of advanced surveillance technology to police poor Black and Latinx neighborhoods: more than fifty thousand surveillance cameras, along with ShotSpotter audio detection devices, automatic license plate readers, Stingray cell-site simulator devices, and social media monitoring software, as well as predictive algorithms, social network analysis, and other advanced techniques of data analysis. The War on Gangs is geographically uneven, with the highest concentration of surveillance on the South and West Sides of Chicago and in pockets of working-class communities of color on the North and Northwest Sides. This demonstrates the centrality of anti-Blackness to the most important police war in the city. Chapters 2 and 3 present our analysis of the War on Gangs.

The *War on Terror* has intensified the surveillance of Arab and Muslim communities throughout the world, including in Chicago. The U.S.-led War on Terror is designed to uphold U.S. empire and Israeli apartheid by containing resistant populations devastated and displaced by settler colonialism, neoliberal restructuring, climate catastrophe, and U.S. support for repressive regimes in the Middle East, North Africa, and Central and South Asia.[71] Strategies in the War on Terror include military invasions, drone wars, extraordinary renditions, counterrevolutions, border securitization, assassinations, and hypersurveillance. Since 2001, the United States and Israel have drawn the European Union, the United Nations, and compliant governments throughout the world into the War on Terror.

Although most discussions of the War on Terror focus on overseas military operations, War on Terror operations also target Arab and Muslim diasporic populations in the United States, along with communities and movements that embrace anti-imperialist politics.[72] The FBI takes the lead on operations related to the War on Terror within the United States, but these operations also incorporate other federal agencies, especially the DHS, as well as local police departments. And the state deputizes residents to monitor each other through programs like Countering Violent

Extremism (CVE) and If You See Something, Say Something. The federal government has actively encouraged coordination and data sharing between local, state, and federal agencies and established new mechanisms for sharing intelligence with partners, such as Israel, to support U.S. imperial projects around the world. High-tech "fusion centers" located in each state and every major city are designed to facilitate interagency data sharing and coordination. Indeed, it was the War on Terror that crystalized dif/fusion as the dominant model of articulation within the webs of imperial policing in the early twenty-first century. We analyze the local War on Terror in chapter 4.

Across the United States, the *War on Immigrants* is designed to control the flow and regulate the behavior of migrants from the Global South displaced by war, repression, and capitalism. The War on Immigrants includes policies designed to draw Mexican and Central American government agencies into the effort to prevent migrants from reaching the U.S. border. It also includes the militarization of the U.S.–Mexican border: the construction of walls, the expansion of the Border Patrol, the incorporation of military technology, the proliferation of detention centers, and support for white supremacist vigilantes. Once inside the United States, undocumented migrants confront constant harassment, surveillance, and threats of deportation.[73]

Federal immigration authorities, including ICE and the U.S. Citizenship and Immigration Services, take the lead on immigration enforcement, but programs like Secure Communities and 287(g) also incorporate local police and sheriff's departments into immigration enforcement.[74] Since the mid-1980s, Chicago has officially been a "sanctuary city," where local government policies prevent city agencies from collecting information about people's immigration status or enforcing federal immigration laws. Nevertheless, a series of exceptions in Chicago's sanctuary city ordinance enabled the CPD to work with ICE to target noncitizens with a criminal mark. Grassroots mobilizations led to the cancellation of these exceptions in 2020, but Chicago police continue to play a fundamental role in immigration enforcement by stopping and arresting young people in immigrant neighborhoods and tagging them with labels like "felon" and "gang member." Chapter 5 outlines our analysis of the War on Immigrants in Chicago.

The Wars on Crime, Terror, and Immigrants are deeply interconnected. Critical scholars coined the term *crimmigration* to highlight the connections between the War on Crime and the War on Immigrants.[75] Much of this scholarship explores the growing role of local police in the War on Immigrants. As we show, the inverse is also true: immigration agents play a key role in Chicago's War on Crime by deporting alleged "gang members." And Black immigrants are disproportionately detained and deported for alleged criminal offenses.[76] Immigration enforcement is also deeply connected to the so-called War on Terror. One of the primary justifications for building the border wall was to prevent "terrorists" from crossing into the United States undetected. And, as we show, immigration agencies use deportation as part of interagency efforts to suppress political radicals tagged as "terrorists." Finally, there are deep ties between the War on Crime and the War on Terror. A CPD lieutenant helped the CIA torture prisoners of war in Guantánamo Bay, and—as mentioned earlier—the CPD operates CIA-style "black sites," such as Homan Square.[77] The CPD calls gang members "terrorists" and floods Black and Latinx neighborhoods with troops in mass deployments that were briefly called "surge" operations, in reference to U.S. military strategies in Iraq and Afghanistan.[78] Moreover, federal funding associated with the War on Terror has enabled local police departments to increase their spending on advanced surveillance equipment and military technology, which they deploy against Black and Latinx residents through the War on Crime.[79]

Criminal Archetypes

Police like to claim that their wars are color-blind. Some scholars, including Michelle Alexander, have argued that the United States now uses criminal records rather than race as a basis for legalized discrimination.[80] But this is merely a displacement. Each of the three police wars is grounded in a racialized criminal archetype: the gang member, the terrorist, and the criminal alien. We borrow the term *archetype* from Joey Mogul, Andrea Ritchie, and Kay Whitlock, who build on the work of Patricia Hill Collins to emphasize the historical longevity, social embeddedness, and emotional power of racialized and gendered discourses about crime, terror, and belonging.[81] In doing so, we also build on the work of Frantz Fanon and Edward Said, who highlight the centrality of culture for colonial and imperial power.[82]

Criminalization is the foundation of the law: defining the limits of legality requires identifying some people or behaviors as illegal.[83] As a result, some forms of subjectivity are categorically outlawed. Migrants may acquire legal status, but the figure of the "illegal alien" cannot be recovered because it is the negative foundation of immigration law.[84] Similarly, individuals can distance themselves from criminalized categories like "gang member" and "terrorist," but the categories themselves are categorically irredeemable. These racialized criminal archetypes draw moral and ontological lines around humanity, marking some people as ineligible for inclusion in the human community. Respectable people are expected to disavow, surveil, and report on anyone tagged with the label "gang member," "terrorist suspect," or "criminal alien." Building on the work of Hannah Arendt, A. Naomi Paik describes these categories as "rightless" and documents the violent forms of exclusion that they enable.[85]

The foundational anti-Blackness of the United States is the basis for the archetype of the "gang member." Using Katheryn Russell-Brown's evocative description, the most enduring and threatening archetype in U.S. history is the "criminalblackman."[86] The racialized and gendered image of Black criminality emerged under slavery and expanded as part of the convict leasing system in the aftermath of the U.S. Civil War.[87] It has shaped police interactions with Black residents in Chicago since at least the early twentieth century.[88] The archetype of the Black gang member or "gangbanger" is a product of the War on Crime and has fueled the mass incarceration of Black people in cities throughout the United States in the late twentieth and early twenty-first centuries.[89] In Chicago, the gang member archetype is almost entirely associated with young Black and Latino men, with women, girls, and femmes increasingly targeted as well. In other cities, the gang member archetype might have Native or Asian expressions, particularly when their cultural expressions—including clothing, music, and language—are coded as Black. As Dylan Rodriguez explains, "the logics and protocols of anti-Black carceral war serve as the premises and templates for the criminalization, policing, and incarceration of (non-Black) Other peoples."[90]

After early associations with European anarchists, the label "terrorist" was increasingly applied to antiracist, anticolonial, and anti-imperialist movements over the twentieth century.[91] In Chicago, mobilizations for Puerto Rican liberation from U.S. colonial rule have been labeled "terrorist," as have Black and Palestine liberation movements. Over time, the archetype of the terrorist has increasingly been racialized as Arab or Muslim. Scholars have documented the orientalist portrayal of Arabs and Muslims in U.S. news stories and popular culture, demonstrating the impact of U.S. imperial interventions in the Middle East and support for Israel's settler-colonial project in Palestine.[92] During the 1990s, the shift from the Cold War to the so-called War on Terror transformed the racialized figure of the "Muslim terrorist" into a primary threat discourse within the United States. Permeated by racialized gendered assumptions about patriarchy in Arab/Muslim communities, this discourse has fueled the intensification of surveillance as well as the global expansion of carceral networks during the early twenty-first century.[93] Though associated primarily with Arabs and Muslims, the archetype of the terrorist still extends to other liberation movements, as demonstrated by the FBI's effort to target so-called "Black identity extremists."

Finally, the War on Immigrants is grounded in the racialized archetype of the "illegal alien" or "criminal alien." The figure of the illegal alien emerged alongside the late-nineteenth-century criminalization of Asian migrants.[94] The archetype expanded to include migrants from Latin America with the creation of the Border Patrol in the 1920s and became overwhelmingly associated with Latinx—especially Mexican—immigrants after the passage of the 1965 Immigration and Naturalization Act.[95] The "criminal alien" is a more recent marker, established as part of the INS Criminal Alien Program in the 1980s. The federal government devised this program to free up bed space within the overcrowded prison system by deporting immigrants convicted of serious crimes.[96] In practice, however, the vast majority of people deported through the Criminal Alien Program are defined as "criminal aliens" based on nothing more than a charge of illegal entry or reentry into the United States.[97] Yet the gendered discourse of the criminal alien links the War on Immigrants with the War on Crime, marking young Latinos identified as "criminals" or "gang members" as priority targets for deportation.

Like the three police wars, the archetypes are deeply interconnected. Individuals are often connected to multiple archetypes simultaneously: immigrants are labeled "terrorists" or "gang members," and street gangs are designated "domestic terrorists." Moreover, as Lisa Cacho explains, neoliberalism and criminalization have created a structure of competition that forces marginalized populations to disavow one another in the quest for respectability.[98] Efforts to uplift immigrants as hardworking, responsible, and family oriented, for instance, often invoke discourses that denigrate and criminalize Black people, and movements demanding rights for Black Americans on the basis of citizenship can reinforce the exclusion of immigrants. Cacho argues that there is no escape from the trap of competitive devaluation that requires vulnerable populations to participate in each other's oppression, even as she imagines the possibility of an "unthinkable politics" that would reject criminalizing stereotypes and the logic of mutual disavowal.[99] Yet, as we discuss in chapter 6, abolitionist movements in Chicago have embraced these supposedly "unthinkable" politics as the foundations for coalition building and radical transformation.

Carceral Liberalism

Nikhil Singh argues that the globalization of U.S. power during the twentieth century blurred the boundaries between policing and warfare, making it "possible to think of war at home and police in the world."[100] By the 1960s, efforts to pacify anticolonial struggles in the Global South and antiracist struggles in the United States relied on similar logics of *counterinsurgency*—low-intensity, asymmetrical warfare combining repressive violence with strategies aimed at "winning hearts and minds."[101] Policing in Chicago relies on a similar combination of repressive and disciplinary strategies. The primary strategies involve the open use of physical, psychic, and symbolic violence. Incarceration, detention, deportation, dehumanization, intimidation, traumatization, bodily injury, and death are celebrated as proper ways to deal with gang members, terrorists, and criminal aliens. Alongside open violence, the three police wars also rely on strategies to promote assimilation, wage discipline, acceptance of the status quo, fear of racialized Others, and even participation in carceral projects. Importantly, the distinction between repressive and productive power is always fuzzy, because disciplinary strategies rest on the (potential) use of violence.[102]

An increasingly common disciplinary strategy involves what we call *carceral liberalism*.[103] To be clear, all forms of liberalism are carceral, because they rely on repressive apparatuses to enforce regimes of racialized dispossession, exploitation, and exclusion. In addition, police have a history of embracing (or at least espousing) politically liberal reforms that they claim will reduce bias and improve community relations.[104] As we describe in chapter 1, every Chicago-based police reform over the last sixty years has involved an expansion of high-tech, data-based policing that promises to make policing more objective and efficient. Despite these liberal promises, however, policing remains a fundamentally violent project grounded in surveillance, incarceration, deportation, and death.

When we refer to carceral liberalism, we are describing a more specific set of disciplinary projects grounded in the logics of individual responsibility, carceral expansion, and police legitimacy. Each of the three police wars includes at least one carceral liberal strategy. As part of the War on Gangs, Chicago police are incorporating community organizations and service providers into a violence-prevention network. They promise support to young people who renounce gang violence but threaten targeted surveillance and enhanced prosecution for those who remain affiliated. Similarly, Chicago's Welcoming City Ordinance offered sanctuary for immigrants without a criminal record but double punishment through incarceration plus deportation for noncitizens identified by police as criminals. Finally, CVE programs offer a supposedly "gentler" yet more expansive approach to the War on Terror by enlisting teachers, counselors, and mental health professionals to identify individuals becoming "radicalized." CVE programs promise support for people who accept an "off-ramp" from radicalism but targeted repression for those who refuse.

Carceral liberal projects are grounded in the logics of individual choice and responsibility. They presume that individuals simply choose between a range of available actions without considering the complexity of subjectivity or the structural conditions that shape people's lives. While offering a narrow pathway to redemption through narratives of innocence or prevention, they hold entire populations responsible for their own repression because they made "bad decisions." Placing the onus of responsibility on individuals also enables the state to deny the need for fundamental structural transformation. Although pitched as progressive approaches to crime, terror, and immigration, these projects all involve an expansion of carceral power. This expansion takes different forms, including enhanced repressive powers, additional punishment, or the incorporation of new actors into carceral networks. Importantly, these programs are designed to add legitimacy to imperial policing by justifying the use of repressive power to punish "real" gang members, terrorists, and criminal aliens. Indeed, carceral liberalism does not exist with violence; the violence is what makes it carceral. We develop our analysis of carceral liberalism in chapter 3 through an analysis of gang violence–prevention work in Chicago.

Weaponized Data

Early-twenty-first-century police strategies increasingly rely on the production, analysis, and circulation of data. Law enforcement agencies use advanced technology to generate data, which they store in massive databases and process through predictive algorithms to determine deployments. They also share data with one another through a range of mechanisms, from bilateral agreements to shared databases. Often referred to as "intelligence-led," "data-driven," or "big data" policing, these strategies are widely celebrated as progressive reforms.

The weaponization of data is key to understanding police practices today. But it is not entirely new and has not fundamentally transformed policing, which remains grounded in the structures of racial capitalism, settler colonialism, white supremacy, and empire. In chapter 1, we trace the roots of weaponized data in Chicago to a series of reforms that promised to professionalize the police and improve trust and legitimacy. We then analyze the role of data in contemporary police wars, a key theme throughout the book. In doing so, we use the term *data-based* policing to highlight the centrality of police databases in the mystical process that transforms racialized surveillance and criminal archetypes into supposedly objective "facts" about individuals and communities. In using this term, we do not want to suggest that the data are factual or the practices scientific. On the contrary, our work exposes the way that police *produce* data through racialized deployments and surveillance; shows how police *cleanse* data through databases, complex analyses, and data-sharing processes; and demonstrates that the *circulation* of data facilitates coordination within the webs of imperial policing. This is how data get weaponized and deployed as a mechanism of articulation within the system of carceral dif/fusion.

Data-based policing may sound progressive, but it remains grounded in racialized deployments, targeted surveillance, and criminal archetypes. In *Imperial Policing,* we introduce you to people identified as "gang members," "terrorists," and "criminal aliens" in police databases. The data erase people's full humanity, reducing them to one-dimensional codes for dangerous subjects whose arrest, deportation, or elimination would make the world safer. In demonstrating how the data are produced, we ask that you look beyond the labels and see real people.

TOWARD THE ABOLITION OF IMPERIAL POLICING

The Policing in Chicago Research Group (PCRG) embraces an abolitionist perspective. This means that we learn from and stand with radical Black and transnational feminist scholars, activists, and organizers who are envisioning and building a world without police, prisons, borders, or war.[105] The PCRG partners with abolitionist organizations and approaches our research questions through an abolitionist frame. Our work builds on and contributes to abolition as a global project, with specific attention to dismantling the structures of imperial policing.

The title of Gilmore's forthcoming book expresses the ethos of abolition: *Change Everything.*[106] As Mariame Kaba explains, "we don't want to just close police departments. We want to make them obsolete. We should redirect the billions that now go to police departments toward providing health care, housing, education and good jobs. If we did this, there would be less need for the police in the first place."[107] For this reason, abolitionist politics is antiracist, anticapitalist, feminist, and decolonial.[108] "What is, so to speak, the object of abolition?" ask Fred Moten and Stefano Harney. "Not so much the abolition of prisons but the abolition of a society that could have prisons, that could have slavery, that could have the wage, and therefore not abolition as the elimination of anything but abolition as the founding of a new society."[109]

Abolitionists insist that the goal is not merely to dismantle the old but to build a new world with new ways of living together and relating to one another. In the language of Critical Resistance and INCITE!, "we seek to build movements that not only end violence, but that create a society based on radical freedom, mutual accountability, and passionate reciprocity. In this society, safety and security will not be premised on violence or the threat of violence; it will be based on a collective commitment to guaranteeing the survival and care of all peoples."[110]

While working to build a new society, we must also appreciate the destructive imperative of abolition.[111] Abolition requires dismantling existing hierarchies and eliminating the structures of organized violence and exploitation that sustain racial capitalism, settler colonialism, white supremacy, and empire. In *Imperial Policing*, we argue that abolitionist politics necessitates ending police wars, rejecting racialized criminal archetypes, refusing carceral liberalism, and dismantling the carceral webs of empire.

Abolitionists critique efforts to fix or improve policing.[112] Liberal reforms always reinforce distinctions between "deserving" and "undeserving" subjects. Some provide relief or protection for people deemed "innocent," "low risk," or "nonviolent," whereas others seek to prevent "good kids" from "going bad." In doing so, they buttress the hegemonic belief that surveillance, incarceration, repression, and death are acceptable for "guilty," "high-risk," "violent," and "bad" people. By promising protections for the "deserving" few, reforms encourage assimilation and reinforce the exclusionary foundations of racial capitalism, settler colonialism, and empire. In the words of Roderick Ferguson, they are "techniques of discipline rather than vehicles toward liberation."[113]

To avoid distinctions between the deserving and the undeserving, abolitionists center the experiences of the most marginalized. As Beth Richie points out, along with Mogul, Ritchie, and Whitlock, centering the most marginalized requires attention to the gender and sexual dynamics of criminalization.[114] Black Youth Project 100 (BYP100), for instance, organizes from a "Black queer feminist lens" that emphasizes the full humanity of all Black people, including people marginalized on the basis of their gender and sexuality as well as people who participate in street organizations and the informal economy. Similarly, the Movement for Black Lives grounds its vision statement in "the experiences and leadership of the most marginalized Black people, including but not limited to women, femmes, queer, trans, gender nonconforming, intersex, Muslim, disabled, D/deaf, and autistic people, people living with HIV, people who are criminalized, formerly and currently incarcerated, detained or institutionalized, migrants, including undocumented migrants, low and no-income, cash poor, and working class, homeless and precariously housed people, people who are dependent on criminalized substances, youth, and elders."[115]

Abolishing the old and building a new society requires what Kaba and Kelly Hayes call a "jailbreak of the imagination."[116] That does not make it a pipedream, for abolitionist projects are happening every day. As Gilmore explains, "groups around the world are coming together to relieve the stress of organized abandonment and its realization through organized violence to change the world in which we live."[117]

Rodriguez points out that abolitionist struggles are grounded in centuries of "(feminist, queer) Black liberation and (feminist, queer) Indigenous anticolonialism/decolonization."[118] Contemporary struggles in Chicago build on a long history of resistance to racist policing, surveillance, and repression. The Black Panther Party was foundational, including its effort to build partnerships with the Young Lords, the Young Patriots, and street organizations like the Blackstone Rangers.[119] The early 1970s witnessed the emergence of the Chicago Alliance against Racist and Political Repression, the Afro-American Patrolmen's League (later the African American Police League), and the People's Law Office. For decades, organizers and activist lawyers fought to hold the FBI and the state's attorney responsible for the assassination of Hampton, to expose the CPD's systematic torture of Black residents and unconstitutional spying by the Red Squad, and to demand sanctuary protections for undocumented immigrants. In the early 2000s, Chicago organizers achieved a statewide moratorium on the death penalty, mobilized massive antiwar and immigrant rights protests, and began building networks of transformative justice and other abolitionist feminist organizations.

The current wave of abolitionist struggle took root from 2013 to 2016, with the emergence of a network of movements resisting the criminalization and murder of Black youth and the deportation of undocumented immigrants, including BYP100, We Charge Genocide, the

#LetUsBreathe Collective, Assata's Daughters, Black Lives Matter–Chicago, Organized Communities Against Deportations (OCAD), Fearless Leading by the Youth, the Ujimaa Medics, Lifted Voices, and the Brave Space Alliance.

In 2014, organizers from We Charge Genocide exposed CPD violence against young people of color at the United Nations.[120] In 2015, organizers achieved a major victory when the City Council passed the Chicago Torture Justice Memorial and Reparations Ordinances.[121] The same year, the acquittal of police officer Dante Servin for the murder of Rekia Boyd and the video of officer Jason van Dyke murdering Laquan McDonald generated campaigns to #FireDanteServin and #JusticeForLaquan.[122] Mass mobilizations led to the firing of the police superintendent, the electoral defeat of the state's attorney, the decision by Mayor Emanuel not to run for reelection, the conviction of Officer Van Dyke for second-degree murder and sixteen counts of aggravated assault, and a U.S. Department of Justice investigation into the CPD that ended with a consent decree.

Meanwhile, the #LetUsBreathe Collective organized the forty-one-day encampment at Freedom Square described at the start of this chapter; OCAD and other immigrant rights organizations fought to free Wilmer Catalan-Ramirez and to resist the federal government's deportation regime; the U.S. Palestinian Community Network and the Committee to Stop FBI Repression led the struggle to free Rasmea Odeh, while the Arab American Action Network organized resistance to Trump's Muslim ban; and transformative justice projects, such as Circles & Ciphers and Love & Protect, emerged and grew with the support of Kaba and Project NIA.

Rather than working in silos, abolitionist movements in Chicago embrace the vision of *political quilting* articulated by Barbara Ransby and Ella's Daughters.[123] Political quilting describes the work involved in stitching together different movements to create a united front. Working together, these organizations have built mass movements to stop the construction of a new police academy, to end the use of CVE, to abolish gang databases, to cancel the ShotSpotter contract, to remove police from Chicago schools and mental health crisis responses, and to defund the CPD. At the same time, the Chicago Alliance against Racist and

Political Repression has continued the long-standing struggle for community control of the CPD, winning a major victory with the 2021 Empowering Communities for Public Safety ordinance.

Although much of this work is intensely local, many of these organizers also embrace an internationalist critique of policing as a global project of racial capitalism and empire. They are connected to national and transnational networks of solidarity that link movements for justice, liberation, and decolonization. At the same time, everyday forms of abolitionist praxis proliferate in the streets of Chicago. Many young people targeted by the police wars offer sharp critiques of policing and visions of a world without police. Some embody insurrectionary and fugitive practices and reject the authority of cops and other carceral agents. In chapter 3, we demonstrate that the critical insights and everyday lives of criminalized young people constitute an important site of abolitionist praxis.

The PCRG has been fortunate to work alongside abolitionist movements, transformative justice organizations, and young people developing innovative struggles against imperial policing. We have learned a great deal about abolition from these partnerships. To be clear, not everyone we work with would call themselves an abolitionist. We ground ourselves in abolitionist politics because reform cannot bring about fundamental social transformation. In chapter 6, we discuss the Expanded Sanctuary and Erase the Database campaigns, which set out to dismantle webs of imperial policing by erasing police databases and eliminating data-sharing processes. In the book's conclusion, we discuss the implications of our analysis for global efforts to abolish imperial policing.

OVERVIEW OF THE BOOK

Imperial Policing is collectively authored by the PCRG. Drawing together multiple threads of research that we have conducted with different social movements and transformative justice organizations, we explore the carceral formations that wage the three police wars in Chicago and excavate the ties that situate these formations within the global structures of imperial policing.

Our movement-based research is informed by feminist, antiracist, anticapitalist, and decolonial methodologies that are grounded in the standpoints of the marginalized, carried out through engagement and dialogue, and geared toward the advancement of social justice.[124] We describe our praxis as *countersurveillant abolitionist research*. Collectivity, multiplicity, and engagement allow our research to be dynamic, relevant, responsive, and accountable to social movements. We believe that activist research should not only be theoretically connected to ongoing struggles for liberation; it also necessitates the creation of relationships of resistance among research team members, movement partners, and marginalized communities.

Imperial Policing is a manifestation of our collaborative approach to research and writing. The content, structure, and authorship of the book were determined through ongoing, open conversations between contributors. We discussed the audience for this book; how it relates to the overall goals of the project; and how it relates to contributors' personal, political, and professional goals. Each chapter is coauthored by two members of the research team, with a grad student or recent PhD as the lead author. Andy Clarno, the PCRG coordinator, made substantial contributions to every chapter as the co–lead author. He is also the lead author of the introduction and chapter 1. As a collective, we discussed outlines and drafts and then workshopped each chapter at least three times. We also incorporated feedback from academics, movement partners, and directly impacted young people. And one of our movement partners, Tania Unzueta Carrasco, is a co–lead author on chapter 6.

In chapter 1, we analyze the genealogy and structure of high-tech, data-based policing in Chicago. We begin by tracing the expansion of data and technology. In doing so, we demonstrate that reforms that promised to address crises of police legitimacy provided cover for the expansion of high-tech, racialized surveillance. We then analyze data-based strategies of imperial policing in the early twenty-first century. In doing so, we challenge the fetishism of police data by showing that data are weaponized through three processes: production, cleansing, and circulation.

In chapters 2 and 3, we turn our attention to the War on Crime/ Gangs. Chapter 2 analyzes the politics of violence prevention in Chicago. We highlight the incorporation of nonprofits, universities, and philanthropic foundations into the carceral network pursuing the War on Gangs. This chapter develops the concept of carceral liberalism to capture the logics of individualism and choice that underpin this emerging strategy of surveillance. Lydia Dana is the lead author of the chapter.

Chapter 3 shows that police gang databases are grounded in racialized archetypes of Black criminality as well as the criminalization of neighborhoods and personal relationships. Drawing on a participatory action research project that the PCRG facilitated with gang-involved young people targeted by the War on Gangs, we uplift marginalized youth as experts on police surveillance. These young people share stories and reflections that demolish the assumption that police data are objective. At the same time, the young people demonstrate their ability to outline alternative safety strategies and imagine a future without police. Haley Volpintesta is the lead author of chapter 3.

In chapter 4, we analyze the War on Terror in Chicago by documenting political repression, the proliferation of surveillance targeting Arabs and Muslims, and the role of data sharing as a mechanism for coordination within a decentralized network of imperial policing. In doing so, we develop the concept of dif/fusion to analyze the multiplication of sites of surveillance as well as the mechanisms for coordination within the carceral webs of empire. Ilā Ravichandran is the chapter's lead author.

In chapter 5, we build on the case of Wilmer Catalan-Ramirez to analyze the War on Immigrants and uncover the limits of liberal sanctuary protections in Chicago. The urban sanctuary regime strengthens police power through two data-based mechanisms of coordination between the CPD and ICE: punitive exceptions written into Chicago's Welcoming City ordinance and disavowed collusion through shared databases. The lead author for this chapter is Enrique Alvear Moreno.

In chapter 6, we discuss the Expanded Sanctuary and Erase the Database campaigns as windows into the dynamics of joint struggle and the challenges of abolitionist organizing against data-based policing. We focus on campaigns to amend Chicago's sanctuary city ordinance and to abolish gang databases, both of which offer lessons in data justice, abolitionist praxis, and countercarceral research. The lead authors for this chapter are Janaé Bonsu-Love and Tania Unzueta Carrasco.

In the conclusion, we review our overall arguments about imperial policing, discuss data-based policing as a new front for abolitionist struggles, and discuss the implications of these arguments for abolitionist organizing today. This chapter was coauthored by the entire collective.

We have also included an afterword by David Omotoso Stovall and a methodological appendix that outlines our approach to countersurveillant abolitionist research. Michael De Anda Muñiz is the lead author of the appendix.

1 Weaponized Data: High-Tech Surveillance in Chicago

In 1995, Chicago opened a state-of-the-art 911 dispatch center in the West Loop. Promising to accelerate response times, the new center was integral to Chicago's emerging high-tech approach to policing. Redesigned after 2001 as the headquarters of Chicago's Office of Emergency Management and Communications (OEMC), the West Loop building houses a joint command center that allows city agencies to coordinate among themselves and with state and federal agencies.[1]

In 2003, the Chicago Police Department (CPD) established the Deployment Operations Center (DOC) at CPD headquarters. Signaling the CPD's deepening commitment to predictive, data-informed policing, officers assigned to the DOC began analyzing the CPD's new Citizen and Law Enforcement Reporting and Analysis (CLEAR) database to provide district commanders with times and locations for "targeted enforcement activities" and lists of "gang member suspects to look out for."[2]

The same year, the CPD began installing surveillance cameras, known as police observation devices (PODs), in "high-risk areas" across the city. Two years later, with a $35 million grant from the U.S. Department of Homeland Security (DHS), the OEMC launched its own camera system, called Operation Virtual Shield. When Mayor Richard M. Daley called for a "camera on every corner," the OEMC expanded its network by incorporating cameras operated by the CPD and other city agencies—including the public schools, public housing authority, and transit authority—as well as private businesses and residents. By 2022, the network included at least fifty thousand cameras monitored by the OEMC and the CPD.[3]

In 2007, the CPD expanded the DOC by building a high-tech "fusion center"—the Crime Prevention and Information Center (CPIC)—with funding from the DHS. Tasked with ensuring the constant flow of data between local, state, and federal law enforcement agencies, fusion centers like the CPIC are key to the federal government's strategy to combat terror attacks through interagency coordination and data sharing. Yet the CPD broadened the mandate of the CPIC to include not just terrorism but "all crimes and hazards" and turned the CPIC into the CPD's centralized control room, where police conduct real-time surveillance, monitor high-tech equipment, analyze data, shape department strategy, inform predictive deployments, and provide up-to-date information to officers in the street.[4]

In 2016, the CPD initiated another massive expansion of surveillance by multiplying and decentralizing its control rooms. Using the CPIC as a model, the CPD installed high-tech Strategic Decision Support Centers (SDSCs) in the city's twenty-two district-level police stations and Area Technology Centers (ATCs) in the three regional offices of the Bureau of Detectives. Analysts in each of these control rooms can monitor video cameras, social media, GIS mapping programs, predictive algorithms, ShotSpotter gunshot detection sensors, and other private- and public-sector surveillance technology distributed unevenly throughout the city, with a concentration on the South and West Sides. In effect, the SDSC/ATC initiative multiplied the CPD's real-time surveillance capacity twenty-five times from 2016 to 2020. Chicago is the first city to attempt something like this. It represents an immeasurable leap in Chicago's long-standing strategy of high-tech racialized surveillance.[5]

Finally, in 2020, Chicago began a three-year, $75 million upgrade to the OEMC 911 dispatch center in the West Loop. The upgrade has enabled the OEMC and the CPD to receive and analyze real-time videos from cell phones and home surveillance cameras.[6]

In short, Chicago is at the cutting edge of advances in high-tech surveillance and data-based policing. Policing remains firmly grounded in the dynamics of settler colonialism, racial capitalism, white supremacy, and empire, yet the weaponization of data has transformed the logics and practices of policing in the early twenty-first century. As part of the investment in carceral strategies to contain the crises and struggles unleashed by neoliberal racial capitalism and empire, the U.S. empire state has invested heavily in high-tech racialized surveillance. Moreover, the long-term U.S. response to the 9/11 attacks prioritized expanded data sharing and improved coordination between law enforcement agencies. In Chicago, each of the three police wars increasingly operates through the production and analysis of data, and interagency flows of data have become a key mechanism for coordination within and between networks of imperial policing. For this reason, it is important to understand how data are weaponized.

In this chapter, we trace the emergence and analyze the structures of data-based policing in Chicago. We begin with a genealogy of technological advances in Chicago that highlights a consistent pattern: the expansion of high-tech surveillance under the banner of liberal reform. Since the 1960s, police have repeatedly responded to crises of legitimacy by promising that new technology and better data will eliminate police bias and racism by allowing for more objective and efficient deployments, but every reform has led to an expansion of racialized surveillance. Next, we analyze the structures and processes of data-based policing in Chicago. Our analysis reveals the fallacy of claims to scientific objectivity by highlighting the weaponization of police data through three processes: production, cleansing, and circulation. We end by arguing that the latest round of police reforms in Chicago will inevitably expand racialized surveillance and subvert the promises of reform.

DATA-BASED POLICING

Policing in the early twenty-first century operates through the collection and circulation of data about individuals, networks, neighborhoods, and more. Law enforcement agencies increasingly use stops, arrests, and high-tech surveillance equipment, such as video cameras, audio sensors, cell-site simulators, social media monitoring, and aerial drones, to compile massive databases; they supplement their own data with information sourced from public databases and private data brokers; they analyze the data using geographic mapping software, social network analysis, machine-learning algorithms, and other emerging technologies; and they use these analyses to determine targets for predictive deployments, heightened surveillance, and aggressive policing.

Big data policing—also known as intelligence-led or data-driven policing—is celebrated as both a cost-saving tool that allows police to efficiently deploy scarce resources and a scientific approach that minimizes the impact of individual biases among officers. Yet critical scholarship paints a different picture. Rather than objective, what we call *data-based policing* is a mechanism of racialized surveillance. The term draws attention to the role of police databases in transforming racialized archetypes into seemingly objective "facts" and facilitating their circulation through the webs of imperial policing.

As Sarah Brayne argues, data-based policing works to "simultaneously obscure and amplify existing inequalities."[7] Using data to determine police deployments and targets may seem more objective than relying on the discretionary power of individual officers, but Brayne shows that data-based policing reproduces inequality by (1) intensifying the surveillance of people already considered suspicious, (2) broadening surveillance to include people who have personal relationships with targeted individuals, (3) concentrating high-tech equipment in particular neighborhoods, and (4) leading people to avoid institutions, such as hospitals, that are seen as sites of surveillance.[8]

Simone Browne reminds us that "surveillance is nothing new to black folks. It is the fact of antiblackness."[9] Challenging Michel Foucault's colorblind genealogy of surveillance, Browne traces surveillance to the context of racial slavery. She demonstrates that the slave ship predated (and may have inspired) Jeremy Bentham's panopticon and identifies precursors to advanced surveillance technologies in the forms of population control deployed to track and punish enslaved Black people in the United States. Plantation owners marked Black bodies with brands and required enslaved people to carry passes.[10] New York City required Black and Indigenous people to carry lanterns when walking at night—ensuring that they would be "constantly illuminated from dusk to dawn, made knowable, locatable, and contained within the city."[11] Rather than providing an alternative to violence, Browne points out, racializing surveillance is always violent.[12]

Building on Browne's argument, Ruha Benjamin offers a blistering critique of advanced technologies that claim scientific objectivity and race neutrality but reproduce racism and inequality. Machine-learning algorithms, she demonstrates, generate racist predictions when the data

FIGURE 3. Police regularly video-record protests as part of their data collection. Our countersurveillant gaze turns the lens back on the police. Photograph by and courtesy of Sarah Jane Rhee (@loveandstrugglephotos).

they analyze are produced by racially discriminatory individuals and institutions. For example, programs that claim to predict ethnicity based on a person's last name actually use zip codes to distinguish white from Black or Latinx from Filipinx names in historically segregated cities. Decades of racial segregation have produced racialized zip codes that now become "data" for what Benjamin calls the "New Jim Code." "Anti-Blackness is no glitch," she concludes. "The system is accurately rigged."[13]

Similarly, Virginia Eubanks demonstrates that high-tech tools of poverty management are not neutral but rather designed to "profile, police, and punish the poor."[14] From automated processes to determine eligibility for welfare to algorithms that forecast child abuse, these high-tech tools are advertised as antidotes to human bias yet systematically distinguish the "deserving" from the "undeserving" poor. Demonstrating that "digital tools are embedded in old systems of power and privilege," Eubanks concludes that the technological aura of scientific objectivity allows elites to "mathwash" the structures of racism and capitalism.[15]

In the face of high-tech surveillance, Benjamin uplifts the work of abolitionist organizations, such as Critical Resistance, Black Youth Project 100, Stop LAPD Spying, and Data for Black Lives, that work to democratize data, demystify technology, surveil the police, and share strategies for resisting and avoiding surveillance.[16] This speaks to the breadth of practices that Browne calls "dark sousveillance," which include tactics to render people and communities invisible, to co-opt or resist the tools of surveillance, and to turn a countersurveillant lens on systems of power.[17] The PCRG is motivated by precisely this vision of countersurveillance and abolition.

Turning a countersurveillant gaze on the empire state, we examine the impact of data-based policing in Chicago. We reconceptualize police databases as repositories of state knowledge that transform racialized discourses about crime, terror, and belonging into "facts" that take the form of a permanent record. Databases codify the devaluation of Black, Latinx, and Arab/Muslim life by tagging people with racialized labels like "gang member," "criminal alien," and "terrorist." Yet the use of predictive algorithms and other advanced tools of data analysis generates an air of mathematical objectivity that allows police to weaponize data while disavowing their reliance on racialized archetypes.[18] By disavowing the racial basis of policing, these mathematical abstractions legitimize police violence against people "on the database." The data then flow through the circuits of imperial policing, becoming further cleansed and enabling multiple agencies to simultaneously target people from different angles with an array of repressive and disciplinary strategies.

TECHNOLOGICAL EXPANSION UNDER THE COVER OF REFORM

In response to grassroots campaigns demanding justice for Rekia Boyd and Laquan McDonald, the CPD promised to carry out a process of "meaningful, tangible, and sustainable positive reform."[19] The reform plan was outlined in a court-ordered consent decree stemming from investigations into CPD practices by the Chicago Police Accountability Task Force (PATF) and the U.S. Department of Justice (DOJ). Given the state of high-tech surveillance in Chicago, it is striking that the PATF and DOJ reports never mention the CPD's use of advanced technology or predictive policing. The only time the reports discuss data and technology is to encourage the rollout of body-worn cameras and the collection of data on police use of force and misconduct complaints.[20] As a result, the expansion of data-based policing is taking place almost entirely beyond the purview of the consent decree. To the extent that police reformers discuss data or technology, they treat them as tools for improving accountability and building trust between police and community members.

Promoting technology as an instrument of police reform is neither new nor surprising. Early-twentieth-century efforts to "professionalize" U.S. police departments led to the incorporation of military technologies, along with military tactics and organizational forms.[21] Since the 1960s, every liberal effort to reform the Chicago police—from professionalization to community policing to body-worn cameras—has incorporated the technocratic assumption that more technology and better data can solve the crisis of police legitimacy. None of these reforms have made policing more just or accountable; all of them have expanded the CPD's capacity for high-tech racialized surveillance, often reproducing the very issues they claimed to address. Technological advances under the cover of liberal reform merely amplify the power of law enforcement to surveil and target Chicago's Black, Indigenous, immigrant, diasporic, and working-class communities. They also feed the technology corporations at the forefront of surveillance capitalism, whose profit models are grounded in the commodification of data.[22]

Laying the Foundations

Between the 1950s and the 1980s, four processes laid the foundation for Chicago's system of data-based policing. Only the first was driven by right-wing forces; the others were grounded in race-liberal reforms. Yet all four constitute a common platform on which the CPD built an iron-fisted, data-based strategy of racialized surveillance cloaked in the velvet glove of community policing. This genealogy contributes to work by radical scholars, such as Naomi Murakawa, Elizabeth Hinton, Jordan Camp, Simon Balto, and Dylan Rodriguez, who demonstrate that liberal reformists established the scaffolding for mass incarceration through projects designed to "modernize" or "professionalize" criminal punishment after World War II.[23]

The FBI and police Red Squad units built the first pillar of data-based surveillance by establishing mechanisms for gathering and using data to suppress radical social movements. From the 1950s through the 1970s, the FBI's Counter-Intelligence Program (COINTELPRO) used covert agents, informants, and technology to monitor and disrupt antiracist, anticolonial, and anti-imperialist movements.[24] At the same time, the CPD Red Squad—officially known as the Subversive Unit—conducted systematic surveillance on community organizations, labor organizers, civil rights activists, and other progressive and radical movements. The Red Squad built a database of 285,000 individuals and 14,000 organizations.[25] Its catalog of index cards provided a precursor to contemporary gang databases and terrorist watchlists.

The second and third pillars of data-based policing are grounded in liberal reforms at the local and federal levels. In 1960, Mayor Richard J. Daley hired superintendent Orlando W. Wilson to "professionalize" Chicago's scandal-plagued police department. A protégé of August Vollmer, Wilson argued that new technology, accountability processes, and merit-based hiring could bring Chicago to the forefront of "modern" policing.[26] The CPD introduced patrol cars with two-way radios, an advanced dispatch system, a hotline for residents to report crime, and an IBM mainframe computer to manage data.[27] These sophisticated new tools enhanced the CPD's ability to criminalize Black residents. Police collected data through aggressive patrols and stop-and-frisk practices and used this information to identify "hot spots" for more intense policing. Wilson's more progressive reforms—around hiring and accountability—were rolled back by a rank-and-file revolt and a reassertion of control by Mayor Daley.[28] But his tenure transformed the CPD into a technologically advanced carceral machine.

The federal government provided further support for data-based policing by funding technology purchases and encouraging data sharing during the 1960s and 1970s.[29] Arguing that Black criminality and unrest were responses to the injustice they faced from racist police, Lyndon B. Johnson's administration launched a "War on Crime" in 1965 with reforms designed to make carceral systems more professional, race-neutral, and procedurally just. Funded by the Law Enforcement Assistance Administration, these reforms involved expanded training, additional officers, and upgraded technology—including computers for collecting and analyzing crime data.[30] Modernization, therefore, added legitimacy and technological capacity to police departments, with the promise that "color-blind" policing would improve police–community relations and diffuse Black-led rebellions. Richard Nixon's "law-and-order" administration merely accelerated the flow of federal funds to local police.

The CPD added the fourth pillar by developing crime-mapping technology through partnerships with academics and community organizations. In the early 1980s, the CPD provided crime data to the Chicago Alliance for Neighborhood Safety (CANS), a community organization that used the data to produce maps for neighborhood watch groups.[31] The goal, as Brian Jefferson explains, was "to convert insurgent spaces into rationally managed microspaces."[32] Later, the CPD partnered with CANS and academics from the University of Illinois at Chicago and Northwestern University to develop the department's first computerized crime-mapping system. This enabled police to create computerized beat maps with information on crime patterns, drug markets, and community violence.[33] In 1991, the CPD began working with the Illinois Criminal Justice Information Authority and Loyola University to incorporate the locations of schools, parks, public transportation, public housing, and other landmarks into its mapping system. Police used the program to build an "early warning system for street gang violence" and envisioned it becoming the "information foundation for community policing" in Chicago.[34]

Race-liberal reformers, therefore, built the foundation on which the CPD established its system of high-tech policing. Starting in the 1990s, "community policing" became the new language of reform through which the CPD transformed data into a weapon of war.

CAPS: A Model and a Justification for High-Tech Surveillance

In 1992, Mayor Richard M. Daley announced that the CPD would develop a "community-based" approach to policing.[35] Offering liberal cover for ongoing police wars in Black and Latinx communities, community policing expanded racialized surveillance, justified investments in advanced technology, and provided an early model for carceral dif/fusion. While the language of community policing has come and gone, the commitment to high-tech, data-based policing has remained consistent.

The consulting firm Booz Allen Hamilton (BAH) developed the blueprint for community policing in Chicago.[36] Hired by Daley to "squeeze the fat out of the department,"[37] BAH produced a remarkable report that weaves together neoliberalism, community policing, and technology. The report argues that the CPD could put sixteen hundred more officers on the street at no additional cost by consolidating districts, reducing bureaucracy, improving accountability, updating its dispatch system, adding flexibility to deployments, and hiring nonunionized civilian employees. It explains that these neoliberal reforms would create the "resource base" for a more efficient, community-based approach to policing. And it insists that information technology and data analysis are essential tools for community policing because they enable police to monitor crime, streamline deployment, and evaluate interventions.

In 1993, the CPD launched the Chicago Alternative Policing Strategy (CAPS), a community policing initiative grounded in advanced technology and data analysis.[38] Like other community policing programs, CAPS emphasized decentralization, partnerships, and prevention. The CPD divides Chicago geographically into three areas (previously six), twenty-two districts (previously twenty-five), and hundreds of beats. Officials claimed that CAPS would decentralize authority from CPD headquarters to district commanders and that patrol officers would spend more time in designated beats talking with residents and business owners.

While presented as a strategy to build trust, community policing creates an expansive structure of racialized surveillance by incorporating residents, businesses, community organizations, and others into a web of criminalizing institutions that operates by distinguishing between innocent/deserving and criminal/undeserving members of a community. Describing residents as the "eyes and ears" of the police, CAPS encouraged residents to monitor their neighbors. As We Charge Genocide demonstrated in a brilliant report, CAPS effectively "deputized" a handful of residents to monitor and report on the most vulnerable members of every community.[39] This is a prime example of a liberal reform that expanded carceral capacity by criminalizing minor signs of disorder, recruiting residents to participate, and multiplying the sites of surveillance. In addition, CAPS enabled police to share information with other city agencies so they could work together to criminalize youth and evict tenants.[40]

Thus, CAPS provided an early model of interagency coordination through data sharing, which later crystalized as dif/fusion.[41]

What distinguished CAPS from other models of community policing was the CPD's commitment to advanced technology and data analysis.[42] Building on the BAH report, the CPD treated information technology as foundational for community policing. At the launch of the program, superintendent Matt Rodriguez declared that "information is power."[43] The CPD established a new 911 dispatch center, installed computers in district stations and patrol cars, developed a new data management system, and introduced a new computerized crime-mapping program described as the "lynchpin of the whole strategy."[44] The technology was designed to enable Chicago police to analyze data and proactively deploy officers to locations where crime might occur.

On paper, the CPD has remained committed to community policing for the last thirty years. In practice, implementation has been highly uneven due to turnover in CPD leadership and an entrenched culture that sees community policing as "soft." According to the 2017 DOJ report, "community policing as a true CPD value and driving force fell away many years ago."[45] Rather than serving as a guiding strategy for the department, community engagement was relegated to small, underfunded, and unsupported offices in each district,[46] while patrol units, mobile strike teams, and detectives relied on violent, antagonistic strategies of crime suppression. As we saw after the murder of Laquan McDonald, Chicago police hold out the promise of community policing after every scandal or uprising. Even when the commitment is real, the promise is a mirage designed to conceal the hard edge of police warfare in communities of color. Data-based policing is no different, promising that objective data can put an end to police racism while massively expanding the capacity for racialized surveillance and interagency coordination.

CLEAR: Essential Infrastructure for Big Data Policing

The technology at the heart of data-based policing in Chicago is the CLEAR data system. The CPD began overhauling its data system with the rollout of CAPS.[47] According to the CPD's Barbara McDonald, "Chicago had mountains of data sitting around in file cabinets or locked in an antiquated, largely inaccessible mainframe computer. We were data-rich, but information-poor." In 2000, superintendent Terry Hilliard called on the CPD to "take CAPS to the next level" with data and technology.[48] The first result was a partnership with the Oracle Corporation to develop CLEAR, a project that cost at least $63 million from 2001 to 2015.[49]

The heart of CLEAR is a "data warehouse" containing tens of millions of entries across hundreds of columns in multiple databases,[50] including arrest records, warrants, contact cards, gang arrest cards, investigatory stop reports, suspicious activity reports (SARs), crime maps, victim information, witness statements, crime scene data, 911 calls, mug shots, tattoos, fingerprints, and more. It also includes data on people's social networks, indicating who an individual was with when stopped or arrested.[51] In short, CLEAR is a digital repository for all of the data collected by Chicago police during stops, arrests, investigations, and other operations. Accessible from police stations, patrol cars, and smartphones, CLEAR is "designed to provide anytime, anyplace access to vast repositories of centralized, relational data."[52]

While supporting the work of patrol and detective units, CLEAR also enabled innovations in predictive policing. In 2003, the department established the DOC to look for patterns in CLEAR data and advise district commanders on when and where to deploy "targeted enforcement activities."[53] The creation of the DOC was accompanied by a centralization of authority from district-level commanders to their bosses, who oversaw area-level and citywide task forces that could saturate "hot spots" and enforce zero-tolerance policies for drugs, gangs, and guns.[54]

Police officials claimed that CLEAR would also support a corporate approach to management. Police estimated that CLEAR would increase the efficiency of entering reports, running names, searching mug shots, pulling rap sheets, and logging evidence—effectively providing the department with "the equivalent of 1.2 officers for every one it had prior to CLEAR."[55] A neoliberal, data-based management system known as Comp-Stat Chicago-Style enabled the superintendent to confront deputy chiefs and district commanders with crime statistics and hold them responsible for developing strategic plans and responding efficiently to shifting trends.[56] The department also promised that data would allow managers to evaluate officers, identify patterns of problematic behavior, and intervene before problems became serious.[57] But, as the 2017 DOJ report emphasized, there was never any accountability.[58]

The CPD and Oracle designed CLEAR to support the circulation of data among law enforcement agencies. Not only does CLEAR contain data provided by the Cook County Sheriff's Office, the Illinois State Police, and other agencies, but the CLEAR Sharing Program encourages other law enforcement agencies to apply for direct access to the data. By 2019, more than five hundred agencies across the country had access to CLEAR. In a 2003 review, Wesley Skogan and his team cautioned, "One issue that bears close watching is whether the administrative safeguards put in place by its many new participants prevent substantial misuse of the data."[59] This warning was apparently unheeded. According to Chicago's inspector general, by 2019, there was not a single data-sharing agreement or other administrative safeguard on the use of CLEAR data.[60]

CLEAR is the technological foundation for all of the advances in high-tech surveillance, predictive policing, and data fusion that define policing in Chicago today. The database received widespread national recognition and was described as a "national model for the future of police information systems"[61] and "a model application that other law enforcement agencies should be learning from if not adopting."[62] CLEAR won awards for innovation in 2004 and 2007, and the DOJ National Criminal Intelligence Sharing Plan upheld it as an exemplary shared record-management system.[63] The centrality of CLEAR inspired our use of the term *data-based policing*.

THE FETISHISM OF DATA-BASED POLICING

Despite assurances from police officials, data-based policing is not objective, and police data should never be accepted as factual. To understand why, it is necessary to look more closely at the structures and practices through which police data are produced, cleansed, and circulated.

Karl Marx famously analyzed what he called the "fetishism of commodities."[64] He used the term *fetish* in the religious sense, to signify the popular belief that certain objects have mysterious or godlike properties. Under capitalism, every item we purchase—every commodity—is produced by workers under exploitative conditions. Capitalists claim ownership over the commodities and sell them for more than the cost of production. It is possible, therefore, to recognize in every commodity the relationships and struggles between workers and capitalists that shaped its production. But people almost never think about these things. All we see is the object that we purchased, not the relationships through which it was produced. In other words, Marx argued, people treat commodities as fetishes that have value on their own, magically erasing the social conditions of their production.

Data-based policing operates through a similar fetishism of data. Police data are produced by documenting people's everyday activities through police stops, arrests, reports of suspicious activity, video surveillance, social media monitoring, and more. The everyday activities as well as the surveillance and reporting take place within a context shaped by race, class, and gender oppression. It is possible to see in every data point the social relations through which it was produced. For instance, we could see crime data as a reflection of concentrated poverty, racial profiling, and targeted surveillance. Instead, people generally accept police data as "factual"—an objective account of the distribution of criminal activity. Michael Rodriguez-Muñiz refers to this attitude as "demographic naturalism."[65] In claiming that their strategies are "data driven," police activate popular assumptions about scientific objectivity that obscure the material and discursive conditions in which data are produced. People accept the data form, like the commodity form, as a fetish that can erase the conditions and relations of production. This obscures the use of police data as a weapon of war. In the words of Stuart Hall, Chas Critcher, Tony Jefferson, John Clarke, and Brian Roberts, "statistics—whether crime rates or opinion polls—have an ideological function: they appear to ground free floating and controversial impressions in the hard, incontrovertible soil of numbers."[66]

To resist the fetishism of police data, we unpack three processes through which data are weaponized: production, cleansing, and circulation. To begin with, we look at the process through which police data are *produced*. Rather than simply collecting statistics, police produce data through strategic deployments, everyday encounters, and sophisticated technology. Racialized criminal archetypes are an essential foundation for the production of police data. Next, we analyze the process of *cleansing* police data to make them appear objective. Databases and predictive analytics transform the messy data produced by police into supposedly objective "facts" that are used to further criminalize targeted communities.

Finally, we describe the *circulation* of data through the carceral webs of empire. As we demonstrate, the circulation of data operates through a collective acceptance that the data are factual. While reinforcing the erasure of its production, the circulation of data has also become a key mechanism of articulation linking together the webs of imperial policing.

Producing Police Data

Statistics should never be mistaken for objective reflections of reality; rather, statistics are produced through identifiable processes in specific social and political contexts.[67] In other words, producing data requires work.[68] For instance, U.S. census data are shaped by struggles over racial and ethnic categories, uneven participation, and politicized analyses.[69] Police data are a product of the Wars on Crime, Terror, and Immigrants, grounded in racialized archetypes and accelerated by new technologies. Production and accumulation are the first steps in the weaponization of data.

Racialized criminal archetypes provide the raw material for the production of police data. Local police and federal agents set their sights on people who "fit the description" of a gang member, a terrorist suspect, or a criminal alien. In pursuit of the War on Gangs, for instance, Chicago police stop young people based on the color of their skin; their clothing, style, and tattoos; and the way they walk, talk, and carry themselves. Similarly, immigration agents target people dressed for work in construction, landscaping, housecleaning, and other low-wage jobs. As part of the War on Terror, local, state, and federal agencies investigate reports of "suspicious activity" based on a person's skin tone, facial hair, religious attire, and spoken or written language. Archetypes provide a shared focal point for surveillance, helping ensure that the various state and private agents involved in each police war target the same populations.

In addition to looks, criminal archetypes have racialized spatial, relational, and behavioral aspects. Chicago police routinely stop young Black and Latinx people for being on a block that police identify as "gang territory" or for being with a person whom police consider a gang member. Immigration agents look for Latinx people at day-labor pickup sites and certain workplaces. The War on Terror has transformed airports, skyscrapers, transit facilities, and tourist locations into sites of particularly intense surveillance for Arabs and Muslims. Everyday activities, such as taking a photograph, looking at a map, or watching a train, can also generate suspicion and attract surveillance when performed by people presumed to be Arab or Muslim. Importantly, locations, relations, and behaviors are criminalized only for people who resemble the archetype. Middle-class white people would almost never be considered suspicious for hanging out on a known drug corner, congregating at a day-labor hiring site, or taking photographs of a train station.

Police provide the labor that transforms archetypes into data. The CPD operationalizes the War on Gangs through tactics like stop-and-frisk, buy-and-bust, corner sweeps, hot spot policing, and surge operations. They concentrate these deployments in working-class Black and Latinx neighborhoods, while focusing increased attention on particular blocks, individuals, and networks. In addition, the CPD profiles young people of color who seem "out of place" in wealthy areas, such as the Loop, and in predominantly white, middle-class neighborhoods. In pursuit of the War on Terror, the FBI infiltrates mosques and community organizations, cultivates informants in Arab and Muslim communities, and entraps young people by provoking violence. Similarly, U.S. Immigration and Customs Enforcement (ICE) agents carrying out the War on Immigrants sweep day-labor sites, raid workplaces known to hire immigrants, and carry out gang operations in Latinx neighborhoods. These racialized deployments generate data through contact that disproportionately targets people who match the archetypes grounding each police war.

An American Civil Liberties Union report on the use of stop-and-frisk tactics by the CPD provides powerful evidence of this unevenness.[70] During summer 2014, Chicago police conducted more than 250,000 stops— four times more than the New York City Police Department. A staggering 72 percent of stops targeted Black residents, who made up just 32 percent of the city's population. A disproportionate number of stops took place in Black neighborhoods, and Black residents were disproportionately stopped in predominantly white neighborhoods.

Police also draw residents, businesses, and community organizations into surveillance networks that transform archetypes into data. Community policing programs like the CPD's CAPS encourage residents to report on potential drug markets and gang activity. In addition, when designing the CLEAR data system, the CPD and Oracle included a publicly accessible version called CLEARpath that allows residents to report crimes, view images of wanted persons, and assist with open cases.[71] The DHS If You See Something, Say Something and CVE programs promote vigilant surveillance and reporting on anything that might be related to terrorism or indicative of "radicalization."[72] Similar programs along the U.S.–Mexican border call on residents to report undocumented migration.[73] All of these programs rely on and reinforce popular associations of Blackness with crime, Islam with terror, and Latinidad with unauthorized migration.

Every time police stop-and-frisk someone, issue a dispersal order, carry out an arrest, raid a workplace, or receive a report of "suspicious activity," the interaction is documented in a police report and stored in a police database. These reports include data on individuals, their associations, and their hangouts. Built up over decades of racialized deployments, police databases are anything but "scientifically objective."[74]

A constantly expanding arsenal of advanced surveillance technology has accelerated the production of police data while intensifying the racially unequal focus on communities of color.[75] New technology generates data in various ways. Sometimes it is as simple as the introduction of computerized reporting. Take, for instance, the digitalization of gang arrest cards. From 1997 to 2003, Chicago police filled out a paper gang arrest card after arresting someone whom they identified as a gang member. During that time, Chicago police entered 16,619 individuals into the gang arrest card database. In 2004, the CPD introduced computerized gang arrest cards as part of the CLEAR data system. From 2004 to 2009, Chicago police entered 70,946 individuals into the database. In other words, digitalization was accompanied by an immediate, massive spike in the number of supposed "gang members" in Chicago.[76] This is one way that technology expands criminalization.

New technologies automate and supercharge the production of police data while intensifying their unequal focus on working-class communities of color. Chicago's most visible surveillance system is Operation Virtual Shield (OVS), an ever-expanding network of surveillance cameras jointly monitored by the CPD and OEMC. CPD PODs—or "blue light" cameras—are heavily concentrated in downtown Chicago as well as in the South and West Sides.[77] The network also includes cameras in public schools, public parks, and public housing complexes as well as on buses, on trains, in transit stations, on highways, at airports, and at tourist destinations. Police can access video feeds in real time—and turn, tilt, and zoom many cameras—from CPD control rooms, police vehicles, and smartphones.[78] In addition, Chicago encourages residents and business owners to link their public-facing cameras to the OVS network.[79] As a result, the OEMC and CPD have access to more than fifty thousand cameras, with the number growing every day.[80] In addition, the CPD deploys dashcams in all CPD vehicles and bodycams on all CPD officers. As Brian Jefferson explains, OVS has enabled the CPD to "'follow' machine-identified individuals and vehicles from camera to camera" as they move through the city.[81]

Many CPD cameras are equipped with automated license plate readers (ALPRs), which record images of license plates along with a time stamp and GPS location.[82] In every police district, the CPD has stationary cameras and at least six vehicles equipped with ALPRs. Every ALPR is "capable of scanning thousands of license plates per hour," generating more than two hundred million records in 2018–19 alone.[83] The technology enables Chicago police to identify patterns of movement and track cars in real time. The CPD can also access the city's network of red-light cameras and speed cameras with a court order. And, in recent years, Chicago Parking Meters Inc.—the private company that operates Chicago's thirty-six thousand parking meters—has required drivers to enter their license plate information when they park. This creates another database that police can use to track people's movement.

In addition, the CPD has an acoustic surveillance network of gunshot detection devices. After testing a gunshot surveillance system in 2007, the CPD began rolling out a new system—ShotSpotter—in 2016, starting in a few districts on the South and West Sides. ShotSpotter claims that its microphones are able to distinguish gunshots from similar sounds (such as fireworks) and identify the location and direction of shots. By 2021, the devices were deployed in the twelve police districts that have the highest proportion of Black and Latinx residents in the city. According to a report by Northwestern University's MacArthur Justice Center, the CPD responded to more than forty-six thousand ShotSpotter incidents from July 2019 to April 2021. Police did not record any gun-related incidents in 89 percent of the deployments; in 86 percent, they found no evidence of any crime whatsoever. But these deployments put communities of color in danger, because police rush to the scene assuming that someone has just fired shots. As the report explains, "any resident who happens to be in the vicinity of a ShotSpotter alert will be a target of police suspicion or worse. These volatile deployments can go wrong in an instant."[84] More deployments to communities of color also generate more police contact with residents, which leads to more reports and therefore more data.

Chicago police also conduct phone surveillance using Stingray devices, which mimic cell towers to intercept signals from nearby phones. The CPD purchased its first Stingrays in 2005.[85] These devices enable police to locate individuals and potentially access their data.[86] In 2016, the Illinois legislature passed the Citizen Privacy Protection Act, which requires a court order to use a cell-site simulator and prevents police from capturing the content of communications. But the CPD has repeatedly denied Freedom of Information Act requests for information about Stingray use, raising questions about whether the CPD abides by the law. In addition, with a court order, local and federal agencies can tap a telephone or access phone company databases, such as AT&T's Hemisphere.[87] Moreover, the National Security Agency conducts dragnet surveillance of phone communication, as revealed by Edward Snowden.[88]

The most recent addition to the CPD's arsenal of advanced surveillance hardware is unmanned aerial vehicles, better known as drones.[89] In 2020, the CPD began purchasing drones using off-the-books cash seized during criminal investigations. Leaked documents from the CPD claim that the drones will be used for vehicle pursuits, crime scene photos, missing persons, and "terrorist related issues."[90] But nothing more is known about the regulation or deployment of this technology.

Police supplement their own data with data sourced from public agencies and private data brokers. Companies like Palantir, PredPol, LexisNexis, Cambridge Analytica, Thomson Reuters, and HunchLab provide police departments with access to nearly limitless data on individuals, their behaviors, and their social networks.[91]

Since 2015, the CPD has deployed programs designed by Oracle, LexisNexis, Geofeedia, and PathAr to monitor social media networks like Facebook, Twitter, Snapchat, and Instagram.[92] Social media monitoring programs enable keyword searches, location-specific geofencing, network mapping, and other targeted operations. Oracle and PathAr both claim that Chicago police successfully used their software to interrupt protests during the 2012 NATO summit. And PathAr advertises the use of its software to map networks of street gangs in Chicago.[93] According to CPD directives, social media monitoring is currently limited to manual searches of publicly available data,[94] but the CPD and the FBI have a secretive Social Media Exploitation Task Force (SOMEX), which may enable Chicago police to bypass the department's own regulations.[95] And the CPD responded to the 2020 uprisings by creating a new Looting Task Force to "monitor posts on social media, looking for posts about looting, violence and other crimes."[96] Closely tied to surveillance capitalism, social media monitoring involves the surveillance of our posts, clicks, likes, and networks.[97] Importantly, social media monitoring leads to a criminalization of mourning because police claim that expressions of grief and loss can be precursors to retaliatory violence.[98]

Facial recognition is a growth field for surveillance technology. In January 2020, the CPD signed a two-year contract with Clearview AI, which uses artificial intelligence to run facial recognition scans on more than three billion images found on social media and across the internet. CPD spokesman Anthony Guglielmi explained that the technology added "jet fuel" to police investigations.[99] Just five months later, Clearview canceled the CPD contract after pressure from activists and a federal lawsuit charging that Clearview's technology violated the 2008 Illinois Biometric Information Protection Act.[100] Nevertheless, the Lucy Parsons Lab obtained documents revealing that the CPD still uses facial recognition software from DataWorks Plus, NeoFace, and Cognitec.[101] This software allows the CPD to compare images captured through its video surveillance network with millions of mug shots in the CLEAR database as well as databases maintained by the FBI and other agencies.[102] Facial recognition algorithms are notoriously inaccurate, with consistent patterns of producing false positives when attempting to identify people of color.[103]

The CPD is also adding DNA to its arsenal of biometric surveillance. The CPD not only collects DNA from people convicted of violent crimes but increasingly collects swabs from people at the time of their arrest. Chicago police are introducing Rapid DNA capabilities at booking stations to allow for DNA collection and processing at the time of arrest.

This feeds into growing federal, state, and local DNA databases, which include samples from crime scenes and repositories of DNA from people convicted and arrested on suspicion of committing violent crime. It has implications not only for people in the system but also for their family members due to familial matching technology.[104]

In a city marked by rampant inequality and intense segregation, with police pursuing a racialized War on Crime, the CPD overwhelmingly trains its surveillance technology on poor and working-class Black and Latinx neighborhoods. The CPD consistently installs new technology in select districts on the city's South and West Sides before expanding its use across the city. The uneven deployment of technology, deployments, stops, and arrests, all of which are grounded in the targeted surveillance of racialized criminal archetypes, ensures that police data overwhelmingly include people who resemble the targeted archetypes. This is an important material foundation for the disproportionate production of data on people of color.

Cleansing the Data

The vast amounts of data that local, state, and federal agencies produce through electronic and other forms of surveillance are stored in police databases and processed through advanced forms of data analysis. This transforms the data into a weapon that police use to wage their wars. Cleansing the data is key to their weaponization. Databases and advanced data analysis codify dehumanizing archetypes as "facts" and generate an air of scientific objectivity, both of which erase the material and discursive conditions of data production. This result is weaponized data, by which supposedly "objective" measures provide "scientific" justification for enhanced targeting of the same people and neighborhoods that the three police wars have historically brutalized.

For twenty years, Chicago police have monitored an arsenal of high-tech surveillance equipment from the DOC/CPIC located in CPD headquarters on Michigan Avenue and 35th Street. By the mid-2010s, the expansion of electronic surveillance had generated overwhelming volumes of data. Like before, the CPD claimed to be "data-rich, but information-poor."[105] In 2016, the CPD began rolling out a novel strategy to address this issue: multiplying and decentralizing the sites for monitoring and analysis. Through a partnership with the University of Chicago Crime Lab, the CPD has built twenty-two SDSCs in district police stations (starting, as always, on the South and West Sides) and three ATCs for the Bureau of Detectives.[106] All of these surveillance hubs have the ability to monitor and analyze the CPD's vast amount of surveillance data in real time and use the information to shape deployments and pursue investigations. In effect, the CPD multiplied its analytic capacity by supplementing the centralized citywide function of the DOC/CPIC with twenty-five local surveillance centers located across the city.

Police strategies transform archetypes into data by treating "gang members," "terrorist suspects," and "criminal aliens" as official populations that can be counted, tracked, and targeted.[107] Police databases are repositories of official state knowledge that codify the devaluation of Black, Latinx, and Arab/Muslim life and reify racialized discourses about crime, terror, and belonging. Tables in the CPD's CLEAR data system, for instance, treat "gang members" and "terrorist suspects" as official populations that can be identified and enumerated. In doing so, they codify dehumanizing racial archetypes as official designations that take the form of "facts." The gang arrest card database, for instance, marks more than 134,000 people with the label "gang member." More than 95 percent are Black or Latinx.[108] Similarly, 77 percent of people whose racial identity is listed in the CPD's SAR database are people of color; 54 percent are identified as Arab, Muslim, Middle Eastern, or "olive skinned."[109] In other words, police cannot see a "gang member" without the presence of a Black or brown body, just as they cannot see a "suspected terrorist" without an "olive-skinned" body.[110] Unlike police reports, which might describe why particular individuals were tagged as "gang members" or "terrorist suspects," databases simply treat the labels as objective "facts." This erases the process through which the data were produced as well as the humanity of the people with the label.

The codification of racialized archetypes has real impacts for individuals and communities. Police record these "facts" on a person's permanent record, which state officials, employers, and sometimes even landlords can access through background checks and public record requests.[111] "In Chicago," Reuben Miller notes, "there are over seven hundred policies that keep people with criminal records unemployed. More than fifty bar them from housing."[112] Devah Pager has documented the racialized economic impact of a criminal record.[113] In Pager's audit study, 34 percent of white people and 14 percent of Black people *without* criminal records received a callback after submitting a job application—but only 17 percent of white people and 5 percent of Black people *with* criminal records received a callback. People with criminal convictions face discrimination and stigma for life—including voting restrictions and limitations on access to public housing, education, food support, and other supports.[114] And Didier Fassin reminds us that the stigma of criminalization is not just produced by a criminal conviction;[115] educators, social workers, and others often attach criminal labels to young people before they have ever been arrested. In Chicago, police enter individuals into the gang arrest card database at the moment of arrest, not conviction, and into the investigatory stop report database after merely stopping and questioning them.

Whereas some databases are purged every five years, others last much longer. SAR data are stored in FBI databases for thirty-five years.[116] The CPD gang arrest card database is never purged. Because the record is permanent, hundreds of people in their seventies and eighties are still in the CPD gang database.[117] In addition, predictive policing can keep people in databases long after their deaths. As we discuss in chapter 2, deceased "gang members" remain in databases so police can target memorials on the anniversaries of their births and deaths. In a world of data-based policing, a criminal label is not just a life sentence; it is quite literally a permanent record.

By transforming racialized archetypes into "facts," police databases reinforce the sense that certain people and places are dangerous while manufacturing a "community" that needs protection. Anthony Hatch refers to this as a racial spectacle: the empire state uses the mass media to disseminate spectacular data about racialized populations that incite white supremacist responses.[118] Stuart Hall and his colleagues, for instance, studied the moral panic that ensued when British police began circulating statistics about mugging, which was popularly understood as a Black crime.[119] Chicago police routinely reference their own data on the number of gang members in the city to remind the public that gang violence is a serious threat, that gang members are concentrated in particular neighborhoods, and that a violent police crackdown is justified.[120] Similarly, federal government officials cite statistics from ICE and Customs and Border Protection to reify the threat of undocumented migrants crossing the southern U.S. border. In other words, police mobilize data built on racialized archetypes as a weapon that justifies further surveillance, violence, and even death.

While databases obscure the production of police data, predictive analytics create an air of *scientific objectivity* that allows police to disavow their reliance on racialized archetypes.[121] Data-based policing uses data analysts, predictive algorithms, and social network analysis to identify crime patterns, anticipate criminal activity, and deploy officers at times and locations considered likely to prevent crime. Police falsely claim that high-tech predictive analytics make policing less biased.

There are two main forms of predictive policing: "hot spots" and "hot people." Hot spot policing is nothing new. For decades, Chicago police tracked crime by placing pins on a wall map—and using them to identify locations for additional surveillance. CPD commander Marc Buslik explained,

> We had a big map on the wall behind you and we'd stick pins in it. And it was a very subjective interpretation by really experienced police officers. We didn't have anybody that we would call an analyst, but people would look at it and they'd say, "It looks like we have a burglary problem here or a robbery problem there." And we'd try to discern some temporal aspect to it, you know, "Is this something happening around midnight or between 10 and 2 during the day?"[122]

Of course, the data on the map—like all police data—were a product of racialized discourses and deployments.

Data-based hot spot policing accelerated with the launch of the DOC in 2003. Analysts at the DOC/CPIC analyzed patterns in the CLEAR database to identify territories for targeted police activity. The DOC/CPIC designated a "Level II Deployment Area" in each of Chicago's then six (now three) police areas where police enforce a zero-tolerance policy for "gangs, guns and drugs."[123] The deputy chief in charge of the area was responsible for saturating these zones with surveillance technology, patrol officers, and special units.[124]

In the mid-2000s, the CPD developed a new crime-mapping system called Caboodle. Whereas earlier maps focused on district-level data, Caboodle was designed to map gang territories and conflicts across the city.[125] More recently, the CPD has added predictive software called HunchLab, which adds spatial and temporal layers to police maps, including the locations and operating times of bars, liquor stores, concerts, sporting events, and more.[126] HunchLab allows police to identify multiple, shifting hot spots for targeted enforcement at different times throughout each shift.

Though hot spot policing is well established, Chicago has become a forerunner in efforts to predict which individuals will engage in criminal activity, specifically gun violence. Chicago police have long targeted particular individuals and their social networks. In 2003, DOC analysts began providing district commanders with lists of "gang members or associates deemed pivotal to an ongoing conflict."[127] And CLEAR was designed to include data on social relationships—including people who were together at the time that they were stopped or arrested.[128]

The 2012 launch of the Strategic Subjects List (SSL) represented the birth of data-based "hot people" policing.[129] The CPD worked with Illinois Institute of Technology (IIT) professor Miles Wernick[130] to develop an algorithm that used CPD data to identify people likely to become involved in violence. The SSL algorithm generated individual risk scores on a 500-point scale, with higher numbers supposedly indicating a greater chance of becoming a "party to violence" as either a shooter or a victim.[131] It calculated these risk scores based on two sets of data stored in CLEAR: (1) an individual's arrest and victimization records and (2) the arrest and victimization records of everyone whom police consider the individual's "associates."

Advances in social network analysis enabled the police to identify these "associates" by mapping networks of people who were arrested together. The SSL focused on two levels of co-arrests. The first level included everyone with whom an individual had been arrested; the second level included everyone arrested with someone in the first level. The result was a regularly updated, ranked list of individuals whom the algorithm determined were at a heightened risk for violence. Police describe the SSL as similar to a credit score, which rises and falls with changes in individuals' records and the records of people in their networks.[132] Police commanders in each district would periodically review the list to identify fifteen people in the district for targeted interventions, including enhanced prosecution.

In response to a study by RAND indicating that the SSL failed to predict violence or generate effective interventions, the CPD/IIT team tweaked the model several times.[133] Police were quick to point out that race, gender, and geography were not factored into the algorithm.[134] Indeed, supporters insisted that the SSL provided "objective" or "race-neutral" guidance about whom to target, yet these claims mask the fact that the SSL was based entirely on CPD data collected through stops, arrests, and other practices grounded in racialized deployments and criminal archetypes.[135] Despite the air of objective neutrality, the data that fed the algorithm were so flawed that the outcome did nothing more than direct police to continue targeting the same people the CPD had already been targeting as part of its War on Gangs.[136] This is how predictive policing generates a vicious spiral of surveillance.

In late 2019, the CPD decommissioned the SSL after negative reviews by RAND and Chicago's inspector general.[137] But we have not seen the end of "hot people" policing in Chicago. CPD officials and community organizations still use CPD data to identify individuals for targeted interventions.

Eubanks uses the term *mathwashing* to describe the way that predictive technologies generate seemingly objective "data" that obscure the conditions of their own production.[138] Companies advertise advanced technology as an antidote to racism because of its supposed ability to bypass human error and bias, and police claim that they are simply targeting the people and places that an algorithm has identified as "hot." But these claims disavow the fact that the data processed through the algorithm are generated by racialized surveillance and targeted enforcement in a neoliberal apartheid city. As Michael Rodriguez-Muñiz explains, data "science" is a very political science.[139] Predictive policing may appear objective, but bias is built into the data collected, the methods of data collection, and the interpretation of the data.

Simon Balto points out that Chicago police arrested two to three times more Black people than white people every year from the 1960s through the 1990s. This changed in the late 1990s, when "the CPD effectively stopped arresting white people and drove Black-to-white arrest disparities to rates about 7:1."[140] It is no coincidence that this enormous racial gap in arrest rates swelled at precisely the moment that the CPD began computerizing its databases and using predictive analytics to determine deployments.

Predictive analytics has reinforced the criminalization of territory and created new possibilities for criminalizing relationships.[141] By relying on proximity to clusters of previous crimes to estimate the probability of future crimes, hot spot policing broadens the scope of hypersurveillance to incorporate larger territories in Black and Latinx neighborhoods.[142] People-centered predictors criminalize social relations, transforming family members and neighbors into criminal associates. As Jackie Wang explains, researchers claim that predictive algorithms can identify people as criminals before they are even born.[143] This helps explain how thirty-three thousand people were added to CPD gang databases as children, some as young as nine.[144]

Ultimately, predictive policing generates a vicious spiral of surveillance: aggressive patrols in Black and brown neighborhoods generate stops and arrests that become "data" suggesting that police should continue targeting the same neighborhoods and populations. Rather than a cycle, it is a spiral that expands as it spins.[145] Predictive policing exposes people to further stops and arrests, each of which makes them more susceptible to future police contact. In Benjamin's words, "crime prediction algorithms should more accurately be called crime production algorithms," because they mass-produce people marked as criminals.[146]

Circuits of Empire

Circulation is the third process through which data are weaponized. Like the production and analysis of data, the circulation of data is always political. Much of the scholarship on data circulation focuses on the public sphere and the cultural politics of numbers. Michael Rodriguez-Muñiz and Leo Chavez, for instance, analyze the ways that actors wield statistics about the growing Latinx population in the United States either to induce fear or to advance political representation.[147] Law enforcement agencies also publicize statistics on the number of crimes, arrests, deportations, gang members, and criminal aliens as weapons of war.[148] As we discussed earlier, the public dissemination of police data constitutes a racial spectacle that shores up support for policing. In this section, we focus on a more private form of circulation, one that remains intentionally hidden from public view: flows of data through the circuits of imperial policing.

Interagency data sharing is not new. Animated by dreams of an omnipotent empire state with unimpeded access to detailed information about individuals, networks, and populations, government officials experimented with various models of data sharing—including interagency task forces and community policing programs.[149] Many of these projects confronted jurisdictional silos, conflicts over power, authority, and recognition and "a culture within the federal system that does not foster sharing of information or trust between agencies."[150] A new approach crystallized after September 11, 2001.

The federal 9/11 Commission argued that U.S. intelligence agencies failed to prevent the attacks due to a lack of information sharing across agencies. The commission called for the adoption of a "decentralized network model" by which agencies would share access to their databases.[151] The DOJ and the DHS responded with guidelines for collecting, analyzing, and sharing information related to terrorism. The International Association of Chiefs of Police formulated what became known as the National Criminal Intelligence Sharing Plan.[152] And the 2004 Intelligence Reform and Terrorism Prevention Act established a new office—the Director of National Intelligence—to facilitate coordination among the seventeen federal agencies that make up the U.S. "intelligence community." As Brandon McQuade explains, "the process of intelligence fusion mobilizes the decentralized surveillance capacities of state and private powers to render the complexity of social life legible as 'intelligence.'"[153]

The federal response to 9/11 popularized and institutionalized the decentralized network model that we call *carceral dif/fusion*, which involves a proliferation of carceral agencies alongside mechanisms for coordination. Within this model, the circulation of data is key to coordination. There are three basic methods of data circulation: shared databases, fusion centers, and data-sharing agreements.

Federal agencies, including the FBI and DHS, maintain shared databases that are sourced from and accessible to law enforcement agencies across the country. State police also maintain databases accessible to local police departments. The Illinois State Police, for instance, maintain the

Law Enforcement Agencies Data System (LEADS) and Violent Crime Information Tracking and Linking (VITAL) database.

As described, the CPD and Oracle designed CLEAR as a shared database. A Chicago police officer served as an "evangelist" or "salesperson" for the CLEAR Sharing Program, actively marketing CLEAR to law enforcement agencies across the country.[154] As a result, officers from more than five hundred law enforcement agencies can access CLEAR without any data-sharing agreements or administrative safeguards to limit their use of the data. Federal agencies use CLEAR data to target people classified by the CPD as "gang members" and "suspected terrorists." As Chicago's inspector general revealed, for instance, ICE searched the CLEAR system more than thirty-two thousand times from 2008 to 2019 to identify "gang members" as priority targets for deportation.[155]

Interagency task forces also create shared databases. Until 2019, the Cook County Sheriff's Office hosted the Regional Gang Intelligence Database (RGID), an electronic gang database created by the Lake County Indiana High Intensity Drug Trafficking Areas (HIDTA) program. The Lake County HIDTA[156] is a regional task force that includes agents from the FBI, the Drug Enforcement Agency, ATF, the Cook County Sheriff's Office, the CPD, and local law enforcement agencies in Illinois and Indiana. The Cook County Sheriff's Office began managing RGID in 2013 and expanded access to more than 367 local, state, and federal agencies, until organizers from the #EraseTheDatabase campaign successfully pressured the Sheriff's Office to decommission the database in January 2019.[157]

Fusion centers are high-tech surveillance centers designed to facilitate information sharing between law enforcement agencies. They represent a second method of data sharing. Building on experiments in data fusion developed as part of the War on Crime, the director of national intelligence and the DHS established the National Network of Fusion Centers to support the War on Terror.[158] Each state has a primary fusion center, and major urban areas have regional fusion centers. Although operated by state or local police departments, fusion centers are staffed by officers from dozens of law enforcement agencies across the country.

The creation of fusion centers was justified as a counterterrorism strategy, and their original mandate involves sharing information related to counterterrorism operations. In practice, officers deployed to fusion centers review SARs, the documents created when people report seeing something that they consider suspicious through the DHS If You See Something, Say Something initiative. When a SAR is filed, analysts at a fusion center review federal, state, and local databases to determine whether the reported activity or individual has a "potential nexus to terrorism."[159]

Fusion centers streamline the process of data sharing by employing dedicated analysts to search databases maintained by various law enforcement agencies, other government agencies, and private data brokers. Some of these databases are shared and therefore already accessible to multiple agencies. Officers on patrol could review these databases on their own, but it would take time. Other databases are restricted to officers associated with particular agencies. Fusion centers bypass these restrictions by placing officers from multiple agencies in the same control room and allowing them to share information. After conducting an initial investigation, fusion center analysts upload the SAR to local, state, and federal databases and send the information to the FBI Joint Terrorism Task Force for further investigation.

Most fusion centers—especially in urban areas—have expanded their missions to include "all crimes, all hazards." As a result, fusion centers have become key nodes in the expansion of racialized surveillance: using federal funding to purchase and monitor high-tech surveillance equipment, sharing intelligence and promoting interagency coordination, and helping to build the web of criminalizing surveillance that crisscrosses the United States.

Illinois has two fusion centers: the Statewide Terrorism Intelligence Center at the headquarters of the Illinois State Police and the CPIC at CPD headquarters. The CPIC began with a focus on counterterrorism, but, like most fusion centers, quickly expanded its mission to include "all crimes, all hazards." Located within the DOC, the CPIC became the central intelligence hub for the entire CPD. CPIC analysts monitor surveillance equipment, provide reports to officers on the street, inform predictive deployments, oversee strategies like the SSL, and develop workups about gang conflicts and incidents of gun violence. But the CPIC is also a fusion center, staffed by agents from the CPD, the FBI, the DHS, the U.S. State Department, the U.S. Secret Service, the U.S. Attorney's Office, the Illinois State Police, the Illinois Department of Corrections, the Cook

County Sheriff's Office, the Metra Police, and suburban police departments.[160] These agents review SARs and share their data with state and federal agencies.

Like all fusion centers, the CPIC is not subject to regulations that limit the collection and retention of information related to political and religious views, associations, or activities. In addition, whereas most law enforcement agencies require "reasonable suspicion" to investigate a person or organization, fusion centers have a lower threshold, known as "reasonable indication."[161] This provides fusion center analysts with tremendous latitude in their approach to surveillance. As the CPIC privacy policy explains, "CPIC may retain information that is based on a level of suspicion that is less than 'reasonable suspicion' such as tips and leads or suspicious activity report information."[162] It is not clear whether this policy applies to the entirety of the CPIC's expansive mission or only to its role reviewing SARs.

Formal data-sharing agreements represent a third method of data sharing. As part of the War on Immigrants, section 287(g) of the 1996 Illegal Immigration Reform and Immigrant Responsibility Act enables local police to enter into data-sharing agreements with federal immigration authorities. Counties that participate in 287(g) run the names of foreign-born people arrested by local police through federal immigration databases and inform immigration authorities when they identify a noncitizen with an immigration violation. Secure Communities expands these checks. Counties that participate in Secure Communities run all fingerprint data collected by local police departments through databases maintained by the FBI and DHS, automatically tagging noncitizens with a "criminal alien" label.[163] Moreover, ICE shares data on the criminal histories of alleged gang members who have been deported with law enforcement agencies in Mexico, Central America, and the Caribbean.[164] Similarly, as part of the War on Terror, the United States and Israel signed a Mutual Legal Assistance Treaty (MLAT) that established a process for sharing information related to particular investigations.[165] Through this process, one country can ask the other for documents or assistance with interrogating witnesses or suspects as part of an ongoing investigation. And the U.S. imperial response to 9/11 included efforts to expand data-sharing agreements with allies and clients around the world.

Within the system of carceral dif/fusion, the circulation of data has become an essential mechanism of articulation linking the webs of imperial policing. To begin with, the circulation of data facilitates coordination among agencies. Interagency task forces create shared databases to support coordinated planning and joint operations. Improved coordination also provided the primary justification for the expansion of data sharing as part of the War on Terror. In addition, the circulation of data enables a swarm of agencies to target people separately and simultaneously. The swarm does not always require coordination, such as when the CPD and ICE use shared data to target alleged gang members despite sanctuary city restrictions on formal coordination. Importantly, the data that flow between agencies comprise more than abstract numbers. They contain detailed information about actual people and their family members, neighbors, friends, and comrades. Data sharing thus intensifies the vicious spiral of surveillance and the mass production of gang members, criminal aliens, and terrorist suspects, ensnaring people in a global web of surveillance, violence, and death.

Data-sharing processes draw schools, social workers, probation officers, child welfare agencies, and even violence-prevention programs into carceral networks.[166] Private data brokers play a growing role in these networks by tracking people's information, interests, and consumption patterns under a system of surveillance capitalism. They claim ownership over our data, run it through predictive algorithms, and sell the results.[167] ICE has made use of surveillance capitalism by establishing a corporate entity that purchases cell phone data to track migrants.[168] The surveillance is ubiquitous, drawing together a constant flow of data from multiple sources that can be studied, analyzed, and weaponized.

As data flow through the circuits of imperial policing, the context of their production disappears entirely.[169] Agencies generally abide by a collective acceptance that data received from other agencies are factual—even when produced through forced confessions or officer discretion. In part, this collective acceptance is grounded in the shared assumptions and racialized discourses that animate policing. But it is also written into the regulations and policies that govern data sharing. Within the United States, the federal regulation that establishes guidelines for the collection, storage, and sharing of information by law enforcement agencies is known as 28 CFR part 23. The guidelines establish a set of standards on which law enforcement agencies base their presumption that data are factual. Similarly, the U.S.–Israeli MLAT treaty has a clause indicating that information shared by a participating country must be accepted in court without "further authentication or certification." These assumptions, standards, and policies reinforce the cleansing of data, ensuring the final erasure of their production.

Although data sharing is a key mechanism for "fusion" within the carceral webs of empire, these criminalizing webs are complex, and data sharing is uneven. There remain proprietary tensions, technological complexities, jurisdictional struggles, policy differences, and privacy concerns that prevent the free flow of information between agencies.[170] CPD officials complain that they share data with the FBI but that the FBI hesitates to share its own data.[171] Although widely embraced in the Wars on Crime and Terror, data sharing is openly contested in the War on Immigrants. Liberal sanctuary cities, such as Chicago, refuse to share certain data with ICE. Nevertheless, flows of data remain important even for sanctuary cities. As we demonstrate in chapter 5, exceptions written into Chicago's sanctuary ordinance allow the CPD to share data with ICE under certain conditions; ICE may be able to access CPD data indirectly through other agencies; and the CPD provides a foundation for immigration enforcement by aggressively surveilling immigrant neighborhoods and tagging young people of color with labels like "criminal" and "gang member."

There remains a powerful drive to expand and ultimately perfect this incomplete system of data sharing. Yet the tensions cannot be overlooked. Some connections are already fragmented or broken, and more can be torn asunder. This is important for campaigns seeking to dismantle the webs of imperial policing.

Chicago's growing reliance on high-tech surveillance is a response to the crises generated by white supremacy and neoliberal racial capitalism. It is an increasingly unstable social order that relies on repression, protecting the powerful by policing the racialized poor. Data-based policing reproduces Chicago's long-standing criminalization of Black, Indigenous, immigrant, diasporic, and working-class communities. Police produce data as part of the three police wars through stops, arrests, and advanced technology. Databases transform racialized criminal archetypes into "facts." The complex subjectivities of real people disappear in the data, and all that remain are "criminals," "gang members," and "terrorists." These data are run through algorithms and other tools that further erase the social conditions of production, providing supposedly objective evidence that police should continue targeting the same people and places. And data-sharing processes enable multiple agencies to target the same populations, expanding the webs of criminalization and surveillance. In this way, data become a weapon of war—a vicious, ever-expanding spiral of surveillance and criminalization.

Rather than reducing the problems that it purports to address, however, data-based policing reinforces the underlying crises. The reification of archetypes and the circulation of seemingly "objective" indicators reproduce the popular imaginary that crime is rampant and that people and property need police for protection. It also helps reinforce the notion that "they" are different from "us" and that "we" need the police to protect "our" neighborhoods from "them." The criminalization of neighborhoods reinforces disinvestment and decline, and the spiral of instability continues to spin out of control. The only fix that elites can imagine is more policing, surveillance, and repression. In response to growing calls to defund or abolish the police, data-based policing legitimizes carceral reforms. Since the 1960s, every attempt to reform the CPD has expanded the department's capacity for high-tech, data-based, racialized surveillance. As a result, communities of color in Chicago confront a police department that deploys an arsenal of advanced technology, relies on the vicious spiral of predictive analytics, and shares its data with an imperial web of criminalizing agencies. Yet none of this has led to a sustained reduction in gun violence.

Attempts to reform the CPD in the aftermath of Laquan McDonald's murder are no different. The CPD rolled out new surveillance technology while outlining plans for "enhanced community policing."[172] As we describe in the next chapter, "enhanced community policing" involves the further incorporation of community-based organizations into the CPD's carceral network. Mayor Lori Lightfoot's administration consolidated a network of organizations that work together to address gun violence through an approach known as "focused deterrence." Police and service providers work hand in hand, using police data to identify people at "highest risk" of gun violence and then extending an offer of support along with a threat of "enhanced prosecution." Legitimized by a discourse of "science," this project expands data-based policing in the name of reform.

At the same time, the consent decree is largely silent about police technology. It says nothing about facial recognition, ShotSpotter, social media monitoring, or the SDSC/ATC initiative. Treating data and technology as a mechanism of police accountability, the consent decree endorses the rollout of body-worn cameras, disregarding their function as a swarm of surveillance cameras that selectively record the perspectives of officers while aimed at Black and brown bodies.[173] And, similar to "professionalization" in the 1960s and CLEAR in the early 2000s, the consent decree embraces the failed promise of using police data to monitor officers and prevent misconduct. This has never materialized and is bound to fail again due to rank-and-file resistance.[174] Regardless of what else happens with the reform process, therefore, the CPD's use of high-tech, data-based racialized surveillance will continue to expand.

Yet Black, Latinx, and Arab/Muslim communities in Chicago are resisting data-based policing. They are refusing to be labeled criminal, alien, or terrorist. Instead of only seeking restitution for individuals who have been wrongfully accused of gang membership or terrorist activity, abolitionist social movements are demanding the eradication of gang databases and SARs, an end to interagency data sharing, restitution for individuals harmed by data-based policing, divestment from carceral agencies, and investment in communities. Exposing the latest developments in data-based policing is part of their strategy to resist criminalization and affirm the full humanity of people whose lives have been reduced to archetypes by their inclusion in police databases. These movements help us envision a pathway to abolition through the erasure of police databases and the affirmation of full humanity for people targeted by police.

2   Focused Deterrence: Carceral Liberalism in the War on Crime

On September 29, 2020, Mayor Lightfoot released Our City, Our Safety—a three-year plan for reducing gun violence in Chicago.[1] The plan grew out of the Police Accountability Task Force (PATF), which was created by Mayor Emanuel and headed by Lightfoot after Chicago police murdered Laquan McDonald. As narrated in the three-year plan, the PATF "spurred a group of philanthropic organizations coming together as the Partnership for Safe and Peaceful Communities to invest in reducing gun violence and improving police legitimacy."[2] Our City, Our Safety claims a "public health" approach that understands gun violence as contagious, learned behavior that spreads through social networks and can therefore be contained and averted.[3] The plan describes dozens of strategies that concentrate on individuals considered "most likely to be victimized or contribute to violence" while simultaneously promoting police legitimacy and encouraging "collaboration, proactive planning, and coordinated efforts" between city agencies, law enforcement, and community-based organizations.[4] The Chicago Police Department (CPD) refers to this as "enhanced community policing."[5]

The strategies in the city's plan focus on young people identified by police and nonprofits as having the "highest risk" of exposure to gun violence. According to the plan, "much of the violence in Chicago is perpetrated by and victimizes a small percentage of people, in small concentrated social networks."[6] This reflects an increasingly popular idea that David Kennedy, director of the National Network for Safe Cities (NNSC), describes as an emerging "science" of violence reduction. This science, he explains, is grounded in the "fact" that gun violence is driven by "very, very small numbers of high-risk people."[7] Rather than an issue of systemic disinvestment in racialized communities, this approach treats gun violence as an individual or group-level problem to be addressed with targeted interventions. As an NNSC brochure explains, "most people in [historically disadvantaged] communities are not at high risk for either victimization or offending. A very small number of identifiable street groups drive the violence, and the people in them face extraordinary risk and trauma."[8] Kennedy coined the term *focused deterrence* to describe programs that seek to identify and intervene with "high-risk" individuals to prevent gun violence.

In Chicago, the Mayor's Office of Violence Prevention established criteria for identifying individuals at "highest risk" of violence. A person is high risk if they are (1) "involved" in street gangs[9] and/or the criminal punishment system and (2) meet at least one of the following criteria: "previous victimization," "violent online behavior," "symptoms of trauma," or "disconnected from school."[10] In practice, this risk-assessment measure depends on data produced through police stops, social media monitoring, and other forms of racialized surveillance. The effort to identify "high-risk individuals," therefore, involves extensive police contact and widespread surveillance in Black and Latinx communities. Citing research from Andrew Papachristos, the report claims that approximately seventeen thousand people are at "highest risk" of violence in Chicago.[11] This is the supposedly "small number" of individuals whom the plan targets.

Overall, the city's plan envisions a coordinated network of public and private organizations using data to develop targeted interventions that address the same high-risk individuals through job training, trauma-informed care, cognitive behavioral therapy, wraparound services, and—notably—the threat of arrest and enhanced prosecution. It is this final aspect, enhanced prosecution, that constitutes the carceral element of *carceral liberalism*—a term we use to capture the logics of individual responsibility, police legitimacy, and carceral expansion that ground these projects. Informed by counterinsurgency strategies, Our City, Our Safety treats service provision and repressive violence as complementary. In this chapter, we assert that although the plan appears to prioritize services for "high-risk" individuals, the services are inseparable from the threat of incarceration. In addition, the plan presumes that people simply "choose" support or punishment. Finally, it calls for "constant collaboration" and "data sharing" between City Hall, the CPD, federal agencies, service providers, street outreach teams, universities, and philanthropic organizations.[12] In other words, it seeks to expand the network of agencies involved in the War on Crime—more specifically, the War on Gangs—and to improve coordination through data sharing.

To lubricate the network, City Hall facilitates weekly "regional coordination meetings" on the South and West Sides, where Chicago police, street outreach organizations, and service providers meet to "leverage each other's distinct but complementary roles in addressing violence."[13] The Office of Violence Prevention also created a digital platform to "share daily crime and violence data . . . with City agencies and community-based organizations who respond to violent incidents. The objective is to make data more accessible and support community partners in using the data to inform decision-making based in real-time."[14] Chicago's emerging network of coordinated agencies sharing data to identify a small number of high-risk individuals for targeted interventions is at the cutting edge of what Kennedy calls the "new science and practice" of violence reduction.[15]

In this chapter, we address Chicago's embrace of this "new science" and examine its material and symbolic impacts on policing in the city. After an introductory discussion of carceral liberalism, we trace the emergence of focused deterrence through violence-reduction projects across the country, including two innovations developed in Chicago. In the next two sections, we analyze the CPD's adoption and rearticulation of focused deterrence and examine the proliferation of violence-reduction projects spurred by carceral science, the nonprofit–industrial complex, and the city's emphasis on coordination. Challenging the narrative of violence reduction as an alternative to carceral interventions, we argue that the emerging networked approach to the reduction of gun violence has created additional pipelines to prison by justifying police stops and surveillance as a way to produce "data" and by drawing community-based organizations into a growing carceral network.

CARCERAL LIBERALISM

It is easy to see the appeal of focused deterrence, particularly in a city where gun violence remains one of the most urgent manifestations of the crises confronting working-class communities of color. Hundreds of young people are killed and thousands are injured in Chicago every year, with heavy concentrations in South and West Side neighborhoods weighed down by decades of racialized abandonment, neoliberal austerity, and state violence. A recent study revealed that young adult men living in some of these neighborhoods face a higher risk of gun-related death than U.S. soldiers deployed to Iraq and Afghanistan during the most intense periods of combat.[16] The trauma of seeing someone shot or losing a loved one to violence is even more widespread. According to another recent study, 56 percent of Black and Latinx Chicagoans—and 25 percent of white Chicagoans—have seen a person shot by the time they turn forty.[17]

There is a desperate need to address the violence claiming and shaping the lives of so many young people in Chicago's working-class Black and Latinx communities. Something must be done to prevent further loss of life and traumatization. Programs that target a few individuals are more affordable than broad-based programs, and their impact is more easily measurable. This helps explain the attraction of focused deterrence to politicians, police officials, philanthropists, and nonprofit organizations. And there is no doubt that community-based violence-prevention programs sometimes help stop shootings, mediate conflicts, negotiate treaties, and forge relationships with young people confronting relentless state, community, and epistemic violence along with racism, gender-based stereotyping, emotional trauma, physical injury, and disability. They help some people change the courses of their lives and help others learn skills for coping with constant exposure to racialized trauma and premature death.

Our research, however, raises serious concerns about the carceral "science," the data, and the partnerships with powerful institutions that support the city's plan, particularly as these coordinated programs threaten to substitute for structural antiracist commitments to equitable investments in communities. When advocates of the new "science" discuss violence, they mean "gun violence." This is evident in the insistence that the "drivers" of violence are small groups of young people. This focus obscures the foundational, structural violence of racial capitalism, white supremacy, empire, and heteronormative patriarchy. By suggesting that the best way to address gun violence is by focusing on a small number of high-risk individuals, the "science" delegitimizes alternative explanations for violence and renders systemic transformation unnecessary. The focus on small numbers also aligns with neoliberal efforts to replace broad-based, publicly financed social welfare programs with narrow, donor-financed public–private partnerships targeting select individuals. It also helps philanthropic organizations justify decisions to fund programs that target young people without addressing the deeper structures of violence or altering their own relationships to power, privilege, and government.

Though presented as an alternative to repressive policing, focused deterrence is a fundamentally carceral project. As we demonstrate in this chapter, focused deterrence projects emphasize police legitimacy, depend on police surveillance, and seek to incorporate community organizations into an expanding carceral network. As outlined, Mayor Lightfoot's three-year plan was a community policing initiative explicitly designed to increase police legitimacy. Focused deterrence projects also rely on aggressive police stops and racialized surveillance to generate the data necessary to identify individuals at "highest risk" of violence. In addition, they always couple the promise of services with the threat of incarceration and "enhanced prosecution." Finally, they operate by drawing nonprofit organizations into a coordinated carceral regime centered on the imperial police. In other words, focused deterrence relies on and supplements the overtly repressive tactics of gang suppression, described in chapter 3, which remain the primary tactics in Chicago's War on Gangs. It is the "soft" side of the War on Gangs, embracing a framework of carceral liberalism.

Our work joins a scholar-activist lineage that challenges the assumption that best intentions and humanitarian interventions necessarily yield positive social change. Rather than reversing oppressive conditions or eliminating inequities, nonprofit social service providers' internal practices, external relationships, and fundraising models can easily reproduce the very inequities they purport to address, effectively becoming counterinsurgency tactics.[18] The term *nonprofit–industrial complex* is used to describe the relationship between academics, philanthropists, and nonprofits that work together to expand social controls, depoliticize grassroots movements, and roll back state spending on social welfare. Throughout the world, U.S. government funding agencies, philanthropic organizations, and academic researchers shape the programming of nonprofits, service providers, and nongovernmental organizations with an eye to controlling dissent and redirecting activists from radical movements into organizations with reformist agendas.[19] This is a useful lens for understanding the challenges facing violence-reduction organizations in Chicago today.

Like the violence-reduction work explored in this chapter, other "soft" forms of policing are often framed as benevolent rather than punitive. The programs that Forrest Stuart calls "therapeutic policing" attempt to restructure policing around the idea of "curing" or "fixing" the poor.[20] Lynne Haney, Victor Rios, Reuben Miller, Nicole Nguyen, Lydia Dana, Kelley Fong, Maya Schenwar, and Victoria Law document the expansion of social control through programs that incorporate educators, social workers, probation officers, child welfare agencies, and even violence-prevention programs and LGBTQ+ service providers into carceral networks.[21] This scholarship helps us understand why meaningful structural change is unlikely to result from these networks.

To be clear, liberalism is always carceral.[22] Liberal beliefs about human beings as autonomous, rational, rights-bearing subjects have always been coupled with racial logics that differentially value human lives and labor and exclude enslaved and colonized people from the category of the fully human. Moreover, military and carceral interventions are increasingly justified on humanitarian grounds. Settler-colonial and imperial regimes carry out racialized wars in the name of protecting women, girls, and LGBTQ+ communities.[23] And liberal reforms promise an end to biased policing, but police continue to uphold racialized regimes of dispossession and exploitation.

Within this more general framework, Ruth Wilson Gilmore refers to "carceral/police humanitarianism" as a domestic counterinsurgency program through which police organizations partner with nonprofits to "identify and attend to the (relatively) innocent victims of too much policing and prison" with "goods and services that in fact everybody needs."[24] What we are calling *carceral liberalism* is closely related to Gilmore's carceral humanitarianism. By "carceral," we mean that these programs rely on threats of arrest, incarceration, or other forms of state violence

The black mans greatest stumbling block is not the KKK or the white citizens council but the white moderate that is more committed to order than to JUSTICE

FIGURE 4. A quote by Dr. Martin Luther King Jr. about the danger of white moderates is held at a #ReclaimMLK protest. Photograph by and courtesy of Sarah Jane Rhee (@loveandstrugglephotos).

and that they attempt to increase the legitimacy and expand the power of the police and the empire state more generally. By "liberalism," we do not mean simply the Democratic Party. Instead, we are pointing to liberal logics of individual choice and personal responsibility that offer a pathway to redemption for individuals who make the "right" choices by rejecting violence. The same logics hold people responsible for their own oppression on account of "bad decisions," thereby erasing the structures of violence that condition these "choices."

Our work is in dialogue with Patrisia Macías-Rojas, Korey Tillman, and Shreerekha Pillai, all of whom use the concept of "carceral liberalism" to describe projects that combine benevolence with coercion.[25] Tillman, for instance, discusses carceral liberal approaches to homelessness that aim to "address the 'behavior' of those on the margins by forcing individuals to make a choice either to move their bodies in ways deemed acceptable by the state and its tangential actors or be disciplined."[26] Importantly, Tillman traces the roots of this strategy to the liberal foundations of colonialism, empire, and anti-Blackness.

Our analysis of carceral liberalism focuses on four sets of actors: carceral scientists, nonprofit organizations, funding agencies, and various branches of the government. University-based social scientists—carceral scientists—developed the general theory of focused deterrence as well as the statistical models and algorithms for analyzing people's social networks using police data. They also provide support with data analysis and program evaluation. Nonprofit organizations carry out the frontline work of violence reduction. They hire former gang members to deescalate conflicts, offer services to those at "highest risk" of violence, and provide standardized training for violence-reduction workers. Public- and private-sector granting agencies—including some of the wealthiest foundations and philanthropic arms of corporations in the United States—facilitate the entire project by controlling the flow of funding to nonprofit agencies and academic researchers. With deep connections to elites and the empire state, most funding agencies support projects that promote liberal reforms rather than radical social transformation. Government agencies that operate at a range of scales—from the local to the federal—help coordinate the entire apparatus and deploy the carceral violence on which it rests.

In other words, focused deterrence is a complex apparatus that combines layers of ideological, financial, bureaucratic, therapeutic, and repressive power that is deployed to contain gun violence while reproducing the violent structures of the liberal order. Importantly, parts of the apparatus also include space for contestation and autonomy. Our critique focuses on the powerful actors working to institutionalize focused deterrence as a form of carceral liberalism: law enforcement; universities; major grant makers; and large, well-resourced violence-reduction organizations whose appeals to middle-class liberal whiteness award them the power to define violence and the platform to narrate its "solution." At the same time, we want to uplift the work of grassroots organizations and frontline workers who are drawn (in)to focused deterrence projects yet still contest criminalization, resist incorporation, and address root causes.

"THE EMERGING SCIENCE OF VIOLENCE PREVENTION"

In 2019, the NNSC at John Jay College in New York City hosted its Tenth Anniversary Conference on the theme "The Emerging Science of Violence Prevention." In his keynote address, NNSC director David Kennedy argued that evidence-based research has proven that certain practices are effective in reducing gun violence. "There are things that, by the highest standards of social science, we *know* work to prevent violence," he said. "We *know* that we can make communities safer and work with communities to be safer. That statement—that we *know* we can do this—that's a new statement. Not long ago, that wasn't true."[27]

These claims to "science" are important for understanding the growing popularity of focused deterrence among police officials and funding agencies. And university-based social scientists—especially criminologists and sociologists—provide the justification for these claims. Several interconnected projects contributed to the notion that there is a "science" of violence prevention. In the 1990s, Kennedy—then at Harvard University—worked with Boston police to develop the strategy he later called "focused deterrence." Gang enforcement officers told Kennedy that they knew nearly every individual involved in gun violence and understood the intergroup dynamics that led to each shooting.

> Every time a kid gets killed, we know them, from the streets. We almost always know who did it—we may not be able to prove it, to take it to a prosecutor, but we know.... And there aren't that many of them and they mostly hurt each other.[28]

These knowledge claims provide the foundation for the so-called science of focused deterrence. Concentrating on the groups considered most violent, police and community-based outreach workers emphasized three messages: (1) don't shoot—gun violence is our top priority; (2) if your group refrains from using violence, police will not actively target your drug sales; (3) but if your group decides to continue using violence, police will aggressively enforce every law against every member of the group—including drug possession, distribution, and loitering. Outreach workers attempted to interrupt violence and offered individuals an "honorable exit" from the gang, while police intensified the collective punishment of groups that refused to comply.[29] From the start, therefore, focused deterrence has been a carceral project grounded in the threat of police violence and incarceration. The program's perceived success attracted funding and led other cities to establish similar programs.

Two other sources of the "emerging science" have roots in Chicago. In 2001, the U.S. Department of Justice funded Project Safe Neighborhoods (PSN), a nationwide interagency initiative coordinated by U.S. attorneys.[30] Tested in Chicago, PSN pioneered three practices that became central to focused deterrence: interagency task forces, call-in meetings, and federal prosecution. PSN began by creating a multiscalar task force that included local and federal law enforcement, local and federal prosecutors, and community-based organizations. The task force identified people on parole who had a record of gun charges and required them to attend a "call-in" meeting. During the meeting, a former gang member spoke about leaving the gang behind, a service provider discussed available forms of support, and a U.S. attorney threatened everyone at the meeting with a "five year mandatory minimum federal sentence if they were caught with a gun."[31] Advancing a liberal framework of individual choice, call-in meetings were designed "to stress to offenders the *consequences* should they choose to pick up a gun and the *choices* they have to make to ensure that they do not re-offend."[32] The promise of support rests squarely on the coercive nature of parole, the threat of federal prosecution, and the individualization of responsibility. This is carceral liberalism.

Finally, focused deterrence programs draw on advanced forms of social network analysis. In a series of articles beginning in 2009, Andrew Papachristos—professor of sociology at Yale and later Northwestern University—transformed the study of gang violence by deploying advanced techniques of social network analysis.[33] Using data sets from the CPD, Papachristos mapped the social networks of individuals who had been arrested together for the same offense (known as co-arrests). He focused on two layers of associations: the first layer included everyone with whom an individual had been arrested; the second layer included everyone arrested with someone in the first layer. Using these network maps to analyze gun violence, Papachristos concluded that shootings and homicides are concentrated within and spread through tight social networks. "Gang members do not kill because they are poor, black, or young or live in a socially disadvantaged neighborhood," he argued. "They kill because they live in a structured set of social relations in which violence works its way through a series of connected individuals."[34] Papachristos thus provided a social-scientific argument for focusing on networks rather than deeper structures. Since that time, police departments, service providers, and others have incorporated Papachristos's model into "focused deterrence"—using social network analysis to identify individuals at "highest risk" of gun violence and targeting them with "data-driven" interventions.

Bringing together these insights, Kennedy founded the NNSC in 2009.[35] The NNSC liaises with law enforcement, academic research centers, and violence-prevention organizations to provide training and support for focused deterrence. As Kennedy explains, focused deterrence is grounded in a few simple "facts": (1) violence is committed by and against very small numbers of very high-risk people; (2) what drives the violence is not primarily about individuals but about groups and networks; and (3) it is possible to identify those individuals, understand the group dynamics, and intervene to transform their behavior.[36]

The emphasis on small numbers and group dynamics is the heart of focused deterrence. "In any place, it's about one half of one percent," Kennedy explains. "That high-risk 0.5% will be consistently connected with 50, 60, 70, 80% of all homicides and gun violence."[37] This means that the vast majority of people in even the most historically disadvantaged neighborhoods will never be either shooters or victims of gun violence. "The principle that there is a small number of high-risk people in the community, and we can tell who they are, and we can pay them a special kind of attention. Everything that works in violence prevention begins with that fact."[38]

The implications are twofold. First, the focus on small numbers and group dynamics shifts attention away from structural dynamics associated with racial capitalism and white supremacy. "As abused as these communities have been," Kennedy says, "they still function remarkably well from a violence-prevention standpoint. They raise their families and govern themselves in such a way that almost nobody in them is violent.

They do a really good job actually."[39] While challenging dominant cultural representations that stigmatize entire communities, this framework stands in opposition to analyses that identify colonialism, capitalism, racism, patriarchy, and heteronormativity as the root causes of violence that must be addressed.[40] Indeed, Kennedy explicitly rejects structural solutions.

> When violence was about cultures of violence and troubled neighborhoods and the historical impact of poverty . . . all of that was not practically useful, at least in any near-term intervention. What has allowed effective intervention is the recognition of the concentration and the group dynamics and then the emergence of interventions that work when focused on groups, network, individuals, and dynamics.[41]

According to Kennedy, "it's infinitely *less* complicated than the traditional root cause story that we have to fix *everything* to fix crime: the economy, the schools, health care, the families, the culture. That idea still has a lot of appeal to a lot of people, but it comes with one nagging and obvious problem: You can't *do* it."[42] Reaching a small number of people, he argues, is something that can actually be done.[43] Instead of "fixing" the system, focused deterrence sets out to "fix" individual subjects.

Second, the focus on small numbers requires targeted interventions to reach those most at risk of becoming victims or perpetrators of violence. "Broad interventions mostly touch people who don't need them as far as violence prevention is concerned," Kennedy explains. "But there's good reason to think that anything that effectively engages with that small number of people and their groups and networks and dynamics is probably worth doing."[44] In line with neoliberal calls for cuts to social spending and the presumption that resources are scarce, this means rejecting universal programs in favor of targeted job training, cognitive behavioral therapy (CBT), and other services. "If you have one thousand CBT-supported job slots and you sprinkle those across Chicago at random, it will be like it never happened. It is not meaningful," explains Kennedy. "But if those job slots are informed by an empirical grounding that says this is the very small number of people who are at risk and therefore they should get these jobs, that makes sense."[45]

Importantly, when it comes to the police, Kennedy suggests that targeted interventions should replace mass surveillance, stop-and-frisk, and other tactics that criminalize entire communities. These programs, Kennedy argues, are too broad to be effective and lead communities to question police legitimacy.[46] He finds it both more effective and more legitimate for police to focus their attention on a few highly active offenders and to use every mechanism in their arsenal to stop them from using violence. According to this logic, focused deterrence is an *alternative* to strategies that criminalize everyone in marginalized communities. As we will see, however, focused deterrence as practiced in Chicago is no alternative. On the contrary, police and nonprofits depend on data collected through racialized surveillance and extensive police contact to identify the "small number" of high-risk individuals. And the incorporation of community organizations into a carceral network is designed to expand surveillance and reinforce police legitimacy, with no change to the project of policing at its core.

The discourse of "science" is important for the expanding popularity of focused deterrence. The discourse is grounded in a description of the practices as "evidence based," meaning evaluated using objective, social-scientific methods—usually by professors at elite research universities. NNSC presentations include a page of statistics from "published, peer-reviewed studies with control groups" that demonstrate the efficacy of focused deterrence. They reference studies demonstrating a 63 percent reduction in youth homicide in Boston during the 1990s and a 37 percent reduction in homicide in Chicago neighborhoods that implemented PSN.[47] The numbers look impressive—and that's the point. Like other data-based policing projects, the "science" erases the social and political conditions through which the data are produced. As Roberto Aspholm notes, "focused deterrence efforts have had no discernable impact on overall levels of homicide in Chicago: The city's average homicide rate of 16.5 per 100,000 for 2011–2015 following the implementation of focused deterrence was nearly identical to its average rate of 16.4 for 2006–2010."[48] Nevertheless, peer-reviewed, evidence-based evaluations by university professors enable Kennedy to claim—"by the highest standards of social science"—that focused deterrence works.[49]

The theory and practice of focused deterrence assume that it is possible to identify high-risk individuals, understand their group dynamics, and intervene to transform their behavior. Aspholm has demolished these assumptions. Ridiculing the notion that police know who is responsible for most shootings, Aspholm points to the CPD's dismal clearance rates. As he notes, "no suspect is even identified in more than four out of five murders and nearly 95 percent of nonfatal shootings in Chicago."[50] Moreover, Aspholm argues that police simply do not understand the importance of personal autonomy among gang members. By this, he means that gang members increasingly reject "the notion that anyone, even their closest comrades, can tell them what or what not to do with respect to violence or any other matter."[51] In this context, he argues, there is little chance that coercive efforts to transform behaviors or "fix" subjectivities will have any lasting effect.

Yet the NNSC insists that focused deterrence is effective when there is a multiscalar network that includes police and outreach workers who know the individuals and groups in each neighborhood, community organizations and service providers that can provide a moral voice and offer support, and local and federal prosecutors that can enforce sanctions. The interventions communicate a dual message—either services and support or targeted enforcement and enhanced prosecution—grounded in a liberal logic of individual choice. This is what we call *carceral liberalism*.

CHICAGO: EXPANDING THE CARCERAL NETWORK

In recent years, Chicago has developed numerous projects grounded in focused deterrence. The CPD operates separate programs in each of the twenty-two police districts across the city, and several donor-funded nonprofit organizations have rolled out programs that attempt to reach the same high-risk individuals with targeted interventions. The city is working to promote coordination between these projects and to further incorporate nonprofit organizations into the carceral network. The effect is a dif/fuse swarm of dispersed yet coordinated carceral interventions that link to the CPD and attempt to "fix" individuals with a promise of support buttressed by the threat of state violence.

Chicago Police

The CPD has been at the center of all focused deterrence projects in the city, dating back to PSN and the advent of data-based social network models. Since 2009, the CPD has worked with NNSC and community organizations on focused deterrence projects as part of its overall approach to gang enforcement: the Gang Violence Reduction Strategy (GVRS).[52] According to CPD directives, the GVRS involves "information gathering, analysis, dissemination of intelligence, linking of gangs to their factions, social network mapping, and a variety of mission-specific operations focused on targeted gang members and their associates."[53] The GVRS brings together local, state, and federal law enforcement agencies; community organizations; and social service agencies and relies on predictive policing and focused deterrence to track and target more than 130,000 people whom the CPD identifies as gang members.[54]

As part of the GVRS, the NNSC helps Chicago police "identify the city's most violently active groups; conduct immediate, targeted outreach to the most at-risk individuals; reduce their involvement in violent crimes; [and] connect them with specialized social services."[55] The NNSC office is embedded within CPD headquarters and linked with community-based organizations across the city, training staff in outreach and overseeing "custom notification" and "call-in" programs—both of which are focused deterrence programs that present community members with the promise of services and the threat of prosecution.

The GVRS began in 2010 in the Eleventh District on the city's West Side. Over the next four years, the project expanded to nine other districts on the South and West Sides before becoming citywide. District-by-district replication means that the CPD operates twenty-two GVRS programs across the city. The decentralization and proliferation of focused deterrence programs is unique to Chicago but consistent with a broader dif/fusion of surveillance in the early twenty-first century.[56]

The foundation of the GVRS is the gang audit, an annual intelligence-gathering process through which each of the CPD's twenty-two district commanders compiles a report on the gang factions, gang members, and gang conflicts in their respective district. As Papachristos explains, "gang audits are a survey or census of a neighborhood's gang landscape—which groups are present, where they hang out, and, most importantly, who's got conflict with whom. The audit emerges from a series of working sessions with law enforcement, community stakeholders, researchers and other gang experts."[57] These audits rely on data generated by Chicago police during stops, arrests, and other encounters. They incorporate social network analysis by identifying supposed leaders and then using CPD data to trace networks around those people. The audits produce data on gang factions, individual associations, social networks, and maps that indicate territorial boundaries and intergroup tensions.

In 2011, Mayor Emanuel hired Garry McCarthy as superintendent of the CPD. Under McCarthy's direction, the CPD carried out gang audits in every district across the city. McCarthy encouraged officers to stop, question, and frisk residents as a way to collect data on their associations and networks, and he transformed social network analysis into "one of Chicago's primary tools in responding to gun violence."[58] Most importantly, McCarthy supervised the rollout of the Strategic Subjects List (SSL), which we described in chapter 1.

Although the SSL has been decommissioned, CPD officials still use data to identify individuals for targeted interventions. This is facilitated by another new mechanism for localized surveillance and deterrence. Since 2016, the CPD has installed high-tech Strategic Decision Support Centers (SDSCs) in each of the twenty-two district-level police stations, starting, as always, on the West and South Sides.[59] The SDSCs have become the decentralized hubs for hyperlocal War on Gang strategies, including focused deterrence. District commanders and district intelligence officers draw on the data collected by the SDSCs to identify people for targeted interventions, and nonprofit organizations doing street outreach work receive notification of gunshots from the local SDSC.

In practice, the GVRS includes three focused deterrence programs: shooting reviews, call-ins, and custom notifications. Shooting reviews are weekly meetings in each police district to discuss every known shooting that took place during the previous week. Led by the NNSC, shooting reviews bring together the CPD district commander and district intelligence officer, along with officers from CPD narcotics, vice, and gang units and representatives of the Federal Bureau of Investigation, the Bureau of

Alcohol, Tobacco, Firearms, and Explosives, and local and federal pros-ecutors.[60] Together, they discuss what they know about each victim, the possible shooters, their social networks, their rivalries, and intergroup dynamics. Describing the people in the room as a "collective body of intel-ligence," an NNSC officer explains, "They give us the information. Who is he up against? What other groups is he running with? Is he in a gang? Does he stay with the gang or does he hang with another group? Those kinds of questions. Then we'll say: who's he connected to?"[61]

Shooting review meetings take place in the SDSCs. During the review, the group consults CPD databases to understand each person's back-ground, associations, and network connections. Frontline officers attempt to correct information from the database that seems outdated or otherwise faulty. All of this knowledge—from databases and human intelligence—is based on stops, arrests, and other forms of racialized surveillance. Gang arrest cards and investigatory stop reports, for instance, provide the data that ground the social network maps. Without stop-and-frisk, constant arrests, and other forms of surveillance, the police would not be able to make knowledge claims about people's social networks and intergroup dynamics. This undermines the notion that focused deterrence is an alternative to repressive policing. In practice, focused deterrence relies on racialized surveillance and constant police contact to generate the knowledge base—or database—that informs shooting reviews and targeted interventions. After reviewing each shooting, the group determines a set of "actionable and accountable deliverables."[62] These actions always include targeted enforcement operations, such as arrests, increased surveillance, hot spot policing, and neighborhood saturation. The response might also involve call-ins or custom notifications.

Call-ins are group-based interventions that target specific gangs or cliques with the threat of collective punishment.[63] When the CPD decides to target a gang in a particular district, the NNSC compares a list of people on parole from that district with CPD gang databases to identify members of the group who are on parole. The NNSC sends the list to the parole office, which requires the individuals to attend a call-in meeting. At the meeting, the CPD area deputy chief and district commander, the Cook County state's attorney, and the U.S. attorney emphasize that the entire group will be held responsible for the actions of every individual associated with the group. If anyone engages in violence, everyone will face sanctions—including aggressive enforcement of every law as well as "enhanced prosecution."[64] For instance, courts are allowed to limit plea bargaining, and a "special understanding" provides federal prosecutors with "enhanced" options to review and adopt cases. They emphasize the possibility of RICO cases and federal charges with long-term sentences. After these threats, speakers from community-based organizations—including mothers who have lost children to violence, former gang members, and service providers—convey a message of "hope and aspiration."[65] They tell the audience that each person is a valued member of the community and offer support if the group chooses to abstain from violence. On the way out, attendees pass tables where service providers offer different kinds of support.

Custom notifications involve similar messages but focus on individuals rather than groups. They were developed to address a limitation to the call-in system, which relies on the carceral system to coerce participation. "Some of the guys, we can't get into the call-in because they're not on paper. They're not on probation or parole," explains a representative from the NNSC.[66] Custom notifications are personalized letters delivered to individuals deemed "high risk." A CPD officer visits the person's home, along with representatives from the NNSC and a community organization. The group shares the letter with the individual or with family members or friends. Each letter outlines an individual's arrest record and informs them that future arrests will lead to enhanced prosecution, including federal charges. "What those individuals need to know if they choose to stay in that lifestyle," explained former CPD superintendent Eddie Johnson, "[is that] we'll come after them with everything that we have."[67] After the CPD delivers the letter, community members and service providers convey the same message as during the call-in. According to the NNSC, the custom notification program involves "bringing services to the house."[68] Yet it also brings threats and surveillance to the house, sidestepping the typical requirement that police would need a warrant to visit a person's home. The CPD has also delivered custom notifications to people in Cook County Jail, magnifying the coercive aspects of the process.[69] And in June 2020, the CPD responded to criticism of its unconstitutional gang database by proposing to use the custom notification process to inform people that their names appear in the new gang database.[70]

Custom notifications and call-ins are framed as offers but grounded in threats. Embracing a liberal logic of individual choice, they are clear examples of carceral liberalism. As the CPD's 2015 directive for the custom notification program explained, "opportunities for seeking assistance will also be provided during the custom notification. However, it is ultimately the decision of the individual to choose not to engage in criminal activity."[71] Though presented as an alternative to generalized surveillance and racialized criminalization, this section has demonstrated that focused deterrence relies not only on the threat of further carceral violence but also on data produced through these very practices. In chapter 3, we examine the process of data production by drawing on the knowledge and experiences of young people targeted by the GVRS.

Multiplicity and Coordination

Starting in 2016, Chicago witnessed a proliferation of grant-funded programs operated by nonprofit organizations that attempt to reach the same high-risk individuals with targeted interventions. Most of these organizations frame their work as an alternative to the carceral. Yet the reality is more complex. Some organizations collaborate with the CPD directly, using call-ins, custom notifications, and police-generated data to reach "at-risk" clients. Others refuse to participate in custom notification programs but have joined a violence-prevention network that encourages "professionalization" and coordination with the CPD. And City Hall is working to further incorporate community organizations into the carceral web. This networked apparatus is the latest iteration of a nonprofit–industrial complex that carries out counterinsurgency operations in coordination with the empire state. But there remains space for contestation and autonomy, even within this network. The overall effect is a swarm of partially autonomous yet coordinated interventions that attempt to identify and "fix" at-risk individuals without transforming the system. This is how dif/fusion generates a spiral of surveillance. After a brief overview of the role of philanthropists and academics, this section discusses Chicago's three highest-profile programs: the Rapid Employment and Development Initiative (READI), Creating Real Economic Destiny (CRED), and Communities Partnering for Peace (CP4P). We focus on CP4P.

In spring 2016, as protesters demanded justice for Laquan McDonald, philanthropic organizations launched two initiatives to fund violence-reduction work in Chicago. First, five major grant makers based in Chicago joined forces to create the Partnership for Safe and Peaceful Communities (PSPC). By 2021, PSPC had grown to more than fifty major funders and had committed more than $90 million to "community-led, evidence-based solutions" to gun violence.[72] While distributing small grants to dozens of community organizations, including restorative justice hubs like Circles & Ciphers, PSPC has provided millions of dollars to two of Chicago's most prominent focused deterrence programs: CP4P and Chicago READI. In the second major philanthropic development of 2016, former U.S. secretary of education Arne Duncan returned to Chicago with a reputed $100 million from the Emerson Collective, the organization run by Laurene Powell Jobs, the widow of Steve Jobs.[73] Duncan used the money to establish Chicago CRED, which joined PSPC to fund violence-reduction programs while simultaneously launching its own focused deterrence program. By controlling the flow of funds, these major philanthropic organizations have established focused deterrence as the hegemonic approach to violence reduction in Chicago.

In a context of neoliberal austerity, funding agencies have tremendous power to shape the agendas of grant-dependent nonprofit organizations that want to address the needs of vulnerable communities. In Chicago, philanthropic organizations provide the material foundation for carceral liberalism. Their power is enhanced by their deep entanglements with the city and state governments and the CPD. Mayor Lightfoot, for example, hired several people from the philanthropic network as part of her revolving administrative leadership team. According to *Crain's Chicago Business,* the grant makers behind PSPC represent the "city's establishment."[74] Their investments align with their vested interests in upholding the social order.

Violence-reduction initiatives grounded in the new "science" of focused deterrence are particularly attractive to this network of private foundations seeking to champion "evidence-based" approaches to social and economic progress. The funding agencies require organizations involved in READI and CP4P to maintain data on their programming and their outcomes, and the grants include funding for the University of Chicago Crime Lab or the Northwestern University Institute for Policy Research (IPR) to evaluate the programs using social-scientific methods.

Here, again, social science researchers from prestigious universities lend legitimacy to policing and facilitate philanthropic buy-in.

Yet there are tensions within the networks. Although Mayor Lightfoot and governor J. B. Pritzker increased public funding to the violence-reduction network, CRED, READI, and others are calling for significantly more public investment. When Lightfoot earmarked $11 million for community-based violence-reduction programs in the 2020 budget, for example, critics pointed to the money earmarked for the CPD ($1.7 billion) and the amount that Los Angeles and New York City spend on violence reduction (roughly $30 million each year) to question the mayor's commitment.[75] Following calls to #DefundCPD, Duncan encouraged the city to shift $150 million to $200 million from the police budget to community-based violence-prevention work.[76] "It's long past time to begin shifting resources from over-policing, prosecutions and prisons and give many more young people a real chance in life through these kinds of programs," he argued.[77] Moreover, the directors of READI and CRED repeatedly point out that community violence is a by-product of systemic oppression. They regularly speak about the need to link violence interruption with long-term structural transformation. And most of their employees are formerly incarcerated men and women who have been impacted by community violence and want to create real opportunities for people in their neighborhoods. Nevertheless, the City of Chicago continues to prioritize punitive approaches to gun violence.[78]

READI and CRED seek to curb gun violence by providing mentoring, counseling, job training, employment opportunities, and wraparound services to people at highest risk of violence. These data-informed, market-oriented programs present as noncarceral alternatives to punitive policing. And there is a great deal to appreciate about their work. Chicago CRED focuses its programming in two neighborhoods in the far South Side of Chicago.[79] Duncan began by visiting young men in Cook County Jail and asking what it would take for them to put the guns down and pursue an alternative path in life. Many explained that it would only take a steady job that paid twelve to thirteen dollars an hour. "Everyone has a price point for changing their behavior, but people don't believe me when I tell them what I learned from these conversations," Duncan says. "It's a myth that everyone's getting rich on the streets. There are so many guys out there that there's no economies of scale for selling. They're getting shot, chased by the police. They're not winning."[80] He insists that thousands of young people are trapped in a vicious circle and would change paths if given jobs, support, and resources.

CRED uses data from the University of Chicago Crime Lab, which is sourced from the CPD, to identify young people in the far South Side considered likely to become shooters or victims.[81] With an annual budget of approximately $10 million, CRED works to prepare young people for the job market through street outreach teams that emphasize violence interruption and conflict resolution; cognitive behavioral therapists who address lifelong and multigenerational trauma; life coaches and educators who provide mentoring and help young people receive high school diplomas; and job trainers who focus on industry-specific certificates as well as "soft skills, like time management, teamwork, and workplace professionalism."[82] But that's not enough, Duncan explains. "We need corporate Chicago to hire our young men," he says. "Our men are going to make a living. It is up to us whether that is in the street economy, which will lead to more violence, or in the legal economy."[83]

Chicago READI is operated by Heartland Alliance, an organization that provides services to Chicago's most "endangered populations." It began as a collaborative project: the University of Chicago Crime Lab would use predictive analytics to identify people most likely to become involved in gun violence; Heartland would provide the men with therapy, job training, and paid employment; and the Crime Lab would evaluate the program's impact.[84] Operated through partnerships with six community organizations in five neighborhoods on Chicago's South and West Sides, READI identifies potential participants through the Crime Lab's algorithm and through referrals from street outreach workers and carceral facilities.[85] The program provides men with twelve months of intensive programming,[86] including cognitive behavioral therapy, life coaching, job training, skills workshops, and a transitional job—all of which are designed to help "ensure a smooth transition to unsubsidized employment."[87] According to the program director, Eddie Bocanegra, "we know what works. And what works is when you're able to build coalitions, for example, people who have boots on the ground and are able to really provide direct services, interrupt some of the violence that we're seeing in the community, and be able to attach individuals to something more promising and tangible."[88]

Though READI and CRED describe their care work as an alternative to the punitive approach of the Chicago police, they also coordinate closely with the CPD. In fall 2020, CRED released a report titled *Reimagining Public Safety,* based on focus groups conducted during the summer of uprisings demanding justice for George Floyd. Although participants expressed a range of ideas about the police, the report called for "not defunding, but reallocating" $150 million to $200 million per year from the CPD to community-based violence-reduction programs.[89] When asked whether CRED supports abolishing the police, Duncan responded in no uncertain terms: "We desperately need the police. While trust at the system level is frankly often broken between police and community, we work with amazing police officers.... We desperately need the police."[90]

CRED and READI participate in regular coordination meetings with the CPD and support the call for closer collaboration between the city, the police, and community organizations. Moreover, READI and CRED make use of databases from the University of Chicago Crime Lab—developed through a partnership with the CPD—to identify potential participants. According to an official with the NNSC, street outreach teams from both READI and CRED receive NNSC training in focused deterrence and participate alongside the CPD in call-ins and custom notifications. In fact, the NNSC official explained, this is one of the ways that READI and CRED make contact with potential participants. "What they need is entry, and a lot of times, they don't get entry unless the police and their community moral voice are bringing them there."[91] This suggests that READI and CRED use their partnerships with the police to recruit clients. And, in the carceral liberal framework, the wraparound services that these organizations provide are available only if people make the "right" choice.

Chicago's third major violence-reduction initiative, CP4P, is even more fully entwined with the CPD. CP4P builds on a long history of community-based approaches to violence reduction in Chicago. The largest, longest-lasting program was CeaseFire (later known as Cure Violence), which began addressing violence as a "public health" issue in the late 1990s.[92] Using an epidemiological model, organizations affiliated to CeaseFire set out to interrupt gun violence through conflict resolution, mentoring, and positive relationships. CeaseFire also distributed state funding to organizations that hired former gang members as "violence interrupters."[93] But throughout its existence, CeaseFire had a volatile relationship with the city and the Chicago police. Police often stopped and harassed CeaseFire outreach workers, demanding information about shootings or accusing them of participation in gang activity. Although CeaseFire/Cure Violence maintains a strong global presence, its local programming dwindled after losing a city contract in 2013 and state funding in 2015. Yet CeaseFire's "public health" approach remains influential, and many of CeaseFire's outreach workers and organizational affiliates now work with CP4P.

CP4P emerged in 2016, when several violence-prevention groups began discussing ways to improve coordination. At the center of these conversations was Teny Gross, director of the Institute for Nonviolence Chicago (INV). Gross was one of David Kennedy's outreach workers in Boston before creating his own offshoot in Providence, Rhode Island. In 2015, he came to Chicago, established the INV, secured a multimillion-dollar budget, and signed a coordination agreement with the CPD. Gross soon began meeting with the heads of other violence-prevention organizations. They outlined plans for the coalition that became known as CP4P.[94] What started with nine organizations has expanded to seventeen organizations in twenty-eight communities across Chicago. As part of CP4P, they receive funding from PSPC and from state and city grants, some of which previously went through CeaseFire.[95]

The centerpiece of CP4P programming is street outreach, which builds on work that many affiliates were doing before they joined CP4P. As a coalition, CP4P emphasizes four pillars of violence reduction: nonviolence, trauma-informed care, hyperlocality, and restorative justice.[96] Outreach workers canvass the streets and build relationships with young people. They try to interrupt the intergroup dynamics that spark shootings and broker nonaggression agreements at the neighborhood scale. In addition, the organizations identify high-risk individuals and attempt to recruit them away from street organizations by offering counseling, legal services, and job training—in part by connecting them with READI and CRED. Each organization has a unique approach and offers distinct services. For example, Claretian focuses on affordable housing; together

Chicago and Southwest Organizing Project provide wraparound services for formerly incarcerated and other marginalized individuals; and ONE Northside focuses on community organizing for justice, including police accountability.

Though each affiliate maintains autonomy, CP4P is dedicated to standardizing and "professionalizing" violence-reduction work. Gross explains that this is something the funders wanted to see. In practice, standardization and "professionalization" take place through the Metropolitan Peace Academy, a mandatory training program for all street outreach workers involved with CP4P organizations. The intensive 144-hour course provides outreach workers with training in structural violence, substance abuse, trauma, adverse childhood experiences, CBT, and the history of gangs in Chicago. The course also includes joint sessions with police officers and outreach workers in an effort to facilitate dialogue, build rapport, and "promote *effective and constructive partnership* towards reducing violence." The nonprofit–industrial complex shapes the effort to "professionalize" street outreach work conducted by individuals "who have troubled histories of their own."[97] Many of these frontline workers come out of prison with a deep desire to create opportunities for young people in their neighborhoods to escape community violence and incarceration. Moreover, most have few opportunities of their own because their police records (stored in databases that are accessible through background checks) create real barriers to employment in Chicago.[98] Certainly, compensating members of racialized and criminalized communities for their knowledge, their time, and their investment in change places material value where unpaid labor is often done. However, imagine what would be possible if state funds were spent on structural change for the very same communities or if violence-reduction initiatives were run by the communities they serve with no obligation to collaborate with police? This would serve an abolitionist purpose and disentangle this crucial knowledge from a law enforcement–mediated network.

Organizations involved with CP4P have diverse relationships with the CPD. Some participate in call-ins and custom notifications. A former leader of one organization explains, "We were like, hey, we're in the community helping people who need the help. I could get CPD to get us to the door, then we can take it from there. They're putting us at the door of people who need the help. Now, if they take it, that's good. But if not, then we tried."[99] In effect, the partnership with the CPD provided an avenue for recruiting clients. She went on to explain, however, that only a few organizations participate in these programs. "Most organizations that are part of CP4P absolutely would not even touch it."[100] The Institute for Nonviolence, for example, refuses to participate in custom notifications. Gross explains, "We think that is still sending a message of a threat. When you threaten people who are all their life being threatened and shot, you're not really reforming the relationship."[101]

Yet the relationship between the CPD and organizations affiliated with CP4P goes beyond custom notifications. There are several distinct layers of engagement. On an operational level, the nonprofits rely on district-level SDSCs to inform them about shootings in the neighborhoods where they operate. As part of CP4P, they also receive information directly from ShotSpotter when shootings take place.[102] On the streets, however, the organizations have strict rules of engagement that limit interactions between police and outreach workers. "They cannot ask us for information," explains Gross. "That's the only red line."[103] When they converge on the scene of a shooting, a CP4P director explains, outreach workers "don't even conversate or communicate with law enforcement because of the optics of how that looks."[104] This is intended to protect the outreach workers from accusations that they share information with the police.

Behind the scenes, the red line on information sharing is less clear. The organizations insist that they do not share information with police about violent incidents or individuals. This shapes the way that outreach workers take notes and organizations store data, on the off chance that the information will be subpoenaed. A senior director of one organization explains, "When I'm going back and reading through mediations and daily logs, I try to make sure they don't put no information that can solve a crime. . . . We just say: 'There's two groups that we're reaching out to,' things of that nature. We don't want to put no names or groups or individuals in there."[105]

Nevertheless, the senior leaders of CP4P organizations participate in regular coordination meetings with the CPD on the South and West Sides. At these meetings, coordinated by City Hall, the directors of the organizations and the supervisors of the street outreach teams sit down with CPD district commanders and area deputy chiefs, along with city officials, to discuss ongoing conflicts, trends, and priorities. By all accounts, the nonprofits do not disclose information about specific incidents. One participant explains, "We would never give information that will incriminate our people because we have firsthand information."[106] Yet the meetings enable the CPD to coordinate interventions with the street outreach teams.

> For example, we have a meeting, and [the CPD] would say, "There was a shooting between this person and that person. Do you guys know these people?" We would say, "Yes, we know the two parties. We'll get on top of 'em. We have some relationships. We got inroads into these particular groups. We'll have a conversation. We'll get back to you." We'll come back and say, "Hey, look, that situation was handled, remediated. He's in services." Or we'll say, "Hey, look, we couldn't get a handle on it. This person is not responding to outreach at all. Then you guys do what you need to do."[107]

> CPD talks about their challenges, right? Like they'll talk about a specific block giving them issues and they try to figure out what's going on over there. They'll say, "Hey, this is going on over there. You work in this beat. Can you guys try to get a hold of it? And we'll focus our attention on another area." We'll do that for a couple weeks. They'll see a reduction, or sometimes, street outreach will be like, "You know what? It's out of our hands. You guys do what you do."[108]

Violence-reduction organizations indicate that the CPD leadership recognizes value in coordination. The manager of an organization explains that "law enforcement, specifically the folks that are in charge, see the value of our work. They want shootings to go down in their beats. We want that too."[109] Nonaggression agreements and interruptions in violence allow CPD to focus its resources in other areas and make the police look good. As Teny Gross explains, "good commanders around the country understand that they're being judged by numbers. If Teny's crew can mediate ten conflicts, that is twenty-five shootings that I don't have on my record. I don't have to explain why. It's really a win-win."[110]

On the other side, closer relationships with police are intended to provide protection for the outreach teams. In theory, they should not be stopped, harassed, and intimidated by police, yet this hasn't always materialized. "There's been a lot of buy-in from the higher ups, the ranking officers," explains an outreach worker. "On the ground level, it's a whole different scene. I've been out there. I've been threatened by police officers to be arrested. There's been a lot of officers, specifically tactical officers, who maybe it hasn't trickled down to them, right? They'll treat you like crap."[111] In part, this stems from police reliance on the "gang member" criminal archetype, which we explore in the next chapter. Police tend to treat outreach workers as gang members because of the way they dress, the way they walk, the places they congregate, and the people with whom they associate. It also stems from tensions around information sharing. As an outreach worker explained, police still lean on them for information: "'If you know who shot somebody, you're going to tell us.' And we're like: absolutely not!"[112]

At the same time, the outreach teams face questions from community members about their relationship with the police. An outreach worker told us that people will say "'they're just playing you guys. They really are getting whatever they need. CPD doesn't do nothing without getting something in return, right?' So there are questions about the leadership of our organization and how trustworthy we are because we are in these conversations with CPD."[113] Another explained that this dynamic existed even during the days of CeaseFire. "It's always been like, 'Oh, you guys work with the police,'" he explained. Whereas some of the suspicion comes from people who do not know the individual outreach workers, other people question whether the outreach workers have gone "soft." "Sometimes people know who you were, and they don't see you move the same way that you used to. So they test you, right? I would get tested all the time where it was like, somebody gets loud with me, somebody gets belligerent with me, might disrespect me. And they're looking for a response to see whether or not I'm still with it, or am I gonna run to the police about it."[114]

CP4P, READI, and CRED are key players in the emerging landscape of violence reduction in Chicago. Grounded in the "new science" of focused deterrence and shaped by the funding priorities of PSPC and

CRED, violence-reduction programs are increasingly entangled with the CPD. And City Hall is working to further incorporate nonprofits into this carceral web through the Office of Violence Prevention, regional coordination meetings, and the Our City, Our Safety plan emphasizing police legitimacy, professionalization, coordination, and data-based interventions. Sociologists and criminologists also play a key role within these networks, through theory building (NNSC), algorithm development (Illinois Institute of Technology), data management and training (Crime Lab), and program evaluations (Crime Lab and IPR).

Interaction between community organizations and the CPD is uneven and complex. For groups that participate in custom notifications and call-ins, the message is clear: "I want to make you a priority. You continue offending, the police will make you their priority. They'll stop you if you make them. We'll help you if you let us."[115] Yet even groups that refuse to participate in these programs still rely on information from the CPD and participate in coordination meetings where they divide up territory and tasks. When community organizations are successful, they say to the CPD, "You can put your attention elsewhere because we got this situation under control."[116] When they're not, they say, "It's out of our hands. You guys do what you do."[117]

The grounding vision is a diffuse but coordinated swarm of organizations with a unified threat and an offer of support to a small number of high-risk individuals. Gross emphasizes the importance of *focused* interventions. "Who should we spend limited resources on? The opposite of lists is what we had in Chicago for the last 20 years, which is, everyone was at risk. If you were Black, brown, and poor, you were at risk. So everyone got funded and never really dealt with the most difficult people. . . . We need to reach the people who are the least desirable for society. They're the most desirable for us, 'cause we know they're not aliens. They're children of the community here."[118]

In response to growing demands for abolition, these organizations situate themselves as alternatives to law enforcement. As an NNSC official explained, the goal of focused deterrence is "to make sure that we never have to have law enforcement's hand in it again."[119] Even David Kennedy recently explained, "We're doing everything we can to replace enforcement with deterrence. We don't want to put hands on people and lock them up. . . . Everybody who is doing this, including the very best folks in law enforcement, want as little law enforcement as we know how to do."[120]

Yet when this framework breaks down, when nonprofits are unable to transform the behavior of the "most difficult people," they fall back on the carceral logic that grounds their work. As a CP4P director explained, "there are some people that you'll go to their house, you can do everything you can try to offer to them. But there's just some people that need to be locked up. You wouldn't even believe how many people I've helped. But there's some times where I just say, 'You've just got to go to jail, dude. I can't do no more for you.'"[121]

Despite these entanglements, there are still tensions and spaces for autonomy within these networks. People in violence-reduction roles find value in their work. They see their interventions as meaningful and distinct from the work of the police. One director explained, "A lot of law enforcement, they still think some people are the bad guys. We don't. There are differences. In all this kumbaya, you gotta also remember you are different. We have different points of view and we have different roles."[122] That difference is an important basis for building radical alternatives. Moreover, by collaborating with the CPD on custom notifications and call-ins, outreach workers are trying to keep their clients away from the punishment that is promised to result from these very programs. This is a harm-reduction strategy. In addition, there are questions of transparency, of what organizations know and understand when they agree to participate in programs alongside the police. The director of one West Side organization, for instance, described being compelled to participate in a custom notification visit without understanding what that meant. He was shocked when the police began issuing threats when they entered his client's house.[123] Yet organizations confront a structure of demands and incentives—from funders, City Hall, and the CPD—that makes it difficult to navigate their ethics and their organizational survival while working to provide meaningful services to marginalized populations in a context of austerity.

On its surface, focused deterrence provides an alternative to the criminalization of entire Black and brown communities. Yet it relies on racialized surveillance to identify "high-risk" individuals, intensifies the criminalization of the "small numbers," and grounds its offer of support in the threat of "enhanced prosecution" with more severe penalties. Moreover, the focus on individuals does not address the lasting forms of structural violence from white supremacy, racial capitalism, and the empire state. The directors of violence-reduction organizations acknowledge this shortcoming but see their interventions as a necessary step toward more transformative projects. In the words of Vaughn Bryant, executive director of CP4P, we must be attentive to structural racism and violence. "Gun violence is only a symptom, a byproduct of larger issues. And we're still not really fully addressing the true root causes just yet. I think all of us, what we're doing is trying to create a place where people can go who want to go to a different path. The healing that is necessary is gonna take a long, long time given how long it took us to get to this point. Because the level of trauma is staggering, it is staggering."[124] Yet targeting jobs and services to a "small number" does not address the structural unemployment confronting huge numbers of criminalized people in working-class Black and Latinx communities.

THE SCOPE AND STAKES OF CARCERAL LIBERALISM

All three imperial police wars in Chicago incorporate carceral liberal tactics that seek to protect the "innocent" by punishing the "guilty." Liberal sanctuary policies offer limited protection for "good" immigrants but double punishment through incarceration and deportation for immigrants with a criminal record. Similarly, Countering Violent Extremism is a War on Terror strategy that relies on an extensive network of surveillance to identify individuals deemed susceptible to "radicalization," direct them toward a different path, and intensify the punishment of those who continue on the course. We focus on carceral liberalism as part of the War on Gangs because the dif/fuse, data-based approach to violence reduction in Chicago has attracted the most extensive investments, built the most extensive networks, and garnered the most support. This is the cutting edge of carceral liberalism.

We appreciate the urgency of addressing the intense violence that confronts working-class communities of color in Chicago today. Gun violence is a destructive reality and an ever-present threat that weighs down on communities battered by decades of state violence and organized abandonment. Many of the people caught up in the growing carceral network understand that gun violence is merely a symptom of deep-rooted crises. Some are exploring ways to link violence reduction with structural transformation.

Rather than addressing the underlying crises, however, the counterinsurgency logics of focused deterrence prioritize participation in a carceral network that uses data produced by aggressive policing to identify a small number of people for offers of support backed by threats of further state violence. Legitimized by social scientists, funded by philanthropists, coordinated by the city, and operationalized by nonprofit organizations, the carceral network extends the reach of the police and creates new pipelines to prison. It offers a pathway to redemption for a select few, who are promised the opportunity to become full members of the community. Yet it does nothing to address the deep crises that the entire community confronts.

At the same time, carceral liberal projects blur the line between support and punishment and expand the spaces and tools for incarceration. Promises of support always come with threats that enhance the surveillance of criminalized communities. Call-ins operate through group-based threats of collective punishment; custom notifications add individualized threats. Both programs set up particularly vulnerable individuals for more severe consequences than they already endure. This reinforces the belief that some people deserve carceral violence and uplifts a liberal logic that holds them responsible for their own punishment. It presumes that individuals in heavily policed Black and Latinx communities can "choose" either to be punished like their peers or to make themselves "exceptions." This logic places responsibility on marginalized individuals and denies the state's responsibility to redress structural harm. Counterintuitively, the "new science" also justifies expanded policing. As we demonstrate in the next chapter, police rely on racialized surveillance, stops, and arrests to produce data about individuals and their networks.

At the same time, focused deterrence projects often attempt to conceal their carceral logics. For instance, an NNSC guidebook suggests that call-ins not be conducted in courtrooms and recommends a "community center or African-American history museum" as an ideal alternative.[125]

The physical setting of the call-in can convey important cues to group members that enhance or detract from the actual messages delivered by the speakers. . . . This may reinforce the overall message that the call-in is a community-led intervention, that the group members themselves are part of the community, and that they can be *agents of change*.[126]

To embed these meetings in Black community spaces—while threatening punitive action on primarily Black individuals—deceptively masks the carceral logic of focused deterrence as well as the anti-Black racism that shapes policing more generally. The implication is that those in attendance are incapable of recognizing the underlying carceral logic.

Moreover, what functions as a threat can pass as legitimacy for the police and the state more generally. Gross explains, "I was in the first call-in in Boston. I participated, and I thought it was fantastic. The government gives you a heads-up that we're coming after you. I said, 'That is great government. That's legitimate government.' I'm giving you a heads-up. I'm not coming to you in 2:00 in the morning, knocking on your door, dragging you out of bed."[127]

Yet the effort to distinguish between punitive policing (knocking on your door and dragging you out of bed) and focused deterrence (knocking on your door and threatening you with enhanced prosecution) obscures the fact that both approaches are grounded in racialized surveillance, criminalization, and incarceration. In other words, the distinction collapses because open warfare and concealed warfare are two tactics within the same police war. Both tactics are deployed simultaneously against the same populations.

Our City, Our Safety acknowledges the need for investments in jobs, housing, wraparound services, and other programs to address what it calls the "safety gap" between Chicago's safest and most dangerous neighborhoods. As the plan concedes, "without addressing the root causes of disinvestment, poverty, and inequitable social policies, Chicago's violence-reduction efforts will fail. Addressing these root causes of violence will take years of sustained effort and coordinated partnership with diverse stakeholders."[128]

Will this actually happen? We can imagine but not predict with certainty what will transpire under Mayor Johnson or future administrations

FIGURE 5. Community safety and health require the rejection of carceral institutions and reinvestment in noncarceral alternatives. Artwork by and courtesy of Monica Trinidad.

with regard to these entanglements. However, it is critical to recognize that targeting "just a few" is a reformist approach geared toward increasing police legitimacy while justifying extensive police contact in Black and brown communities. As we document in chapter 6, communities of color in Chicago are working together to reject the carceral logics embedded in data-based policing and to envision and build alternative forms of safety that do not rely on the police.

Radical alternatives would include funding for community-based organizations and violence interruption that does not require or incentivize participation in carceral networks, the provision of wraparound services that are not grounded in a threat of enhanced prosecution, and interventions that seek to transform structures rather than just small numbers. Above all, it is crucial to reject Kennedy's assertion that fundamental structural transformation is impossible. We cannot address the urgency of gun violence without also confronting the underlying crises of racial capitalism and the empire state. Campaigns to defund police departments and invest in communities are a critical step in that direction. However, it would be a mistake to assume that turning to nonprofits represents real progress. We have to attend to their reliance on funders and their limited ability to provide unconditional support. Funders must part with the status quo, stop individualizing social problems, and find ways to fund groups that seek to upend existing systems and institutionalized violence.[129] Above all, we must recognize that multiscalar interagency entanglements are central to the system of policing in Chicago and beyond. This both enriches and complicates existing understandings of power and strategies for resistance.

3 Strategic Subjects: Predictive Policing and the Gang Member Archetype

It was a Sunday morning, the ninth of June, when we learned that Marquise had died. The previous day, Marquise, Brianna, and their neighbors were on the block honoring the life of their friend Gerald, who was sixteen years old when he was shot and killed in 2008. According to police and the media, Gerald was just another dead gang member. But to Marquise and his neighbors, Gerald was a peacekeeper, a problem solver, and an important presence in their neighborhood.

The community gathered every summer to remember Gerald. Chicago police see these memorials as dangerous and closely monitor the gatherings. Indeed, the Chicago Police Department (CPD) keeps track of the deaths of alleged gang members and uses these data to deploy officers for heightened surveillance as part of its predictive policing strategy. According to neighbors, Chicago police had a heavy presence on the blocks near Gerald's home the first week of June 2019. Early Saturday evening, police approached seventeen-year-old Jaquan and called out his name. "We hear you like to go on high speeds," they taunted, invoking his reputation for evading police and implying that they were ready to chase him down.[1] Jaquan tried to brush off the officers' antagonism, but their words were both a provocation and a harrowing prediction.

Later that night, Jaquan and Marquise were driving to meet friends. Police reports indicate that officers were "touring the area for [Jaquan]" because they had "observed several of [Jaquan]'s close acquaintances in the area."[2] According to a statement released by the Fraternal Order of Police, an unmarked vehicle pulled alongside their car, and the officers "confirmed with each other that it was [Jaquan]."³ Perhaps out of fear and perhaps in response to the earlier provocation, Jaquan drove away.

Chicago police are supposed to weigh the risks of engaging in a chase by applying a "balancing test," which requires that officers account for the offense, the danger of the pursuit, traffic on the sidewalks and streets, and environmental conditions before initiating a chase. Importantly, officers are instructed to "consider *not* initiating or terminating an active motor vehicle pursuit whenever the suspect's identity has been clearly established."⁴ Despite their identification of Jaquan, the police initiated a chase that continued at high speeds for more than a mile and a half through primarily Black neighborhoods on Chicago's West Side. They crossed multiple residential blocks with pedestrian traffic, stop signs, stop lights, and limited streetlights. The officers evidently decided that detaining Jaquan outweighed the risks of the chase.

During the chase, Jaquan lost control of the car and collided head-on with another vehicle. The driver and passengers in the other car survived, but Jaquan died on impact. Marquise fought through the night with arms and legs broken and ribs fractured, his internal injuries too severe to repair. Police and hospital security contained Marquise's family and friends in the hospital parking lot, explaining that they could not go inside because they were a security risk. Marquise's father was allowed inside the following morning, after Marquise was pronounced dead.

The deployment of police to monitor Gerald's memorial demonstrates how data-based policing can lead to injury and death. Predictive policing does not just anticipate reality; it helps shape it by influencing the deployment of officers and surveillance technologies, identifying people and places as targets for aggressive policing, and informing officers' interactions with the people they stop. When surveilling a memorial ends in the loss of life, these deaths become new data points that justify additional deployments in subsequent years. Predictive policing becomes self-fulfilling, and the spiral of surveillance continues to grow.

Haley met Marquise a year before he died. Marquise had been released from Cook County Jail after fighting a murder case for two and a half years. In 2016, when he was nineteen years old, Marquise was arrested and charged with the murder of his childhood friend. Newspapers reported that Marquise was a killer, claiming that he and the victim were from rival gangs. The eyewitness and the victim's family members repeatedly told police they had it wrong; Marquise was not the shooter. Despite their pleas, the assistant state's attorney prosecuting the case focused on Marquise's gang membership and deployed a narrative about gang conflict and vengeance that marked Marquise as always already criminal. Marquise faced forty-five years to life in prison. Then, in June 2018, the charges against Marquise were dismissed. Exactly one year later, he was killed in the police-initiated high-speed chase.

The experiences of criminalized Black youth inspired the Policing in Chicago Research Group (PCRG) to work with gang-involved young people to better understand the processes and effects of the CPD's data-based gang enforcement practices. These practices are central to the so-called War on Crime, the first of three interconnected police wars that together constitute imperial policing. In chapter 2, we showed that focused deterrence depends on widespread surveillance and extensive police contact in Black and Latinx communities to identify people at "highest risk" for violence. In this chapter, we draw on the situated knowledge and experiences of young people of color targeted by police to reveal how police produce data through racialized surveillance and aggressive police stops. We developed a countersurveillant abolitionist methodology, in part, by working alongside young people who are the direct targets of the War on Gangs.[5]

We begin this chapter by discussing our research with young people and the relentless epistemic, state, and community violence they experienced. We then examine the "gangbanger" archetype and discourses that deny the humanity of Black youth and allow police to justify their deaths. Then, we uplift the voices of young people whose experiences shatter myths about data-based policing by demonstrating how police produce and deploy their data to intensify racialized surveillance, state violence, and community conflict. Finally, we explore the everyday forms of resistance that Black youth in Chicago use to navigate the material effects of the gang member archetype and predictive policing. We focus on funerals and memorials as sites of fugitive motion where youth resist criminalization and state violence. Throughout the chapter, we show that the everyday lives of young people of color are key sites of abolitionist praxis.

YOUTH-LED RESEARCH AND THE LIMITS OF CRITICAL SCHOLARSHIP

When we began meeting with organizers to discuss the gang database, gang-involved youth were typically not present. Organizers are working with young people to represent their interests and develop organizing strategies that include youth, but gang-involved youth reflected on power dynamics that contributed to their exclusion. Concerns about "safe passage" generally assume that the threat to young people's safety is interpersonal. But youth shared that the threat of arrest and state violence also informed how they could participate in public conversations about the gang database. Because of their absence, we sought to include in our research youth who are the targets of the CPD's gang enforcement.

The analyses in this chapter are rooted by the experiences and knowledge of young people of color—especially Black youth, but also Latinx, Muslim, Indigenous, and immigrant youth—who are included in the CPD's gang database. Through their everyday encounters with police, young people of color develop a critical awareness of and strategies for navigating racialized surveillance. Simone Browne refers to this as *dark sousveillance,* which includes the tactics people use to render themselves invisible, to resist the tools of surveillance, and to turn a countersurveillant lens on systems of power.[6] This section introduces our research with young people, addresses a limitation of radical methodologies, and discusses the politics of loss that shaped our experiences.

Our work with young people was facilitated by Circles & Ciphers, a youth development organization that fuses hip-hop arts and culture with restorative justice principles and practices to support youth entangled in the criminal punishment system. In November 2017, Circles & Ciphers invited PCRG members Haley and Andy to a community circle with their youth members. Haley has worked with Circles & Ciphers since the founding of the organization in 2010. During the community circle, we discussed our research while young people shared their experiences with predictive policing, high-tech surveillance, and police violence. The circle began a dialogue that led to a series of collaborative research projects about the surveillance of gang-involved youth.

Through in-depth qualitative interviews with young adults, archival research, Freedom of Information Act (FOIA) requests, and participatory action research, we sought to understand the construction of gang members as a criminal archetype and the operationalization of predictive policing in communities of color.[7] We interviewed eighteen young people of color and held numerous informal conversations with other youth.[8] Youth described how their identities as Black, Muslim, Latinx, and/or immigrant situated them as objects of surveillance and violence. Their experiences of racial profiling and police antagonism became part of our ongoing dialogue and led to the decision to conduct a youth-led participatory action research (YPAR) project. Including a participatory action component was important to us because gang-involved youth have extensive experience with forms of surveillance and police violence that those in power are not generally willing to discuss. Studying policing from the perspective of its primary targets provides an essential corrective to dominant narratives about gangs, crime, and community violence.

We understand that surveillance and criminalization impact Black and brown youth regardless of whether they are involved with street organizations. Innocent people are inevitably profiled, harassed, charged, and labeled as gang members. But centering the harm experienced by people *mistakenly* identified as gang members suggests that people who *really are* gang members deserve to be criminalized and incarcerated.[9] Building on an abolitionist framework, we center the experiences of gang-involved youth to disrupt the dominance of the innocence narrative and the impulse to respond to gangs with policing and punishment. Youth who are gang members help us see harms caused by policing that are not visible when we focus only on the wrongfully accused. When we expand our sphere of concern by recognizing the humanity of gang-involved young people, it becomes clear that abolition is the only solution to the harm administered by imperial policing.

Our youth-led team consisted of two young Black women and four young Black men, including Marquise. Haley and Andy facilitated skill-building workshops on research methods and provided support to the research team as they developed the study. Young people set out to analyze the gap between "official" narratives of policing and gun violence and their own experiences and understandings. Tati and Wayne were from rival factions of a street organization on Chicago's North Side. Together, they planned to reclaim the North Pole by conducting media research and interviews to create an alternative narrative about the historical origins of intergenerational conflict in their community. Devell and Reef were contending with the ongoing barriers of reentry after prison and frequently experienced antagonistic interactions with police tied to their criminal records. Through autoethnography and qualitative interviews, they hoped to expose surveillance practices that prevent young people from rebuilding their lives after incarceration. Marquise and Brianna sought to collect oral histories from folks in their community who were affected by the tragic loss of their friend Gerald and the ongoing surveillance since Gerald's death.

The YPAR team began by conducting media research, writing FOIA requests, and developing skills for qualitative interviews. But the research itself was difficult to sustain because of the relentless state and community violence that youth leaders encountered. Research objectives fell away to more pressing concerns, including the arrests of youth leaders and their loved ones and instances of gun violence. During the first year of the project, six young Black people with whom we developed relationships were shot, and four were arrested. The YPAR ultimately ended when Marquise was killed. During the following year, four more Black youth associated with the project, all survivors of state violence, were shot and killed, including our team member Devell. And the violence continues to devastate and eliminate our friends.

We wanted the YPAR to provide an opportunity for criminalized young people to examine and address biased representations of their lives, their loved ones, and the impact of policing on their communities. But the unrelenting volatility created by police, state, and community violence made this feel impossible. The tremendous impact of violence on the lives and deaths of gang-involved youth required that we reckon with the limits of carceral violence-reduction strategies and critical scholarship. The people who carried out this research were stopped, harassed, arrested, and even killed by the institutions they were studying. Even critical research methodologies like YPAR presume a degree of stability and the taken-for-grantedness of life. The young people we met and with whom we worked live/d rich, complex, and full lives but experience/d extreme levels of insecurity, uncertainty, and impermanence. This precarity calls into question the basic presumption of life itself. It informs our analysis of predictive policing and memorials as sites of death and life making.

Our relationships and solidarities emerged from a deep, mutual respect and recognition of the profound inequities that shaped our life chances. As researchers, Haley and Andy could enter and exit the lives of the young people, while they faced what felt like an impossibility of crossing. Collectively, we were able to leverage resources to support the work, but despite our race and class privileges, the team faced challenges that required reflection, reorganization, and problem solving, at times successfully and other times not. For example, safe passage was a concern for several youth leaders who did not feel safe entering or moving through certain neighborhoods. We decided, as a team, to meet at the University of Illinois at Chicago (UIC) campus so we could have space to gather and youth could access computers and the internet with relative safety. But getting to UIC was a challenge. Some young people could not take public transportation without crossing oppositional borders or being stopped by police. Haley provided transportation when she could, and we called taxis at other times. On one occasion, a taxi driver canceled a ride because he would not drive to a West Side neighborhood where one of our team members lived. As a research team, we attempted to think through the barriers and identify solutions, but we could not always predict or control the conditions that created vulnerability.

The work was thus shaped by a *politics of loss,* where PCRG members could enter and exit research sites, while Black youth were disappeared through systematic separation, incarceration, and death. The loss we experienced as a research collective was multifaceted and, in many ways, brought our collective together at the onset of this project. Over time, we began to understand how, in a very real sense, a politics of loss marks the deep divide between the relative security of academic researchers and the extraordinary vulnerability of young, poor, and working-class people of color.

Though a gut-wrenching reminder of the urgency for abolition, the deaths of friends and colleagues has forced us to reflect on what it would take for a project like this to have real, transformative impacts. We spent time learning how to ethically navigate forms of epistemic, state, and community violence and extend radical vulnerability, love, and reflexivity in

FIGURE 6. A North Side memorial honors those killed by police. Photograph by and courtesy of Sarah Jane Rhee (@loveandstrugglephotos).

our relationships. We had to grapple with the tensions and contradictions of participatory research, activist scholarship, and epistemic hierarchies while embracing the risks that shape the everyday lives of young people of color. Our work together was enabled by hope and trust. We return to these issues in the conclusion of this chapter by extending love and radical relationship building as tools for social engagement that can help us imagine new political possibilities for community-engaged, activist scholarship with criminalized youth.

Although we did not complete all of the tasks that we set out to accomplish, the project mobilized a group of young people who were otherwise excluded from conversations about the gang database. Youth leaders saw themselves as knowledge makers and built relationships with other youth whom some viewed as opposition, and together we learned a great deal about policing, surveillance, and violence. Rather than claiming expertise about the lived experiences of gang-involved youth, we draw on their knowledge and expertise to document police practices and challenge official narratives. In doing so, we demonstrate how predictive policing codifies dehumanizing archetypes; justifies targeted surveillance, violence, and death; and contributes to the very conditions that police claim to address. We also uplift gang-involved young people as experts whose dark sousveillant knowledge and everyday forms of abolition are indispensable to efforts to dismantle the carceral webs of empire and build a world without police.

GANG MEMBER: A MAGIC WORD

The former mayor of Chicago Rahm Emanuel regularly referred to young people as "gangbangers," including three times in his agenda-setting 2016 speech on crime and policing.[10] After Marquise and Jaquan were killed, the Fraternal Order of Police released a statement defending the actions of the police officers. They described Marquise and Jaquan as "gang members," "the worst criminals," and "a dire threat to the innocent."[11] Reflecting on more than ten years of experience working with gang-involved youth in Chicago, a criminal defense attorney described the term *gang member* as a "magic word that makes everything OK." He explained, "If you say 'gang member' in Chicago, reporters will be OK with it, general citizens will be OK with it, everyone will be OK with whatever it is that police want to do to the gang member. Shooting? OK, the person was gang involved. It somehow justifies it."[12]

Conversations about violence and policing in Chicago are grounded in anti-Black racism. At the forefront of these conversations is the racialized and gendered criminal archetype of the "gang member." Criminal archetypes involve recurring representations that evoke powerful emotional responses.[13] Within discourses of criminality, the image of the "gang member" is based on the most enduring criminal archetype in U.S. history: "criminalblackman."[14] The image of Black male criminality has oiled the wheels of white supremacy and heteropatriarchy for hundreds of years, from fugitive slave patrols to lynch mobs, from restrictive covenants to gentrification, from mass incarceration to police-involved shootings.[15] Whenever law enforcement officials, city officials, the media, and others discuss "gang members" or "gangbangers," they invoke threatening images of dangerous young Black and Latino men. The archetype is captured in mug shots, crime alerts, and daily news stories depicting hardened male criminals of color with cold eyes and face tattoos, often accompanied by references to clothing, colors, and symbols.

The racialized figure of the gang member also produces an image of gang-involved women, girls, and femmes. Most female gang members are portrayed as victims in need of saving: young women without parental supervision searching for a surrogate family; survivors of childhood sexual violence being manipulated and exploited by male gang members.[16] Others are portrayed as ruthless, masculine killers. These tropes discount how heteronormative patriarchy and white supremacy shape the choices young women make.[17]

The young women we interviewed revealed complex histories of violence, vulnerability, victimization, criminalization, and resilience. Tati, a young Black woman, discussed how her experiences with sexual violence shaped her resistance to gendered traps, like taking a charge and doing time for a boyfriend, which two other young women we met had done. To protect herself from being victimized again, Tati decided she would be as tough as the men she knew. "G.," a masculine-presenting young white woman, was arrested as a suspect in an attempted murder case. Although G. was a victim of sexual, gender-based, and state violence, the media and the police referred to her as a "ruthless" gangbanger and circulated images of a masculine, gun-toting figure with face tattoos to instill bias and justify her incarceration. Media accounts often misgendered G. by referring to her as a man.

Racial constructions of femininity shape the boundaries of womanhood, protecting white women and girls and denying those protections to Black women and children. Gendered and racialized differences articulate who is human and therefore entitled to rights and protections and who exists outside of those boundaries.[18] The young women with whom we spoke, across racial categories, resisted normative ideologies of femininity for myriad reasons. But the media and the police portrayed them in masculine terms and characterized them as more violent than heteronormative white women. Young women and girls like Tati and G. are further expelled from the protected category of "women and girls" as gang members, justifying surveillance, incarceration, and death.

The archetype of the "gang member" is thus a mechanism of dehumanization that erases the complex subjectivity of young people and the structural conditions and inequalities they navigate. Stripped of their humanity, people described as gang members are presented as evil, violent, and degraded, with the capacity to kill. The gang member archetype leaves no space for understanding the reasons young people do or do not become affiliated with street organizations; the rewards, harm, and contradictions they experience if they do affiliate; or the aspects of their lives that extend beyond their affiliation. Moreover, the archetype obscures the material conditions of white supremacy, heteropatriarchy, racial capitalism, and settler colonialism that laid the foundations for the development of street organizations, the reliance on criminalized survival strategies, and the perpetuation of community violence.

Critical scholars who conduct ethnographic research with gang-involved youth in cities across the world consistently show that street organizations are best understood as responses to oppression and marginalization. Gangs emerge in neighborhoods assaulted by generations of racial and colonial domination; stripped of institutional supports, educational opportunities, and career possibilities; subjected to organized abandonment, targeted surveillance, and state violence; and immersed within a U.S. society defined by militarism and hypermasculinity. Young people join peers in street organizations for mutual support and self-defense, economic and social empowerment, and a collective identity in resistance to a hostile society.[19]

Echoing this analysis, the youth with whom we spoke identified community ties, friendship, loss, and safety as key reasons for why they joined gangs. Several young people described joining gangs because they were "hanging out with certain people," were "living in certain neighborhoods," and "grew up with it." A twenty-four-year-old Black man who joined a gang when he was fourteen said, "I got attached to the people I grew up with, and when my closest friend died . . . that's what changed me." A twenty-five-year-old Black man described racial tensions between Black and Latinx youth. He joined a gang at the age of twelve to feel safer in his neighborhood.

> We grew up being chased by [Latin Kings]. Chased in the park, chased in the street, and um, we started fighting back eventually. Then we came across this group of dudes that was actually [Gangster Disciples] and they was like, "We'll walk you home." And that was how it started.

Being a gang member meant something in their communities and gave them a sense of belonging.

The racialized archetype of the gang member subjects all Black youth and other young people of color to presumptions about criminality. In the words of Robert Durán, young people of color are treated as "constant criminals even when following the law."[20] Several young people we interviewed expressed similar sentiments. As one young person explained, "it's like people just think that gang members just always bad." Devell, a youth leader in our research team, described a time that police harassed him and his family at a neighborhood barbeque: "You know, it's our family block. We was doing illegal stuff, but at the time we *wasn't* doing illegal stuff. We was just kickin' it and everything was shut down. But now they messing with us." The dehumanizing archetype erases that complexity and normalizes surveillance, harassment, incarceration, and other forms of police violence against people presumed to be gang involved.

The gang member archetype is also a discursive and affective tool to differentiate "community members" from "criminals" and to incorporate the former into a network of criminalizing surveillance that targets the latter for incarceration, expulsion, and death. The state uses "community safety" and "innocent children" as twin tropes to produce gang members as dangerous, racialized others. In doing so, it reinforces an us-versus-them logic and contributes to the notion that police exist to protect "us" from "them." Within the logics of white supremacy, community safety is not equally produced for all, and the police decide who lives and who is left to die. Gang enforcement becomes a mechanism that police use to then make determinations about life and death.

Every six years, the Chicago Crime Commission publishes a *Gang Book* that summarizes the information that local police have compiled on gangs in the city. *The Gang Book* presents a fear-provoking portrait of gang violence and lawlessness in Chicago. Reifying the gang member archetype, *The Gang Book* publishes mug shots that label individuals as gang leaders and maps that identify neighborhoods as gang territories.

In a letter celebrating the publication of the 2012 *Gang Book,* Cook County sheriff Tom Dart noted that "innocent children are too often caught in crossfire, and too many long-time residents have had to watch as their neighborhoods were overtaken by gang activities."[21] President of the Chicago Crime Commission and former CPD superintendent Jody Weiss called on "community-members" to help police identify and target "gang members."[22] The overall message of *The Gang Book* is consistent: "they" are not a part of "us," and we—the community and the police— must do whatever it takes to reclaim "our" neighborhoods from "them." In the 2018 *Gang Book,* Michael J. Anderson, special agent in charge of the Federal Bureau of Investigation (FBI) in Chicago, expressed this argument in just a few lines:

There are some individuals and violent criminal gangs whom, as a result of their actions and threats, not only inflict serious bodily harm and death upon citizens, but directly interfere with community members' rights to safe housing, school, health care, employment, and a criminal justice system free of witness retaliation, intimidation, and tampering. Consequently, the environment of fear created by these individuals and gangs poses the greatest challenge to law enforcement officials in securing cooperation from the community to reclaim so many neighborhoods in Chicago.[23]

Two recent investigations into CPD practices provide further evidence of the dehumanizing impact of the gang member archetype. In 2019, the City of Chicago inspector general published the results of an investigation into CPD gang databases, which confirmed PCRG research on the extensive and racially discriminatory use of gang designations by the Chicago police. The report included a telling note about how Chicago police officers view alleged gang members. Gang arrest cards, which Chicago police fill out when they arrest someone they consider gang affiliated, include a space for officers to enter the person's occupation. According to the inspector general's report, "CPD officers entered occupations for individuals on gang arrest cards including 'SCUM BAG,' 'BUM,' 'CRIMINAL,' 'BLACK,' 'DORK,' 'LOOSER [sic],' and 'TURD.'"[24] Labels such as these represent the biased attitudes of the Chicago police and highlight the failure of Chicago police to view alleged gang members as fully human.

In 2017, the U.S. Department of Justice (DOJ) published a report documenting the unconstitutional use of excessive force by the Chicago police and the CPD's failure to hold officers accountable. Buried at the end of the report is an important note about dehumanizing language:

> Black youth told us that they are routinely called "n_____," "animal," or "pieces of shit" by CPD officers. A 19-year-old black male reported that CPD officers called him a "monkey." Such statements were confirmed by CPD officers. One officer we interviewed told us that he personally has heard co-workers and supervisors refer to black individuals as monkeys, animals, savages, and "pieces of shit." Residents reported treatment so demeaning they felt dehumanized. One black resident told us that when it comes to CPD, there is "no treating you as a human being." Consistent with these reports, our investigations found that there was a recurring portrayal by some CPD officers of the residents of challenged neighborhoods—who are mostly black—as animals or subhuman.[25]

Significantly, the DOJ report indicates that this language was directed not just toward alleged gang members but toward Black residents generally and entire Black communities. Such language desensitizes officers to the humanity of Black people, "setting the stage for the use of excessive force."[26]

As our research demonstrates, the use of gang databases and predictive policing reinforces and stabilizes these archetypes, treating them as facts that justify surveillance, violence, and death. The dehumanizing term *gang member* is indeed a magic word that underpins an us-versus-them logic, helps construct the notion that police are protecting "us" from "them," and expands the web of surveillance.

GANG ENFORCEMENT: RACIALIZED SURVEILLANCE, VIOLENCE, AND MANUFACTURED CONFLICT

The so-called War on Gangs is the primary local manifestation of carceral efforts to protect white supremacy, racial capitalism, and empire by policing the racialized poor. This police war targets young, working-class Black and brown people whose lives and labor are so devalued that capital and the state treat them as disposable. Local police provide the frontline officers for carrying out the War on Gangs, while state and federal agencies provide support with investigation, prosecution, and incarceration. And, as we discuss in chapters 1 and 2, high-tech corporations and community organizations are also linked to this carceral project.

In Chicago, even the most seemingly race-neutral approaches to gang enforcement remain fundamentally rooted in anti-Blackness and the racialized archetype of the "gang member." Advanced forms of data-based policing manufacture "criminals" by producing data, treating the data as "fact," and using the data to determine police strategies and deployments. In practice, CPD gang data are largely a product of criminalized *archetypes, associations,* and *neighborhoods.* In this section, we demonstrate how data-based policing intensifies racialized surveillance and police violence and enables the police to manufacture conflict within neighborhoods. To do so, we draw on the dark sousveillant knowledge of young people of color, whose experiences challenge the official narrative about gangs and crime. Their critical awareness of racialized surveillance grounds our countersurveillant analysis of state power.

Policing Gangs in Chicago

The CPD is at the center of all efforts to suppress street organizations and community violence in Chicago. Yet gang enforcement is operationalized through a network of local, state, and federal law enforcement agencies as well as community-based organizations and service providers that collaborate with the CPD. And it draws on tactics and technologies developed through other police wars and military interventions around the world.[27] The overall approach to gang enforcement is the CPD's data-based Gang Violence Reduction Strategy (GVRS). Here we focus on the data that inform the GVRS, to demonstrate how data-based policing is grounded in racialized archetypes and anti-Black racism. Indeed, data-based policing manufactures criminality through targeted surveillance, transforming archetypes into official designations and erasing their production so that they operate as "facts."

As we explained in chapter 2, the GVRS is grounded in the production and analysis of data about gang members, their associations, their conflicts, and their territories. The data are produced through stops and arrests and analyzed during an annual gang audit in each of the CPD's twenty-two police districts. Gang audits result in databases of people associated with each gang faction, maps of gang territories, and "interactive link capabilities to allow social network analysis."[28] These maps, databases, and network analyses in turn shape CPD strategies and deployments, including stop-and-frisk, dispersal orders, gang probation, targeted surveillance, focused deterrence, gang arrests, and enhanced prosecution. The emphasis on data collection, data analysis, and data-driven deployments suggests a level of scientific objectivity uncontaminated by racism.

The CPD maintains multiple gang databases, the two most important of which are the gang arrest card database and the investigatory stop report (ISR) database. Whenever police arrest a person whom they determine to be gang affiliated, officers complete a gang arrest card, which indicates the person's gang faction, their known hangouts, and whether they "self-admitted" to gang membership. According to the inspector general's 2019 report, the CPD gang arrest card database included more than 134,000 people.[29] Police and the media publicize figures like this to foment fear of gangs in Chicago.[30] Yet, as we discuss later, the CPD does not require evidence to support gang designations. Instead, police manufacture these designations based on racialized archetypes and the criminalization of associations and territory. This is why 95 percent of people on the list are Black or Latinx (69.8 percent Black; 25.2 percent Latinx).[31]

ISRs are produced when police detain and question a person but do not carry out an arrest. This includes the infamous practice of stop-and-frisk, which has a long history in Chicago but became increasingly prevalent as a result of data-based policing. Starting in 2011, superintendent Garry McCarthy urged officers to carry out stops to generate data on people's associations and hangouts.[32] In 2015, the American Civil Liberties Union exposed the abuse of stop-and-frisk tactics by Chicago police. In summer 2014 alone, Chicago police carried out more than 250,000 stops.[33] Police regularly failed to provide legal justification for the stop. In response to this scandal, the CPD introduced ISRs, which require officers to provide a "reasonable articulable suspicion" for the stop. One option they can select is "gang and narcotic related enforcement."[34] Each year, the CPD issues more than five thousand ISRs that label people gang members.[35] Like gang arrest cards, ISRs are overwhelmingly used to designate young Black and Latinx people as gang members.

Along with gang databases, the CPD designates geographic areas as gang territories. According to the inspector general's report, "CPD may designate areas as gang-involved based on any of the following: the type of graffiti in the community, the number of gang-involved individuals living in the area, and CPD's understanding of the gang-related history in the area."[36] The department creates gang maps for each district that outline the territories that police associate with each faction. Officers can access gang maps through a program called Caboodle, and the Chicago Crime Commission publishes the maps in its *Gang Book*. The department uses these maps—along with designations like "hot spot"—to identify particular areas for targeted, predictive deployments, including what the CPD calls "aggressive patrol and violence suppression missions."[37] Aggressive patrols are unevenly distributed, with the highest concentrations in Black neighborhoods on the South and West Sides of Chicago. Although "predictive deployments" appear to be data driven, this is merely a displacement—and disavowal—of the underlying anti-Blackness that grounds the gang member archetype codified in the data.

The CPD uses these data to deploy targeted enforcement actions against individuals. As we describe in chapter 1, the CPD pioneered the use of individualized predictive policing by feeding its arrest and contact data into an algorithm known as the Strategic Subjects List (SSL). The algorithm was designed to identify people likely to become a "party to violence" by analyzing individual arrest and victimization records as well as the records of people whom police consider to be part of their social networks. Despite its apparent mathematical objectivity, the SSL was based entirely on data created through a history of racist police stops and arrests.

As a defense attorney explained, the CPD treated people with high SSL scores as the "supervillains of the city."[38] In 2017, nearly four hundred thousand people were on the SSL, including nearly half of all Black boys and men aged ten to twenty-nine in Chicago. Of the sixty-five thousand listed as "gang affiliated," 74.5 percent were Black, 21.4 percent were Latinx, 60.7 percent were younger than thirty years old, and 96.9 percent were male.[39] Yet two-thirds of the people identified as "gang affiliated" had no documented arrests for violent offenses or unlawful use of a weapon.[40] In late 2019, after a critical investigation by Chicago's inspector general, the CPD decommissioned the SSL.[41]

The CPD maintains another database of high-priority individuals as part of an enforcement strategy known as the Targeted Repeat Offender Apprehension and Prosecution (TRAP) program. The CPD and the State's Attorney's Office work together to "identify repeat offenders with the high propensity toward violent, gang-related crime" and subject them to "enhanced prosecution."[42] People on the TRAP list confront more intense surveillance, more regular police stops, increased obstacles to securing a bond, enhanced charges with longer sentences, and additional obstacles to sentence mitigation. As the defense attorney quoted earlier explains, "if this person is stopped, under no condition will law enforcement give them any breaks. They are to be prosecuted to the fullest extent of the law, no matter what."[43]

By describing its gang enforcement strategy as "data driven," the CPD suggests that it is determined by objective measures. We refer to this as data cleansing or mathwashing. But treating CPD data as objective—as an accurate representation of reality—would require us to overlook their production. As we document in the next section, the data are produced through stops and arrests that are informed by racialized archetypes and anti-Black racism as well as the criminalization of associations and neighborhoods. Moreover, the CPD uses these data to identify people and places for heightened surveillance, aggressive patrols, and enhanced prosecution. This, in turn, generates new data that help justify targeting the same people and the same neighborhoods that are already deemed suspect. Beneath its aura of scientific objectivity, therefore, data-based policing manufactures "criminals" out of archetypes, associations, and segregated neighborhoods.

Racializing Surveillance

Racializing surveillance is a technology of social control whereby surveillance practices produce racialized norms about who belongs inside or outside of a neighborhood, citizenship, and/or the category "human."[44] As a form of racializing surveillance, CPD gang enforcement strategies rely on databases that transform racialized archetypes into so-called facts and facilitate the circulation of data between criminalizing agencies. Our research reveals how gang designations provide the police with justification to treat people as subhuman. Yet the data themselves are anything but factual. Instead, we demonstrate in this section how data are produced through policing practices grounded in a racialized criminal archetype and the criminalization of associations and neighborhoods.

Reporting on the first publicly available information on CPD gang databases, Mick Dumke concluded that the databases are "riddled with dubious entries, discrepancies, and outright errors." For instance, two people were listed as 132 years old, and another thirteen were 118 years old.[45] The inspector general reached a similar conclusion, chastising the CPD for the errors and inconsistencies in its gang arrest card database. In addition to ninety records of people born before 1901, the Office of Inspector General found eighty records in which the person's age was listed as zero, more than twenty thousand individuals with multiple birth dates, and fifteen thousand listed as gang members without identifying a gang.[46]

Far more revealing, however, are the data that the inspector general exposed about the reasons that officers provided for adding individuals to the gang database. The CPD has official criteria for identifying gang members: self-admission, tattoos and markings, signs and symbols, or identification by an informant or gang expert.[47] But the department requires no evidence to support a gang designation. According to the inspector general, 88.18 percent of people in the gang arrest card database "self-admitted" to gang membership.[48] But arresting officers are not required to document this admission. Instead, they just click a box on their report indicating that the person admitted belonging to a gang.[49]

Another 11.66 percent of people in the database were added without the officer providing any justification. This means that 99.84 percent of the 134,242 people in the gang arrest card database were added at the discretion of the officer. This helps explain why almost everyone in the database is Black or Latinx.

In our interviews, we asked gang-involved youth whether they had admitted to the police or officers in jails and prisons that they were members of a street organization.

> Have I self-reported? No. I didn't admit it, but they knew I was a gang leader.

> They tell me that I'm in a gang. I say, "No." They look at me like I'm laughing, like I'm lying. I'm like, "Nah, I'm not in a gang. Why would I tell you I'm in a gang in the first place?" I'm affiliated with people because I grew up with them. But I never say I was in a gang.

> I didn't really tell them. It was more like I kept it a secret, knowing it would be used against me for my background.

Several young people reported that officers pressured them to admit membership. The young man who shared the last quote told us that he eventually admitted he was a gang member, but only because he feared for his safety after officers at Cook County Jail confined him with people affiliated with another organization. But every other person we interviewed insisted that they never admitted to gang membership. A defense attorney shared similar reflections. When he talks with clients about information in their police records, he often asks if they reported being in a gang. "A lot of times, I say, 'Well, they have you here as being a self-admitted Four Corner Hustler.' And they'll look at me and start laughing. 'There's no way I'm a Four Corner Hustler. I'm a this' or 'I'm nothing.' To be honest, there's quite a few of those: 'I've never told the cops I'm part of this!'"[50]

These statements cast serious doubt on CPD records suggesting that more than 88 percent of people in the gang arrest card database self-admitted to membership. And these are the same records on which arresting officers fabricated occupations such as "SCUM BAG," "CRIMINAL," and

"BLACK." Rather than objective facts, gang designations should be read as the codification of criminal archetypes and the product of racialized police strategies that concentrate surveillance and enforcement on particular people and neighborhoods. The impact is devastating, particularly for young Black people and communities of color.

Data-based policing remains firmly grounded in racialized criminal archetypes. Many people report being stopped just because of the way they look. Race, age, and gender are the primary determinants—with clothing style providing a secondary justification for police stops. Many youth report being stopped by police and identified as gang members simply because they present as young, Black, and masculine.

A young Black man from the West Side described a childhood of constant police stops. He estimates that he was stopped "maybe five hundred times" and arrested thirty to forty times before turning eighteen, although he was only convicted of a crime twice. Another young Black man described a summer before he turned eighteen when police picked him up five or six times a month. "But me being a juvenile, a parent could come get [me]," he explained. After turning eighteen, he was detained "probably like twenty-five times." Each interaction with the police could have landed these young people in a gang database.

Young people also discussed receiving gang designations based on their associations. Youth described how police used contact cards[51] and ISRs to criminalize their friendships and associations. "Being in a community where there are gangs and stuff, that led me into being in the gang database because the friends I was with at the time were gang affiliated," explained a young Latino. A young Latina explained that officers accused her of being in a gang after she was shot. "They were laughing and being rude," she explained, "saying things like 'Oh, this just happens to little girls who thinking they tough' or whatever. They told me, 'You know your boyfriend is a Spanish Gangster Disciple [SGD].' And they accused me of being in the gang too."

A Black man explained that his younger brother was given a false gang designation as a result of his own affiliation. "Now, I tell everybody—when they walkin' with me outside or drivin' with me—just to be aware," he explained. "The police are gonna say what you is, but you're not really what they say. We don't know what they put in the system because they go in the computer and do what they do behind the computer. But let's say you was a neutron and got locked up, maybe on a DUI. They'll say: 'Oh, he's a SGD.' You'll say, 'I'm a SGD? My friend is a SGD!'"

As these statements demonstrate, the criminalization of associations is a key mechanism through which people receive gang designations. It also grounds the practice of using social network analysis to identify individuals for heightened surveillance, as the CPD did with the SSL.

In addition to criminalizing individuals and associations, the police criminalize neighborhoods. Young people maintain friendships and relationships that crisscross police-identified gang boundaries, yet Chicago police regularly issue gang designations based on where people happen to be stopped. In chapter 5, we discuss the case of Wilmer Catalan-Ramirez, an immigrant detained by Immigration and Customs Enforcement in 2017 because of his inclusion in CPD gang databases. During his trial, Wilmer's lawyers discovered that police listed him as a member of two rival organizations during two different stops. These designations reflected CPD maps that associate particular factions with the neighborhoods where Wilmer was stopped.

Yet Wilmer is not alone. One young man told us, "There were times when they would mark me down as a Latin King or times they would mark me down as a Black Stone. You know, when they used to pull us over, they would give us these gang cards, these little yellow cards. We'd give them our name, our address or whatever. And then they would ask [if we were gang affiliated] again. And of course, we all said no. And then they'd be like, 'fucking liar' and just mark some shit down based on where we were at, the colors we got on." We asked him how many contact cards he'd received. "A lot," he replied. "I can't even remember. Those things were like second nature. And each time they gave me one, I was a member of a different gang."

The inspector general's report documented more than twenty-five thousand people listed as members of multiple gangs in the gang arrest card database. "For example," the report points out, "one individual has been classified as a member of nine different gangs, and according to CPD's own training materials several of these groups are rivals."[52] To be sure, there is growing evidence that gang affiliations have become more fluid in recent years and that some groups "clique up"—or link up—with former rivals.[53] Yet this cannot possibly account for twenty-five thousand cases of multiple affiliation.

Despite these issues, the CPD treats the data as fact, and so do other agencies that access CPD data. As a young person explained, "it puts you in a position where you gotta go out of your way to prove you're *not* affiliated. So how the hell do you do that?"

Along with the gang database, the CPD uses predictive tools like the SSL to legitimate targeted surveillance, mask due process violations, and build cases against youth. Analyzing the SSL data, *Chicago Magazine* reported that only 3.6 percent of people on the list had become a "party to violence."[54] Yet police were disproportionately arresting people with a Strategic Subjects score on the South and West Sides of the city. The documentary *Pre-Crime* highlights the case of Robert McDaniel, a young Black man who had been arrested only for minor offenses but ended up on the SSL because CPD databases linked him with people who had violent offenses on their records. "If I was to commit a crime or murder right now, they would parade themselves," he points out in the film. "They've got a job to do, and they want to do it. If they've got to breed crime, if they've got to make criminals, if they've got to sit here and convince you that you are a criminal and provoke you to do it, they'll do it."[55]

McDaniel's critique resonates with Marquise's experience fighting a murder charge. During Marquise's trial, his defense team learned that Marquise had a Strategic Subjects score. Gang enforcement officers had created network maps based on Marquise's arrest history and previous contact with the police as well as the arrest histories of his friends and family. Prior to the murder charge, Marquise had four adult arrests, none of which were violent, and the majority of his police contact occurred when he was between the ages of thirteen and fifteen. Yet the algorithm gave Marquise a Strategic Subjects score of 449 out of 500.

Two days before Marquise's friend was killed, Marquise received a custom notification letter that stated, "The Department believes that you are at risk for gun violence, either as an offender with a propensity for engaging in retaliation against others or as a victim. . . . If you engage in gun violence, rest assured you will be subject to arrest and prosecution to the fullest extent of the law." The letter served as a "notice that law enforcement action would not be random, but targeted and specific."

The use of the term "rest assured," often deployed to reassure people that things will be OK, is here used as a guarantee of surveillance, harassment, and death-making entrapment.

After the shooting, police arrested Marquise and charged him with murder. The police and state's attorney used the custom notification letter to manufacture a narrative that not only supported their case but also suggested that the SSL had provided an accurate prediction. The defense team, on the other hand, believed that police targeted Marquise as a result of the algorithm's prediction. Perhaps they even manufactured the charges to validate the SSL, which was relatively new and controversial at the time.

The young people with whom we worked echoed McDaniel's insightful critique of the SSL as a tool for making criminals. The assignment of gang designations based on racialized archetypes that criminalize individuals, associations, and neighborhoods demonstrates how police manufacture criminality. Social network analysis and predictive algorithms, like the SSL, claim objectivity yet rely on data collected through long-standing practices of racialized policing. And officers are never held accountable for fabricating data that circulate as fact and have real implications for people's lives.

Police Violence

Young Black people in Chicago are the primary subjects of dehumanization and violence by Chicago police. From 2011 to 2016, Black people were the targets of 76 percent of documented use-of-force cases by the CPD, including 80 percent of firearm cases and 81 percent of Taser cases.[56] But gang-involved young people face particularly intense forms of violence because they are the *intended* targets of policing practices. We found that the gang database amplifies their exposure to violence by (1) intensifying interactions during "routine" police stops and (2) expanding the surveillance of young people whom police identify as gang members.

When the subject of a police stop is believed to be a gang member, police attitudes about gangs appear to impact the interaction. Youth reported that the police regularly exercise power through threats, provocations, and physical violence, which young people commonly characterize as "extra." The day before one of our interviews, police stopped a young Black man on his way to a concert with other young Black men who work together at an organization that supports people returning from jail. "So, all of us in the car, we all felons, but we all got jobs. We all got IDs, all our credentials. We're correct, you feel me? There ain't no weed, no liquor, nothing in the car," he explains. The police ran the names of everyone in the car, despite not having cause to do so, and discovered that some were in the gang database. The young men began asking questions, and the officers responded by threatening arrest and escalating the stop.

> They were irritated by our knowledge of the law, you feel me? And they were getting real irritated, so now they was doing extra stuff—like saying, "Since you all felons, you not supposed to be together. We could take y'all in if we want to." But we not disrespecting you. We didn't do nothing wrong, so what y'all stopping us for? 'Cause we was in this neighborhood and you see four Black guys in a car. That's why you stopped us.

The police told the men to step out of the car. "They like, 'Step out of the car now. We have the right to search y'all cause y'all felons.'" The police searched the car but didn't find anything. Then they began questioning one man about his record:

> "Why is you on parole?" But they already knew what he was on parole about, so why ask him? He said, "I don't have to tell you that. And y'all already know. Y'all already looked it up, right? You put the ID in your system—why you all want me to tell y'all?" Now they looking under the hood for a gun, because this guy got a murder in his background. But, you know, we all legit. We working. We all—everything—we came correct. It's too good to be true. Like, we all offenders, but we all doing something. We all working, we're on a productive roll. They couldn't get past the fact that we was doing something good, something different.

This story reveals the vicious spiral of data-based policing: racially motivated stops and the criminalization of associations land young people in police databases; their inclusion in a database prevents them from associating and justifies further harassment. Again, we see a critical awareness of both racialized surveillance and the law as well as the spiral of surveillance through which gang designations and arrest databases increase people's vulnerability to future police harassment, violence, and arrest.

A young Black man described how the police stopped the vehicle he was in while returning home from a memorial. From the back seat, he asked the officers why they stopped the car. The officer replied, "Because your muffler was loud." Knowing that was a pretense, the young man started asking more questions: "'You telling me you pulled us over because the muffler is loud? But I don't hear nothing.' The car is packed, they see the car is packed, you know what I'm saying. That's the only reason why they pulled us over, you feel me?" The officers ran everyone's names, then came back to the car and asked the passengers about previous arrests. One officer questioned the young man about pending charges involving a weapon. "I told 'em straight up, 'The firearm wasn't there. They didn't have no firearm. Whatever pops up in your computer system, that's not true—that's alleged.'" Next, the officers began making everyone get out of the car so they could perform a search. The young man responded, "You don't have the right to pull me out the car! Whatever my homie gave you, as far as his insurance and his license, that's all you guys need. What's the reason you pulled us over? Now you just extra with it—all this extra stuff you guys doing—it's uncalled for." His knowledge of the law and his critique of police data demonstrate a critical awareness or dark sousveillance that emerges through everyday interactions with police.

Gang-involved youth also reported that once they were identified as gang members and recognized by the police, police encounters and harassment increased. A twenty-two-year-old Black man described being stopped fifteen times over the previous year. The CPD stopped him a week and a half before our interview. "They were harassing me, asking me where some guns at? Where some more guns at? Why you run?" Another time, he says, "me and my homie, we got in a little shit with the police. My homeboy was singing in the back seat, and they told him, 'If you don't shut up, we gonna Tase yo ass' and shit like that. All that extra shit. They just take advantage of they authority."

Another young Black man, who was on the SSL, described similar harassment. After he was arrested and charged with a misdemeanor, he bonded out of jail. The police who arrested him, he says, were upset to see him back in the neighborhood. He believes that they manufactured evidence to arrest and charge him with a second offense. "When I bonded out, the police seen me. The police officer they come harassing me. I was out seventeen days—seventeen days—they put another case on me, because they seen that I bonded out." He describes having to relocate to another neighborhood to avoid the constant harassment.

Over a one-month period, the police harassed one young Black man on three separate occasions. The first time, he was locked up for violating a parole condition that prevented any "gang contact." He explained, "They tell me that I was with somebody four hours ago. I didn't know it was a gang contact. I mean, there's gangs everywhere, especially in Chicago. Everybody a gang member now. But they don't care." Another time, the police targeted his girlfriend. "One of the police jacked my girlfriend. They stopped her 'cause they thought I was in the car. And they was asking her, like, 'Where he at?' So, I count that as a harass 'cause you come harass my girlfriend to look for me."

One young man described how he was stopped three times, leading to two separate arrests in one day. Others described how police park on their blocks, call them out by name, and escalate what could be routine stops. A young Black man described being repeatedly harassed by detectives when he was outside of his high school. "If it's the blue and whites [patrol officers], they treat me like a human being. But the D-Boys [detectives], no. They don't care." He explains that detectives seem to be on a mission to arrest him. "That's what irritates me," he says. "You assuming that I did something wrong. And it's not even assuming—it's like *hoping* I do something wrong. So that's what you harass me for. Anything I might have, you hope I got it, just to get me locked up. That's a lot of harassment. The police trying to make it worse for me." This aligns with McDaniel's critique and Marquise's experience with predictive policing, which can lead police to assume—or even hope—that their predictions are correct.

Many of the young people with whom we spoke were also targeted by federal agents because of their gang involvement. In recent years, federal agencies like the FBI, the Bureau of Alcohol, Tobacco, Firearms, and Explosives, and the Drug Enforcement Agency have intensified the use of RICO charges against alleged gang members in Chicago.[57] Relying on techniques of social media surveillance and social network analysis first developed in Iraq and Afghanistan, federal agencies manufacture claims of a conspiracy when there is not enough evidence to prosecute individuals. Prosecution in a federal court enables harsher sentences than would be possible in a Cook County court. As discussed in chapter 2, focused deterrence programs allow prosecutors to threaten young people with federal changes during custom notifications and call-ins. Moreover, during summer 2020, Chicago mayor Lori Lightfoot and U.S. president Donald Trump arranged to deploy additional federal agents to Chicago to prosecute more gun cases—including nonviolent gun possession—in federal courts.[58]

A young Black man whose family migrated from West Africa began carrying weapons for protection after he was shot. Chicago police did not investigate his shooting, nor did they offer anything to help him feel safe, yet the police contributed to his vulnerability by antagonizing neighborhood conflicts. He understood that carrying was a risk but felt he had no other way to protect himself and his family. Despite having no history of violence, he was arrested and charged with possessing a gun as a minor, foreclosing any legal pathways to gun ownership as an adult. At age twenty, he faced federal charges for gun possession. Federal agents referred to his gang membership as evidence of his dangerousness, ignoring his underlying need for safety. A second young Black man described a similar story, where his nonviolent arrests led to federal gun charges. While incarcerated, he was issued a custom notification letter by the CPD and interrogated by federal agents. He was eventually indicted in a RICO case where the state argued that he was part of a criminal enterprise based on his network ties with other members of a street organization, many of whom he'd grown up with.

Through experiences such as these, young people develop dark sousveillant knowledge and strategies to mitigate potentially violent interactions with the police. A Latina college student explained how her inclusion in the gang database made her careful about what she said to police. "Like if I get pulled over or have an encounter with the cops, or if the cops are called on me, the cops would treat me differently than before I was on the gang database. It puts me in a position where my voice and what I say would be criminalized." A Black man, formerly gang involved, says,

"If I'm stopped, I gotta be extra careful. With my background coming up, the police got their hands on their guns. Even though it's been a long time, they're more cautious when they stop me. It's not, 'Hey, how you doing? You was speeding.' No. They're drawing their guns walking up to you." Our interviews with gang-involved young people illustrate that the gang database and other data-driven policing strategies intensify dehumanization by producing an ever-expanding spiral of surveillance and violence. Young people of color—especially Black youth—are regularly stopped, harassed, beaten, arrested, and even killed. And because they are seen as subhuman, their arrests and even their deaths are treated as insignificant or celebrated.

Manufactured Conflict

Chicago police play a role in manufacturing not only criminality but also the conflicts that they claim to address. This is not entirely surprising, because gang conflict is the justification for the CPD's $1.9 billion annual budget.[59] But Chicago mayors and police superintendents are routinely criticized for failing to stop gun violence. Still, researchers have identified several ways that CPD contributes to gang conflicts. In this section, we build on this work to highlight the role of data in perpetuating community violence.

David Stovall argues that the City of Chicago has "engineered conflict" in Black working-class neighborhoods by supporting gentrification, eliminating public housing, and closing public schools, all of which have forcibly dislocated the city's Black population.[60] At the same time, he argues, the CPD/FBI strategy of using RICO statutes to target gang leaders has fractured existing street organizations. By eliminating the ability of gang leaders to enforce discipline within the ranks, the CPD/FBI policy has contributed to a fractured landscape of gang conflict. Building on insights from Frantz Fanon, Stovall argues that "enemies are manufactured as the result of continued displacement, hyper-segregation and dispossession. In these instances, people are often quicker to punch each other before they identify the enemy as white supremacy and capitalism."[61]

This aligns with research by Roberto Aspholm, who analyzes recent shifts in Chicago gang conflicts.[62] The hierarchical gang organizations that dominated drug sales in Chicago from the late 1970s through the

1990s have been fragmented because (1) the collapse of drug markets has eliminated opportunities for entry-level gang members to advance within the organizations, (2) the destruction of public housing and the incarceration of gang leadership disrupted existing territories and hierarchies, and (3) rank-and-file rebellions destabilized long-standing hierarchies. In place of large street organizations, Chicago now has a fractured landscape defined by small, localized cliques and alliances based on personal relationships. Police intensified these conflicts by incarcerating the upper echelons of the gang leadership, which weakened the capacity of organizations to enforce discipline on members and enabled individuals to enact violence without requiring approval from above.

Robert Vargas has documented other ways that Chicago police intensify neighborhood conflicts.[63] Targeting drug sales on a particular block can trigger competition when other cliques attempt to assert control over the space. In addition, Chicago police often expose—intentionally or not—people who call to report a crime. For instance, police might announce the person's name over the scanner or approach the person's house for a witness statement. These practices can generate cycles of retaliatory violence.

These studies provide important insights into ways that Chicago police intensify conflicts. Our research corroborates these findings. A young Black woman told us that the CPD and FBI conducted a drug raid in her neighborhood based on information they received from a teenage informant. When police and federal agents were leaving the house, the woman and her neighbors heard an officer thank the informant by name. The identification of the young person led to threats of retaliation against the informant and his family.

We want to highlight another troubling way that Chicago police incite or intensify conflict, as described in the 2017 DOJ report. The gravity of these findings justifies quoting the report at length:

> CPD will take a young person to a rival gang neighborhood and either leave the person there or display the youth to rival members, immediately putting the life of that young person in jeopardy by suggesting he has provided information to the police. Our investigation indicates that these practices in fact exist.

We were told by many community members that one method by which CPD will try to get individuals to provide information about crime or guns is by picking them up and driving them around while asking for information about gangs or guns. When individuals do not talk, officers will drop them off in dangerous areas or gang territories.

We reviewed a publicly available video that appears to capture one instance of an officer displaying a youth in police custody to a group of individuals gathered in a rival gang territory. The video shows CPD officers standing around a marked CPD vehicle with the back doors wide open and a young male detained in the rear. Officers permit a crowd of male youths to surround the car and shout at the adolescent. The crowd can be seen flashing hand gestures that look like gang signs and threatening the cowering teenager in the backseat. One of the males in the crowd appears to have freely recorded the interactions all while CPD officers stood beside the open vehicle doors. The video does not show any legitimate law enforcement purpose in allowing the youth to be threatened.

Residents told us that this has happened for years, with several individuals recounting their personal experiences. A young black man told us that when he was 12 or 13 years old, he and his friends were picked up by CPD officers, dropped off in rival territory, and told to walk home. Another black teen told us that his brother was picked up in one location, dropped off in another location known for rival gangs, and told: "Better get to running." . . .

A pastor at a Latino church told us that his congregants reported being picked up by CPD officers seeking information regarding guns or drugs, but when they either could not or would not provide such information, the officers removed the congregants' shoelaces and dropped them off in rival neighborhoods.[64]

Simon Balto traces this tactic to the early years of the CPD's War on Gangs in the late 1960s. Along with sweeps, arrests, and raids, he points out, CPD antigang strategies included the infiltration of street gangs and the "exacerbation of intergang tensions." In Balto's words, "gang members repeatedly reported being picked up by police officers who demanded information from them and, if they failed to give it, dropped them, vehicle-less, deep in a rival gang's turf."[65] The longevity of these practices forces us to acknowledge that the Chicago police have played a role in manufacturing gang conflict for decades.

Our research suggests that the CPD's use of this tactic to exacerbate gang conflict today—as documented by the DOJ—is informed by the rise of data-based policing. Gang databases allow police to identify individuals as members of particular street organizations; gang maps inform the way that police think about neighborhoods or blocks as belonging to different gangs; and gang audits shape their understanding of existing gang conflicts.

Our interviews with young people demonstrate that police efforts to exacerbate conflict are not limited to dropping suspected gang members in rival neighborhoods. Taunting is another mechanism that Chicago police use to antagonize conflicts. A young Black man explained:

> The majority of the time, when I be by myself, what the police do when they approach me, um, they just go off what they have in my record, or whatever the case may be. I don't know what pops up in the computer system. "Are you still affiliated? Where the rest of your brothers? I just see you out here." And then they mention other rival hoods, um, just to see what we'll do. "Well, I know your homie died. I know about that. Whatcha gonna do about it?" Or the police just pull up on us. They say like, "Oh, well, the kids [from a rival organization] is up the street. What are you guys gonna do?"

These accounts demonstrate how police use data to identify individuals as members of particular gangs and make claims about their associations, their fallen comrades, and their rivalries. The police use these data to taunt and provoke young people and initiate further acts of community violence. For a department that claims to take gang conflict seriously, these accounts illustrate an incredible lack of respect for the lives and deaths of young people who are gang involved.

Gang-affiliated young people also described the impact of gang designations on their experiences in jails and prisons. Sometimes young people are wrongfully identified as members of a particular gang and housed with members of oppositional gangs based on the information contained in police databases. One young man described being misidentified as affiliated with a particular faction because of where he was arrested. This set him up for problems in Cook County Jail.

> They don't care what happens to you. They just send you in and then you go on deck. Then you get separated from there: they assign you to a particular floor based on contact cards. See like me, when I go to jail, I'm in the system as a [member of one gang], but I'm not [affiliated with that gang]. All my cases got caught in their neighborhood, so the police automatically link you: "You gotta be [in that gang] 'cause that's where you caught your cases at." But that's not how it is.

Another man described how misidentification follows people from the county jail to the Illinois Department of Corrections. In this case, false assumptions or administrative errors can lead to violence.

> In the joint, whatever in your background they automatically just try to place you. Like: "Alright, he this [gang], he that [gang]. We're gonna place him here, 'cause that's where all these people at." And the whole time, the county probably mess up. I'm in the system as [a member of a particular gang], when I'm not. When you get to the joint, they like, "We see you was a [gang member] in the system from the county, so we gonna put you where all [the members of that gang] at." And then you not [in that gang]. Now you somewhere what you not. And then you gotta tell them, like, "I'm not this" and then you get banked. So, they kick you off the deck. Either you gonna bank yourself or they gonna bank you. Or, they gonna beat you up and roll you and make you go.

To "bank yourself" refers to asking for a housing reassignment. In the process, individuals may be forced to admit a gang affiliation to justify their request. One young man discussed the complex social rules he had to navigate when he was housed with members of an oppositional gang.

> The corrections officers put me on a deck full [of one gang], and I wasn't feelin' it. We was gonna fight inside the room. I told them what I was and they told me, "There ain't [anyone from your gang] on this deck." There was more of them than there was of me. And, um, they

was like, "If I was you, I would just bank yourself, man." I ain't gonna lie, I was scared. So, I'm like, just skip it, I just do what I do. So, I did it. I banked myself. The sergeant was like, "We got a bitch on the deck. We got a bitch on the deck who's bankin' himself. What you bankin' yourself for?"

The young person, who was a member of a Latinx gang, suspected that the officers housed him with Black gang members because of his appearance, pointing to how gang designations can be based on assumptions about identity and race. The young person identified the risk to his safety if he remained in the unit and faced social consequences, degrading comments, and violence for acknowledging his vulnerability. In February 2020, nineteen-year-old Pedro Ruiz was killed after being housed in the Cook County Jail with a young person with whom he had existing conflicts.[66] Police insist that a working gang database is crucial for understanding and interrupting these conflicts. This raises important questions: was the information about Ruiz in the database incorrect, or did the officers make assumptions that he would be safe with people who looked like him? Regardless, the use of gang information can aggravate existing conflicts with potentially life-threatening consequences.

Gang designations turn race and class inequality into a permanent record, and assumptions about the objective, scientific nature of data help erase the conditions of data production and legitimize aggressive policing in Black and Latinx neighborhoods. Moreover, inclusion in the gang database has serious consequences regardless of whether a person is actually involved in a street gang. Inclusion makes people vulnerable to more regular and violent police encounters. It has a negative impact on bail, bond, sentencing, and parole decisions. It can also create barriers to housing and employment. People in the database have been denied jobs because some background checks include gang designations, and people with family members in the database can be prevented from leaving jail or prison because they have no place to live due to probation or parole conditions that prevent association with other gang members.

The youth we interviewed also described how the police negatively impacted their relationships to other institutions and their access to resources. During our research, Circles & Ciphers staff were advocating for a high school student to reenroll in his neighborhood school after a juvenile arrest and period of incarceration. As a restorative justice organization, Circles & Ciphers was working to repair the relationship between the student and school administrators. The principal ultimately agreed to reenroll the student. A Chicago police officer then contacted the principal and advised that the student be prevented from attending based on his gang membership. Barred from his neighborhood school, the student enrolled in a school in a different community. A month later, outside of his new school, he was the victim of a shooting.

Young women also described how the police used claims of gang membership and threats of child separation to force their compliance with investigations.[67] When a young Black woman was arrested for gun possession, the police interrogated her about her boyfriend, who was on the SSL. The police said they would pursue a gun case against her if she didn't provide information to incriminate her boyfriend. If incarcerated, she would be separated from her young child, and her gang membership would be used as an aggravating factor to make reunification with her child more difficult. Navigating the tightrope between protecting her boyfriend, her child, and her own safety, the young woman decided to plead guilty, even though the gun did not belong to her. Her incarceration resulted in the loss of her apartment, security deposit, and employment and forced her to consider kinship care for her child. Luckily, she had family to house and care for her son, averting a child protection case. Many of the young parents with whom we spoke had lost custody of their children during periods of incarceration and had to meet extensive conditions for reunification.[68] The gang member archetype complicated these processes by shaping how courts evaluated their parenting and made decisions about their children's needs.

Overall, the data that police produce through racialized stops and arrests are used to determine police strategies, to incarcerate people in jails and prisons, and to exacerbate conflicts and forms of punishment. The experiences of gang-involved youth provide further evidence that police and carceral authorities expand webs of surveillance by creating conflict and contributing to the conditions that they claim to address. Next, we explore how data-based policing creates a permanent record, enabling the CPD to target funerals and memorial events.

THE POSTMORTEM EFFECTS OF THE PERMANENT RECORD

In *Precarious Life,* Judith Butler reflects on the fundamental vulnerability and interconnectedness of human life and asks whether it is possible to build community through mourning.[69] Butler points out that the unequal distribution of vulnerability to death is accompanied by prohibitions on public mourning for those considered not fully human. She argues that we must resist these prohibitions by naming, grieving, and acknowledging our relationships with people whose lives are treated as having no value.

For young people navigating Chicago's fragmented gang landscape, Aspholm explains, "the loss of a member is typically experienced among his surviving comrades as profoundly sorrowful."[70] In this section, we uplift the analysis from young people that their allegiances and rivalries are shaped by personal relationships and the deaths of loved ones, not by territorial or economic competition. Gang-involved youth write lyrics, produce songs, and record videos to memorialize the dead.[71] They name their cliques after loved ones who have been killed, a critical variable in the construction and changing nature of gangs that remains undertheorized. We show how funerals and memorials are sites of world making that are viewed by the CPD as dangerous and captured in the spiral of surveillance.

For gang-involved young people and their friends and relatives, funerals and memorials are particularly important spaces to honor the dead and build community. Youth use these spaces to celebrate the lives of their comrades by sharing stories. Memorials also enable people to renew their commitments to one another and challenge the dehumanizing portrayal of their loved ones. By creating space for living, grieving, and healing, memorial events create ephemeral traces of loved ones lost and fugitive possibilities for building community, resisting criminalization, and embodying complex subjectivities erased by the gang member archetype. In this context, mourning is a political act of celebrating the lives of people who were not recognized as fully human. Memorials are public acts of defiance against the prohibition on mourning for people whose lives and deaths were not supposed to matter.

To the state, therefore, funerals and memorials are dangerous, and the logic of predictive policing has transformed these events into sites of intense racialized surveillance. Youth report that places of mourning become sites of surveillance and arrest. In 2017, the Cook County sheriff created the Funeral and Cemetery Violence Task Force to keep western suburban cemeteries safe during funeral processions for young people who had been murdered.[72] The task force encouraged data sharing between funeral directors and police to help anticipate violence, suggested predictive deployments to secure funeral homes and burial sites, and called on state legislators to enhance penalties for crimes committed at funeral and memorial events. The CPD created an intelligence bulletin to share predictions about potential disruptions with funeral directors, cemeteries, and suburban police departments.

Police officers are deployed inside funeral homes, during processions, at wakes, and at burial sites. On September 28, 2019, Derrick, a young Black man and comrade, was at a traffic light when a man approached the car and fired shots that struck him in his head and chest. Derrick was pronounced dead at the hospital. No one was arrested for Derrick's murder, but police obstructed Derrick's funeral on the pretext of protecting the bereaved from threats of violence. Unmarked police cars sat in the lot across from the funeral home. A paddy wagon waited in a nearby parking lot. A white officer sat in an unmarked car wearing plain clothes and a bulletproof vest with his firearms visible, and a tall Black officer in plain clothes stood at the entrance to the funeral home, questioning people as they entered the building. During the funeral, police confronted a group of young people who went to their car to smoke, asking questions, demanding to search their vehicle, provoking a confrontation, and ultimately arresting the young people.

Police also track the dates of birth and death of alleged gang members and deploy police to surveil memorial gatherings around these dates. This surveillance is significant for several reasons. First, the policing of funerals and memorial events demonstrates the permanence of a gang designation. According to the CPD, Chicago police have no way of removing names from the gang arrest card database; people remain in the database for decades. As of 2019, more than four thousand people older than fifty years of age were in the database.[73] A separate gang database maintained by the Cook County Sheriff's Office included hundreds of people listed as "deceased."[74] A database of deceased gang members demonstrates the permanence of a police record.

Second, by surveilling memorials, the police impede the ability of the bereaved to mourn the loss of loved ones. The police obstruct a fundamental right to assembly and a deeply human need to grieve. Policing funerals and memorials hinders the effort to heal and denies the deceased's loved ones the time and space to mourn. Deploying police to monitor memorials also heightens the surveillance of the deceased's family, friends, and neighbors and increases the likelihood of police encounters that could end in violence.

During Marquise's funeral, family members and friends joined a procession to the burial site. On the way, police pulled over Marquise's relatives after a white woman reported that a group of Black youth stopped her car and climbed on the hood. Marquise's cousin Brianna and his sister Jasmine, both of whom were involved in our YPAR project, were in the car that police stopped. The police drew their weapons, forced the passengers out of the vehicle, and accused them of vandalizing the woman's car. Brianna, Jasmine, and the other people in the car did not match the descriptions that the woman provided—nor did their vehicle—but the police questioned them anyway. While their car was stopped, the vehicles behind them in the procession were also forced to stop. By the time the police allowed them to leave, Brianna, Jasmine, and other friends and family had missed Marquise's burial.

Finally, the deployment of police to monitor memorials demonstrates another way that data-based policing leads to injury and death. When Marquise and Jaquan died, they were gathering with neighbors at a memorial for their friend Gerald. The police viewed Gerald's death as a predictive data point. They deployed police to the annual memorial, which led to a high-speed chase and the deaths of two young men. For the police, their deaths became new data points that justified additional surveillance in subsequent years. On the first anniversary of Marquise's death, loved ones planned a small balloon release in his memory. A police vehicle circled the block while Marquise's family gathered. The balloons and a life-sized cardboard cutout of Marquise identified the event as one of mourning. Yet, the police interrupted the event and interrogated Marquise's father. They eventually left the family to grieve, but the surveillance of Marquise's memorial signifies the postmortem effects of a gang designation.

Predictive policing and gang databases produce these postmortem effects by entangling death and mourning with carceral logics. Police lean into the archetype to attack the humanity of the deceased and devalue their deaths—"just another dead gang member"—while criminalizing associations by surveilling their loved ones at funerals and memorials. They transform death into data to expand the spiral of surveillance and disrupt the resistance of the bereaved who honor the lives of the dead. Yet the deceased leave behind fugitive traces, creating new epistemic possibilities for the living who share dark sousveillant knowledge and reclaim the humanity of their loved ones. The postmortem effects of the gang member archetype thus produce a paradox: while they impede the ability of the living to mourn and heal, the bereaved resist by celebrating life, building community, and uplifting the fugitive traces of escape in death.

DO WE DARE LOVE THE SHOOTER?

Our intent in this chapter is not to minimize the impact of community violence or downplay the tremendous losses that poor and working-class Black and brown communities confront. Gun violence is indeed a problem that has devastated communities in Chicago. Yet predictive policing grounded in a "gangbanger" archetype obscures and disavows the foundational violence of racial capitalism, white supremacy, and heteropatriarchy that leads to the development of street organizations and community violence. It also obfuscates the role of police in upholding a fundamentally unequal and violent social order through criminalization, incarceration, and death.

Despite the conditions that shape the lives of Black youth in Chicago, they are cast as perpetual threats to society, particularly when they challenge social norms and the rigidly gendered, raced, and classed social order. Youth who are gang involved, who have lost loved ones to police and gun violence, are seldom seen as knowledge makers and experts positioned to resist criminalizing archetypes and build transformative solutions. Yet their dark sousveillant knowledge and everyday fugitivity situate gang-involved young people as experts capable of dissecting the empire state and imagining a future without police.

A transformative response to community and state violence requires that we affirm the complex humanity of gang-involved young people and support youth who are often victims of violence *and* perpetrators of harm. In the conclusion of her book *Social Death,* Lisa Marie Cacho narrates the loss of her cousin Brandon.[75] While the primary frames available for ascribing value to the life of a young person of color are either racial exclusion or resistance, Cacho concludes that both frameworks are too narrow to account for the fullness and complexity of Brandon's life or the emptiness left behind by his death. The gang member archetype is so totalizing that it admits only one possibility for redemption: a decision to renounce the gang and "turn your life around." We want to emphasize the importance of challenging the gang member archetype by honoring the fullness of human life and insisting that gang membership does not make the lives of gang-involved youth any less valuable.[76]

Haley met Devell five years before we began the YPAR. He had been called to testify against Taivon, a childhood friend. Taivon was charged with aggravated battery; Devell was the victim. Although victims of crimes are entitled to services when they cooperate in prosecutions, the state treated Devell like a gang member whose only value was his testimony against another gang member. Haley was in court supporting Taivon when Devell testified. After his testimony, Devell exited the courtroom. Haley was surprised to see Devell in the hallway because victims are often separated from the public during a trial. Haley asked Devell if he was OK. Devell expressed feelings of betrayal and disposability. Haley later learned that Devell was a ward of the Department of Children and Family Services (DCFS). His mother struggled with homelessness, substance abuse, intimate partner violence, and state violence. He often spoke about being born into chaos. "I was in DCFS since I was four years old," he explained. "I came out the womb and [my life was] just chaotic." But narratives of violence and victimization do not fully capture his life. "Even though I was on the streets, I stayed in school," he explained. "I was on the honor roll, principal's lists. So, I was always smart, but I just stayed in trouble and fightin' and stuff, you know, defending myself."

Devell was shot and killed on January 29, 2020, near the intersection where his brother Devin was killed two years earlier. At Devell's funeral, a well-known community organizer and former gang leader offered a redemptive narrative of achievement and self-improvement. Attempting to counter the gang member archetype, he claimed that Devell was

FIGURE 7. Reef leads a community line dance at a peace circle event. Photograph by and courtesy of Edvetté Wilson Jones.

in recovery, no longer gang involved or selling drugs. He claimed that Devell had turned a corner, was mending his mistakes, and was on his way to becoming the man he was supposed to be. Despite the speaker's clear affection for Devell, this redemptive narrative did not tell the whole story. Like the archetype that the speaker rejected, his narrative erased aspects of Devell's subjectivity to create a liberal subject worthy of grief. Devell was a young Black father, a circle keeper, and a boxer who was on the SSL and struggled with the consequences of a criminal record, mental illness, and addiction. Acknowledging the troubling aspects of Devell's life should not make him any less valuable and worthy of our grief.

Like funerals, court proceedings become scenes of redemption. Judges expect defense witnesses to activate scripts about a young person's character to gain sympathy in the hope of receiving a bond or a reduced sentence. But liberal discourses cannot contain the subjectivities of human beings. In 2019, Reef was arrested, charged with murder, and held without bond. At a bond hearing, Haley and several other people testified as character witnesses. Haley discussed Reef's involvement in the YPAR as one of many indicators of Reef's humanity and ties to the community. After hearing the witness testimony, the judge announced that Reef was "a man with two faces" and implied that he deceived the character witnesses. The judge insisted that Reef could not be a loving, caring father and organizer, a valuable member of the community, and a gang member at the same time. The judge rejected the assertions of Reef's humanity, holding him on a $700,000 bond. Reef was found not guilty of the murder nearly four years after his arrest.

Young people like Reef and Devell demand that we acknowledge the complex reality of human subjectivity. The metaphor of two faces demonstrates the subjective erasures that stem from the dehumanizing gang member archetype and its redemptive alternative. The knowledge that Devell, Reef, and other youth shared with us emerged from their experiences as individuals situated by multiple and overlapping identities and intersecting systems of power and violence and their experiences as victims of violence and perpetrators of harm. We had so much more to learn together, but their lives and insights inspired and strengthened the work of abolitionist organizing against the database and of the PCRG.

To make life-affirming changes, we need to lean on the decades-long work of grassroots organizers and restorative and transformative justice practitioners. In Chicago, organizations like Project NIA, Black Youth Project 100 (BYP100), and Circles & Ciphers have developed practices that acknowledge the complex lives of young people and the role of the police in perpetuating violence. Project NIA, founded by Mariame Kaba in 2009, has campaigned to close youth prisons and develops popular education tools about community accountability, community safety, and a world without prisons. BYP100, established after the murder of Trayvon Martin, has organized for decriminalization and abolition while developing resources for community safety—such as "She Safe, We Safe"—that do not rely on the criminal punishment system.[77] And Circles & Ciphers facilitates restorative and transformative justice circles with gang-involved youth, including conflict-resolution processes and victim–offender dialogues. Responding to the devastating violence that communities of color experience from the empire state, these organizations are building safety through solidarity and mutual aid, popular education, and campaigns to transform the political conditions that reinforce oppression and violence.

This chapter does not offer straightforward solutions to gun violence in Chicago but aims to challenge the disavowal and abandonment of gang-involved youth and gestures toward radical love, relationships, and collective care as transformative pathways. The violence that Black youth face in Chicago is multidimensional and intersectional. Expecting youth to "just say no" to gang membership or to pick up and leave when they feel unsafe or receive a promise of services is not realistic. Learning from feminist, queer disability justice projects, we suggest resisting and address-ing violence together, with no one left behind.[78] What would change if we were to reframe the violence that youth perpetuate as a response to white supremacy, racial capitalism, and heteropatriarchal oppression? What could we accomplish if we were to focus our organizing around youth who cause harm, rather than the innocent? What would it mean to embrace gang-involved youth in their entirety, to love them while acknowledging their participation in violence? What could we build and what could we become if we were to love the shooter?

In 1996, sixteen-year-old "Jamie" was arrested, charged with the mur-der of his friend "Freddy," and sentenced to life without the possibility of parole. In 2012, the U.S. Supreme Court held that the mandatory sentenc-ing of life without parole is unconstitutional for people under eighteen.[79] After the ruling, Jamie, one of more than twenty-five hundred "juvenile-lifers," received a resentencing hearing. Freddy's daughter, whom Jamie had held as an infant, prepared a victim impact statement. On the stand, however, she put down her letter, looked at Jamie, and forgave him. As Jamie cried, Freddy's family members stood in the courtroom and told the judge to send him home. We can learn from Freddy's daughter and the young people whose voices and insights are centered here; we need to rethink violence, its impact on human lives, and its solutions.

The experiences of the young people we interviewed and with whom we worked demonstrate how carceral solutions like data-based predictive policing manufacture criminals and perpetuate conflicts. Youth resist surveillance and adopt everyday abolitionist praxis because they believe they are more likely to be harmed than helped by the police. The experi-ences of gang-involved youth challenge us to interrupt narratives that center the innocent and reinforce the notion that police can protect "us" by punishing "them." By recognizing the full, complex humanity of gang-involved youth, we can disrupt othering narratives and learn from the young people who live on the front lines of the struggle for a world without police.

We can think about ways to be in relationship with youth that are not limited by the rules of the academy or the boundaries of research and embrace our responsibility to act with radical love. In the words of Paulo Freire, "love is an act of courage, not fear . . . a commitment to others . . . [and] to the cause of liberation."[80] Radical love privileges the experiences and perspectives of the marginalized, requires a commitment to dialogue and care, and demands a willingness to take risks to redistribute power.

Though associated with different gangs, the young people who worked together in the YPAR shared a mutual recognition and love for one another. After the deaths of Marquise, Devell, and Taivon, Reef recalled a moment they shared together while Marquise recovered from an abdominal gunshot injury. When the team gathered, Marquise wore a colostomy bag, and Reef and other youth leaders shared knowledge about caring for gunshot injuries. "It's crazy, because the only time Marquise and Taivon met was at the church," remembered Reef. "It was me, Taivon, Marquise, and Devell. Yeah, it was just different. It was the only time that I seen us all together." Remembering this moment of fugitive possibility, of caring for one another in the face of dehumanization and death, we shared in the grief that Reef expressed at the loss of our friends and research partners. The deaths of Marquise, Jaquan, Derrick, Deven, Devell, Taivon, and Deshawn remind us what is at stake and why it is necessary to disrupt violence and build a world without exploitation and oppression.[81] We hope this chapter stands as a memorial to their lives and as an act of defiance against everything that says their deaths do not matter. We must demand more of each other to move toward transformative possibilities.

4 Manufacturing Terrorists: Palestinian Americans and the Dif/Fusion of Surveillance

In October 2013, the U.S. Department of Homeland Security (DHS) arrested Rasmea Odeh at her home in Chicago and charged her with unlawful procurement of naturalization. A prominent activist in the struggle for Palestine liberation, Rasmea had lived and organized in Chicago for ten years, helping to build a powerful community through her visionary leadership as coordinator of the Arab American Action Network's (AAAN) Arab Women's Committee. She worked with Arab women and girls to address issues within the community; resist the racist repression of Arabs and Muslims; and build connections with Black, Latinx, and other communities struggling for social justice in Chicago and beyond.[1] Rasmea's commitment to joint struggle and the liberation of Palestine makes her dangerous to the U.S. empire and the Israeli apartheid state.

As we document in this chapter, Rasmea's arrest and eventual deportation were the culmination of a series of coordinated investigations led by federal agencies that targeted Palestinian leftists and socialist internationalists throughout the Midwest. U.S. attorney Barbara McQuade charged Rasmea with making false statements on her 2005 application for U.S. citizenship because she denied having a previous criminal conviction. Recycling a label pinned on Rasmea by the Israeli government, McQuade designated her a "terrorist."[2] The government's case rested on decades-old documents obtained from the Israeli government that indicated that Rasmea had been arrested in Jerusalem, confessed to a bombing, and was convicted by an Israeli military court. The Israeli documents, however, said nothing about the twenty-five days of torture, threats, and sexual violence that Rasmea faced during her interrogation

FIGURE 8. Rasmea Odeh at an April 28, 2015, emergency action in solidarity with Baltimore after the killing of Freddie Gray. Photograph by and courtesy of Sarah Jane Rhee (@loveandstrugglephotos).

by Israeli Shin Bet (Internal Security) agents. Rather than allowing the Israeli documents to stand as "facts," Rasmea set out to demonstrate the social construction of the "terrorist" label by describing the Israeli state violence that led to her confession and conviction. But the judge blocked Rasmea from testifying about her torture and challenging the legitimacy of her conviction. Despite efforts to overturn the judge's decisions, the court covered up Rasmea's experiences of sexual violence, accepted the Israeli documents without question, and treated Rasmea's conviction as a simple and undeniable "fact." In doing so, the U.S. government validated and concealed the sexualized, gendered, racial violence through which Israel pinned the label "terrorist" on Rasmea. The U.S. government's treatment of Rasmea underscores the impact of settler-colonial violence, sexual violence, and imperial state violence across time and space. Finding her guilty of unlawfully procuring U.S. citizenship, the United States deported Rasmea to Jordan in October 2017.

Highlighting the connections between Israeli settler colonialism and the U.S. empire, Rasmea's case reveals key mechanisms in the multiscalar structure of surveillance operating to police Palestinian freedom struggles and other movements for liberation. In particular, it signals the emergence of an imperial network of carceral agencies led by the U.S. federal government that coordinates counterinsurgency projects based on the racialized archetype of the "terrorist"—a dehumanizing archetype rooted in counterinsurgency campaigns by colonial and imperial powers. When any agency tags an individual with the "terrorist" label, it becomes a data point that is stored in a permanent record, circulates within the network, and is accepted as a matter of fact—concealing the conditions and discourses through which the label was produced.

Repressing political activists like Rasmea is an essential part of the so-called War on Terror, the second of three interconnected police wars that we examine in this book. The War on Terror is a joint counterinsurgency project of the U.S. empire state and the Israeli settler-colonial state to target a wide range of political opponents—from political Islamists to Arab nationalists to socialist feminists. U.S. federal agencies assume primary responsibility for War on Terror operations within the United States, especially the U.S. Attorney's Office, the Federal Bureau of Investigation (FBI), and the various arms of the DHS. Over the last twenty years, however, the empire state has expanded the War on Terror by incorporating additional state agencies and encouraging the private-sector surveillance of Arabs and Muslims.

We theorize this emerging structure as the *dif/fusion* of surveillance to place emphasis on two distinct but interrelated moments: diffusion and fusion. *Diffusion* points to the proliferation and decentralization of surveillance by numerous state and private-sector actors that participate in the War on Terror. Promoting and activating a shared archetype, diffusion leads to the mass production of "terrorist" labels stored as permanent records in law enforcement databases. *Fusion* refers to the mechanisms that enable coordination within the multiscalar networks of imperial policing. Fusion centers, such as the Chicago Police Department's (CPD) Crime Prevention and Information Center (CPIC), are key nodes in the system because they enable the analysis of information from the databases of multiple agencies and the dissemination of data across agencies. As we demonstrate throughout the book, fusion centers and data-sharing agreements have enabled the emergence and expansion of a multiscalar network of carceral surveillance that includes a constantly growing number of local, state, and federal agencies; private-sector corporations; academics; mental health professionals; nonprofits; philanthropic organizations; and global partners of the U.S. empire state, such as Israel's Shin Bet. Importantly, when data circulate through this network, the conditions of their production disappear, and what remains is seemingly objective data that are used to target the same racialized populations that have historically been targets of imperial policing.

To be sure, dif/fusion is not limited to the War on Terror. In practice, dif/fusion is one of the primary models of articulation through which the carceral agencies of empire are linked into a complex unity. But the War on Terror provides an excellent window into the operation of this model. This chapter, therefore, will draw out the dif/fusion of surveillance as it operates through this particular police war. Because the webs of imperial policing are global, dismantling these webs is a core component of abolition.

We begin by documenting the consolidation of the "Arab terrorist" archetype after 1967 and its post–Cold War consolidation and expansion to include Arabs and Muslims. We then analyze the dif/fusion of surveillance after 2001, documenting the emergence of a decentralized, data-based, coordinated, and global network of imperial policing. Analyzing local manifestations of the War on Terror in Chicago, we examine the investigations that led to the deportation of Rasmea Odeh and document the use of suspicious activity reports (SARs) as a tool of racial surveillance. In doing so, we demonstrate that dif/fusion generates an ever-expanding spiral of surveillance that has devastating impacts on Arab and Muslim communities.

THE EMERGING WAR ON TERROR AND THE ARCHETYPE OF THE ARAB/MUSLIM TERRORIST

The U.S. War on Terror did not begin in 2001. Since the late nineteenth century, the United States has used the label "terrorist" to describe resistance to U.S. colonial and imperial rule—in the Philippines, Puerto Rico, Vietnam, and beyond—as well as radical challenges to capitalist state violence. For the last fifty and more years, the logics and practices of the War on Terror have increasingly linked U.S. imperialism with Israeli settler colonialism.[3] Indeed, the dehumanizing archetype of the

"Arab terrorist" and experiments in multiagency coordination can both be traced back to the late 1960s, when the Palestine liberation movement built strong connections with Black radicals and internationalists in the United States.[4] As a project of the U.S. empire, the War on Terror is truly global—targeting Arab and Muslim communities with surveillance and repression in the Middle East and across their global diasporas. The Palestinian diasporic community in Chicago has remained a consistent target of this imperial police war.

A long history of orientalist representations and strong Zionist currents in the United States facilitated the construction of the "Arab/Muslim terrorist" as a criminal archetype.[5] We use the term *criminal archetype* to highlight the historical longevity of this figure, the emotional weight that it carries, and the deadly state violence that it legitimizes. Threat discourses centering the figure of the "Arab/Muslim terrorist" emerged alongside Zionist settler colonialism, were crystalized by the U.S. government and mainstream media, and now circulate globally through the networks of the U.S. empire.[6]

In the 1960s and 1970s, archetypical terrorists were Arab secular nationalists and leftists, especially those associated with the Palestine Liberation Organization (PLO), formed in 1964 to coordinate struggles for the liberation of Palestine and the return of Palestinian refugees displaced during the *nakba* (catastrophe) that marked the 1948 formation of Israel as a settler-colonial state. After Israel occupied the West Bank and Gaza Strip along with the Golan Heights and Sinai Peninsula in 1967, U.S. media increasingly portrayed Israelis as "civilized, predestined, and striving people," while invoking "strong derogatory racial overtones towards Arabs."[7] Nation-based racism, cultural racism, and an image of Arab women as oppressed by a backward patriarchal culture became important pillars for this racial project, as did the shifting global dynamics of the U.S. empire.[8]

In 1973, the Israeli consul in Chicago publicly claimed that "all of the city's Arab community were 'potential terrorists.'"[9] The dehumanizing label placed targets on the backs of Chicago's diasporic Arab communities. It also obscured and delegitimized their political critiques of U.S. imperialism, racism, and Zionism[10] as well as their partnerships with other communities fighting for social justice.

The Cold War produced early experiments in coordinated, multi-agency surveillance programs that targeted people based on this archetype and therefore reified the archetype. In 1972, Richard Nixon created the Cabinet Committee to Combat Terrorism (CCCT), which instructed the State Department, the FBI, the Central Intelligence Agency (CIA), the National Security Agency (NSA), and the U.S. Immigration and Naturalization Service (INS) to establish "special measures" for monitoring Arabs and Arab Americans.[11] These measures included Operation Boulder, a three-year program designed to intimidate, silence, and deport Arabs critical of U.S. policy in the Middle East. INS agents conducted stringent reviews of visa applications from Arab countries and interviewed every Arab in the United States on a student visa. They asked questions about coursework, employment, and political activities and reported "suspicious" cases to the FBI.

Immigration enforcement and deportation were primary tools of the early War on Terror. In the early 1980s, the INS attempted to deport two Palestinian community organizers based in Chicago: Samir Odeh and Mahmoud Naji.[12] The INS also developed emergency plans for the mass detention of "alien terrorists and undesirables" from eight Arab countries and Iran and initiated deportation proceedings against one Kenyan and seven Palestinian socialists—the Los Angeles 8—for handing out literature associated with the Popular Front for the Liberation of Palestine (PFLP), a left-wing faction of the PLO.[13]

The Cold War surveillance of Arabs and Palestinians also involved coordination between the U.S. government, the state of Israel, and Zionist organizations. In 1981, at the request of Israel's Mossad intelligence agency, the FBI arrested a young Palestinian named Ziad Abu Ain visiting his sister in Chicago. Federal authorities held Abu Ain in Chicago for two years before extraditing him to Israel.[14] At the same time, the Anti-Defamation League (ADL)[15] built a nationwide surveillance network that employed former police and CIA agents to surveil organizations and individuals supporting Palestinian and South African liberation. The ADL compiled reports on 950 organizations and nearly 12,000 individuals and shared its data with South African and Israeli intelligence.[16] The Jewish Defense League resorted to more violent tactics, including the bombing of Arab American organizations and the murder of Palestinian American organizer Alex Odeh.[17] These privatized forms of surveillance and repression were never officially condoned. But, as Louise Cainkar notes, "the FBI did little to investigate these incidents; Arab lives mattered to law enforcement only as potential terrorists."[18]

The end of the Cold War led to three shifts in the War on Terror. First, the collapse of the Soviet Union, along with growing anti-Muslim sentiment, led to a shift in the primary U.S. national security discourse from "communism" to "terrorism." As the "Arab/Muslim terrorist" became the primary threat to U.S. "national security," anyone presumed to be Arab, Muslim, or "Middle Eastern" became the target of hypersurveillance and criminalization.[19] Second, the U.S. government began adopting legislation to disrupt funding and "material support" for groups designated "foreign terrorist organizations" (FTOs).[20] This produced another layer of surveillance by criminalizing solidarity with Palestine liberation and resistance to U.S. imperial policy in the Middle East. Finally, moving away from an emphasis on interagency coordination, the FBI took the lead on all domestic counterterrorism operations. The first two shifts were consolidated after 9/11, but the third was reversed when the federal government embraced carceral dif/fusion.

During the 1990s, all three shifts were evident in the surveillance of Muhammad Salah and Operation Vulgar Betrayal, both of which focused on Chicago's Palestinian community. In 1993, Israel arrested Muhammad Salah, a U.S. citizen from the Chicago suburb of Bridgeview,[21] as he crossed into the Gaza Strip with humanitarian aid collected by Islamic charities in the United States.[22] The Israeli state has always used surveillance and arrest to criminalize stateless people living in exile who attempt to return or even visit their homeland. Israel labeled Salah a "terrorist" by claiming that he was a military commander of Hamas, the Palestinian Islamic Resistance Movement, distributing money to support violence. Beaten, threatened, held incommunicado, and subjected to weeks of arduous torture, Salah signed a forced "confession" written by the notorious Shin Bet. On the basis of this evidence, Israel sentenced Salah to five years in prison and insisted that the United States clamp down on financial flows from charities in the United States to occupied Palestine.[23]

In 1995, the Clinton administration declared Salah a "specially designated terrorist" and outlawed financial support for Hamas. The next year, Congress passed the Anti-Terrorism and Effective Death Penalty Act, which criminalized the provision of "material support or resources" to those labeled FTOs. In 1997, the United States added Hamas—along with the PFLP and other Palestinian groups—to the list of FTOs, creating severe restrictions on flows of financial aid to Palestinians in the occupied territories and refugee camps.[24] And in 1998, the United States signed the Mutual Legal Assistance Treaty (MLAT) with Israel to promote cooperation between law enforcement agencies in the two countries.[25] Salah's attorneys, Michael Deutsch and Erica Thompson, describe these policies as a "joint venture" by Israel and the United States to expand surveillance, criminalize Palestinian resistance, and establish dangerous legal precedents and mechanisms for coordination.[26]

When Israel shared Salah's "confession" with the U.S. government, the Chicago field office of the FBI launched Operation Vulgar Betrayal (OVB), a wide-ranging operation seeking to uncover networks of financial support for Hamas.[27] Treating the southwest suburbs of Chicago—home to many Arabs, especially Palestinians—as the epicenter of these networks, the FBI focused its attention on the Mosque Foundation in Bridgeview. Salah was a leading member of the Mosque Foundation, and Israeli interrogators incorporated damning claims about the foundation in Salah's forced confession. Using wiretaps, informants, and provocateurs, OVB produced widespread distrust and anxiety, fragmented social ties, and disrupted community organizing. When Salah was released from Israeli prison in 1997, an FBI informant infiltrated his welcome party, befriended him, and began recording conversations and submitting reports to the FBI. "By the late 1990s," the *Chicago Tribune* explains, "federal agents were knocking on doors, trading leads with investigators in other cities and flying to Israel to interview authorities. At FBI offices in Chicago, investigators hung on the wall a 30-foot-long chart listing the names of people and organizations nationwide believed to have ties to Hamas."[28] Despite its repressive tactics, the FBI was forced to close OVB when a grand jury determined that there was no credible evidence for an indictment.

The long-standing interests of the United States in the Middle East created the need for internal policies to support its global imperial activities, including collusion with Israel. Shifting policies and discourses after the Cold War revealed an expanding War on Terror that was concretized after 9/11. Salah's case and OVB shed light on how the U.S. empire built transnational surveillance networks that were expanded, reorganized, and deployed to manufacture "terrorists" after 2001.

THE DIF/FUSION OF SURVEILLANCE AFTER 9/11

The U.S. political landscape underwent a dramatic transformation after September 11, 2001. The administration of George W. Bush used the attacks in New York City and Washington, D.C., to formalize the War on Terror as an endless, expansive, global project that includes military invasions, drone wars, assassinations, extraordinary renditions, torture, and surveillance. Defining political Islam as a global enemy, the War on Terror targets Arabs and Muslims everywhere, including in Chicago.[29] The War on Terror also provides cover for the United States and Israel to target antiracist, anticapitalist, anti-Zionist, and anti-imperialist movements throughout the world. Palestinian organizers and their allies in Chicago have been key targets due to long-standing connections between Palestinian, Black, Indigenous, and Puerto Rican liberation movements.

Policies like the USA PATRIOT Act, the Homeland Security Act, and the National Security Entry–Exit Registration System (NSEERS) fortified the structures for surveilling and criminalizing Arabs and Muslims at U.S. borders and airports and throughout the United States. The empire state expanded broad-based surveillance of Arabs and Muslims as well as targeting repression of community organizers and political activists. Federal agencies supplemented long-standing practices of infiltration and wiretaps with the expanded use of data-based surveillance tools like terrorist watch lists, no-fly lists, and dragnet phone surveillance.[30] Mosques, community centers, Islamic schools, and airports became sites of racial profiling and political repression. Supposed "random" searches at airports, for instance, were informed by pregenerated lists as well as efforts to flag anyone with brown skin, a Muslim name, stereotypical clothing, or facial hair.

Government policies concretized and activated the archetype of the "Arab/Muslim terrorist" in the American imagination, justifying surveillance, criminalization, and death as necessary to create an illusion of safety for the citizens of the United States. This, in turn, provided legitimacy to private-sector fearmongering, harassment, and violence against Arabs and Muslims throughout the country, including in Chicago.[31]

In 2002, the FBI reopened OVB and renewed its investigation of the Mosque Foundation and the Palestinian community in the southwest suburbs of Chicago.[32] After two years of FBI surveillance, federal prosecutors, led by U.S. attorney Patrick Fitzgerald, filed new charges against Muhammad Salah and two other Palestinian men for racketeering and material support for terrorism. For the first time, the U.S. government combined RICO statutes with material support charges, extending the notion of racketeering to implicate the defendants in a conspiracy to finance a FTO.[33] Originally developed to target the Mafia, RICO statutes became a weapon in the War on Gangs in cities like Chicago during the 1990s. Salah's case marked the expansion of RICO statutes to the War on Terror.[34] This was also the first time that U.S. courts permitted the introduction of coerced confessions made to a foreign government—a data-sharing practice that would recur in Rasmea's case.[35] Yet even with secret evidence, anonymous witnesses, wiretaps, and the obliteration of due process, OVB never led to any terrorism-related convictions. Nevertheless, the prosecutorial joint venture revealed the growing importance of data sharing as a mechanism for coordinating the interconnected projects of the U.S. empire and Israeli settler colonialism. OVB also demonstrates expanded criminalization and manufacturing of terrorist subjects through RICO and material support charges.

Although OVB and other early post-9/11 counterterrorism cases remained centered on the FBI and the U.S. Attorney's Office, the empire state soon broadened the network of federal and local agencies through what we call carceral dif/fusion. The federal 9/11 Commission that investigated the attacks provided official justification for dif/fusion. The *9/11 Commission Report* concluded that U.S. intelligence agencies failed to anticipate September 11 because they operated in silos without sharing information:

> The U.S. government has access to a vast amount of information. When databases not usually thought of as "intelligence," such as customs or immigration information, are included, the storehouse is immense. But the U.S. government has a weak system for processing and using what it has.[36]

The commission called for the adoption of a "decentralized network model" for data management in which "agencies would still have their own databases, but those databases would be searchable across agency lines."[37] Although the report does not mention Nixon's Cabinet Council on Combating Terrorism, the 9/11 Commission proposed a dif/fuse model of surveillance facilitated by data sharing that replicated the coordinated, interagency approach to the suppression of the Palestinian and Arab left enacted by the CCCT. As documented in chapter 1, the CPD's Citizen and Law Enforcement Analysis and Reporting (CLEAR) data system soon became an award-winning model for data sharing. The decentralized model enabled not only a diffusion of surveillance but also a circulation of tactics between police wars, such as bringing tools of social media monitoring developed for counterterrorism purposes into operations targeting Black and Latinx communities.

As a mode of articulation through which the various carceral agencies of empire are linked, dif/fusion involves two interrelated moments: diffusion and fusion. As mentioned previously, *diffusion* refers to the logics, policies, and practices of multiplication and dispersal that enable an ever-expanding proliferation of surveillance agents, whereas *fusion* refers to the structures and processes that facilitate coordination within a decentralized, multiscalar surveillance network.

Diffusion

Federal agencies retain primary responsibility for most operations related to the War on Terror within the United States. The U.S. Attorney's Office and the FBI oversee targeted investigations; the DHS operates no-fly lists, border controls, and deportations; and the NSA conducts massive surveillance of telephone and electronic communication. But policies like the USA PATRIOT Act and the Homeland Security Act were designed to multiply the agents of surveillance and encourage interagency coordination. The USA PATRIOT Act removed the so-called wall that previously separated "domestic" investigations headed by the FBI from "foreign" investigations headed by the CIA.[38] The twenty-two agencies that make up the newly created DHS all expanded their capacity for investigations and surveillance.

The federal government also increasingly recruits local and state police departments to participate in the War on Terror. The FBI has partnered with local police departments to create nearly two hundred Joint Terrorism Task Forces (JTTFs) across the country, including one in Chicago.[39] Many metropolitan police departments, including the CPD, have established counterterrorism bureaus. And cities, counties, and states have received federal funding to create departments of homeland security and emergency management.

Along with expanded state surveillance, the federal government draws private-sector actors into the surveillance network by activating the "terrorist" archetype within the popular imagination and encouraging civilians, service providers, and lawfare organizations to monitor and report on neighbors, family members, students, and patients.

Countering Violent Extremism (CVE), for example, was initiated under the Obama administration, which defined its approach to counter-terrorism as gentler than the Bush regime's. Modeled on community polic-ing and consistent with what we call carceral liberalism, CVE programs encourage educators, librarians, religious leaders, mental health workers, and social service providers to report expressions of Muslim culture, Is-lamic religious belief, support for Palestine liberation, and critiques of U.S. foreign policy in the Middle East. They also deputize "good" Muslims to report on potential "bad" Muslims.[40] These disciplinary efforts intensify the surveillance that Muslims confront on a daily basis, transforming even places of worship and trusted religious advisers and mental health profes-sionals into deputies of the surveillance state. CVE targets Muslims in the diaspora, including Black Muslims, and a proliferation of this model is seen in the FBI's Black Identity Extremism program, which targets Black political movements. As we discuss later, SARs also deputize the public to identify potential "terrorists," thereby reinforcing the archetype of the "Arab/Muslim terrorist."

And, since 2001, federal courts have greenlighted surveillance by Zionist organizations that use lawfare to disrupt support for Palestine liberation. Lawfare stems from the legalization of private spying by Zionist organizations. In 2000, attorney Nathan Lewin and the ADL introduced a landmark $600 million civil case against Muhammad Salah and four Islamic charitable organizations, accusing them of responsibility for the death of an American teenager allegedly killed by Hamas in the West Bank. Lewin argued that anyone donating money to an FTO should be held liable for violent actions carried out by people associated with the organization. The case ended in 2008 when the Seventh Court of Appeals determined that donors can be held liable if prosecutors show that they knew the "character" of the organization they were supporting.[41] This incentivized surveillance by private organizations that use civil law to manufacture "terrorists" and disrupt the flow of humanitarian aid to Palestinians.

Fusion

Alongside the proliferation of surveillance through processes of diffusion, the empire state incorporates *fusion* mechanisms that enable coordination. The 2004 Intelligence Reform and Terrorism Prevention Act established two key fusion mechanisms. First, it created a new position—the director of national intelligence—to coordinate the U.S. "intelligence community." Second, it established the National Network of Fusion Centers to facilitate interagency data sharing. Flows of personnel, training, expertise, discourse, and technology have contributed to interagency coordination for decades.[42] In the early twenty-first century, however, data circulation has become an essential fusion mechanism connecting dispersed sites of surveillance. And as information circulates through the carceral webs of empire, the data are cleansed: the practices of imperial policing and the racialized archetypes that ground the data's production are erased. All that remains are seemingly incontrovertible "facts."

The dif/fusion of surveillance has exponentially increased reports of potential terrorist activity, reinforcing the claim that fusion is effective. The "terrorist" archetype provides a shared focal point for surveillance, which helps ensure that reports submitted by a decentralized network of state and private-sector actors continually identify the same populations as suspects. This is how imperial policing manufactures terrorist suspects. In the following sections, we focus on the case of Rasmea Odeh and on SARs to demonstrate how dif/fusion leads to coordinated repression and the mass production of terrorist suspects.

RASMEA ODEH AND THE DIF/FUSION OF SURVEILLANCE

Rasmea Odeh's experience demonstrates how dif/fusion operates through multiagency networks of imperial policing that carry out linked investigations based on shared data. The 2003 U.S. invasion of Iraq generated massive worldwide resistance. Antiwar protests in the United States were met with an iron fist and ramped up surveillance of activists and organizers. Rasmea's arrest and eventual deportation stemmed from this surveillance as well as the earlier investigations targeting Palestinians in the Chicago area. Linking the War on Terror with the War on Immigrants, Rasmea's arrest and deportation involved a coordinated web of investigations and data sharing between multiple agencies within the United States and beyond, including federal prosecutors, immigration authorities, national security agencies, local police, and Israel's Shin Bet.

During the 2008 Republican National Convention, the Minneapolis fusion center became a hub for multiple agencies surveilling protesters, gathering data, and sharing intelligence.[43] An undercover FBI informant known to the group as Karen Sullivan infiltrated the antiwar committee and later the Freedom Road Socialist Organization (FRSO).[44] In 2009, "Sullivan" joined a delegation to Palestine coordinated by the General Union of Palestinian Women (GUPW) to witness the gendered impact of the occupation. When the delegation arrived at Ben Gurion International Airport, they were denied entry by Israeli officials—presumably based on a tip from "Sullivan." The FBI's informant also manufactured evidence that U.S.-based solidarity activists were providing monetary support to the PFLP through the GUPW and to the Revolutionary Armed Forces of Colombia (FARC). This allegation became the basis for a series of witch hunt–style FBI raids in 2010.

In September 2010, FBI agents performed coordinated raids on the homes of antiwar leftists in Chicago, Cleveland, and Minneapolis who were connected to the FRSO and Palestine solidarity movements.[45] In Chicago, targets of the raids included Hatem Abudayyeh, executive director of the AAAN, and Joe Iosbaker, a Palestine solidarity activist and union organizer. The FBI search warrants contained explicit references to information from "Sullivan."[46] They also referenced a documentary film titled *Women in Struggle,* which focused on the contributions of

Palestinian women to the liberation struggle.⁴⁷ At the same time, Carlos Montes, a longtime Chicano activist in Los Angeles, was arrested by the Los Angeles Police Department's SWAT team and the FBI on false charges of weapons possession. During the arrest, an FBI officer asked Montes about his involvement with FRSO, which connected Montes's arrest to the raids in the Midwest and revealed the extent of cross-country interagency coordination.⁴⁸

The government convened a grand jury to consider indictments for providing "material support" to FARC and the PFLP, both of which are U.S.-designated FTOs.⁴⁹ The lead prosecutor was U.S. attorney Barry Jonas; his supervisor—Patrick Fitzgerald—led Salah's investigation. Although the grand jury eventually threw out the case for lack of evidence, the experience of targeted surveillance and the possibility of reopening the case remained real threats to the organizers. The 2010 raids exposed the collaboration between fusion centers, the FBI, local law enforcement, and U.S. attorney's offices for targeted surveillance, data sharing, and coordinated interagency attacks on Palestinian activists. These efforts also demonstrate the priorities of the empire state, which utilized extensive resources to tag Palestinians and their supporters with the "terrorist" label. Yet no one foresaw that Rasmea Odeh would become the next target of imperial policing.

In 2013, three years after the FBI raids, the DHS arrested Rasmea at her home in Chicago. Barry Jonas was present at Rasmea's arraignment, signaling that her arrest was a link in an ongoing chain of investigations. The U.S. attorney charged Rasmea with misrepresentation on her December 1994 application for admission to the United States and on her 2005 citizenship application, alleging that she concealed a previous criminal conviction. The government based its case on documents obtained from the Israeli government through the 1998 MLAT, which facilitates the transnational circulation of law enforcement data and requires courts to accept the data without "further authentication or certification."⁵⁰ The Israeli government shared fourteen hundred pages of redacted documents that painted Rasmea as a convicted terrorist who confessed to a bombing in 1969.⁵¹

Rasmea's trial demonstrates how the circulation of data conceals its production. As mentioned, the MLAT requires courts to treat shared evidence as "fact" without questioning the methods used to obtain and manufacture the evidence in the first place.[52] Rasmea's "confession" was the result of torture, threats, and rape, a well-documented practice that Israeli Shin Bet agents have used against Palestinians for decades.[53] Her "conviction" was a product of Israel's fundamentally unequal military court system, a pillar of legal apartheid deployed to uphold Israeli settler-colonial domination throughout historic Palestine.[54] Nevertheless, the federal judge in the U.S. District Court refused to exclude the Israeli documents and prevented Rasmea from challenging the legitimacy of her "confession" and "conviction." Accepting Rasmea's conviction as simple "fact," the judge concealed the racialized sexual violence and apartheid legal system that produced the data indicating that Rasmea was a "terrorist." Rasmea was found guilty, imprisoned, and later deported to Jordan.

The circulation of intelligence files, with conditions that required U.S. courts to accept as "fact" the terrorist label pinned on Rasmea by Israeli military courts, highlights the oppressive power of data sharing as a fusion mechanism within the carceral webs of empire. Israeli government representatives were present at every hearing to ensure that the court concealed the Israeli military's use of torture. Representatives from private-sector lawfare projects were also present at the trial, indicating their collaboration with Israel and the United States in the War on Terror.[55]

Rasmea's case also demonstrates that gender-based state violence is a key site of connection between the U.S. empire state and the Israeli settler-colonial state. As Rasmea experienced firsthand, Israel uses gendered sexualized violence on Palestinian women as a strategy of war and ethnic cleansing. Decades later, the United States validated Israeli torture and extended Rasmea's trauma by disavowing the violence she and other Palestinian women endure(d). Among the evidence presented against Rasmea was the same documentary film—*Women in Struggle*—that the FBI used to justify the 2010 raids.[56] This demonstrates a direct, material link between the FBI raids and Rasmea's arrest, while also highlighting the gendered and racialized surveillance of leftist Palestinian organizers. On the frontlines of Palestinian liberation since before the *nakba*, Palestinian women present a threat to Israeli settler colonialism. For many Palestinian women, feminism has meant care work through an abundance framework, participation in all forms of resistance, and connecting struggles for national liberation with women's liberation from patriarchy.[57] Progressive Arab and Palestinian women's movements have participated in coalitional struggles with Black liberation, Puerto Rican independence, and other anti-imperialist movements. Their resistance is in direct opposition to the narratives of victimhood and terrorism that Israel and the United States use to justify settler colonialism and empire.[58] Data sharing allowed the United States and Israel to jointly target women on the front lines and deport a Palestinian feminist socialist organizer as part of the so-called War on Terror to curtail resistance, spread fear, and reassert imperial power.[59]

Dif/fusion allows a taken-for-granted and flexible approach to interagency coordination, empowering different agencies to take the lead on different cases or pieces of an investigation with shared goals and shared archetypes. This makes it hard to trace where an investigation or a "terrorist" designation began or how the data flowed between agencies. Indeed, state agencies want the circulation of data to remain invisible and investigations to appear distinct.[60] Yet political mobilizations and legal processes can sometimes expose the hidden mechanisms of data sharing. Indeed, much of what we know about the circulation of data was revealed by organizers contesting the 2010 raids and Rasmea's deportation. And our analysis of SARs was possible only because of a legal contest fought by organizers after the state refused to grant Freedom of Information Act (FOIA) requests. Although we do not know everything about how data circulate, we have learned a great deal from organizers, lawyers, and scholar-activists.

SUSPICIOUS ACTIVITY REPORTS AND FUSION CENTERS

In 2010, the DHS rolled out a nationwide If You See Something, Say Something campaign that is the epitome of dif/fusion, highlighting the proliferation of surveillance agents, the activation of racialized archetypes, and the role of data sharing across the dispersed network of the carceral empire.

First established by New York City's Metropolitan Transit Authority, the If You See Something, Say Something campaign is designed to recruit individuals to participate in the War on Terror by monitoring and

FIGURE 9. *Above and right.* In this art piece, Hoda Katebi and Mary Zerkel highlight the use of SARs to police Muslim communities. Photograph by and courtesy of Sarah Jane Rhee (@loveandstrugglephotos).

reporting on one another.[61] The binary logic that grounds the War on Terror—most clearly expressed by George W. Bush, "you are either with us or with the terrorists"—promotes diffusion by encouraging people to identify with the benevolent U.S. empire and participate in the surveillance of dangerous Arabs and Muslims.[62] Defining suspicious activity as "any observed behavior that could indicate terrorism or terrorism-related crime," the federal program encourages everyone to "stay vigilant and say something when you see signs of suspicious activity."[63] Sociologist Brendan McQuade explains that the goal is to make it "as easy and natural as possible for lay individuals to be the 'eyes and ears' that listen to and watch their neighbors, family members, and fellow shoppers, travelers, and sports fans."[64]

Whenever someone calls to report something that they consider suspicious, it generates a SAR. Police and other law enforcement officers can also file SARs after encounters that they consider potentially related to "terrorism." SARs are collected and reviewed by analysts at fusion centers, high-tech surveillance centers operated by local police and staffed by officers from multiple law enforcement agencies. Responding to the

9/11 Commission Report, the U.S. government created a National Network of Fusion Centers, the primary objective of which was to promote data sharing between federal, state, local, and tribal law enforcement agencies. Operating as key nodes in the new system, fusion centers bypass existing limitations on access to restricted databases by placing officers from multiple agencies in the same control room and allowing them to share information. This also encourages officers to treat data from other agencies as "facts" without questioning how the data were produced.

In the Chicago area, If You See Something, Say Something is managed by the Cook County Department of Homeland Security and Emergency Management. SARs are collected and reviewed by analysts at one of the two fusion centers in Illinois. Chicago's fusion center is the CPIC, located at the headquarters of the CPD and staffed by the CPD, FBI, and DHS, along with the Illinois State Police (ISP), Illinois Department of Corrections, Cook County Sheriff's Office, U.S. Department of State, Metra Police Department, U.S. Secret Service, U.S. Attorney's Office, and suburban police departments.[65] The ISP operates another fusion center, known as the Statewide Terrorism Intelligence Center (STIC), at its headquarters in Springfield.

Through FOIA requests submitted by the AAAN, the Lucy Parsons Labs, and the Policing in Chicago Research Group, we gained access to 112 SARs from CPIC and 123 from STIC from 2016 to 2020.[66] Alongside young people from the AAAN's Youth Organizing Program, we analyzed these SARs to understand what prompts a SAR, to examine the tools that fusion center staff use to conduct their initial investigation, and to learn what happens after the fusion center investigation. Our analysis demonstrates that SARs are tools of racialized surveillance used to repress dissent and criminalize the everyday lives of people of color, particularly Arabs and Muslims.

SARs rely on and activate the archetype of the "Arab/Muslim terrorist." Official SAR guidelines explain that "factors such as race, ethnicity, gender, national origin, religion, sexual orientation, or gender identity must not be considered as factors creating suspicion (but attributes may be documented in specific suspect descriptions for identification purposes)."[67] In practice, the data clearly demonstrate that race, ethnicity, religion, and national origin are factors that create suspicion.[68]

Because of the overwhelming association of Arabs and Muslims with terrorism in popular culture, the majority of SARs filed by police and civilians involve suspicions about people who are assumed to be Arab, Muslim, or from the Middle East. This allows us to understand how surveillance, based on racialized archetypes, is diffused through the population. More than half of all SARs that include markers of racial identity listed the suspects as Arab, Middle Eastern, Muslim, or "olive skinned" (53.6 percent at CPIC; 49.4 percent at STIC), and even more are identified as people of color (76.8 percent at CPIC; 63.9 percent at STIC).[69] The actual percentages are almost certainly higher, because people identified as "white" on SAR forms might be Arab, Muslim, or Latinx.[70] This provides evidence that the archetype of the "Arab/Muslim terrorist" provides the discursive foundation for suspicion.

The use of SARs as a tool of racial profiling can also be seen in some of the examples of activities that people considered "suspicious." In June 2016, a "concerned citizen" called CPIC to report seeing two men and a boy—all of whom "appeared to be Middle Eastern"—sitting on a bench at a Chicago Transit Authority train station during rush hour on two different occasions. The group did not board a train and eventually got up and left the station. Video surveillance confirmed that, on both occasions, the group exited a train, sat down on a bench for about fifteen minutes, and then left. One of the men was "carrying a black duffel bag."

Days later, security contractors for the Art Institute of Chicago contacted CPIC about two suspicious men standing outside of the Symphony Center. A witness "observed a male (possibly Middle Eastern) individual holding a possible hand drawn map consisting of a circle with a point in the middle with lines pointing outward. The individual was mumbling something and a second male individual (possibly Middle Eastern) then approached the man with the alleged map." Both men had "medium olive skin complexions."

The same year, STIC received several other dubious reports: a man with a "Middle Eastern accent" called a fertilizer store to ask about purchasing fertilizer; two "Middle Eastern" men went to a gun shop and spoke Arabic to one another; and four "Middle Eastern" men spoke Arabic while purchasing shoes. In the last incident, STIC analysts determined that purchasing shoes constituted a "potential nexus to terrorism."

One of the primary functions of SARs is to criminalize dissent and suppress political critique of U.S. foreign policy in the Middle East. One of the shocking SARs we reviewed involved a student carrying a flier related to the boycott, divestment, and sanctions campaign to isolate Israel for violating Palestinian rights. In 2019, a college police department notified STIC of an incident that began when someone turned in a backpack to lost-and-found. The reporting officer searched the backpack to identify the owner. He explains, "I discovered in an envelope several different printed images. One image showed a barcode with part of the bar code [sic] highlighted. I discovered through an internet search that this image was encouraging boycotting products from Israel by recognizing the highlighted section of the bar code [sic] to know what products are from Israel." The officer identified the student who owned the backpack and questioned him about the contents of the envelope. The student said that he did not want to speak with the officer and left. The officer then reported the incident to STIC.

Other SARs relate to political critiques of U.S. foreign policy in the Middle East. In 2017, for instance, the Illinois National Guard contacted CPIC to report a former U.S. soldier who posted on social media that he "realized I was an oppressor" while deployed in Afghanistan and had become "an anarchist, abolitionist, anti-capitalist, anti-imperialist." CPD investigators spoke with the man's ex-girlfriend, who reported that he had talked about going to Rojava, Syria, to fight against ISIS alongside Kurdish socialist militias.

In 2019, a school resource officer contacted STIC to report a sixteen-year-old Arab American high school student who went to see his school guidance counselor because he was upset that he would never see his grandparents again. The counselor reported that the student claimed that his grandparents were political Islamists living in Syria. The counselor spoke with the student's father, who confirmed that the grandparents were in Syria but did not address their political views. The counselor and the school resource officer reported both the student and his father to STIC. Rather than focusing on the child's anxiety, the school filed a SAR that treated the counselor's secondhand claims about the grandparents' political views as a fact, potentially opening the door to further investigations of the student and his father, as well as family members in the United States and Syria. Indeed, SARs are designed to promote information sharing that can enable multiple law enforcement and intelligence agencies to conduct their own follow-up investigations.

The most common pattern in the SARs is people being reported for taking photos while olive, brown, or Black. People submitted SARs after observing people of color—especially people they identified as Arab or Muslim—taking photographs of churches, trains, fire stations, the State Capitol, the Art Institute, and other locations around Chicago and across the state. In September 2016, during the Major League Baseball playoffs, a man reported a "suspicious male individual, possibly Middle Eastern" at the L Station across from Wrigley Field. The suspect "appeared out of place while taking various photographs" and was "typing or texting, possibly in Arabic." Earlier that month, CPIC received a SAR after an Algerian man entered the building formerly known as the Sears Tower, followed an employee into a secure area, and was stopped on the sixty-sixth floor taking pictures of the city. In August 2019, a Black woman "wearing clothing consistent with those worn by women of the Muslim faith/religion" was reportedly taking a video of the State Capitol in Springfield. A witness contacted the police, who filed a SAR with STIC. Analysts identified the woman through the registration plates on her rental car. In these and at least ten other cases, CPIC and STIC shared SARs with the FBI about people taking photographs that only raised suspicions because the photographer was Black, brown, or olive skinned.

SARs are regularly used to criminalize work, mental health crises, protected speech, and an incredible range of behaviors when performed by people of color. A "M/E" (Middle Eastern) male made illogical claims about superpowers while trying to withdraw money from his bank account. A woman out for a walk reported being "aggressively hip checked" by a South Asian man. Two "Middle Eastern" men were observed going in and out of a church before leaving the area. A man at a bowling alley who looked "either middle eastern or Hispanic" was watching people bowl and play video games. A Saudi family told the local police that their passports were missing; police filed a SAR with STIC, which forwarded the report to the U.S. State Department.

Along with the focus on Arabs and Muslims, SARs are also tools for targeting Black people—especially if they are associated with Islam. In

2016, a woman called the CPD to report that she was looking at apartments when she saw "[ISIS] propaganda posters in English." She noted that "there was an African American male present when she was touring the apartment." In 2019, a U.S. Customs and Border Protection officer called CPIC to report seeing a Black man sitting in a Dunkin' Donuts parking lot "taking photos of law enforcement officers and writing notes in a notebook." In 2020, a Black male entered a synagogue in Chicago and spoke with a greeter while a security guard searched his belongings. He left after a few minutes, at which point congregants alerted a police officer, who stopped and questioned the man. In 2018, a police officer contacted STIC to report a suspicious vehicle that he mistakenly thought had been involved in a previous incident. The vehicle was registered to a Black man and covered in bumper stickers that read "In the name of Allah, the merciful," "I'm willing to die for my country and Allah," "God hates cowards," and "No surrender or retreat" as well as "additional Arabic writing . . . that could not be translated."

All of these examples indicate that the deputization of individuals to participate in the War on Terror relies on the racialized archetype of the "Arab/Muslim terrorist." The effect is to reify racialized suspicion among the public. The empire state expands racialized surveillance by inculcating a racialized definition of who and what is suspicious and encouraging individuals to monitor and report on one another, with particular attention to people who seem to match the archetype.

After receiving a SAR, analysts at CPIC and STIC conduct an initial investigation by searching databases maintained by multiple law enforcement agencies, other government agencies, and private data brokers. If the original report does not include the suspect's name, fusion center analysts first attempt to identify the person using the information they have available. They run license plate numbers (even partial numbers) through state databases, use facial recognition technology operated by the CPD or the Office of the Illinois Secretary of State, review the databases of mass transit authorities (such as VENTRA cards), and contact private companies (including car rental agencies and phone carriers) to identity the person described in the report. Through these and other techniques, fusion centers are able to identify a suspect in half or more of the SARs they receive (49 percent for CPIC; 66 percent for STIC).

Next, the fusion center analysts search a wide range of state and private-sector databases for information about the person. During these investigations, CPIC and STIC analysts often obtain some or all of the following:

driver's license image from the Illinois Secretary of State
firearm owners identification from the ISP
criminal history through multiple databases, including the
>   CPD's Citizen and Law Enforcement Reporting and Analysis (CLEAR)
>   ISP Law Enforcement Agencies Data System (LEADS)
>   FBI National Crime Information Center (NCIC)
>   FBI National Data Exchange (N-DEx)
>   FBI Law Enforcement Online (LEO)
>   U.S. Secret Service's Targeted Violence Information Sharing System (TAVISS)
>   U.S. Drug Enforcement Agency's (DEA) El Paso Intelligence Center (EPIC)

immigration history through DHS Immigration and Customs Enforcement databases, including country of birth, history of border crossings, naturalization status, and removal status
incarceration records, including history of visitation, through the Illinois Department of Corrections Offender Tracking System (OTS)
public assistance records
employment records and earning statements
credit reports
LexisNexis Accurint reports, which include public records and nonpublic information like date of birth, Social Security number, phone number, current and previous addresses, email accounts, real estate titles, motor vehicle registrations, previous names and aliases, employment history, and possible associates
auto insurance claims history through the Verisk Insurance Services Office database

CPIC and STIC searched all of these databases in their investigations of the SARs that we reviewed. But this is merely a sample of the kinds of databases that fusion centers access. Some are owned by private-sector data brokers, such as LexisNexis and Verisk, that compile information on people and sell it to law enforcement agencies and other clients. CPIC and STIC also analyze people's social media accounts and contact their friends, family members, and others in search of "derogatory" information. Data circulation and corporate partnerships are core infrastructures for the dif/fusion of surveillance.

After their initial investigation, fusion center analysts develop what they call a "workup" on the individual—a document that compiles all of the information that the analysts consider relevant. They upload the SAR along with the workup and related documents to the FBI's eGuardian database and send the information to the FBI-led JTTF for further investigation.[71]

The FBI has a policy requiring that every lead be investigated. As a result, every one of the "suspicious" incidents discussed in this chapter has been fully investigated by a local FBI field office or JTTF. In addition, SARs are stored for decades in FBI databases. eGuardian is an unclassified FBI database accessible by fusion centers and members of JTTFs across the country. Information is stored in eGuardian for 180 days. SARs are also added to a second FBI database: Guardian. This is a classified data system used by the FBI and JTTFs for investigations and for maintaining records from other agencies, such as the DEA, the Secret Service, the NSA, and the CIA. The FBI stores records in Guardian for five years before moving them to the FBI's Sentinel Case Management System, where they are held for thirty years. This means that all of the SARs discussed in this report will be stored in FBI databases for at least thirty-five years.[72]

The creation of fusion centers was justified as a counterterrorism strategy, and their initial mandate focused on sharing information related to terrorism. But most fusion centers—including CPIC—soon expanded their missions to include "all crimes, all hazards." As we discussed in chapter 1, CPIC is a key player in the CPD's War on Crime. The logics of U.S. empire and the fear of the "Arab/Muslim terrorist" thus paved the way for the expansion of racialized surveillance more broadly: using federal funding to purchase and monitor high-tech surveillance equipment; sharing intelligence and promoting interagency coordination; and helping to build the web of criminalizing surveillance that crisscrosses the United States and targets Black, Indigenous, immigrant, diasporic, and working-class communities.

Other data-sharing processes, such as shared databases and MLAT treaties, lubricate the imperial networks of policing by facilitating the circulation of data and the recycling of terrorist designations. Treaties that require manufactured data to be accepted as "fact" promote collaboration between states and extend the boundaries of persecution for Arabs and Muslims, especially Palestinians. Collaboration between U.S. and Israeli intelligence agencies, made clear in the cases of Muhammad Salah and Rasmea Odeh, lays bare the apparatus of global surveillance and empire.

CONCLUSION: MANUFACTURING TERRORIST SUBJECTS AND THE SPIRAL OF SURVEILLANCE

While the surveillance of Palestinians and anti-imperialist Arabs is a long-standing practice of the U.S. empire, the early years of the twenty-first century saw the expanded deployment of War on Terror logics to support and justify U.S. imperial interventions and wars in the Middle East and beyond. Embracing *diffusion,* the state ramped up its surveillance apparatuses, including broad-based state surveillance and multilayered privatized surveillance. At the same time, the U.S. state concluded that 9/11 stemmed from a lack of coordinated intelligence and thereby established policies to promote *fusion* or coordination through data-sharing mechanisms like fusion centers. Dif/fusion has accelerated the manufacture of terrorist subjects and generated a spiral of surveillance that feeds the expansion of the U.S. empire.

The dif/fusion of surveillance leads to the mass production of Arab and Muslim terrorist subjects. From OVB through the FBI raids to the arrest and deportation of Rasmea Odeh, we can see how interagency coordination grounded in a shared "terrorist" archetype allows the carceral webs of empire to manufacture terrorists and target Arab and Muslim communities with racialized, gendered, and sexualized violence. The criminalization of "material support" and the use of RICO statutes also facilitate the manufacturing of terrorist subjects, as do the multiplication and proliferation of surveillance agents and technologies. Programs like CVE and SARs deputize teachers, counselors, religious leaders, and the entire population as agents of imperial policing.

All of these programs depend on and activate the dehumanizing racialized archetype of the "Arab/Muslim terrorist," which emerged and expanded as a result of the shifting dynamics of U.S. empire and Israeli settler colonialism. As a result, the proliferating surveillance agencies and technologies all concentrate on the same communities. This generates an accumulation of data, which are stored in police databases and treated as "fact." Transforming racialized archetypes into "facts," databases conceal the conditions of data production and provide "proof" that Arabs and Muslims really are what the government always already knew them to be. For example, by training mental health professionals to identify and report signs of radicalization, CVE programs reify the notion that there are terrorists in Arab and Muslim communities; by soliciting SARs and investigating incidents like an "olive-skinned" person taking pictures of an elevated train, the archetype of the "Arab/Muslim terrorist" is reinforced in the popular imagination and provides proof that the War on Terror is necessary. The data both codify and reify the underlying archetypes that treat Arabs and Muslims as always already terrorists.

Dif/fusion also facilitates the circulation of these "facts." Muhammad Salah and Rasmea Odeh were both labeled "terrorists" by Israel. Mechanisms of data sharing allowed these labels to travel across borders, along imperial pathways. When U.S. agencies gained access to Salah's confession and Rasmea's conviction, they launched new domestic investigations and surveillance operations. Both cases demonstrate the permanence and global reach of labels like "terrorist," which stick to people and circulate as "facts" while erasing the social and political contexts of their production. Prosecutors and judges treated Rasmea as a "terrorist," silenced her experiences of rape and torture, denied her posttraumatic stress disorder diagnosis, and attempted to paint her as a violent, untrustworthy "criminal," erasing Rasmea's dedication to uplifting women and challenging racism. Dif/fusion results in continual marginalization and expulsion, while reproducing fear within Arab and Muslim communities.

Fusion centers, shared databases, and other data-sharing agreements also enable the circulation of data. Targeted surveillance of activists by the state and lawfare organizations, along with more generalized forms of state and privatized racial surveillance, creates troves of data that serve as raw material for police, investigators, prosecutors, and fusion center analysts. These processes allow the empire state to translate the "facts" stored in dispersed databases into decentralized yet coordinated efforts to achieve the same imperial goals.

The result is a spiral of ever-increasing surveillance that feeds itself and justifies the logics and structures through which the spiral is maintained. The U.S. empire legitimizes investments in surveillance to target people who fit the archetype of the "terrorist"; more investments and diffused and targeted surveillance generate more data and manufacture more terrorists; the creation of more terrorists justifies further investments in surveillance and U.S. imperial interventions across the world, including collaboration with Israel. The spiral is anxiety producing and inescapable for Arabs and Muslims, making them ever more vulnerable to criminalization, deportation, and death. We can see this in Rasmea's case: a radical brown woman was deemed a "terrorist" by a settler-colonial state and thereby subjected to gendered sexualized violence and incarceration; the permanence of this manufactured label placed her at heightened vulnerability to arrest and deportation; and the circulation of the label intensified her surveillance and exposed her to the imperial War on Terror forty-four years later. By utilizing legal processes to criminalize and deport Rasmea, separating her from her community, the United States and Israel legitimized the weaponization of gendered and sexual state violence against "terrorist" subjectivities. Utilizing the dif/fusion of surveillance to criminalize, dehumanize, and dispose of Palestinians and their allies underscores the brutality of a system constructed to support empire, racial capitalism, settler colonialism, and white supremacy.

The research that informs this chapter also led to a report on SARs and the surveillance state, coauthored by the AAAN and the PCRG.[73] On the basis of its findings, the AAAN launched a campaign on July 1, 2022, demanding that the CPD and ISP end the use of SARs and close their fusion centers.[74] The AAAN is now developing and implementing a curriculum to educate community members about the report and its findings as the first step in a campaign to resist and abolish the SARs program in Illinois and beyond. As we explore in more detail in the conclusion to this book, thinking abolition globally requires an expansive vision that sets out to delink and dismantle all of the carceral agencies of empire.

5 Welcoming City? Punitive Exceptions and Disavowed Collusion in the War on Immigrants

In September 2012, Mayor Emanuel and the Chicago City Council passed the Welcoming City Ordinance (WCO), a sanctuary policy that aimed "to make Chicago the most immigrant-friendly city in the country."[1] Building on existing sanctuary laws, the WCO set out to "clarify the communications and enforcement relationship between the city and the federal government."[2] Under the WCO, no city agency could ask questions about, disclose information regarding, or condition city services on people's citizenship status. Insisting that immigration enforcement is the responsibility of the federal government, the WCO prevented the Chicago Police Department (CPD) from detaining people due to civil immigration violations or from providing U.S. Immigration and Customs Enforcement (ICE) access to or information about people in CPD custody.

Yet there was a catch: a list of punitive exceptions written into the WCO. None of the limitations on CPD–ICE cooperation would apply when a person "(1) has an outstanding criminal warrant; (2) has been convicted of a felony in any court of competent jurisdiction; (3) is a defendant in a criminal case in any court of competent jurisdiction where a judgment has not been entered and a felony charge is pending; or (4) has been identified as a known gang member either in a law enforcement agency's database or by his own admission."[3]

As Mayor Emanuel made clear when introducing the WCO, Chicago's new sanctuary regime would provide protections only for "those who play by the rules, contribute to our economy, and help make Chicago the incredible city that was envisioned by its first immigrant settlers."[4] Juan Rangel of the United Neighborhood Organization, which helped draft the ordinance, made explicit the criminalizing distinction between "good" and "bad" immigrants that informed the sanctuary policy: "There is a difference between people who come here to contribute to the well-being of their families and in the process contribute to the well-being of their city, [and] those who engage in criminal activity, and in the process, destroy our quality of life. This new ordinance makes that distinction even clearer."[5]

In the United States, the War on Immigrants is somewhat more contested than the Wars on Crime and Terror because capitalism relies on the low-wage labor of immigrant workers, especially undocumented people. In general, whereas the Republican Party espouses an expansive war on all undocumented migrants, the Democratic Party embraces a more limited war on immigrants labeled "criminals," "gang members," or "terrorists." Under president Barack Obama's Priority Enforcement Program (PEP), for example, the federal government used police databases to prioritize people with criminal records for targeted immigration enforcement. In 2017, Donald Trump ended the PEP in favor of a more aggressive approach that treated *all* undocumented immigrants as "criminals" to be deported. Joe Biden's administration returned to the Obama-era policy of using criminal records to prioritize people for removal while promising also to consider mitigating factors.[6]

These political differences conceal a more fundamental agreement. Obama, Trump, and Biden all disavow the role of U.S. imperial projects and neoliberal racial capitalism in generating flows of migrants from the Global South through starvation wages, flooded markets, land grabs, political repression, and environmental catastrophes.[7] They share a commitment to controlling the flow, regulating the behavior, and exploiting the labor of migrants, and they rely on criminality to distinguish between "good" and "bad" immigrants. The difference is that Trump embraced a more expansive definition of criminality. In one of his many infamous speeches, Trump depicted Mexican immigrants as criminals, rapists, and drug dealers before adding disingenuously, "And some, I assume, are good people." Threatening to withdraw federal funding from sanctuary cities like Chicago, Trump declared, "The predators and criminal aliens who poison our community and prey on our young people . . . will find no safe haven anywhere within our country."[8]

FIGURE 10. The chalk graffiti states that ICE and the police are the same "bullshit." Photograph by and courtesy of Sarah Jane Rhee (@loveandstrugglephotos).

In Chicago, Trump's policies intensified debates over the city's sanctuary policies and cooperation between the CPD and ICE. Mayor Emanuel argued that dismantling sanctuary policies would violate the Constitution and undermine efforts to build trust between communities of color and the CPD. As we describe in the next chapter, immigrant and U.S.-born Black and Latinx social movements argued that Chicago's existing sanctuary policies did not provide enough protection. Led by Organized Communities Against Deportations (OCAD), Mijente, and Black Youth Project 100 (BYP100), the Expanded Sanctuary campaign called on the mayor to end all coordination between the CPD and ICE and argued that a true sanctuary city would ensure the safety and well-being of all immigrants and all communities of color rather than distinguishing between the deserving and the undeserving, the good and the bad, the law abiding and the criminal. One target of the campaign was the exceptions—or "carve-outs"—in the WCO that eliminate sanctuary protections for immigrants classified as criminals and gang members.

These questions gained urgency in March 2017 when ICE detained a

Chicago resident named Wilmer Catalan-Ramirez because of his inclusion in a CPD gang database. As the Expanded Sanctuary campaign mobilized for Wilmer's release, his lawyers charged ICE and the CPD with unlawful entry, excessive force, and denial of due process. The movement demanding Wilmer's freedom intensified the call to eliminate the exceptions from the WCO. It also exposed a second form of coordination between the CPD and ICE that is disavowed by the WCO but made possible by data-sharing processes. In doing so, Wilmer's case revealed the limits of reform and the importance of abolishing gang databases and data-sharing agreements as a step toward abolishing imperial policing.

In this chapter, we examine collaboration between ICE and the CPD to demonstrate that Chicago is a decidedly unwelcoming city for immigrants with the mark of a criminal record or a gang designation. We argue that Chicago embraces a regime of liberal sanctuary that uses police data to fabricate a distinction between "law-abiding" and "criminal aliens," offering sanctuary protections to the former and aggressively policing the latter. In this context, we document two major mechanisms through which the local police engage with the War on Immigrants—punitive exceptions and disavowed collusion—both of which involve interagency data-sharing processes. We begin by examining Chicago's sanctuary policies, which have always incorporated *punitive exceptions* that explicitly deny protection to criminalized immigrants, including those classified as "gang members." Next, we draw on the experiences of Wilmer Catalan-Ramirez to reveal a more hidden mechanism of *disavowed collusion* between police and immigration enforcement that relies on the production and circulation of data. Wilmer's story demonstrates how everyday interactions between local police and immigrants lay the foundation for deportation by producing criminal labels that are stored in databases and circulate as "facts." We end the chapter by reflecting on the limitations of reforms and the paradox of liberal sanctuary.[9]

POLICING THE "CRIMINAL ALIEN" IN A SANCTUARY CITY

The Criminal Alien Program (CAP) is a federal immigration policy that sutures the connections between the War on Crime and the War on Immigrants in the United States. Between 1988 and 1996, the U.S. government codified the figure of the "criminal alien" as a priority target for deportation and built the infrastructure to enforce this mandate. Patrisia Macías-Rojas shows that the original motivation for the CAP was to remove migrants from jails and prisons to make space for young Black and Latinx people targeted by the War on Crime.[10] Although justified as a way to remove people convicted of murder, rape, and drug trafficking, the legal definition of *criminal alien* ballooned to include people convicted of drug possession, driving without a license, and reentering after deportation. According to Amada Armenta, CAP is now responsible for the majority of deportations from the interior of the United States each year.[11]

Immigration enforcement is geographically uneven because the federal structure of the United States enables municipal and state governments to determine the degree to which local police cooperate with ICE. This has generated a "multijurisdictional patchwork"[12] of policies and practices, with some localities adopting openly anti-immigrant policies while others claim to provide "sanctuary" for immigrants.[13] *Sanctuary* is a term claimed by liberal cities in the United States that enact laws and policies to limit the participation of local authorities, including police, in the enforcement of federal immigration laws.[14]

Urban elites and liberal scholars celebrate sanctuary cities as a form of local resistance to federal immigration enforcement.[15] Emerging critical studies, however, have challenged the notion that sanctuary cities like Chicago are truly sites of resistance to the War on Immigrants. Indeed, recent research demonstrates that sanctuary cities reinforce hierarchies and participate in disciplining and displacing migrants.[16] Interdisciplinary scholars A. Naomi Paik and Ananya Roy advance the notion of *liberal sanctuary* to describe the paradox of sanctuary cities that offer rights and protections for "law-abiding" immigrants while denying these rights to noncitizens classified as "criminals."[17]

Importantly, the same criminalizing distinction between "good" and "bad" immigrants grounds the CAP. Describing CAP as a form of "carceral liberalism" that protects some immigrants and punishes others, Macías-Rojas explains that "not all undocumented immigrants are uniformly denied rights and classified as dangerous or punishable by the state. Indeed, some are deemed 'worthy' of state protection, while others are branded permanently 'rightless' by virtue of a criminal conviction."[18] Those considered worthy, she notes, are labeled "workers" as opposed to "criminals."[19]

To be sure, all undocumented immigrants live in conditions that Daniel Kanstroom describes as "eternal probation," constantly constrained by the threat of deportation whenever the government decides.[20] Yet the threat is not evenly distributed. As Nicholas De Genova argues, Mexican migrants face a heightened risk of deportation because they are disproportionately constructed as "illegal." For De Genova, deportability—the ever-present possibility of being removed from the United States—renders Mexican labor a "distinctly disposable commodity."[21]

Previous research has demonstrated how local police activate the threat of removal. On the basis of ethnographic research in Nashville, Tennessee, for instance, Armenta shows that local police criminalize migrants through practices like investigatory traffic stops.[22] And the county sheriff participates in 287(g), a federal program that authorizes local police to enforce immigration laws. Through this program, the Sheriff's Office runs the name, date of birth, and fingerprints of every foreign-born person arrested by local police through Federal Bureau of Investigation and U.S. Department of Homeland Security (DHS) databases.

Unlike Nashville, Chicago claims to be a "sanctuary city" that limits cooperation between the local police and ICE. Yet our research shows that data-based policing creates multiple pathways for local police to participate in the criminalization and removal of immigrants. Local police construct the distinction between "worthy" and "rightless" immigrants in a sanctuary city by transforming racialized archetypes into criminal labels. As we demonstrate throughout the book, criminal labels like "gang member" and "terrorist suspect" are data produced by uneven police deployments and racialized criminal archetypes. In Chicago, the archetype of the "gang member" is an important foundation for the construction of noncitizens as "criminal aliens." Local police patrol immigrant neighborhoods, stopping and arresting people who fit the profile of a "gang member"; police databases cleanse the data by erasing the conditions of their production; and the flow of data between agencies enables ICE to identify, target, detain, and deport immigrants tagged with a criminal label. We focus on two pathways of data circulation: punitive exceptions and disavowed collusion. Through these entanglements, local police participate in the War on Immigrants by activating the condition of deportability while ICE supports the War on Crime by targeting alleged "gang members" for deportation.[23]

LIBERAL SANCTUARY AND PUNITIVE EXCEPTIONS

In the aftermath of Hurricane Katrina, tens of thousands of undocumented migrants converged on Louisiana to help rebuild the Gulf Coast. Wilmer Catalan-Ramirez joined this migration, leaving Guatemala to search for opportunities in Baton Rouge. Within weeks of his arrival, ICE arrested Wilmer during a workplace raid and charged him with fraud and misuse of documents. He served seven months in jail and was then deported. After returning to the United States, Wilmer found work in Georgia and met his future wife, Celene Adame. In 2009, Wilmer and Celene relocated to Chicago. As Wilmer told us, "they said that it was a sanctuary city, and that it would be better for us."[24]

Chicago and other cities first adopted "sanctuary" policies in the 1980s in response to grassroots efforts to protect Central American immigrants from deportation by the administrations of Ronald Reagan and George H. W. Bush. While recognizing the imperative of local protection from federal agencies, it is important to understand that municipal sanctuary policies effectively deradicalized the demands of grassroots movements.[25] Liberal sanctuary policies adopted by municipalities have serious limitations. Most importantly, municipal ordinances cannot prevent federal immigration agencies from operating in the city; they can only limit the support that city agencies provide to federal authorities. In addition, liberal sanctuary policies do not provide equal protection for all immigrants; instead, they rely on criminalization to distinguish between "good" immigrants who deserve protection and "bad" immigrants who do not.[26] Sanctuary policies that include this distinction work as mechanisms of carceral liberalism: they extend disciplining opportunities to the "deserving," while subjecting anyone with a criminal mark or gang affiliation to incarceration and deportation. We refer to these distinctions as punitive exceptions; by suspending sanctuary for certain immigrants, they lay the foundation for coordinated efforts by local police and federal agents to aggressively police "rightless" noncitizens.[27]

In 1985, mayor Harold Washington introduced Chicago's first sanctuary city law by signing Executive Order 85-1. Four years later, mayor Richard M. Daley reinforced this policy through Executive Order 89-1.[28] Both orders sought to ensure "equal access by all persons residing in the City of Chicago, regardless of nation of birth or current citizenship, to the full benefits, opportunities, and services, including employment and the issuance of licenses, which are provided or administered by the City of Chicago."[29] For the first time, sanctuary city laws prevented city agencies—including the police—from asking about citizenship status or sharing citizenship data with federal agencies. But the orders also introduced the logic of punitive exceptions, stating that the city would share data with federal agencies *if* it was "required to do so by statute, ordinance, federal regulation or court decision."[30]

In 1992, Mayor Daley and police superintendent Matt Rodriguez revealed another punitive exception to liberal sanctuary. The Chicago Crime Commission had petitioned the mayor to allow the CPD to share citizenship information with the U.S. Immigration and Naturalization Service (INS) to control street gangs in the city. In doing so, the Crime Commission embraced the emerging emphasis on targeting "criminal aliens" for deportation. Immigrant and refugee rights organizations pushed back, calling on Daley "not to provide city information on residents' citizenship to federal agencies without court orders to do so."[31] Daley said that the police department would share information with the INS only in cases in which the defendant was accused of committing "serious crimes."[32] Superintendent Rodriguez then announced that "the department's practice of turning over information on criminal activities *has been standard policy*, even under the executive order, and will continue."[33] These statements exposed the long-standing CPD practice of using criminal records to limit sanctuary protections.

In March 2006, the Chicago City Council responded to mass mobilizations for immigrant rights by passing the city's first sanctuary ordinance. Adding chapter 173 to the Municipal Code, the City Council confirmed the principle of equal access to services, opportunities, and protection without regard to citizenship status. Rejecting federal efforts to expand the role of local police in immigration enforcement, the ordinance declared that CPD participation in immigration enforcement would undermine Chicago's efforts to promote trust and cooperation between law enforcement agencies and immigrant communities.[34]

Six years later, Mayor Emanuel and the City Council renamed chapter 173 the "Welcoming City Ordinance." As noted, the 2012 WCO prevented city agencies from asking about, disclosing, or conditioning services on people's citizenship status and prevented the CPD from giving ICE information about or access to people in CPD custody. Yet none of these protections applied to people with an outstanding warrant, a felony conviction, pending felony charges, or a gang designation in a law enforcement database.[35] Through these four exceptions (also known as "carve-outs"), the WCO reiterated a formal distinction between noncriminal and criminal, or deserving and undeserving, immigrants. This marked a critical shift in immigration policing by defining entire groups of people as "criminal aliens" who are categorically ineligible for sanctuary protections. The liberal sanctuary ordinance expanded the use of criminal labels to distinguish between good and bad immigrants and to justify coordination between the CPD and ICE to police noncitizens who have criminal records or are considered gang members.

As a form of carceral liberalism, Chicago's municipal sanctuary policies also operate to promote assimilation and discipline. To begin with, they encourage immigrants to comply with the law and cooperate with local police. Indeed, this was Mayor Emanuel's primary objection to Trump's attack on sanctuary cities.[36] Moreover, the rollout of the first sanctuary policies represented by Washington's Executive Order 85-1 and Daley's Executive Order 89-1 coincided with the neoliberal restructuring of urban governance, including a renewed emphasis on wage discipline and cuts to government spending on welfare, education, housing, and other services. In this context, sanctuary policies provide immigrants with minimal protection from deportation in exchange for their willingness to provide for themselves through low-wage labor with minimal government support. Defining "good" immigrants as compliant with the law and their employers, they subject "bad" immigrants to deportation.[37]

Some scholars celebrate liberal sanctuary policies for preventing municipal and law enforcement agencies from using local resources and information to support federal immigration enforcement.[38] But an emerging critical literature cautions against excessively optimistic analyses by unpacking how liberal sanctuary perpetuates social hierarchies and exclusionary politics.[39] Our research confirms that Chicago's liberal sanctuary policies explicitly enable coordination between local and federal agencies to police and remove "undeserving" immigrants based on their criminal records or gang designations. The logic of punitive exceptions reinforces and expands existing social hierarchies between so-called good and bad immigrants, activates the deportability of "undeserving" people with criminal records and gang designations, and obscures the larger structural conditions that make crime and street gang organizations possible to begin with.[40] At the same time, liberal sanctuary policies subjugate "good" immigrants to a disciplinary regime by promoting assimilation, authorized forms of low-wage labor, and cooperation with the police while discouraging participation in antisystemic struggles or underground economic activities.

DISAVOWED COLLUSION AND THE CIRCULATION OF POLICE DATA

The exceptions written into Chicago's sanctuary ordinance provided an explicit mechanism for collaboration between the CPD and ICE. But another, more insidious form of collaboration operates alongside yet distinct from these punitive exceptions. The difference is subtle but important. The WCO codified punitive exceptions by allowing Chicago police to provide ICE with information about individuals under certain exceptional conditions. At the same time, however, ICE had direct access to CPD's Citizen and Law Enforcement Analysis and Reporting (CLEAR) data system, which was designed to be shared with other agencies. In other words, ICE agents could perform their own searches of CPD's extensive databases rather than waiting for CPD to provide them with information about individuals. We refer to this mechanism of collaboration as *disavowed collusion*. Liberal sanctuary policies conceal this collusion by making connections between local police and federal immigration authorities appear exceptional. Yet Chicago police produce data every day through stops, arrests, and other encounters, and ICE agents use these data on a regular basis to inform their operations. In other words, there is nothing exceptional about collusion grounded in the production and circulation of data. Disavowed collusion highlights the role of data sharing for coordination among the decentralized agencies that constitute the carceral webs of empire.

The case of Wilmer Catalan-Ramirez helps visualize the mechanisms that enable coordination between agencies that officially disavow cooperation. The production, cleansing, and circulation of data allow local police and federal agencies to carry out distinct strategies against immigrants who fit the profile of the "gang member" and "criminal alien." Wilmer's experience provides a window into the process through which local police activate deportability by turning racialized archetypes into "data" as well as the processes that allow ICE to access these data, treat them as "facts," and use them to target immigrants with a criminal mark. It demonstrates that local police in a sanctuary city lay the foundation for the War on Immigrants by manufacturing "criminal aliens." At the same time, federal immigration authorities pursue the War on Crime by detaining and deporting alleged "gang members."

Chicago Police Department

As we discussed in chapters 2 and 3, the CPD's data-driven approach to the War on Gangs includes long-standing efforts to build databases of gangs and gang members. The CPD draws on racialized deployments and the criminalization of archetypes, geography, and associations to manufacture gang labels and record them in databases.[41] As long as ICE has access to these databases, the data produced by local police become a weapon of immigration enforcement.

Sitting in their living room in 2018, Wilmer and Celene described how Wilmer was classified as a gang member. They underscored that Chicago police focused on his associations, his geography, and his looks to pin a gang label on Wilmer. When Wilmer moved to the Back of the Yards neighborhood on the Southwest Side of Chicago, he found work as a mechanic. People from the neighborhood brought cars to be painted or repaired and asked Wilmer to install alarms or sound systems. Wilmer told us that the police began seeing him as a gang member because of associations he had formed through his work. Wilmer noted, "This is how people in the neighborhood started getting close to me. But I was not asking them whether they were a gang member or not. They gave me work and I said, 'Yes, why not?'" As part of his job, Wilmer would buy paint at one store in the neighborhood, parts at another, and equipment at a third. Before long, police started coming to the garage and asking him questions. As Celene recounted, "The police told him, 'We always see you in the street, walking around, looking after the neighborhood.'" According to Wilmer, the police would stop him up to three times a week. When we asked if other people in the neighborhood encountered similar treatment, Wilmer said, "Yes. Everyone."

In June 2015, Wilmer was outside a neighbor's home, speaking with a friend while their children played. The CPD had designated the area a "hot spot" and deployed extra officers to aggressively target drug sales and gang activity.[42] Two Chicago police officers approached Wilmer and his friend, questioning them about "narcotics activity" and issuing contact cards.[43] On his contact card, the officers indicated that Wilmer "was loitering with another individual in a known Latin Saints street gang/narcotic area while also being in an area of recent gang violence." As a result of this stop, Wilmer was added to a CPD gang database as a member of the Latin Saints. Importantly, Wilmer's presence in his neighborhood with his friends was considered criminal. This illustrates the racialized nature of surveillance; within Black and Latinx neighborhoods, police treat young people as potential criminals. Gang designations transform the presumption of criminality into a "fact." In other words, police manufacture criminals on the basis of racialized archetypes. And by storing criminal labels in shared databases, police obscure the social relations through which the "facts" were produced.

The next year, Wilmer and a friend drove to a store to purchase paint so Wilmer could paint his friend's car. On their way back to the garage, Chicago police stopped them, frisked them, and ran their names through CPD databases.[44] When the police saw that Wilmer's friend was in the gang database, they began interrogating him. Wilmer tried to assist his friend by translating the officer's English messages into Spanish, but the officer told him, "Shut up! I'm not talking to you." Pointing out that Wilmer did not have a driver's license, the officer added, "If it was you driving, I would arrest you." Wilmer tried to deescalate the situation and reassure the officer that he and his friend were on their way to the garage. But the officer threatened Wilmer a second time: "If I catch you again, I'll arrest you!" His friend was later deported.

A month later, in November 2016, Wilmer drove past the same officer. Remembering the officer's threat, Wilmer parked the car and got out before the officer could pull him over.

> When he came behind me to grab me, I was already walking. And that's when he told me, "Come here! I saw you driving." And I said, "But you didn't catch me driving. The car is parked." That made him so angry

that he put me in the back of his car and began saying, "I'm going to put you under arrest. I'm going to arrest you." And I said, "But why?" He said, "Because you were driving without a license." And I said, "But I'm walking." And he said, "But I saw you and I followed you." "But you didn't catch me in the car. The car is parked." He searched the car—he turned it over and found nothing. That was the moment that I think he put me into another gang database.

The officer charged Wilmer with failing to stop at a stop sign and driving on a suspended license. This marked Wilmer as a "criminal alien," adding evidence to the growing recognition that traffic stops play a key role in funneling immigrants into deportation proceedings.[45] The officer filed a gang arrest card indicating that Wilmer was a member of the Satan Disciples.[46] Although the Satan Disciples and the Latin Saints were rivals, CPD records now indicated that Wilmer was a member of both organizations. The gang arrest card notes that Wilmer did not "self-admit" to membership. As we discussed in chapter 3, 88.18 percent of people in the CPD gang arrest card database supposedly self-admitted to gang membership. But not Wilmer. Instead, he is among the 11.66 percent of people who police added to the database without providing any explanation for why they were labeled gang members.[47] Wilmer thinks the officer listed him as a member of the Satan Disciples out of frustration at Wilmer's effort to assist his friend during the first stop and his noncooperation during the second stop. An additional factor could be the location where Wilmer was stopped. On CPD gang maps, he was stopped in a liminal zone between neighborhoods identified with the Satan Disciples and the Latin Saints.[48]

Wilmer's experience reveals that the inclusion of a name in CPD gang databases does not depend on empirical verification of the person's affiliation with a street gang organization.[49] A person can be designated a gang member—even a member of multiple gangs—without any evidence. Like the stories documented in chapter 3, Wilmer's experience reveals how local police transform racialized discourses about crime into "facts" that take the form of a permanent record. As street-level agents of the empire state, police officers use their symbolic power during everyday encounters to apply gang labels to Wilmer and other young people of color in similar positions. In doing so, local police lay the foundations for immigration enforcement in a sanctuary city.

The CPD attached an official gang designation to Wilmer based on his *associations, geography,* and *looks.* Police criminalized Wilmer on the basis of his associations—both informal relationships and labor relations—with people in the neighborhood. Having friendships with and doing work for people whom police identified as gang members enabled the police to transfer the gang label to Wilmer. To use Wilmer's expression, "everything started here."

Geography was also important. Not only did Wilmer live and work in a neighborhood that CPD identified as "gang territory," but his work also required him to circulate through the area, purchasing supplies from various stores. Police began harassing, stopping, and frisking Wilmer when he was driving or walking in the neighborhood. The first time the police stopped him, Wilmer was standing with a friend in an area that police had designated a "hot spot." This justified the police decision not only to stop-and-frisk Wilmer but to add his name to a gang database. His second gang designation may also have been shaped by the location of his arrest, as Wilmer was stopped while moving between areas that the CPD considers the territories of rival gangs.

Underlying all of this is the racialized criminal archetype of the "gang member." Wilmer repeatedly stated that police considered him a gang member because he "looks like" a gang member. When we asked what that meant, he explained, "The police just look at your face. I mean, it doesn't matter. Although I dress in a normal hat, they look at you as being young, Latino, and they say, 'Ah, this is a gang member.'" Stereotypes about clothing, style, aesthetics, and a performance of racialized masculinity serve as evidence that allows police to confirm prefabricated beliefs and justify adding a gang label to immigrants like Wilmer. In Chicago, the "gang member" archetype has become an important foundation for the legal category of "criminal alien."

Once Wilmer had been designated a gang member, Chicago police began treating him as such during every interaction. In January 2017, Wilmer was hit by a stray bullet while leaving a restaurant. He suffered a fractured skull, a broken shoulder, and partial paralysis. As a result of the shooting, Wilmer should have been eligible for a U visa, which provides a pathway to citizenship for victims of crime. But, Wilmer recounted, "They were accusing me of being a gang member. Here everyone is supposedly a gang member." In other words, the police did not treat Wilmer as a victim eligible for support because they considered him a gang member who deserved punishment. He went on to question the police response to his shooting. "Where they shot me, there are cameras. I was coming out of a restaurant and there are cameras in back. There's a liquor store on the corner too and it has cameras all the way around. But the police have not been able to figure out who did it. They are putting more police and more security, and what good is it?" Like the young people discussed in chapter 3, Wilmer demonstrates here a critical awareness of racialized surveillance.

Wilmer's treatment by police in the wake of the shooting is important because Wilmer frequently expressed concerns about how to protect himself, not from gangs but from the police. "I swear to you, I'm not afraid of gang members, neither here nor elsewhere. I'm worried about the police," he explained.

> They walk down the street, and they just look at your face to see how you will respond. If you look Hispanic and you live around here, they stare at you. And obviously if you look at me, I am going to look you in the eyes. And when you make eye contact, they turn around and bang! "Why are you looking at me?" No, you looked at me first. "I can look at anybody—and you look suspicious."

Discussing this provocation, Wilmer described the Chicago police as "a gang with authorization."

Wilmer's experience helps us understand why gang databases do not reflect actual gang membership. In the absence of empirical evidence, local police officers relied on three forms of "evidence" to claim that Wilmer was a gang member: associations, geography, and looks. A core activity of gang enforcement is the symbolic work of labeling people "gang members." On the basis of prefabricated and stereotypical "evidence," police officers anticipated Wilmer's gang membership, designated him a gang member, and deployed enforcement actions including surveillance, investigatory stops, threats, and arrests. Gang enforcement becomes a self-fulfilling prophecy,[50] concealing the state's agency in producing the gang members whom it is supposed to track and punish. For noncitizens, a gang designation comes with a "criminal alien" label, and incarceration is coupled with deportation. Racialized archetypes provide the foundation for local police to activate deportability.

Overall, then, this section demonstrates that the CPD fabricates gang labels that take the form of a criminal record. Local police store these labels in databases, which are then shared with federal agencies. This is the foundation of the disavowed collusion between the CPD and ICE.

Immigration and Customs Enforcement

Since its inception, ICE has built infrastructure to support the War on Gangs. ICE has its own National Gang Unit, which is part of the agency's investigative division, and maintains its own gang database, known as ICEGangs, which is sourced from local and federal agencies. The National Gang Unit oversees Operation Community Shield (OCS), a transnational initiative that involves multiagency collaborations targeting alleged gang members and their cross-border connections.[51] Each year, OCS task forces carry out military-style operations targeting specific organizations or issues: Southern Tempest, Project Nefarious, Project Southbound, Project Wildfire, Project Shadowfire, and Operation Raging Bull.[52] According to ICE, OCS has led to the arrest of more than seventy thousand gang members since 2005. The ICE official who helped design OCS insists that "you have to apply the scorched earth methodology to gang enforcement—really zero tolerance."[53]

To carry out its gang enforcement strategy, ICE relies on local police databases and data-sharing processes to identify priority targets for detention and deportation.[54] ICE is one of more than five hundred agencies that could access the CPD's CLEAR data system, which includes its gang databases. According to a report by Chicago's inspector general, immigration authorities searched CPD gang databases more than thirty-two thousand times from 2009 to 2018.[55] Accepting CPD data as factual, ICE weaponizes the data for targeted enforcement actions.

In a rebuke to Trump's aggressive immigration policies, the Chicago City Council began considering a renewed sanctuary city ordinance on March 22, 2017. Four days later, the Chicago field office of ICE launched a six-week operation as part of a nationwide sweep targeting "foreign born members of violent street gangs." Nationally, the operation led to the arrest of 1,378 people, more than two-thirds of whom were U.S. citizens.[56] On the morning of Monday, March 27, ICE agents shot a fifty-three-year-old man—a legal permanent resident—while attempting to detain his twenty-three-year-old son on Chicago's Northwest Side.[57]

The same morning, ICE agents violently raided Wilmer Catalan-Ramirez's home on the Southwest Side, where he lived with his wife and three children. ICE agents stopped Celene outside of their home while she was taking the older children to school. The officers did not identify themselves as ICE agents, and Celene assumed that they were CPD detectives. The agents claimed that they were looking for criminals in the neighborhood and showed her an image of a Latino man with the last name Rubio. She said that she didn't know him and turned the agents away. When she returned, she found ICE agents in her yard, on the stairs to her apartment, and inside her home.

According to Wilmer's attorneys, ICE officers unlawfully entered Wilmer's home without a warrant or permission and used excessive force against him.[58] After dragging Wilmer out of bed and into the living room, the agents asked, "Where are the guns and drugs?" and demanded Celene's and Wilmer's IDs. Three agents then surrounded Wilmer, who pleaded with them to be gentle because he was still recovering from being shot. Nevertheless, the agents pulled Wilmer's arm behind his back and slammed him to the ground, causing Wilmer to cry out in pain and insist that he needed medical attention.

Detaining Wilmer, the ICE agents drove him to Loyola University Medical Center, where doctors confirmed that the violent arrest had dislocated Wilmer's shoulder, fractured his clavicle, and exacerbated his head injury. The same agents then transported Wilmer in handcuffs but no seat belt to the McHenry County Jail, sixty miles away, which serves as an ICE detention center. Wilmer told us that the driver kept stopping abruptly, slamming Wilmer's head against walls and causing further brain trauma that still generates seizures. During his detention, immigration authorities systematically denied Wilmer the medical assistance that he needed for the injuries he sustained during the raid.[59]

Wilmer described a conversation with an ICE agent at the detention center. The officer asked, "'Do you know why you are here?' And I said, 'No, I have no idea.' And they said, 'You are in a gang, right? That's the information that we received from the police.'" That was the moment Wilmer first learned that Chicago police had identified him as a gang member. The fact that Chicago police do not inform people of their gang designations helps to obscure the collusion between the CPD and ICE.

Although Trump announced an end to the PEP in February 2017, ICE agents assessed Wilmer's priority status hours after his detention on March 27, 2017. The assessment concluded that Wilmer was a "Priority 1" target for deportation because he was "at least 16 years old and intentionally participated in an organized criminal gang to further its illegal activities."[60]

The documents that ICE submitted in response to Wilmer's lawsuit indicate that this assessment was based on a search of the CPD's CLEAR database.[61] ICE submitted a copy of Wilmer's arrest records from the CLEAR database, including the gang designation listed on his gang arrest card from November 2016, when a police officer charged Wilmer with running a stop sign and identified him as a member of the Satan Disciples. To support its assertion that Wilmer's gang membership was a threat to public safety, ICE also submitted photocopied pages from the Chicago Crime Commission's 2012 *Gang Book* with a profile of the Satan Disciples.[62] Wilmer described his surprise when the ICE agent told him that he was listed as a Satan Disciple: "I said, 'But I don't even live in that neighborhood. And I am not a gang member.' If he had said the [Latin] Saints here in my neighborhood, I would have told them that I know them or something. But he was putting me down as something from a place where I had never lived."

Wilmer's case reveals the mechanisms of disavowed collusion, where the CPD and ICE share a commitment to gang enforcement as well as resources, practices, and data while carrying out distinct strategies to target immigrants with criminal records and gang designations. Young immigrants of color in heavily policed neighborhoods confront regular stops by the local police that generate criminal records and gang labels on the basis of their associations, geography, and look. Local police apply the criminal labels; immigration authorities use the labels to track and detain immigrants. On the basis of data collected through decades of racialized stops, the CPD labeled Wilmer's neighborhood a gang hot

FIGURE 11. Wilmer, Celene, and their children celebrate Wilmer's release with community members. Photograph by Antonio Gutierrez; courtesy of Organized Communities Against Deportation.

spot and saturated the area with aggressive patrols, looking for people who "fit the description" of a gang member. The Chicago police officer who filed Wilmer's gang arrest card had previously threatened Wilmer and had a history of antagonism toward residents of the neighborhood. All of this context is erased by the CPD data system. It is not taken into account when officers from the CPD, ICE, or other agencies search the database. For ICE agents, CPD data are simply a set of "facts" that can be used to assess a person's history and determine their eligibility or priority for deportation. Wilmer received a gang arrest card when he was charged with running a stop sign and driving without a valid license, yet it was this gang arrest card that ICE agents referenced in their assessment that Wilmer "intentionally participated in an organized criminal gang to further its illegal activities" and was therefore a top priority for deportation.

Chicago's WCO implies that coordination between the CPD and ICE is limited to exceptional circumstances. Yet Wilmer's experience has revealed that punitive exceptions exist alongside another form of collusion made possible by data-based policing. This collusion involves the production of criminal labels by local police, the recording of these labels in police databases, and data-sharing processes that allow federal agencies to weaponize the data. A mutual commitment to gang suppression informed by racialized archetypes lays the foundation for the CPD–ICE alliance. Neither the CPD nor ICE shies away from this commitment, but they disavow the routine collusion that operates through the everyday production and circulation of police data. Disavowed collusion demonstrates the importance of behind-the-scenes data sharing for coordination within the webs of imperial policing.

WHEN WE FIGHT, WE WIN!

The fight for Wilmer's freedom began during the ICE raid. When ICE agents tackled Wilmer to the ground, Celene began recording and live-streaming his detention. She then linked up with OCAD, which mobilized support for Wilmer's family while building a campaign for his release. Celene began meeting with lawyers from the MacArthur Justice Center, the National Immigration Project of the National Lawyers Guild, and the National Immigrant Justice Center. Lawyers soon learned that ICE detained Wilmer because of his CPD gang designation, but they did not know why the CPD identified him as gang affiliated or how ICE gained access to that information. Over the next ten months, political and legal mobilizations on Wilmer's behalf brought about his release while also uncovering the disavowed alliance between ICE and the CPD and exposing the limitations of liberal sanctuary protections for immigrants in Chicago.[63]

Wilmer's legal team filed a lawsuit against the Chicago police, ICE, and the McHenry County sheriff. While demanding access to medical care for Wilmer within the detention facility, they charged ICE and the CPD with unlawful entry, excessive force, and denial of due process. Through litigation, Wilmer's lawyers gained access to CPD records indicating that Wilmer was a member of multiple rival gangs as well as the documents that ICE used to assess the priority of Wilmer's removal. Celene recounted,

> The surprise was that, when the lawyers began to inquire about Wilmer's gang membership, the police said that Wilmer did not belong to only one but to two gangs at the same time. It was kind of illogical. So I responded: "Well, I need them to present the evidence that they

have." I know that Wilmer is not a gang member and I have proof that he was working in a formal job and didn't spend his time on the streets or at home.

The legal team pushed the CPD to provide proof of Wilmer's gang membership. Wilmer remembered challenging the police reliance on racial archetypes:

That's what I told the judge: OK, the police look at me, seeing how I dress. That doesn't matter, right? If I dress like a lawyer and I go to dinner as a lawyer and I say to you, "Oh, I'm a lawyer." They are going to want proof, right? And I should say, "Here is the proof that I am a lawyer." And the judge started to say, "Oh, you're right about that."

He continued, "We asked the city for explanations. We said, 'OK, you say that I'm a gang member. Where is the evidence that I'm a gang member?' They didn't have anything. Never. They presented nothing."

At the same time, OCAD, BYP100, and their partners in the Expanded Sanctuary campaign fought tirelessly for Wilmer's release. Through teach-ins, rallies, workshops, press conferences, and meetings with elected officials, organizers challenged the ideology of a so-called sanctuary city where ICE can carry out raids based on information obtained from the local police. They called on the Chicago City Council to eliminate the exceptions in the WCO that enable the CPD to help ICE detain noncitizens labeled criminals and gang members. They fought the system of racialized surveillance that disproportionately criminalizes Black and Latinx communities through gang designations. And they demanded an investigation into the CPD gang database by the City of Chicago inspector general.

Inside the detention center, Wilmer fought the denial of medical care. Officers threatened him with solitary confinement for enlisting the support of other inmates and as retaliation for the community-based mobilizations for his release. As a statement from OCAD explains, "these aggressions culminated with a hunger strike led by other men in deportation proceedings. Wilmer's release was among the demands that came as a result of the hunger strike."[64]

After months of delay and obfuscation, the CPD acknowledged having no proof that Wilmer was involved with either of the street organizations with which he was associated in its records. In November 2017, lawyers for the CPD signed a letter declaring that the Chicago police have no evidence that Wilmer "is a self-admitted gang member" and that they cannot verify that he "actually and in fact belongs to a gang."[65] The CPD sent this letter to ICE and U.S. Citizenship and Immigration Services (USCIS), indicating that Chicago police had no objections to Wilmer's application for a U visa. They also added the letter to Wilmer's police record in the CLEAR data system. Six weeks later, ICE agreed to release Wilmer from detention and promised that he would not face deportation while awaiting his application for a U visa. Reunited with his family, Wilmer dismissed the lawsuits against ICE and the CPD.[66] But the brutality that Wilmer faced during his arrest and incarceration continues to affect his health and his interactions with the state. These repercussions will impact Wilmer for the rest of his life. And neither the CPD nor ICE has offered any reparations to help Wilmer live with the consequences of legalized state violence.

The political and legal struggle to free Wilmer helped expose the collusion between the CPD and ICE. First, it provided new insight into the tactics ICE used to identify priority targets for deportation. CPD officials were insistent that Chicago police did not "tip off" ICE about Wilmer, but legal submissions by ICE revealed that a tip-off was unnecessary because the federal immigration agency already had access to the CPD's CLEAR data system. A simple records search brought up Wilmer's gang arrest card.

Second, it exposed the permanency of gang designations in CPD databases. Despite acknowledging that there was no proof of Wilmer's gang affiliation, the CPD explained that it would not be able to remove Wilmer's gang designations from the database. Police claimed that it was not technically possible to remove the gang designation or delete the record. As an alternative, the CPD included a copy of its lawyer's letter to USCIS/ICE in Wilmer's record. A search of the CLEAR database will still show that Wilmer is a member of multiple street gangs, but it will also link to the letter indicating that there is no evidence to support these designations.

Wilmer says that his gang label still creates problems. "For example, if the police stop me and I give them my ID, there it appears: he's a gang member. If the officer is really interested, he has to go all the way down to find the letter that says I am not a gang member. When they stop me, I can tell them that I am not a gang member, but it doesn't matter because the label will appear." This highlights the permanency of a designation that even the CPD admits is baseless. As *Chicago Tribune* reporter Jacqueline Serrato notes, "the gangbanger label will follow a person for life. Once a resident is identified as a documented gang member—whether justifiably or not—it will never come off their record, not even through expungement."[67]

As we describe in chapter 6, erasing the CPD gang database became a top priority of the Expanded Sanctuary campaign as a result of Wilmer's case. The movement combined harm reduction through the effort to secure Wilmer's release and prevent his deportation with the abolitionist goals of eliminating gang databases and ending interagency collaboration. In response to a campaign demand, Chicago's inspector general revealed that Wilmer was not alone in being listed as a member of multiple gangs. More than twenty-five thousand individuals in the CPD gang arrest card database have multiple gang affiliations.[68] That means that one out of every five people in the database is considered a member of multiple gangs. This is the same report that revealed that immigration agencies had searched the CPD gang databases more than thirty-two thousand times in a ten-year period.[69] On the basis of these and other findings, the Office of Inspector General report slammed the CPD for not requiring any evidence to support gang designations and raised serious concerns about the lack of control over access to CPD data.

According to an assessment by OCAD, "through this campaign we have been able to concretely demonstrate how the City of Chicago is complicit in the deportation of our communities, how police are an extension of the deportation pipeline, and the harms that surveillance technologies and databases cause."[70]

The fact that Wilmer was ultimately released could be used to suggest that the system actually "works" to differentiate the "law abiding" from the "criminal," the "good" immigrant from the "bad." But Wilmer's case is unusual, and innocence narratives are problematic. Wilmer and Celene had extraordinary organizational and legal support. Lawsuits challenging a criminal label are rare, and they often fail, even when the labels are completely baseless. Moreover, legal challenges cannot confront the harm that criminalization and collusion inflict on people who really are affiliated with street organizations. Innocence narratives legitimize the dehumanization of gang-associated individuals by obscuring the social conditions that produce street organizations and justifying the enduring violence of imperial policing, which reduces poor immigrants of color to archetypes and erases their full humanity. Rather than reproducing the distinction between "innocent" and "criminal," we need to address the regime of imperial policing itself. To truly confront the power of punitive exceptions and disavowed collusion means to address the fact that police manufacture criminality by transforming racialized archetypes into data and disseminating these data through a web of carceral agencies.

THE LIMITS OF REFORM AND THE PARADOX OF LIBERAL SANCTUARY

Collaboration between the CPD and ICE is grounded in a shared commitment to the transnational War on Crime, including the effort to remove "criminal aliens" from the United States. Responding to grassroots mobilizations, Chicago has embraced liberal sanctuary policies, including a less expansive definition of *criminal alien* than other cities. But Chicago collaborates with ICE to target "gang members" through both punitive exceptions and disavowed collusion grounded in everyday forms of data circulation.

Like the War on Terror, the Wars on Crime and Immigrants are transnational projects of empire. Chicago police saturate Black and Latinx neighborhoods, relying on racialized archetypes and the criminalization of geography and associations to tag young immigrants of color with labels like "gang member" and "felon." The CPD stores these labels as "data" and shares them with ICE through the two mechanisms we highlighted in this chapter. In turn, ICE uses CPD data to carry out "gang surge" operations as part of OCS, targeting alleged gang members as top priorities for removal. At the same time, federal agencies militarize the U.S.–Mexican border, train Latin American military and police forces, destroy crops in South America and Central Asia, enlist neighboring governments to prevent migrants from reaching U.S. borders, and deport alleged gang members and drug traffickers.

During the struggle for Wilmer's freedom, OCAD organizer Rosi Carrazco highlighted the contradiction in Chicago's claim to be a sanctuary city. "Every time that the Chicago Police Department shares information about any of us with immigration enforcement," she explained, "they are violating Chicago's promise to be a Sanctuary City and to protect us from President Trump's policies. The City of Chicago must look at how its policies criminalize people of color and feed us into Trump's deportation machine."[71]

As we discuss in the next chapter, Wilmer's case helped galvanize the Expanded Sanctuary campaign in Chicago—which demanded ending the exceptions in the WCO, abolishing Chicago's gang database, and eliminating ICE access to CPD data. After years of grassroots organizing, the Chicago City Council revised the WCO in January 2021, removing the four categorical exceptions and preventing the CPD from sharing data directly with ICE. These are major victories for the Expanded Sanctuary campaign and for immigrant rights more broadly, addressing both the explicit and disavowed forms of collusion between the CPD and ICE.

Yet there remain important loopholes, as documented in a 2021 report by OCAD and Just Futures Law.[72] To begin with, the ban on data sharing applies only to the enforcement of "civil immigration law." The CPD can still share data with ICE for the purposes of enforcing "criminal law." This could allow the CPD and ICE to continue working together to target immigrants with a criminal record or gang designation. Moreover, the archetype of the "criminal alien" blurs the distinction between civil and criminal law, opening the possibility for collaboration against immigrants accused of "criminal" offenses, such as illegal reentry to the United States. Finally, there remain multiple pathways through which ICE may be able to access CPD databases. First, CPD's fusion center—CPIC—is staffed by officers from the DHS. In addition, the CPD still shares the CLEAR database with the DHS. It is possible, therefore, that ICE has indirect access to CPD data through its parent agency. All of these loopholes constitute further mechanisms of disavowed collusion. They demonstrate the limits of sanctuary reforms in a city that remains committed to protecting "good" immigrants and punishing the "bad."

In February 2021, the Biden administration announced interim guidelines for immigration enforcement while working on more permanent regulations.[73] The interim guidelines represented a return to the Obama-era policy of prioritizing particular categories of immigrants for deportation. The three priority areas were national security, border security, and public safety. Under the guidelines, a noncitizen could be considered a "public safety enforcement priority" if they have a conviction for a gang-related crime or "intentionally participated in an organized criminal gang or transnational criminal organization." After pushback from immigrant rights organizers, the Biden administration removed this language when publishing its formal guidelines in September 2021.[74] While focusing on the same priority areas, the new guidelines explain that DHS personnel should exercise discretion by considering circumstances that might mitigate the factors that make someone a priority for deportation. In other words, they should not just accept local police data as "fact." As the guidelines explain, "our personnel should not rely on the fact of conviction or the result of a database search alone. Rather, our personnel should, to the fullest extent possible, obtain and review the entire criminal and administrative record and other investigative information to learn of the totality of the facts and circumstances of the conduct at issue."[75] Further research, however, should investigate the extent to which ICE abides by or reworks these guidelines through immigration enforcement on the ground.

The new guidelines embrace a commitment to interagency coordination, data sharing, and criminalization. Through everyday interactions, CPD officers produce the criminal records and gang labels that activate deportability by differentiating between "law-abiding" and "criminal" immigrants—and they do so by relying on racialized archetypes and the criminalization of associations and neighborhoods. This reveals how the state actively fabricates much of the gang population that it claims to control. Wilmer's story highlights the mechanisms through which the symbolic production of "gang members" in a liberal sanctuary city lays the foundation for targeted immigration enforcement. It is through these everyday encounters that the CPD funnels Black and Latinx residents into immigration control, forced confinement, and mass deportation. This demonstrates why abolishing gang databases and data-sharing agreements is an important step toward abolishing imperial policing.

Moreover, criminalization is closely related to neoliberal restructuring. The threat of deportation based on a criminal record works as a disciplinary force, encouraging noncitizens to keep a low profile and support themselves through low-wage labor. In this sense, as Macías-Rojas argues, labor is constructed as the opposite of criminality. We see this in Celene's insistence that Wilmer's pay stubs are proof that he was a "worker," not a gang member. Celene pointed to Wilmer's labor as evidence that he was a "law-abiding" immigrant. Yet it was Wilmer's work that first exposed him to suspicions of gang membership. This demonstrates that racialized criminalization threatens to put all young Latinx immigrants—even those who submit to wage discipline—at risk for a criminal mark and heightened vulnerability to deportation.[76] But even this contradiction can be productive, encouraging all noncitizens to keep a low profile by reminding them that anyone, at any time, can be labeled a criminal or gang member and thus subject to deportation.

Chicago claims to be a sanctuary city invested in protecting immigrants from deportation. But this protection applies only to immigrants without a criminal mark or gang designation. Like other forms of liberal inclusion, liberal sanctuary embraces the paradox of providing limited protection from deportation based on the criminalizing distinction between "deserving" and "undeserving" immigrants. While the former are conceived of as willing to cooperate with local police and submit to exploitative labor practices, Chicago's urban sanctuary simultaneously facilitates the expulsion of "undesirable" immigrants through punitive exceptions and disavowed collusion. In the words of scholar-activist Ruth Gomberg-Muñoz and OCAD organizer Reyna Wences, Chicago's sanctuary regime is "a tale of two cities: one a bold proponent of protection for immigrants and the other a nucleus of racialized policing practices that entrap immigrant men of color."[77]

6 Expand Sanctuary! Erase the Database! Joint Struggle against Criminalization and Deportation

with Tania Unzueta Carrasco

Sanctuary movements and abolitionist movements have rich, interwoven histories that stretch back generations. The meanings and contexts of sanctuary are ever evolving, but it is grounded in resistance practices that provide a semblance of safety to people targeted by the state. Abolition is the theory and practice of chipping away at a vast system of formal social control through punishment and surveillance, while also building new practices and systems that affirm people's humanity. As defined by Critical Resistance, a national organization at the forefront of efforts to abolish the prison–industrial complex, abolition is a political vision that aims to eliminate imprisonment, policing, deportation, and surveillance by creating lasting alternatives that make punishment obsolete.[1] An abolitionist framework entails, more specifically, dismantling structures of organized violence and exploitation while developing and implementing projects, institutions, and conceptions for collectively regulating our social lives and redressing shared problems—interventions that can render policing, imprisonment, and surveillance insignificant methods for ensuring relative peace and security.

As complementary as the concepts of sanctuary and abolition are, they are rarely discussed together as a cohesive praxis. In her recent work, A. Naomi Paik proposes "abolitionist sanctuary" as a radical alternative to the liberal sanctuary policies that we discussed in chapter 5.[2] Abolitionist sanctuary combines the logic and practice of sanctuary, which leverages community to provide safety from imminent harm, with abolition, which seeks to transform the conditions that create harm. Strategically, it is both defensive and offensive: responsive to the world as it is while building toward the world as it should be, where all people are able to live equitably in their full dignity regardless of citizenship status, race, gang affiliation, "criminal" history, or any other markers that are used to disenfranchise and oppress.

In developing the framework of abolitionist sanctuary, Paik drew inspiration from the Campaign to Expand, Defy, and Defend Sanctuary (or the Expanded Sanctuary campaign), a national campaign launched by Black and Latinx grassroots organizations in January 2017 as part of a broader movement to abolish local police and immigration agencies. As conceptualized by Mijente, a team that includes Tania Unzueta Carrasco—a co-lead author of this chapter—the campaign to Expand, Defy, and Defend Sanctuary was an effort to incorporate policing and incarceration into conversations about safety for immigrants and a challenge to cities that claimed to provide "sanctuary" for immigrants while targeting Black and brown residents with racialized surveillance and aggressive policing. The use of the word *sanctuary* referenced the history of resistance and protection that it carries while representing a strategic effort to disrupt and rethink a widely used term. As Mijente noted, sanctuary "can be a call that unites broad swaths of institutions and civil society if it is based in the belief that collective protection should extend to *all* communities facing criminalization and persecution and defend against all the agencies that threaten us."[3] The call to Expand, Defy, Defend Sanctuary forced movements to grapple with tensions between co-optation and resistance while working toward harm reduction and abolition.

In Chicago, the Expanded Sanctuary campaign was grounded in a joint struggle against interconnected police wars and co-led by three Black and Latinx organizations: Black Youth Project 100 (BYP100), Mijente, and Organized Communities Against Deportations (OCAD). The lead organizers were the coauthors of this chapter, Tania Unzueta Carrasco and Janaé Bonsu-Love. Our initial demands, which evolved over the next four years, were to (1) protect all Chicagoans from immigration enforcement by eliminating the exceptions or "carve-outs" from the Welcoming City Ordinance (WCO), Chicago's sanctuary city ordinance;[4] (2) eliminate the Chicago Police Department's (CPD) gang database; (3) create policies that decriminalize and reduce arrests; and (4) decrease police funding and invest in Black and Latinx communities.

Joining forces to protect our communities while building toward abolition, the organizations leading the Expanded Sanctuary campaign in Chicago focused on the CPD gang database and data sharing between the CPD and U.S. Immigration and Customs Enforcement (ICE) as racist tools for criminalizing Black and Latinx communities and creating a pipeline to both incarceration and deportation. The strategic value of unifying in this effort was to make it harder for the state to play us against each other. Dismantling the institutions that oppress marginalized communities requires movements for immigrant justice, racial justice, and economic justice to be as collaborative as the carceral institutions that target our communities. This chapter describes an effort to radicalize resistance to the War on Crime and the War on Immigrants by building ties between immigrant justice and Black abolitionist movements and working to sever the flows of data that enable coordination between local and federal agencies. These mobilizations informed many of the insights developed in this book. In this chapter, we explore the vision, strategies, challenges, and tensions of abolitionist sanctuary. Next, we discuss the campaign to amend the WCO before turning our attention to the primary focus of this chapter: the Erase the Database campaign. We end with reflections on visions and strategies of organizing for abolitionist sanctuary in the context of high-tech, data-based policing.

DEFY, DEFEND, AND EXPAND SANCTUARY

When we build links between different sectors of radical and progressive movements, the path to victory becomes clearer. Barbara Ransby uses the term *political quilting* to describe the work of bridge building between movements and among organizers, scholars, activists, and artists to create spaces where "trust and collaboration can be forged and collective thinking can occur."[5] Political quilting is necessary for building a sustainable movement against criminalization, surveillance, and the carceral webs of empire that extend from Chicago across the country and around the world. It happens not in a single moment but over a series of events and interactions during which communities, organizers, and the institutions that we have built learn to trust each other and mobilize collectively. In the early days of the Trump administration, the inflammatory rhetoric and aggressive law-and-order politics emanating from the White House led to a rise in strategic alliances among progressive movements committed to joint struggle. In Chicago, we used that moment to harvest the seeds of practical solidarity between U.S.-born and immigrant Black and Latinx communities that had been sown long before Trump's inauguration.

A formative moment in the cross-racial, cross-issue political quilting in Chicago took place in fall 2015 with an action led by BYP100—an organization of eighteen- to thirty-five-year-old Black activists and organizers—to shut down the annual conference of the International Association of Chiefs of Police (IACP). The IACP conference brought together police from more than eighty countries, along with their corporate backers, to share tactics and strategies. We felt that the decision to hold this conference in Chicago, a city with chronic disinvestment from Black and brown neighborhoods that spends 40 percent of its budget on police, was an affront to our communities.

In response to the IACP conference, BYP100 gathered Black-led organizations and close allies, including Southside Together Organizing for Power and Fearless Leading by the Youth, and mobilized a series of high-visibility civil disobedience actions where organizers put our bodies on the line to disrupt the event. Using the hashtags #StopTheCops and #FundBlackFutures, we pushed back against the dominant narrative of public safety: *investment in policing does not keep us safe.* Although the action was Black led, OCAD and the #Not1More campaign (which later became Mijente) demonstrated practical solidarity by providing direct action training and assisting with strategy. These undocumented-led immigrant rights and Latinx groups had been experimenting with civil disobedience to protest deportations under the Obama administration and were instrumental in shaping the strategy. Because it involved civil disobedience, the planning and implementation of the event were effectively a trust-building exercise. We leaned into friendships and shared values among individuals and organizers to build institutional relationships and deep trust by sharing both risk and tactics to respond at this strategic moment.

We continued building relationships at a collaborative direct action in February 2016, when Assata's Daughters (a grassroots intergenerational collective of radical Black women) supported OCAD and Mijente in shutting down the highly trafficked street in front of ICE headquarters in

FIGURE 12. The February 2016 coalitionary action that shut down the street in front of ICE's Chicago headquarters. Photograph by and courtesy of Isaac Silver.

Chicago during the morning rush hour commute. The action was initially planned as a protest against continued deportations under Obama, but the growing relationship between undocumented-led organizations and Black-led organizations like Assata's Daughters expanded the message to emphasize connections between policing and immigration enforcement. The action resulted in an iconic photograph of Black and Latinx people, U.S. born and immigrant, blocking the street with a sign that read "Dismantle ICE, Defund Police." In a statement, Assata's Daughters explained why Black women with citizenship privilege would participate in this civil disobedience action:

> [It is because of the] intrinsic ways in which our struggles are connected. This doesn't mean we mistake our struggles as being the exact same: we know settler colonialism and anti-blackness are distinct, but united under white supremacy. . . . Solidarity is as much to do with difference and self-reflection, as a shared commitment to end oppression. It is, at its best, a verb: It means the ongoing work of appreciating

another communities [*sic*] oppression and resistance even when it has nothing to do with you, building deep relationships, developing shared analysis and strategy, taking action together, studying and being transparent about the ways we are complicit in each others [*sic*] oppression, showing up for each other and practicing accountability.[6]

Marisa Franco, founder and national director of Mijente, echoed this sentiment, saying, "The threats we face require collaboration. We can't fend off the threats we face, much less advance, if we fight alone in our own sectors and silos. It is time for a new era of collaboration across communities. We must now name common enemies and common goals and broaden our organizations and alliances accordingly."[7] This principle of joint struggle brought Black-led, Latinx-led, documented, and undocumented grassroots organizations into strategic alliances to resist criminalization, deportation, and surveillance. Moreover, these organizations, actions, and movements were led largely by women and nonbinary people.

Our alliances grew more intentional under the Trump administration, particularly with the expansion of police state powers through executive actions like the so-called Muslim ban, the effort to cut federal funding for liberal "sanctuary" cities, and the threat to "send in the feds" to target already criminalized Black and brown communities in Chicago. The political moment called for a framework that would highlight the interconnectedness of the criminal punishment system and the immigrant deportation system, as well as the need to bring multiple targeted communities together to strategize about how to keep ourselves safe and free ourselves from carceral violence in all its forms. Anticipating the violence of the Trump regime, Mijente, BYP100, and OCAD came together with different bases but connected goals to build a campaign to redefine and expand what it means for Chicago to be a "sanctuary city." In our strategy sessions, we critically appraised the idea of "sanctuary," focusing on who was protected, who was excluded, and how. Newly elected U.S. president Donald Trump was attacking even the mildest, government-defined "sanctuary cities," such as Chicago, while propping up the unions of police and immigration agents as part of his base.[8] The campaign, therefore, set out to push Chicago's Democratic mayor to expand sanctuary, while also defending the concept from the federal government.

As organizers embedded in criminalized Black and Latinx communities, we knew that the mainstream, liberal understanding of sanctuary applied to only some immigrants, excluding people involved in the criminal punishment system. This exclusion is grounded in liberal respectability narratives that distinguish between "law-abiding" and "criminal" citizens and noncitizens to evaluate worthiness of rights, protections, and punishability. We also understood that we would have to tackle police violence, stop-and-frisk, and the criminalization of Black residents to provide sanctuary for all.[9] Addressing criminalization helped us move past the respectability narratives and politics that dominated conversations about crime and public safety, including within the immigrant rights movement. Above all, we understood that ICE and CPD were two sides of the same coin. As we demonstrate in chapter 5, the pipeline to both incarceration and deportation begins with local police interaction, regardless of whether the local police work openly with ICE.

We developed the concept of Expanded Sanctuary to push for policies that would protect all residents—immigrant and U.S. born, Black and Latinx—by limiting contact with and the power of all law enforcement agencies. To build a grassroots campaign that embodied this vision of abolitionist sanctuary, we needed a tactical approach to onboard organizations and communities beyond those that already identified as abolitionist. By leaning into the dominant frame and language of "sanctuary," organizers were able to leverage and subvert the public's familiarity with the concept to inject their own meanings. For example, a coauthor of this chapter, Janaé Bonsu-Love, sought to develop a counternarrative of sanctuary as a U.S.-born Black organizer, saying,

When I hear the word "sanctuary," I envision a place that is safe for everyone—regardless of citizenship status, gender, religion, or any other marker that deems one "other" in this country. That vision does not include Donald Trump, the National Guard, Immigration and Customs Enforcement, Border Patrol nor local police departments. I envision self-sustaining, well-resourced communities with strong bonds and networks of people who call on each other in times of need. Without addressing safety and protections for all targeted communities, sanctuary is a misnomer.[10]

FIGURE 13. The updated banner at the Expanded Sanctuary campaign launch press conference. Photograph by and courtesy of Sarah Jane Rhee (@loveandstrugglephotos).

In January 2017, a multiracial group of organizers, scholars, and community members met on the fourth floor of Chicago's City Hall to announce the launch of the Expanded Sanctuary campaign to make Chicago a "real sanctuary" for all members of our communities. The launch marked a shift in the conceptualization of sanctuary. For more than a year, immigrant rights groups had been organizing to amend the WCO. At every protest, the group of mostly older, first-generation Latinx immigrants organizing with OCAD carried a sign that read "Make Chicago Safer & More Welcoming for ALL Immigrants." The slogan reflected the dominant way that sanctuary had historically been understood. Recent conversations about redefining and expanding sanctuary led them to shift their demands. To reflect their new understanding of sanctuary, they cut off the bottom of the sign. At the campaign launch, immigrant justice organizers held a sign that now read simply "Make Chicago Safer & More Welcoming for ALL" (Figure 13). This was a small yet significant and tangible indication of how joint struggle was transforming the meaning of sanctuary.

The campaign to Expand, Defend, and Defy Sanctuary was national, with both local and national organizations involved in the launch, creating campaigns across the country with local demands and varying levels of success. In Philadelphia, a coalition led by the grassroots organization

Juntos discovered and ended a ten-year contract between ICE and the city's arrest and arraignment database.[11] In Louisville, Mijente fought for an ordinance that separated local police from ICE and pushed back against the state's prohibition of local sanctuary policies. In Santa Ana, California, organizers challenged the deportation of immigrants with criminal records and fought for local policy changes to address criminalization.[12] In Chicago, the Expanded Sanctuary campaign called for an end to the exceptions in the WCO, the elimination of gang databases used by Chicago police and other law enforcement agencies, the adoption of policies to decriminalize and reduce arrests, and cuts to police funding and investment in Black and brown communities. The first two items were our top priorities. In the next section, we discuss our campaign to amend the WCO, which began in 2017 and achieved a major victory in 2021. We then return to 2017 and trace the development of our ongoing campaign to erase the CPD gang database. We focus on the Erase the Database campaign because of the possibilities it opened for joint struggle and the challenges it revealed for abolitionist sanctuary in an era of data-based policing.

SANCTUARY FOR ALL IMMIGRANTS THROUGH THE WELCOMING CITY ORDINANCE

Prior to the launch of the Expanded Sanctuary campaign, efforts were already under way to amend the WCO to remove clauses that categorically excluded criminalized populations from sanctuary protections. Adopted in 2012 as Chicago's flagship sanctuary ordinance, the WCO promised protection for immigrants but excluded those with arrest warrants, felony convictions, and pending felony charges and those whose names appeared in a law enforcement gang database.[13] Since 2015, a coalition of immigrant rights organizations had organized to remove these four punitive exceptions—or "carve-outs"—from the WCO.[14]

Immigrant rights organizations saw the campaign as an effort to limit the circulation of data about immigrant communities while rejecting dominant narratives and policies that offer protection to "good" immigrants while excluding "bad" immigrants based on their relationship to the criminal punishment system. In this sense, the fight to eliminate exceptions from the WCO was already an abolitionist campaign.

The Expanded Sanctuary campaign brought new energy, ideas, and organizations into the fight to amend the WCO. In February 2017, allies on the City Council introduced an amendment to remove the carve-outs. But without support from Mayor Emanuel, the amendments stalled in committee. Meanwhile, Emanuel sued the U.S. Department of Justice over Trump's threat to eliminate federal grants for sanctuary cities. The lawsuit painted Emanuel as a defender of the undocumented and Chicago as a sanctuary for immigrants. But Emanuel continued blocking grassroots demands to remove the WCO exceptions, effectively aligning with Trump's vilification of immigrants as criminals. Rather than defending undocumented Chicagoans, Emanuel's lawsuit was merely an attempt to preserve federal funding for the CPD and uphold his image as an immigrant-friendly mayor. In the lawsuit, the city proudly noted its policy of punitive exceptions, stating that "undocumented individuals will be detained at the federal government's request *only when Chicago has an independent reason to believe they might pose a threat to public safety.*"[15] Organizers pointed out contradictions in Chicago's liberal sanctuary policies but decided to wait for a better political moment to amend the WCO. This gave us more time and energy for the struggle to eliminate the CPD gang database, described in the next section.

A new opportunity to amend the WCO finally arrived in 2019, when Chicago's municipal elections coincided with growing demands to "abolish ICE." Organizers used the #AbolishICE energy to toxify the city's relationship with ICE and amplify the need to amend the WCO. At the same time, the movement turned the WCO amendments and the gang database into election issues. In coordination with other progressive organizations, we asked mayoral candidates to take a stand on the removal of the carve-outs and the abolition of the gang database. This generated commitments from the top candidates for mayor, including the eventual winner, Lori Lightfoot.

On January 27, 2021, forty-one of fifty City Council members voted to eliminate all exceptions from the WCO and to end formal collaboration between ICE and all city agencies, including the CPD.[16] The revised WCO extended sanctuary protections to all immigrants without regard to criminal record. In addition, the city eliminated ICE's direct access to the CPD's Citizen Law Enforcement Analysis and Reporting (CLEAR) data system, a disavowed form of collaboration exposed by the Expanded Sanctuary campaign.[17] It took six years of protesting, mobilizing, and grassroots lobbying to move the city to stop using felony convictions, charges, warrants, and gang designations as reasons to collaborate with ICE and to end the data-sharing processes that allowed ICE to access CPD data. These important victories severed key links in the web of imperial policing.

But the work is not done. When the WCO was amended, we began working to document how city, state, and county agencies still share data and information with the Department of Homeland Security and, therefore, indirectly with ICE. Mijente's "No Tech for ICE" campaign has uncovered how data brokers contracted by the federal government buy information from local light and gas companies, which ICE uses to track immigrants and conduct raids.[18] In addition, the new WCO does not include enough protections to effectively prevent ICE from indirectly accessing CPD data.[19] Moreover, ICE uses devious means to access other data, including tapping a private database containing hundreds of millions of utility records, to pursue immigration violations.[20] As long as ICE has indirect access to CPD data and can simply buy information from private data brokers, protections like those in the amended WCO will not provide true sanctuary for criminalized immigrants. For these reasons, data sharing—especially when the private sector profits from punishment—remains an important frontier in the battle against imperial policing. Above all, we recognize that gang designations remain a mechanism by which the CPD criminalizes Black and Latinx U.S.-born and immigrant Chicago residents. Abolishing gang databases, therefore, remains a top priority.

THE CAMPAIGN TO ERASE THE GANG DATABASE

Along with efforts to strengthen the WCO, the Expanded Sanctuary campaign prioritized the struggle to erase the CPD gang database. The Erase the Database campaign emerged from Black-led organizing against police violence and criminalization in Chicago as well as from Chicago's antideportation immigrant justice movement. It therefore provided common ground for political quilting by Black and Latinx organizations.

For years, Black-led groups like BYP100 had been resisting criminalization and police violence against Black communities. BYP100's very first campaign, the Campaign to Decriminalize Black Lives, was

FIGURE 14. The official logo of the Erase the Database campaign. Image courtesy of the Erase the Database campaign.

launched in 2014 with the goal of ending the CPD's racially targeted and unjust enforcement of drug laws by decriminalizing marijuana. The racially biased War on Crime had created what the *Chicago Reader* called a "grass gap," meaning that Black people were disproportionately arrested for low-level possession despite the similar rates at which people of all races consume marijuana.[21] The Campaign to Decriminalize Black Lives was rooted in the understanding that petty marijuana possession served as a convenient guise to stop, search, and harass Black people in the city, just like the gang database.

On the immigrant justice side, OCAD was founded by undocumented immigrants—youth and adults—to resist the War on Immigrants under President Obama. Similarly, Mijente was founded by organizers from the #Not1More deportation campaign, an undocumented-led effort to end all deportations, including of people with criminal records.[22] This marked a break from the respectability politics that informed the immigrant rights movement at the time.

The gang database gained visibility with the violent arrest of Wilmer

Catalan-Ramirez in March 2017, which we discuss in chapter 5. ICE agents arrested Wilmer from his home without a warrant as part of a gang operation. When Wilmer's wife, Celene Adame, posted a video of the arrest on social media, it caught the attention of OCAD, which had mobilized high-visibility campaigns to stop deportations for years. Organizers contacted Ms. Adame and offered to figure out why her husband was taken and to assess whether an organizing campaign would help his case. Documents obtained from ICE showed that Wilmer was targeted because he was labeled a gang member. Organizers and lawyers soon discovered that ICE learned of his gang designation from a CPD database. Although OCAD had previously seen gang designations in immigration cases, no one had publicly challenged these designations. This time, however, Wilmer and Celene demanded answers. Wilmer's case could have remained narrowly focused on getting Wilmer out of detention and back with his family; instead, it became a centerpiece in the emerging campaign to dismantle the entire gang database.

Over time, the Erase the Database campaign grew from three organizations to an expansive coalition of grassroots, legal, labor, and research groups. We attracted organizations like the MacArthur Justice Center, which led the legal strategy on Wilmer's case and a class-action lawsuit against the city; the Policing in Chicago Research Group (PCRG), which led the research and data analysis; and organizers with groups like the Brighton Park Neighborhood Council and Beyond Legal Aid, which helped organize Freedom of Information Act (FOIA) drives for people to check whether they were on the gang database.

Campaign Goals and Principles

As its name suggests, the ultimate goal of the Erase the Database campaign is to completely eradicate gang databases in Chicago. This goal is grounded in abolitionist values agreed upon from the start by the founding organizations. Every organization that was recruited into the effort was specifically told by organizers that this was not a reformist campaign in which we figured out *who* should be on the gang database or how to improve it. We were out to eliminate the database. When we started the campaign, we also had to figure out how to focus on both Wilmer's release and our longer-term abolitionist goals. Antideportation and abolitionist organizers had long committed to harm-reduction strategies that would get people released while exposing the systematic reasons why they were detained to begin with. After many conversations, we created a campaign to expose the hidden operations of data-based policing, mobilize communities directly impacted by the gang database, advocate for abolition, and seek restitution for the harmful effects of the database.

As a campaign led by abolitionist organizations, we wanted to center several interconnected principles. These are the points to which we return when making decisions. To win against the city, we needed to build a broad campaign that could bring new organizations into the fight—which meant that we needed to be clear with them about the values that should guide our organizational decisions. Although not every organization that joined the coalition would call itself abolitionist, we work together under these principles:

1. We demand the abolition of gang databases. Instead of trying to reform or improve the CPD gang database, we want to erase the data and eliminate gang databases altogether.
2. We refuse to distinguish between "good" and "bad," "innocent" and "guilty." Instead of fighting for people mislabeled as gang members, we reject the "gang member" label altogether, knowing that it is a racial frame that criminalizes and harms our communities.
3. We want to sever the connections between local police and federal law and immigration enforcement agencies. We do that by calling for an end to data sharing, which is a key mechanism that grounds interagency collaborations.
4. We demand the defunding of police and immigration enforcement agencies and a reinvestment of these funds in the communities most harmed by policing.

By establishing these principles based on shared values and relying on relationships that we had built with each other and with the new organizations involved in the fight, we were able to create a broad campaign with clear abolitionist goals, expand the number of people and organizations working on the campaign, and make demands that would create tangible change for our communities. All of this is part of our larger vision of abolishing the police, ICE, and all other agencies of imperial policing.

Strategies: Multiple Fronts

The Erase the Database campaign was conceptualized as an open source campaign with a steering committee and multiple working groups. Over time, organizers developed a multipronged strategy that included (1) research, (2) community education and outreach, (3) litigation, and (4) organizing and policy. In developing each strategy, we wanted to stay true to our abolitionist politics. How could we end the gang database completely, ensure that the state does not reinvent the database under another name, and repair the harm done to individuals and communities in a comprehensive way? The answers to these questions were never easy, and we often had to navigate the trap of "reformist reforms" that reinforce the status quo by achieving small gains for some people while upholding false dichotomies of good–bad and criminal–innocent. We also had to balance long-term goals and visions with short-term strategies that would advance part of our goals. In this section, we reflect on our overlapping strategies, including victories, unintended consequences, and remaining questions.

Research is a highly valuable strategy in community organizing and grassroots campaigns. Organizers need information to develop solid platforms and to affirm our base's instincts and lived experiences. We also need research to develop counternarratives to the misinformation campaigns that seek to discredit and undermine the knowledge of our community members. Because of the urgency created by Wilmer's detention and potential deportation, we launched the campaign to Erase the Database before we knew much about the database itself. At the beginning of the campaign, we met with city officials and asked questions about Wilmer's case, but we did not know how many people were in the database, how they got there, or whether their names could be removed. As organizers, we wanted to be able to describe the database in detail, to respond to questions from community members and policy makers, and to understand exactly how the database created harm in our communities. For these reasons, we dedicated the first year of the campaign to research.

Additionally, we understood that research findings can generate press and provide advocacy tools to advance campaign goals; thus we formed a research working group to facilitate access to the information necessary to make decisions about targets and policy demands. This included researching existing policies, writing new policies, and gathering and analyzing data through FOIA requests and other methods. Organizers knew that some additional capacity and resources were needed to carry out these tasks, and the PCRG was being formed at precisely the same moment.

Andy Clarno, coordinator of the PCRG, had been in conversation with OCAD and BYP100 about strategic research support. To organizers, the prospect of partnering with this university-based activist research collective was attractive not just because of need but also because Andy was clear that the research team would follow the organizers' lead and that the research would happen only to the extent that it could actually help the campaign. Additionally, Janaé Bonsu-Love was both a BYP100 organizer who helped launch the campaign and a core member of the PCRG. This helped establish trust between the PCRG and the campaign organizers. Taken together, the elements of timing and some foundational trust were aligned. In February 2017, OCAD and BYP100 began a partnership with the PCRG to examine the ways that gang databases were being constructed and used to target Black and brown youth by both the CPD and ICE. This research would help shape the campaign's strategies and solutions.

We developed four approaches to researching the database. First, the PCRG set out to learn everything possible about gang databases in Chicago. Students and faculty from the University of Illinois at Chicago scoured the internet; conducted interviews with current and former employees of the CPD, directly impacted people, investigative journalists, defense attorneys, public defenders, and others; wrote FOIA requests to the CPD, Chicago Public Schools, the Cook County Sheriff's Office, ICE, and the Federal Bureau of Investigation; and collected archival materials that began to reveal the contours of the CPD's mysterious data system. Campaign organizers met regularly with the research team to discuss emerging findings and new questions and to decide on next steps for the research. Several important preliminary findings emerged from this research. We learned that electronic databases were just the latest iteration of the CPD's gang tracking; the CPD has been collecting gang information since the 1980s. Over time, we came to understand that what we were calling the "gang database" was not a single, stand-alone system but rather a combination of databases and tools for storing gang designations within the CPD's CLEAR data system. We also learned that more than 135,000 people were designated gang members in CLEAR, and the vast majority (95 percent) of individuals were Black and Latinx. Put another way, 11 percent of Chicago's total Black population and 4 percent of the Latinx population, compared to just 0.6 percent of the white population, was in the gang database.

These numbers were astronomical compared to other jurisdictions with large populations. For example, California, a state with fifteen times the population of Chicago, has approximately 90,000 people in its state-wide CalGang database,[23] and New York City's Criminal Group Database is estimated to house records for between 17,500 and 42,000 people.[24] Even more troubling, we learned just how subjective gang designations were in practice. Chicago police officers have virtually unlimited discretion in determining who is and is not a gang member. Subjective criteria like tattoos, clothing, the use of signals or symbols, and information provided by a "reliable" third party and social media, in addition to where one lives or congregates, were all used to make designations. These criteria amount to racialized archetypes of primarily Black and Latinx people as dangerous gang members to be constantly surveilled, harassed, and disenfranchised. In contrast to the ease of getting into the database, we found no policies governing how one could get out. In November 2017, the PCRG shared a draft of its initial report at a teach-in organized by BYP100, OCAD, and Critical Resistance.[25] Organizers included a list of demands in the report, one of which was a formal investigation by the City of Chicago inspector general into the CPD gang database.

While the PCRG continued conducting research, the call for an investigation by the inspector general marked the beginning of our second research strategy. The campaign understood that the inspector general would have more resources and access to CPD data than the PCRG. Moreover, the Office of Inspector General (OIG) had a new Public Safety Division to provide independent evaluations of the CPD and related agencies. The Public Safety Division was established in response to mass protests after the police murder of Laquan McDonald. Staff of the Public Safety Division attended the November 2017 teach-in and responded to the campaign's call by initiating a review of CPD gang databases. In April 2019, the OIG finished its investigation into CPD gang databases and concluded that (1) the CPD lacked sufficient controls for generating, maintaining, and sharing gang-related data, (2) the CPD's gang information practices lacked procedural fairness protections, (3) the CPD's gang designations raised significant data quality concerns, and (4) the CPD's practices and lack of transparency regarding gang designations strained police–community relations.[26] In short, the OIG's report confirmed the findings of the PCRG and lent credence to the demands of the campaign.

For our third research strategy, we organized a series of FOIA workshops for people to request documents from the CPD to find out whether their names were included in a CPD gang database. Working with attorneys at Beyond Legal Aid, we developed an online FOIA tool through which individuals could request their records from the CPD. Then we organized ten workshops in Black and brown communities across the city, at which we discussed the database and helped community members submit their FOIA requests.

Finally, the campaign called for public hearings into the database as both an organizing and a research strategy. If done properly, public hearings could require police officials to answer questions about their practices. As described later, the Cook County Board held a public hearing into a regional gang database maintained by the Sheriff's Office. However, the board did not require the sheriff to attend or to respond to questions. In July 2021, the Chicago City Council held a public hearing on the CPD gang database, after two years of public demands and a request supported by twenty-five alderpeople. Organizers and community members were able to share concerns about the database, while supportive members of City Council questioned CPD officials about the existing gang database and plans for a new database. But the CPD officials evaded the most difficult and pressing questions. Although promising, public hearings did not prove to be a generative method for exposing the database.

Nevertheless, the OIG investigation, the FOIA workshops, and the partnership with the PCRG have been effective research strategies. In the context of data-based policing, research became an important tactic in exposing hidden mechanisms of racialized police surveillance and pressuring the city to address the harm created by the database.

As we learned more about the database, the campaign initiated the second part of its strategy: *community education and outreach*. We organized teach-ins and community meetings to promote political education about the CPD gang database, racialized surveillance, and the interconnected police wars targeting our communities. From large, citywide events to smaller, neighborhood-based gatherings, the campaign shared knowledge about the database with the communities most directly impacted. Community leaders, organizers, journalists, defense attorneys, and residents—including people identified as gang members by the CPD and ICE—learned about data-based policing and its impacts while also sharing their knowledge and experience with organizers. The FOIA workshops provided an innovative and interactive tool for teaching and learning about the database. Another memorable event included a Christmas-themed zine that doubled as a coloring book to provide political education for our youngest community members. The zine told the story of the Grinch, who broke into CPD headquarters, stole the gang database, and dumped it into the Chicago River, "where it would surely be destroyed forever." Under Covid-19 conditions, our teach-ins became webinars. But we returned to in-person events in summer 2021, including block parties and gatherings in local parks. Throughout the campaign, we have maintained the same goal: to ensure that everyone in our community becomes an expert on how gang databases criminalize our communities and why they should be destroyed.

The third aspect of our strategy—*litigation*—was key to navigating tensions between abolishing the database altogether and providing immediate material relief to individuals impacted by it. In 2018, the MacArthur Justice Center at Northwestern Law School filed an injunctive civil rights class-action lawsuit against the City of Chicago and the CPD on behalf of everyone who currently or in the future will be included in the CPD's gang database.[27] Plaintiffs included four individuals—three Black and one Latino man who suffered adverse consequences as a result of being wrongfully listed in CPD gang databases—along with six Black- and Latinx-led organizations[28] that sought declaratory and injunctive relief by virtue of our missions and the interests of our members.

Taking direction from community organizations and drawing on information from a second PCRG report, the lawsuit asserted the unconstitutionality of the database. There were three primary constitutional claims. First, the database was unconstitutional because it violated individuals' Fourteenth Amendment right to due process, as people were entered into the database with no notice, no opportunity to contest the designation, and no way to be removed. Second, the database was racially discriminatory because it disproportionately targeted Black and Latinx communities, therefore violating individuals' Fourteenth Amendment right to equal protection. Finally, the database violated people's Fourth Amendment protection against unlawful search and seizure, as individuals with gang designations are frequently followed, stopped, and targeted by police. This put the harms identified by community members into legal terms and added the threat of a lawsuit.

The lawsuit also alleged that (1) the CPD began engaging in discriminatory policing practices and rapidly expanding the gang database as a response to public pressure to combat violence; (2) the CPD maintains a racially discriminatory gang database, riddled with errors, in which it falsely and permanently labels individuals "gang members"; (3) the gang database unlawfully discriminates because of its disparate impact on Black and Latinx people; (4) the CPD's targeting of Black and Latinx people for inclusion in the gang database is motivated by racial and ethnic animus; (5) labels in the gang database are permanent and impose harm; and (6) the CPD relies on its own false gang designations and knowingly shares these false designations with third parties, including ICE, despite the city's claim to be a "sanctuary" for immigrants.

We knew from the start that litigation was a limited tool because we did not have a viable constitutional claim to ask the court to abolish the gang database. As organizational plaintiffs, our goals were to make it more difficult to put people in the gang database, to give people already in the database a fighting chance to get out of it, to cease data sharing between the CPD and third parties, and to provide transparency so individuals in the database would know that the CPD was targeting them. In addition, the lawsuit could reduce the harm and begin to remedy the violations that the gang database perpetrated. We were looking for concrete relief for people in the database. The lawsuit also provided the city with our second comprehensive presentation of arguments against the gang database after the PCRG reports, allowing us to increase pressure on the city to consider our proposed solutions.

Organizational plaintiffs called on the court to enforce four specific provisions that would transform CPD practices related to the gang database. The first provision would make it more difficult for police to add an individual to the database by requiring a sworn declaration from two or more detectives that there is proof beyond a reasonable doubt. The second would require the CPD to provide written notice to every individual who has been designated a gang member in one or more of CPD's databases in the last twenty years. The third would provide any person who contests their designation as a gang member with the right to an administrative hearing to determine whether the CPD can prove, beyond a reasonable doubt, that the individual is a gang member. The final provision would prohibit the CPD from sharing gang designations with any third party and require the CPD to publish disaggregated data about its gang designations on a quarterly basis. These provisions were tactics within our legal strategy to make using the gang database so onerous that the CPD would simply stop using it. In this way, we hoped that the provisions would advance the abolitionist goal of making the gang database obsolete.

After two years of litigation backed by pressure from community organizations and the publication of the OIG report, the city and the CPD proposed creating a new gang database to be known as the Criminal Enterprise Information System (CEIS).[29] Rather than addressing the community's demands, the city simply attempted to create a *constitutional* gang database by resolving the most egregious violations outlined in the lawsuit. Our first response was to organize. We discussed the new database with community members and provided information about how people could send comments about the proposed database to the city. We then filed a FOIA request to release those comments, which demonstrated an overwhelmingly negative response to the proposed CEIS.

In turn, the lawsuit became a mechanism for engaging with the city to push for as many protections as possible in the new CEIS. The city ultimately conceded to several of our demands: stricter criteria for entry; regular purging of data; notices of inclusion; the ability to appeal designations; annual audits; no data sharing with any third parties for immigration, employment, education, licensing, or housing purposes, as well as required user agreements before allowing other agencies access; and annual publishing of aggregate data on the number of people included in the CEIS, the number of people added and removed, and the number of appeals granted and denied. Additionally, the CPD agreed to stop using gang arrest cards and to technologically "wall off" existing cards so that they cannot be accessed.

With these concessions in place, the plaintiffs collectively decided that we had taken the lawsuit as far as we could and that the rest of the fight had to be won through organizing or other means. On September 2, 2020, the lawsuit closed with settlements for the individual plaintiffs and a voluntary dismissal by the organizational plaintiffs. The organizations and the individual plaintiffs did not reach this decision lightly. We were hesitant about the city's potential to frame the individual settlements and the dismissal as a win and as proof that the city was serious about reform. Ultimately, the decision was about balancing immediate relief and recompense for the individual plaintiffs and others in the database with the limited possibilities for what ongoing litigation could accomplish. The relief that the settlement brought to the individual plaintiffs was a drop in the bucket compared to the tens of thousands of Chicagoans who remain in the database without the same opportunity to pursue a lawsuit.

The organizational plaintiffs' decision to dismiss the lawsuit against the CPD was in part designed to maintain our right to file another lawsuit if the CPD continues to designate people as gang members in a discriminatory and unconstitutional manner. It also allowed us to avoid a formal settlement, which we knew that the city would spin as an endorsement for the CEIS by the Erase the Database campaign. Understanding that the lawsuit would not lead to abolition, we found it useful as a tool to put pressure on the city. As a result of this engagement, the city agreed to protections that could reduce the harm to community members caused by the CPD's gang designation practices—protections that the city would not have conceded without the pressure of the class-action lawsuit. However, these protections do not go far enough. In our notice of dismissal, we made it clear that "a complete abolition of CPD's gang database" is what we ultimately seek.

We tried to use the law as strategically as possible while recognizing the tensions between abolitionist and reformist reforms. Although we knew from the start that the court could not abolish the gang database, we still fell into the trap of wins for a few. For example, all four individual plaintiffs were "wrongfully included" in the gang database and experienced material harm as a result. Focusing on those who were "wrongfully" included (i.e., not actually in a gang) left space for the city to claim that the new database will be "accurate" and that the people in the CEIS are "actual" gang members. At the end of the day, there are still thousands of people who have been criminalized, incarcerated, deported, and surveilled and who deserve recompense *regardless of* whether they have ever actually been a gang member. And the institutions that are responsible need to be abolished, regardless of whether they sometimes "get it right." By appealing to the courts on behalf of those who were wrongfully included, we won some relief for individuals but are still seeking reparation on a broader scale and the erasure of the entire gang database.

The CEIS is an example of how policing and surveillance are always shape-shifting and illustrates the lengths to which the state will go to criminalize communities and retain its carceral technologies. The coalition will continue working to abolish these systems because we know that we—as community members and neighbors—keep each other safe, not criminalizing databases, predictive algorithms, and racist policing.

Finally, and most importantly, the core strategy of the Erase the Database campaign has always been *organizing*. The campaign is led by organizers who are also researchers, policy strategists, media makers, and legal thinkers. Research, political education, litigation, and mobilization all work together to move community members toward abolition and to transform public policy. We organize protests, press conferences, and community events; we meet with alderpeople and political caucuses; and when there are elections in Chicago, we participate in forums with the candidates and put the issue on the map. All of this is designed to build momentum and a mass base for ordinances that will abolish the gang database.

In summer 2018, we drafted a City Council ordinance when we launched the lawsuit. The MacArthur Justice Center, our legal partner, drafted two ordinances. One articulated our overall goals of abolition and reparation; the other proposed a temporary fix that we believed would prevent harm, chip away at the database, and move us toward abolition. The temporary ordinance would stop the CPD from adding new people to the database, provide notifications to people on the database, add data transparency, and stop data sharing pending the outcome of the inspector general's audit. The coalition decided to start with the temporary ordinance based on what we thought we could achieve at the time, believing that the pending release of the OIG report would strengthen our ability to push for permanent abolition.

We focused on members of the Black and Latino aldermanic caucuses because they represent (at least theoretically) the people who are disproportionately harmed by the gang database. This strategy came with challenges. Members of the Black caucus insisted that the city needed a way to track gangs and gang members. In addition, most members of the Black caucus seemed uninterested in issues related to immigration. And we had little success getting the Latino aldermanic caucus to support our abolitionist vision. One alderman, for example, expressed concern that our ordinance would help "illegals."

Before long, however, we found people on the City Council who were willing to sponsor the ordinance and to try to get Mayor Emanuel on board. Ricardo Muñoz, who was then a longtime alderman in Little Village, offered to help move the ordinance. He had helped our parallel working group amend the WCO, so we thought he might do well as a sponsor for the gang database ordinance. Muñoz had also announced that he would not be running for another term, so he had little to lose by using his political muscle.

Recognizing that the ordinance would undergo changes before a final vote, we tried to remain vigilant in our conversations with Muñoz about what was nonnegotiable. We also worked closely with alderman Carlos Ramirez-Rosa, a longtime ally and supporter of the campaign, to monitor meetings inside City Council. We were prepared to pull the plug on the ordinance if it was edited in ways we did not endorse, and we were prepared to make Muñoz a target if need be. Again, we saw this ordinance as temporary, pending what we had yet to learn from the OIG. Muñoz introduced the temporary ordinance in July 2018 and quickly garnered cosponsorship from forty-six of the fifty members of the Chicago City Council. While introducing the ordinance, he spoke about his own relationship to gangs as a youth in Little Village and provocatively wondered aloud if he himself could be in the gang database. Muñoz was by no means a champion of abolitionist causes, but sharing his story and moving to support the ordinance are testaments to the impact of our combined research, legal, and organizing strategies.

Despite garnering aldermanic support, we were cautious in our optimism. Over time, we learned that Muñoz was not aligned with our long-term vision. Whereas the coalition saw the ordinance as a step toward abolition, Muñoz was devoted to reforming the database. He was concerned that the city would be attacked as lax on "law and order." In a meeting, he even said, "We want to make sure we can say that we don't want the database to stop existing, we just want a better database." At that point, we realized that Muñoz was undermining our message. The process of pushing for the temporary ordinance showed us that we needed to be clearer that our goal is to challenge the criminalization of Black and brown communities and to resist the disposal of people via incarceration and deportation for gang affiliation.

In fall 2018, the Erase the Database campaign began meeting with Cook County commissioner Jesus "Chuy" Garcia and soon-to-be commissioner Alma Anaya to discuss possibilities for abolishing a separate gang database maintained by the Cook County Sheriff's Office (CCSO). The Cook County Board of Commissioners is the legislative body that governs the county, similar to a city council. After learning that the CCSO hosted an online gang database known as the Regional Gang Intelligence Database (RGID), Commissioner Garcia called on the county's Office of the Independent Inspector General (OIIG) to investigate whether RGID was a tool for racial discrimination, and Commissioner Anaya introduced an ordinance demanding that the CCSO stop adding names to the database and stop sharing gang designations with other agencies until the OIIG completed its investigation. The Erase the Database campaign mobilized support for the ordinance among the Board of Commissioners.

With growing public attention on RGID, the CCSO began to distance itself from the database. Then, in early January 2019, sheriff Tom Dart suddenly announced his plan to decommission RGID.[30] On January 15, 2019, RGID was taken offline and stored on encrypted hard drives in a vault.

Concerned about what the CCSO was concealing in its rush to remove RGID from public scrutiny, the Erase the Database campaign called on the Cook County Board to ensure that the abolition of the database took place in a responsible, publicly accountable, and permanent manner. To support these demands, the PCRG analyzed thousands of pages of CCSO communications related to the decision to decommission the database.[31] These documents raised new questions about what abolition looks like in a context of data-based policing.

A month before RGID was decommissioned, the CCSO sent a request to hundreds of law enforcement agencies asking one of them to take over the database's management. An officer with the Indiana High Intensity Drug Trafficking Area Task Force followed up with an "urgent" appeal to find a new host for RGID, explaining that "the information contained within the database is highly valuable and would be devastating to lose completely." Officers from multiple agencies expressed interest in acquiring the database, and CCSO officials had telephone conversations with several of these agencies to discuss a transfer of RGID. A supervisor from the Mid-States Organized Crime Information Center (MOCIC) said that MOCIC would be "very interested" in taking over RGID.[32] Yet the CCSO never publicly acknowledged these expressions of interest in hosting the database nor explained whether the database had indeed been transferred.

Moreover, after the sheriff announced that RGID would be taken offline, CCSO received multiple requests to download Excel versions of the database before the data were destroyed. One of these requests explained that RGID was "designed with that capacity on the back end." At the same time, the CCSO was actively expanding the number of agencies with access to the database. During December 2018 and January 2019, the CCSO signed access agreements with several new agencies and issued dozens of new user accounts for RGID. Two new user accounts were created on January 14, 2019—the day before the database was decommissioned. The CCSO never explained whether these new users—or existing users—were able to download, print, or save screenshots of the database.

In February 2019, the Cook County Board responded to community concerns by unanimously passing an ordinance requiring the permanent destruction of RGID, prohibiting the CCSO from sharing gang designations in the future, and demanding public hearings about the gang database and its impact. Rather than seeking to reform or improve the database, the board decided to abolish the database and ensure that it is not revived. In the words of Commissioner Anaya, who sponsored the ordinance, "the passage of the ordinance will be a major step forward for Cook County. We will serve as a national model."[33]

On January 8, 2020, the hard drives storing the RGID database were destroyed. But questions remain: Were the data transferred, downloaded, printed, or saved? Are the data still being used to track and criminalize communities? One of the biggest questions about abolition in the context of data-based policing remains the difficulty of ensuring that data are ever really destroyed—especially when they have been shared with hundreds of other agencies.

During the Cook County campaign, organizations involved with the Erase the Database campaign began seriously to consider the politics of notification and restitution. Notifying people that their information appears in a gang database is a complicated process—it must be done in a secure manner that does not cause further harm. Yet notification is important for accountability because it enables individuals to seek restitution for harm and helps them challenge their designation in other gang databases, including those maintained by the CPD. This marked the beginning of long discussions about the politics of notification and about restitution for individuals and communities harmed by the database.

During summer 2020, as communities across the country rose up to protest the police murders of George Floyd, Tony McDade, Breonna Taylor, Rayshard Brooks, and other young Black people, organizations in Chicago united behind the demand to #DefundCPD. Building on long-standing abolitionist visions, the #DefundCPD campaign incorporated demands to abolish CPD gang databases, cut police funding by 75 percent, and "re-invest those funds into non-carceral social services and community programs" in Black and brown communities.[34]

#DefundCPD added energy to the Erase the Database campaign, including a new partnership with the youth-led organization Good Kids, Mad City (GKMC). Seeking to create fully resourced, sustainable communities and to uplift approaches to violence that do not rely on the police, GKMC has proposed the creation of a Peace Book Commission. The Peace Book would divert funding from the CPD toward noncarceral initiatives designed to address community violence by providing wraparound services to criminalized youth and paying peacekeepers to facilitate treaties between street organizations.[35]

In 2021, GKMC and the Erase the Database campaign came together to introduce a joint Community Restoration Ordinance (CRO) before the Chicago City Council. The CRO is a combined ordinance that would disrupt criminalization by dissolving the CPD's existing gang databases; prevent the CPD from creating a new gang database or sharing its data with federal agencies; provide compensation to individuals harmed by the database; and invest in long-term reparations/restitution to Black and Latinx communities through wraparound services, restorative justice programs, community-led peacekeeping, and remedies to gun violence that provide services without the threat of incarceration—"including but not limited to free college tuition, free drug treatment centers, employment priority preferences when applying for city jobs, trauma centers, trauma-informed schools, mental health care clinics, standby psychiatrists or therapists, restorative justice, community centers, transformative justice, fair housing, food justice and economic justice."

Through this new partnership, the Erase the Database campaign has linked demands for the abolition of repressive carceral systems with calls for the creation of community-led, noncarceral initiatives that address the root causes of gun violence. The campaign has developed tools for envisioning restitution not only for individuals but for communities harmed by high-tech, data-based policing. In doing so, it has rejected distinctions between the deserving and the undeserving, the innocent and the guilty.

Mayor Lightfoot and her City Council allies maneuvered to prevent the introduction of the CRO. As we go to press, Chicago has a new mayor—Brandon Johnson—who made a campaign promise to support the goals of Erase the Database and other anticarceral campaigns. In September 2023, the interim Chicago Community Commission on Public Safety and Accountability—an oversight body created by the 2021 Empowering Communities for Public Safety ordinance—placed a vote that effectively blocked implementation of the proposed CEIS.[36] While anticipating pushback, we celebrate this vote as a partial victory for the Erase the Database campaign and a significant milestone toward reimagining public safety under the Johnson administration. With renewed energy and hope for the future, the struggle to end imperial policing continues.

LOOKING BACK AND LOOKING FORWARD: ORGANIZING FOR ABOLITIONIST SANCTUARY

Offering an important lens for thinking about the Expanded Sanctuary campaign, Angela Davis, Gina Dent, Erica Meiners, and Beth Richie argue that "an abolition feminist lens teaches us that our work is not simply about 'winning' specific campaigns but reframing the terrain upon which struggle for freedom happens. Indeed, one of the fundamental precepts of abolition is that winning a campaign is not the only measure of success: *how* we struggle, how our work enables future struggles, and how we stay clear about what we are fighting for matters."[37]

Efforts to amend the WCO and to erase the gang database are part of a broader campaign to expand the meaning and practice of sanctuary through an abolitionist framework. Ultimately, this is a struggle to fundamentally transform liberal sanctuary policies that offer conditional protection for "good immigrants" while intensifying the punishment of immigrants whom police consider "criminals" or "gang members" and providing no support at all to Black and Latinx populations with citizenship. What would it mean for Chicago to be a true sanctuary city where all residents can live in their full humanity without fear of persecution due to race, class, gender, sexuality, citizenship status, gang affiliation, or criminal history?

As we have documented in this chapter, campaigns to expand sanctuary must grapple with tensions between abolition and harm reduction. Recognizing this tension from the start, the Erase the Database campaign established four clear goals that served as bedrock abolitionist principles to ground our strategies and shape our decisions as we fought for policies that could provide protection for our people in the short term. The need for sanctuary at the municipal level was particularly urgent in light of the extremist policies enacted by federal agencies under the Trump administration. This forced our movement to confront the challenge of fighting for reforms that would provide real protection and chip away at the system of imperial policing without deepening the oppression of the most marginalized people in our communities. In other words, we set out to achieve what Critical Resistance calls "non-reformist reforms," which weaken the empire state and refuse distinctions between "good" and "bad," "innocent" and "guilty." Navigating these tensions became most acute in our litigation strategy and our efforts to transform public policy. While offering the most concrete possibilities for constitutional protection, courts and legislative bodies are dangerous minefields of co-optation and "reformist reforms" that strengthen the state. We have fallen into these traps more than once, but we are learning from our mistakes as we continue the struggle.

The Expanded Sanctuary campaign has helped open a new front in the struggle by turning an abolitionist lens on data-based imperial policing, including massive databases, advanced technology, and data-sharing practices. The goals of the WCO and Erase the Database campaigns focus on abolishing databases and other tools of high-tech surveillance, eliminating data-sharing practices that enable coordination between local and federal agencies, defunding all carceral agencies, and rejecting criminalizing labels like "gang member." While uplifting this abolitionist approach to data and technology, it is important to recognize that data-based policing poses new challenges for abolition. As we discussed in the case of the CCSO, what does it mean to abolish a shared database? How do we know that the data are truly gone? Similarly, the CPD's proposal to create a new gang database reveals the way that the state reinvents itself to hold on to its tools of criminalization and surveillance. In addition, it is absolutely crucial to remember that the struggle to abolish imperial policing in all its forms goes much deeper than data and technology. Even if we take away some of their tools, we still confront a regime of policing grounded in settler colonialism, racial capitalism, white supremacy, and empire.

Cross-racial, cross-issue coalitions of organizations committed to joint struggle are essential building blocks for abolitionist sanctuary. The carceral regimes that we confront are similar, yet distinct and deeply intertwined. Our struggles must be connected as well. The Expanded Sanctuary campaign recognized that gang databases provide a useful focus for building a Black–Latinx coalition owing to the racialized archetype of the "gang member" and the focus on gangs by both local police and federal immigration authorities. Linking the campaigns to erase the gang database and amend the WCO also helped ensure that immigrant rights groups remained accountable to Black-led organizations. And our embrace of political quilting enabled the campaign to build a large coalition of groups that are differently situated in skill, constituency base, and relation to the empire state, including community organizations, legal clinics, university-based research teams, and more. All of this is key to building a successful movement.

But we also missed opportunities to expand the campaign. The Erase the Database campaign has struggled to build connections with young people directly targeted as gang members. There are many obstacles to their participation, including movement between neighborhoods and heightened exposure to police surveillance. But the campaign could have done more to address these challenges, such as more intentionally organizing in the neighborhoods we know to be most impacted by gang policing, incorporating more transformative justice centers into our coalition, and working to coordinate accessible places to strategize. In addition, while focusing on links between the War on Crime and the War on Immigrants, we did not sufficiently address connections with the War on Terror. There were openings for building these connections. The Arab American Action Network participated in both the WCO and the Erase the Database campaigns. And when Arab and Muslim communities organized at O'Hare International Airport to protest Trump's Muslim ban, there were conversations between organizers about how to build connections. However, we fell short in practical solidarity in real time. Perhaps the emerging campaigns to eliminate fusion centers and end the use of suspicious activity reports will provide the basis for building these links.

Despite these shortcomings, the Expanded Sanctuary campaign has had a number of achievements and provides an important window into abolitionist organizing against imperial policing. It has helped to eliminate the punitive exceptions in the WCO, end direct access to CPD data for ICE, decommission the RGID database, introduce some constitutional protections to CPD gang databases, and ultimately secure support needed to end the city's use of the gang database. More broadly, the campaign has built connections between Black- and Latinx-led organizations in Chicago and moved immigrant rights organizations toward a more radically inclusive orientation that rejects respectability politics and criminal archetypes. Still, major questions remain. What would real sanctuary look like in an imperial city like Chicago? How can sanctuary be extended to address the three police wars: the War on Crime, the War on Terror, and the War on Immigrants? And what will it take to abolish imperial policing altogether?

Conclusion

For the Abolition of Imperial Policing

Abolitionist praxis addresses carcerality as a logic of power
that generates multiple, overlapping, and differently scaled
carceral regimes (reservations, plantations, segregated
cities/towns, prisons, military bases, and so forth). Thus,
eliminating carceral-state violence via prisons, jails, police,
detention centers, and military bases is but one aspect
of a broader rethinking—and remaking—of collective,
insurgent "power" that simultaneously asserts a liberated
autonomy from and posits a radical challenge to long
historical relations of gendered, racial-colonial dominance.

> —DYLAN RODRIGUEZ, "Abolition as Praxis of Being
> Human: An Afterword"

The carceral structures of the U.S. empire state are vast webs of repressive
and disciplinary agencies that have similar but distinct missions and carry
out overlapping, interconnected projects. These webs crisscross the globe
but congeal in context-specific formations at a range of geographic scales
to pursue joint projects. We call these projects *police wars* to emphasize
their violent nature. In *Imperial Policing,* we analyze the three principal
police wars in twenty-first-century Chicago—the War on Crime, the War
on Terror, and the War on Immigrants—as windows into local formations
and global networks of imperial policing. Although the details may differ,
many of the same agencies, discourses, policies, practices, technologies,
and databases shape policing at other scales and in other locations.

Neoliberal restructuring has concentrated wealth in the hands of
billionaire capitalists while intensifying the crises confronting Black,

Indigenous, immigrant, diasporic, and working-class communities. In this context, the three police wars are best understood as imperial strategies to contain crises, enforce order, and protect the powerful. The War on Crime is primarily an effort to contain or eliminate the Black poor rendered disposable by white supremacy and neoliberal restructuring; the War on Terror is an imperial project to support U.S. hegemony in the greater Middle East, corporate access to inexpensive oil, and Zionist rule in Palestine; and the War on Immigrants is a project to control the flow and regulate the subjectivity of people seeking opportunities in the imperial mainland after being displaced from the Global South. These police wars are deeply intertwined. The War on Gangs targets immigrant as well as U.S.-born Black and Latinx youth; the War on Terror pursues not only Arabs and Muslims but also Black radicals, Marxists, and solidarity activists; and the War on Immigrants subjects noncitizens (and some citizens) labeled "terrorists" or "gang members" to detention and deportation.

Distinct combinations of carceral agents come together to wage each war. This generates context-specific formations that take the form of hierarchically organized networks. But there is extensive overlap between these networks. In part, this is because some agencies are engaged in multiple wars and/or operate at multiple scales. It is also due to shared goals, strategies, technologies, discourses, and data. These multiscalar formations are articulated together to form the complex unity that we describe as the *webs of imperial policing*.

This does not mean that the networks are seamless or operate in unison. On the contrary, there are always tensions between agencies over jurisdiction, recognition, resources, and data as well as strategic and political disagreements. Moreover, while there is broad political consensus in the United States supporting the War on Crime and the War on Terror, the War on Immigrants is more contested. This is because the racial capitalist demand for low-wage labor creates openings to resist exclusionary nationalism and because grassroots mobilizations have pushed some cities, such as Chicago, to adopt liberal sanctuary policies that offer partial protection for some noncitizens by limiting cooperation with federal immigration authorities.

Each police war is discursively grounded in a *racialized criminal ar-*

chetype: the gang member, the terrorist suspect, the criminal alien. The archetypes are informed by globally circulating threat discourses that largely associate Blackness with criminality, Islam with terror, and immigrants with a wide range of social ills. They mark people as suspicious based on their bodies, their social networks, and their geographies. Thus, archetypes provide a shared focal point for surveillance. This helps explain why dispersed carceral agents so consistently identify the same populations as suspicious: Black people as gang members; Arabs and Muslims as potential terrorists; Latinx people as criminal aliens. Police databases reify and codify these racialized archetypes by attaching official labels to individuals, treating them as "facts" and enabling their circulation through the webs of imperial policing.

All three police wars are materially grounded in the physical violence of arrest, incarceration, detention, deportation, beatdowns, torture, rape, and death, fused and entangled with traumatizing and dehumanizing forms of psychic and symbolic violence. Each war also incorporates a range of disciplinary strategies that promote assimilation, wage labor, and cooperation with the police. We focus on an increasingly popular disciplinary strategy that we call *carceral liberalism,* which espouses a neoliberal ethic of individual choice and self-responsibility while relying on and expanding police violence. Programs like "focused deterrence" and Countering Violent Extremism incorporate service providers into carceral networks, offering minimal support to individuals who make "good" choices while blaming entire populations for their own repression and threatening further violence against people who make "bad" decisions. Liberal sanctuary policies provide minimal protection to "good" immigrants who are willing to accept wage discipline and remain politically docile, while targeting "bad" immigrants for arrest and deportation based on police records. Rather than addressing the root causes of crime or violence, carceral liberal programs all reinforce the status quo.

To contain the crises caused by racial capitalism, colonialism, and empire, the United States has directed massive investments to state- and private-sector carceral agencies. Police, prisons, immigration enforcement, national security, and military agencies are immune from neoliberal demands for cuts to public spending. The budgets of repressive agencies have ballooned while social services face permanent austerity. At the same time, privatized security, prison, military, and intelligence companies have built global markets for repression. High-tech security corporations and private data brokers contribute to and profit from police wars by arming carceral agencies and facilitating the weaponization of data. Moreover, community organizations, educators, social workers, and everyday residents are drawn into networks of surveillance.

Our work draws attention to the *dif/fuse* structure of twenty-first-century imperial policing. The empire state has multiplied the agents and sites of policing not only by proliferating state agencies but also by incorporating tech companies, educators, social workers, mental health professionals, community organizations, social service agencies, and everyday residents into decentralized carceral networks held together by the circulation of data. Flows of data provide an increasingly essential mechanism for coordination—or fusion—within these decentralized networks.

While policing remains firmly rooted in the dynamics of settler colonialism, racial capitalism, white supremacy, and empire, recent advances in the *weaponization of data* have contributed to cutting-edge strategies of imperial policing. Data-based policing has an air of scientific objectivity that allows police to disavow their continued reliance on racialized archetypes and targeted deployments. Our research helps dismantle this myth by demonstrating exactly how data are produced, cleansed, and circulated through the carceral webs of empire. Police data are a product of the Wars on Crime, Terror, and Immigrants, largely arising from discourses, policies, and technologies that train police attention on criminalized people and places. Police databases and advanced techniques of data analysis cleanse the data by erasing the social conditions of data production, while simultaneously transforming the data into weapons that police use to wage war on the racialized poor and adjacent communities. And the circulation of data between agencies has produced swarms of carceral agents that use the data to target the same populations with a vast array of repressive and disciplinary tactics. The result is a self-fulfilling spiral of surveillance that heightens the vulnerability of the most marginalized: racialized police stops generate data that justify deploying more police to target the same people and neighborhoods.[1]

RESISTING DATA-BASED IMPERIAL POLICING

The rise of data-based policing has presented new targets for resistance. From one angle, organizations like Stop LAPD Spying, Mijente, Data for Black Lives, Our Data Bodies, Action Center on Race and the Economy (ACRE), and the Detroit Community Tech Portal are building campaigns against data-based surveillance. These campaigns include efforts to regulate or eliminate police databases and surveillance technology, to expose and target tech companies that work with law enforcement, and to demand community oversight of police technology.

From another angle, some organizers and data scientists are using the tools of data-based policing against the police. A growing number of community-based organizations and investigative journalists are creating their own databases and tools to map police misconduct and abuse using story collection, video documentation, social media posts, and data visualization. These countersurveillant databases create a public record and support efforts to resist the violence of policing. In Chicago, the Invisible Institute has created a database of police misconduct allegations called the Citizens Police Data Project and is using social network analysis to identify networks of abusive officers.[2] Other databases include the Evidence of Violence website by Kilometro 0, Mapping Police Violence, and Open Police Complaints.

Andrew Ferguson argues that turning data-based tools on the police can be an effective way to reduce police violence, increase police effectiveness, and improve police accountability. Ferguson also argues that data can support targeted, noncarceral interventions to address community violence.[3] As we demonstrate in chapter 2, however, many so-called alternatives—such as focused deterrence programs—cannot be described as noncarceral because they rely on police data and (threats of) carceral violence.

In a more explicitly abolitionist vein, Ruha Benjamin uplifts creative efforts to demystify and democratize technology so that marginalized communities can develop high-tech tools to support emancipatory struggles against white supremacy, racial capitalism, and the empire state.[4] She highlights a countersurveillant mapping project carried out by Stop LAPD Spying, the Digital Defense Playbook developed by Our Data Bodies, and the subversive clothing and accessories developed by Hyphen-Labs.

In Chicago, an important precursor to contemporary struggles against data-based policing was the effort to dismantle the Chicago Police Department (CPD) Red Squad (aka Subversive Unit). Through a seven-year lawsuit, organizers with the Chicago Alliance against Racist and Political Repression and the Citizens Alert Coalition exposed the unconstitutional surveillance practices through which the Red Squad built a database of index cards on more than 285,000 individuals and 14,000 organizations involved in labor, civil rights, and liberation struggles.[5]

More recently, organizations like ACRE, the Lucy Parsons Labs, the Invisible Institute, the StopCVE coalition, the Expanded Sanctuary campaign, and the coalition to EndSARs are developing innovative struggles against data-based surveillance. The Policing in Chicago Research Group has been fortunate to work alongside these campaigns. From these partnerships, we can discern four aspects of the challenge to high-tech, data-based policing in Chicago: rejection, elimination, separation, and reparation.

First, there's an outright *rejection* of criminalizing archetypes. Black, Latinx, and Arab/Muslim communities are rejecting labels like "gang member," "criminal alien," and "terrorist suspect." Rather than organizing demands based on claims of innocence or false accusation, movements are refusing the negative archetypes altogether because of the harm that they cause to communities of color. In doing so, they are affirming the humanity of the most marginalized by refusing to distinguish between the innocent and guilty or the deserving and undeserving.

Second, and closely related, movements are demanding the *elimination* of police databases and advanced data analytics. Rather than working to ensure that "innocent" people are not "wrongfully" included in the databases, movements are demanding the abolition of gang databases, suspicious activity reports, and other weapons of data-based policing. They reject the scientistic assumption that police data, predictive algorithms, network analysis, and other tools of what Benjamin calls the "New Jim Code" are neutral or objective.[6] Recognizing that police databases have real impacts on people's everyday lives, movements are calling for them to be erased, not improved. The demand for erasure is in part a response to the permanence of police records. In this sense, it is related to what European and Latin American social movements call the "right to be

▶ **DOMESTIC** ◀

+

▶ **GLOBAL** ◀

POLICE

Militarism is the use of violence and coercion to control people and resources. Militarized US forces and institutions include police, prisons, ICE, and the military. We demand an end to both domestic and global warfare waged by the US – from police killings in our neighborhoods, to drone strikes abroad.

FIGURE 15. Resistance to imperial policing must be domestic and global. Art by Alec Dunn, Justseeds.org; courtesy of Dissenters.

forgotten." But erasure goes deeper. It challenges what Dean Spade calls the "administrative classification systems that distribute life chances."[7] Fulfilling the abolitionist vision will require an expansive focus not only on databases maintained by carceral agencies but also on private-sector data brokers that sell data to carceral agencies.

The third demand is for *separation*. Movements are demanding an end to data sharing as a way to break the criminalizing webs that ensnare the most marginalized. Because data fusion facilitates interagency co-ordination, the elimination of data sharing can sever links in the carceral webs. Organizers have worked to eliminate data-sharing processes that allow U.S. Immigration and Customs Enforcement (ICE) and the Chicago Public Schools to access CPD data. They are also attentive to private data brokers as well as data flows between the police and service providers. As the Interrupting Criminalization collective explains, "it is vital to EXPLICITLY decouple social programs from policing. We need firewalls. For example, youth programming should not be tied to policing. Ever."[8]

Finally, movements are demanding *reparation* for the harms caused by data-based policing. For the Erase the Database campaign, calls for reparations include individual restitution for people included in the data-base and broader efforts to redirect investments from policing toward the communities most harmed by the database. Here there is potential to use police databases in ways that Benjamin describes as emancipatory. Mapping the neighborhoods of people on CPD gang databases, for instance, could demonstrate where to redirect the most funding. The call for reparation is part of a broader effort to reimagine justice, develop resources, and build relationships and communities without relying on imperial state violence.

Overall, Black, Latinx, and Arab/Muslim communities in Chicago are exposing the latest developments in data-based policing as part of their strategy to resist criminalization and reaffirm the humanity of people whose lives have been reduced to archetypes. These movements are calling for the abolition of police databases, an end to interagency data sharing, restitution for individuals harmed by the databases, and a broader divestment from the carceral state and investment in communities. As these movements demonstrate, abolition involves destroying existing structures and practices while simultaneously building a new world that is not rooted in violence.[9]

In doing so, social movements are identifying new challenges for abolition in a context of high-tech, data-based policing, including the permanence of data, the multiple circuits of data sharing, and the continual (re)invention of technologies. The question of permanence emerged when the Cook County sheriff decommissioned a shared, regional gang database. Although the sheriff eventually destroyed two hard drives containing the database, the Erase the Database campaign confronted the possibility that other agencies downloaded and saved the data before they were taken offline. The 2021 amendment to Chicago's Welcoming City Ordinance presented the issue of multiple data-sharing circuits. Although ICE no longer has direct access to CPD's CLEAR database, there remain several possible circuits for ICE to access CPD data: (1) in pursuit of a "criminal" (rather than "civil") case, (2) through the CPD's fusion center, and (3) through ICE's parent agency—the Department of Homeland Security—which retains access to CLEAR.[10] Finally, the CPD has attempted to outmaneuver abolitionist campaigns by reinventing its technologies of surveillance. After the Erase the Database campaign revealed the egregious constitutional violations in the CPD's gang arrest card database, the CPD proposed creating a new gang database that would include basic constitutional protections for due process. The permanence of data, the multiple pathways of data circulation, and the constant reinvention of technology mean that grassroots campaigns must articulate precise demands, exercise caution about claiming victory, and remain vigilant about emerging technologies and practices.

These movements also confront tensions between the urgent need for decarceration and harm reduction and longer-term abolitionist goals. The proposal for a new CPD gang database, for instance, would purge thousands of names by requiring police to provide evidence that the people on the list are active gang members. At the same time, it would justify the surveillance, incarceration, and death of people on the new list, whom Chicago police claim "really are" gang members. Through a lawsuit, the Erase the Database campaign worked to achieve as many protections as possible but refused to compromise on its demand for an end to all gang designations.

In navigating these challenges, the Erase the Database campaign found helpful direction in Ruth Wilson Gilmore's distinction between *reformist reforms* that expand the reach of the carceral state and *nonreformist reforms* that "unravel rather than widen the net of social control through crimi-nalization."[11] The campaign made use of questions developed by Critical Resistance and Dean Spade as tools for analyzing the potential impact of proposed reforms. Critical Resistance asks whether a proposed reform (1) reduces funding to the police, (2) challenges the notion that police increase safety, (3) reduces the tools/tactics/technology that police have at their disposal, and (4) reduces the scale of policing. Dean Spade adds, (1) Does the proposed reform provide material relief? (2) Does it leave out an especially marginalized group? (3) Does it legitimize or expand a system we are trying to dismantle? (4) Does it mobilize the most affected for ongoing struggle? These questions help organizers determine whether a proposed reform would "expand the reach of policing" or "chip away and reduce its overall impact."[12]

ABOLISHING IMPERIAL POLICING

Organizers understand that data and technology are simply the latest tools of the police and that abolishing these tools is merely one step along the path to liberation. Targeting the tools of data-based policing is key to countering the dominant strategies of imperial policing today. But real transformation requires abolishing the deeper structures of imperial policing—including multiple police wars, racialized criminal archetypes, carceral liberal strategies, and carceral webs of empire—and, ultimately, the underlying structures of white supremacy, racial capitalism, settler colonialism, and empire.

To begin with, we must abolish police wars as a strategy for addressing the crises that confront contemporary society. Deploying the organized violence of empire to contain, displace, exploit, or eliminate the racialized poor is never the answer.[13] The three police wars have not, cannot, and maybe never really intended to meet their stated objectives of creating safe, secure, and peaceful communities. Instead, they perpetrate physi-cal, administrative, and ideological violence on racialized communities whose liberation depends on the abolition of the U.S. empire state as we know it. Rather than carceral violence, we must develop structurally transformative solutions that change material conditions and bring an end to exploitation, dispossession, displacement, and death.[14]

The "invest/divest" framework introduced by the Movement for Black

Lives (M4BL) outlines a pathway toward abolition.[15] The M4BL vision statement calls for a reallocation of funding from the carceral system to educational, economic, infrastructural, and transformative justice projects in Black communities. Importantly, the M4BL statement includes not only police and prisons but also the military–industrial complex and U.S. military support for Israel as core components of the carceral empire to be targeted for divestment. Similarly, as Janaé Bonsu-Love explains, the Black Youth Project 100 (BYP100) Agenda to Fund Black Futures calls for "divestment from systems that punish our people and investment in the things we need to survive and thrive," including a living wage, reparations, comprehensive health care, and universal childcare.[16]

Transformative justice organizations are also developing crucial alternatives to carceral violence. Dean Spade explains: "Abolitionists are trying to build models for dealing with harm that do not rely on exile, expulsion, or caging, but instead examine the root causes of harm and seek healing and transformation for both people experiencing and people responsible for harm."[17] As practiced by Critical Resistance, INCITE!, Project NIA, Just Practice Collaborative, Circles & Ciphers, Generation 5, and the Safe OUTside the System Collective, transformative justice provides healing and reparations for people who are harmed while holding people who commit harm accountable to their communities and promoting the transformation of society as a whole. The Interrupting Criminalization "Defund Toolkit" outlines numerous examples of efforts to address mental health crises and interrupt violence without relying on police.[18] And the BYP100 "She Safe, We Safe" campaign promotes community-based strategies and resources to ensure the safety of Black women.[19] "These approaches," Ejeris Dixon explains, "work to prevent violence, to intervene when harm is occurring, to hold people accountable, and to transform individuals and society to build safer communities."[20]

Along with the abolition of police wars, we must dismantle the dehumanizing archetypes that provide the discursive foundation for these wars. Archetypes like "gang member," "terrorist," and "criminal alien" obscure people's humanity by reducing them to outlawed categories. Recognizing people's humanity requires moving from liberal logics to radical love. Whereas liberal logics flatten people's lives with narrow subject categories (innocent or guilty, deserving or undeserving), a politics of radical love sets out to build real connections with people by embracing the full complexity of their subjectivity.[21] It also means recognizing, in the words of Dylan Rodriguez, "the radical possibility that the historical targets of incarceration are also the complex embodiment of its imminent undoing, hence its abolition as such."[22]

Abolitionist movements are practicing radical love to affirm the full humanity of the most marginalized. The Immigrant Youth Justice League, a precursor to Organized Communities Against Deportation, held "coming-out" rallies where young immigrants identified themselves as "undocumented, unafraid, unapologetic." Members of BYP100, Black Lives Matter–Chicago, and other Black freedom movements proudly proclaim themselves "unapologetically Black." Moreover, through strategies of political quilting, movements have worked to overcome the trap that Lisa Cacho calls "competitive legibility," in which uplifting one community requires demeaning another.[23] The Expanded Sanctuary campaign, for instance, is grounded in joint struggle and the assertion that everyone should be safe from policing, surveillance, and violence regardless of race, gender, citizenship status, criminal history, or gang involvement.

Carceral liberal strategies claim to embrace people's humanity. For instance, Countering Violent Extremism is premised on helping people find a pathway from radicalization to redemption. Practitioners of focused deterrence incorporate a message of love into their meetings with gang members: you are a part of this community, we care about you, and we want to help. And liberal sanctuary policies identify immigrants as important contributors to the city. But all of these projects fall short: love, support, and inclusion are conditioned on individuals making "good" choices by rejecting violence, embracing wage discipline, and severing social connections. Moreover, carceral liberal projects endorse individual morality rather than structural transformation. They are disciplinary, assimilationist projects that seek to incorporate people into the structures of racial capitalism, settler colonialism, and empire without radically transforming these structures. This aligns with concerns raised by Grace Hong about political projects that seek to "reintegrate" the marginalized into the existing social order.[24] Because we need noncarceral alternatives and structural transformations, it is imperative to target carceral liberal strategies as part of a broader effort to abolish imperial policing.

FIGURE 16. Abolition requires a radical imagination of new ways of relating to each other and addressing our problems. Photograph by and courtesy of Sarah Jane Rhee (@loveandstrugglephotos).

Finally, abolishing imperial policing requires dismantling the diffuse carceral webs of empire. Angela Davis, Gina Dent, Erica Meiners, and Beth Richie use the concept of "delinking" to describe the important work of challenging the "migration of carcerality" from police and prisons to diffuse sites of surveillance and discipline.[25] Movements are working to defund, dismantle, and abolish all state- and private-sector carceral agencies, including local police departments, ICE and the FBI, and the prison– and military–industrial complexes. Along with the individual agencies, it is imperative to confront the policies, practices, and structures that link these agencies together as carceral webs. Data-sharing practices and racialized criminal archetypes are key links within these networks. The circuits of imperial policing also involve interagency task forces, joint training, expert consultants, shared technology, criminalizing discourses, and other processes. Movements are already targeting many of these, such as the Deadly Exchange campaign to end Israeli training of U.S. police forces. But we must do more.

Ultimately, all of this requires a struggle to abolish racism, colonialism, capitalism, heteropatriarchy, borders, war, and empire. In the words of

Nadine Naber and Clarissa Rojas, "in order to abolish the prison–industrial complex we are going to need to dismantle the colonial heterosexist, racial and imperial underpinnings of carcerality."[26]

GLOBAL SOLIDARITY AND ABOLITION

The carceral webs of the U.S. empire state and the racialized discourses that ground the police wars are global in reach; so, too, is the struggle against imperial policing. Circuits of imperial policing are being met by circuits of transnational solidarity linking struggles for liberation across the world. Davis and her colleagues argue that "internationalist engagements are imperative to illustrate the continuing and global repercussions of colonialism and imperialism embedded in police and carceral institutions."[27]

Abolitionist visions have long been informed by internationalist struggles against racist, colonial, and imperial violence. And organizers in the United States have forged connections with anticarceral movements in Palestine, South Africa, Chile, Argentina, Australia, and beyond. These connections expand as organizers work together to build another world.

Of course, not all organizers adopt "abolition" as a framework for envisioning and building political resistance. Other radical frameworks—"liberation," "dignity," "revolution," "sovereignty," and "decolonization"—may resonate more fully with other organizers, especially in the Global South. It is helpful to think of these frameworks together and find ways to use the overlaps and productive tensions to strengthen global resistance against empire.

Conceptualizing abolition as a practice of resisting and eliminating all forms of carceral violence helps us envision and build relationships that are liberatory in nature. Reflecting on years of organizing with INCITE! Women of Color against Violence, Naber and Rojas note,

> Against the capitalist approach that urges us to produce—Presto! You made an abolitionist society!—INCITE taught us that movement work is constantly becoming, that we build on legacies and lessons learned through practice. The goal, then, of a decolonial abolitionist feminism is not a liberated utopian world without police, prisons, or

FIGURE 17. Abolition is possible only through solidarity. Artwork by and courtesy of Monica Trinidad.

war, but rather a process where over time we learn and remember the skills for living better, in better relation with one another and all life, on the path to ending violence.[28]

Visions for abolition are always in process, subject to revision, and inclusive of multiple—often overlapping—struggles. It is through collective work and global solidarity that we begin envisioning and building alternatives and practicing the skills we need to live in a world without policing, incarceration, capitalism, and racist, heteropatriarchal violence. Coalitional mobilizations committed to joint struggle and political quilting are key.[29] These mobilizations build on the decades-long work of grassroots organizers and restorative and transformative justice practitioners, creating local networks of resistance that are connected to national and transnational formations. For comrades in the Global South, struggles to transform patriarchal, authoritarian, and apartheid states must contend with the local manifestations of the U.S. empire state, including support for neoliberal policies, counterrevolutionary forces, and right-wing coups. Through principled forms of revolutionary solidarity, movements are developing visions of liberation and abolition that stretch from local police and private security companies to federal immigration authorities and national security agencies to the prison- and military–industrial complexes and, ultimately, to the racial capitalist, settler-colonial, heteropatriarchal U.S. empire state.

Abolitionist research has an important role in these mobilizations.[30] By working alongside and supporting abolitionist organizations, scholar-activists can contribute powerful tools for resistance. Countersurveillant abolitionist research can help shape and validate demands and also monitor their implementation. Scholar-activists connected to universities can leverage institutional power and resources. We want to encourage academics to think creatively about how our work can contribute to dismantling systems of power and violence. But it is crucial to do so in ways that are led by and accountable to movements and communities. Moreover, by working alongside people directly impacted by policing, scholar-activists can help young people see themselves as researchers and experts, rather than as sources of the problem. Conducting abolitionist research often requires focusing on specific questions and concrete problems that need to be addressed. We need to honor and support these concrete struggles while keeping an eye on longer-term goals.

THE FIERCE URGENCY OF ABOLITION

The work of abolition is incredibly urgent because racialized working-class communities in Chicago and across the world are facing multiple, intersecting crises that cannot be addressed without fundamental social transformation. Combinations of permanent unemployment, contingent labor, school closures, inadequate health care, unaffordable housing, environmental degradation, segregation, gentrification, and eviscerated social services shape the lives of working-class Black, Indigenous, and diasporic communities of color in Chicago. Immigrant and diasporic communities also contend with the devastating consequences of neoliberal capitalism, (settler) colonialism, climate catastrophe, and warfare in their homelands. All of these forms of oppression are grounded in racial capitalism, settler colonialism, white supremacy, empire, and heteronormative patriarchy.

Without question, gun violence is the most intense expression of the crises confronting communities in Chicago today. The crisis is all too real: young people of color—especially young Black men—are shot and killed nearly every day in Chicago. Most of the violence is concentrated in working-class Black and Latinx neighborhoods on the South and West Sides and in pockets of the North and Northwest Sides. But the impacts are never distant, and the people are not statistics, for the violence often hits close to home. We all have friends, neighbors, and loved ones—even members of our research team—who have been hurt or killed by gun violence. We are members of the community, all of us are affected, and we cannot ignore what is happening.

We will never successfully address gun violence without confronting political, economic, epistemic, and state violence. It is irresponsible and unjust to continue blaming young people for the violence. As we have demonstrated throughout this book, imperial policing perpetuates violence by concealing systemic crises, intensifying suffering, and manufacturing conflict in working-class communities of color. As activists and community-engaged scholars, we believe that it is critical to seek transformative and life-affirming solutions to violence. The latest technologies and data-based practices—even carceral liberal forms—merely intensify the police wars targeting our communities. The white supremacist–racial capitalist–heteropatriarchal–carceral empire is fundamentally unjust and cannot be reformed or recovered. Rather than more accurate data or more objective policing, we need to resist the underlying dynamics of dehumanization and criminalization as well as the belief that police can protect "us" from "them." Abolition is the only solution.

We can do more to build relationships based on mutual respect and recognition for people whose humanity has been reduced to criminal archetypes. There is potential in the simple act of creating spaces for people to feel safe coming together and in the day-to-day choices we make about how to relate to one another. As Mariame Kaba states, "everything that is worthwhile is done with other people."[31] Our research and our struggles for abolition must center the people directly targeted by imperial policing. Dark sousveillant knowledge and everyday abolitionist praxis situate gang-involved young people on the front lines of that struggle. To build a different world, we must engage with and care about all of the people who live in our communities. And this requires emotional vulnerability, because being in relationship with people targeted by the empire state opens us up to relentless trauma and devastating loss. But as we mourn, we build radical hope and rise.

Afterword

Abolition Dreaming in Chicago: Channeling Refusal in Unsettling Times

David Omotoso Stovall

Among the paranoia of popular media musings about Chicago's "crime problem," few are willing to discuss the city's white supremacy conundrum in the form of isolation, containment, disinvestment, and dispossession. Where the Policing in Chicago Research Group has taken careful and thoughtful steps to name the police wars waged in Chicago, the consequences for those of us who remain in its boundaries are local and international. In a global city, neoliberal powers are worried that multinational corporations are looking for other spaces to locate their headquarters because workers are "concerned for their safety." Ironically, the mass media travel and leisure conglomerate Condé Nast has ranked Chicago the number one tourist destination in the United States. To Chicagoans who can read between the lines of this strange irony, the top ranking means that *Chicago is a great place to visit, as long as you go only to the recommended spaces—everything else is too dangerous.* Taking into account the absurdity of being declared too dangerous and a great destination in the same breath, I am in line with the authors' inquiry through the following questions: *What about the people who live in those dangerous places? Who are they? How have they been made disposable?* Most important, *why do we continue to depend on the state—especially imperial police—to regulate this population at all costs and to preserve the city for the wealthy and powerful?* I am pleased that the authors do not pivot away from these questions. Their examinations throughout the book serve as a perpetual reminder of the fact that we cannot run from the realities of the day, no matter how daunting they may appear. As the three pandemics of white supremacy, capitalism, and Covid-19 are historical and continue to provide warnings for the present and the future, the police wars on crime, terror, and immigrants continue to rage through our hearts, minds, and streets.

In offering a parting note of sorts, the goal here is not to leave readers with a putrid disdain for any hope for the future. To the contrary, it is to remind us of the work required to dream, build, and protect the structures and formations that will provide us shelter from the storm of late-stage capitalism and burgeoning totalitarianism, sometimes clothed in the neoliberal rhetorical wool of making our streets "safe." In many ways, this book has unearthed what many Black, Latinx, Indigenous, and Arab Chicagoans live daily. It is for these reasons that the promise and necessity of abolition loom so large in the visions of activists, organizers, and scholars.

When imagining a world without imperialist, capitalist power as the sole arbiter of human existence, moving toward abolition requires a number of considerations. In Chicago, where police violence is central to the operation of power, we must remind ourselves that the primary function of police is to serve as the militarized arm of the state. Because their primary duty is to fulfill the desires of the powerful, they operate primarily as a functionary (albeit an important one) of the state. Rarely are police departments given free rein to operate outside the auspices of state power. Abolition teaches us that there is no such thing as a rogue police department or "bad apples." As many members of the Chicago Police Department will state off the record, "the police are only here to do the mayor's bidding." Despite the realization by many white residents in summer 2020 that police operate with carte blanche authority over Black bodies, the authors are correct to name the historical function of police. Because their first "assignments" from the state were to retrieve human beings escaping enslavement in the South and to disrupt labor organizing in the North, we should understand that little has deviated from the institutional formation of police departments. Again, these are not by-products of policing; they are their *origin story*. Federal, state, and local governments are not designed to punish themselves. Instead, because their duty is to protect themselves first, the imperialist order must be understood for its racist, classist, patriarchal, and homophobic beginnings. When the state moves to protect police departments accused of wrongdoing, they are complicit only in what they were designed to do in the first place.

We should also understand police to function as a primary arbiter in the engineering of conflict between and within racial and ethnic groups in Chicago, creating rationales by which to target and hunt Black, Latinx, Indigenous, and Arab residents in the name of law and order. Through obstruction and failure at the government and administrative level, the city's recent and historical maneuvers in education and housing, as well as law enforcement, continually operate as material and ideological sites for the containment and marginalization of large groupings of Black residents on the South and West Sides of the city. Because school closings, the destruction of public housing, and local law enforcement are usually investigated as singular entities, their grouping under the auspices of an "engineered" or planned instability allows us to consider the legal, spatial, and educational conditions of Black, Latinx, Indigenous, and Arab residents of Chicago. Schools and housing are soft targets for the regulation of certain bodies, especially if those spaces have experienced similar disinvestment and isolation. Because schools and housing often mirror each other in large cities like Chicago, it does not take long to identify patterns of disinvestment and planned abandonment. When schools and housing in the same community are left in disrepair, coupled with minimal access to health care and living-wage employment, stress levels can run high. Because Chicago is hypersegregated and many of these communities are contained, the tendency is for people to displace their stress and trauma on each other, often increasing levels of violence. If we couple this with a city that is depopulating itself of Black people, we soon see those "dangerous" areas as the result of decades-long policies aimed at ridding the city of its most undesirable residents. The police wars mentioned in this volume should be considered as part and parcel of engineered conflict.

I agree with the authors' treatise that isolation in the form of hypersegregation and gentrification creates enclosures designed for police to contain and/or isolate Black, Latinx, Indigenous, and Arab populations. It is also critical to understand that the police wars detailed in the manuscript are soundly rooted in anti-Blackness. Again, this is not to suggest some sort of oppression Olympics in terms of who is targeted the "most" or the "worst" or to state the obvious. Instead, Saidiya Hartman reminds us that anti-Blackness positions the bodies of Black people as the naturalized sites of gratuitous punishment. Additionally, those who are punished in Chicago are most often proximal to Blackness (racially, economically, and spatially) and are rewarded when they can proclaim their distance from it. Geographically, this is most evident on the South and West Sides of the city, where Black and Latinx populations often reside in adjacent neighborhoods experiencing the various police wars. When we spatially map wrongful arrests or convictions, torture, or other egregious acts by police in Chicago, the vast majority remain in predominantly Black neighborhoods that are in proximity to Latinx spaces, where populations are also wrongly persecuted and hunted by law enforcement. Historically, many of these spaces were created as racial enclosures by the city to limit the access of Black people by way of restrictive covenants and other Black codes created to remind Black residents that they were never to encroach on spaces designated for whites. The current spatial relationship of Black, Latinx, Indigenous, and Arab people to imperial police violence alerts us to the target of white racial animus, designating marginalized and often disinvested spaces for said populations to reside. In light of the historical continuum, acts of solidarity are seen as the most dangerous when Latinx, Indigenous, and Arab residents outwardly reject anti-Blackness and work to develop conjoined actions to combat the tentacles of the police state.

For the aforementioned reasons, *abolition* is not a word to be taken lightly. I understand it as a collective determination that certain things are unacceptable (e.g., imperial policing, prisons, corrupt nonparticipatory government) and must be abolished. At the same time, because these things are unacceptable, there is the responsibility to replace them with something else. The authors are correct that these cannot be programs, systems, or institutions that make for a "nicer" carceral state that determines who is acceptable and who must be banished. Instead, at this moment, we are pushed to consider our work to be fugitive, where traditional rules may not work and require rethinking. It is what Fred Moten and Stefano Harney reference as incomplete work in that we do not rest on the laurels of the latest victory but solemnly remind one another that there is always work to be done. An embrace of fugitive work allows us to envision an abolition practice that might not be as clean or acceptable to the masses at first. Nevertheless, it requires us to rethink and reimagine what we're trying to do and who we're trying to do it with. As a born-and-raised Chicagoan, I know that it is counterproductive in any revolutionary struggle to run from the realties presented by the current moment. Instead, we must contest the practices of the state that facilitate the engineering of conflict between groups in the name of keeping in the "good" while expelling the "bad." Now is not the time to dismiss the seriousness of the moment. Instead, if we are willing to confront the realities we see on the street and tie them back to the desires of the neoliberal state to dispose itself of the undesirable, we can begin to do our work earnestly, with integrity and humility. This type of liberatory engagement will often sit in contradictions and mistakes, but it is imperative that we continue to wrestle with the process and commitments that provide the greatest chances to do things differently.

I admit that it is deeply challenging to remain hopeful in a world that can often feel like it's crumbling beneath our feet. At the same time, the sobering realities can provide an offering of possibility if we are willing to make demands on our world while working to change it. We are without question in a state of upheaval. Many moments feel chaotic and restless, but on the other side of upheaval is a clearing. The work to get there will be rough at times. It's easy to feel as if we'll never get there, but we need to pay attention to the ruptures. Acts of solidarity are a rupture. The end of cash bail is a rupture. Permanently closing prisons is a rupture. Building sustainable housing and food delivery systems is a rupture. All of them exist because they are reflective of a willingness to work.

For Black, Latinx, Indigenous, and Arab residents of Chicago who reside in gentrifying neighborhoods or in communities on the outer edges of the city, the intersection of school closings, public housing, and law enforcement provides the material conditions from which to grow resistance to imperial policing. If there is one thing of which we can be sure, it is that there is no greater time than the present to be counted in the multitudes of those who overstand the imperative of dedicating our blood and bone to the work. The ability to determine healthy, life-affirming spaces free of fascism, white supremacy, misogyny, ableism, imperial power, Zionism, neoliberal regimes of surveillance, patriarchy, and homo/transphobia is in our line of sight. It is work that requires a deep sense of honesty and vulnerability. Rest assured, we cannot fool ourselves into believing that this will come easily. Right now, it is without question that many of us are tired and deserve rest. In a struggle like ours, it is in our weariness that we find the collective will to breathe and build strength to move forward. Abolition reminds us that it is a joyous struggle where there are no throwaway people or people to be ignored. It is a reminder that all fugitive work has a purpose and becomes clearer by the second if we are willing to do it.

Methodological Appendix: Countersurveillant Abolitionist Research

Although historically marginalized by positivist aspirations to "scientific objectivity," politically engaged scholarship has deep roots in sociology and related fields. In the face of growing inequality and brutality, many scholars are building on traditions of political engagement to produce and advocate for research that has an impact beyond academic circles. Among sociologists, this work is called *public sociology.*[1] Beyond the discipline of sociology, politically engaged research often falls under the rubric of *activist scholarship.*

The Policing in Chicago Research Group (PCRG) emerged in the space opened by the resurgence of public sociology and activist scholarship. The PCRG is an activist research collective composed of current and former faculty and graduate students at the University of Illinois at Chicago (UIC). As part of a wave of cross-movement organizing that has galvanized the streets of Chicago since 2013, we came together to support mass mobilizations by conducting research on policing in dialogue with social movements and transformative justice organizations. We seek to amplify marginalized voices while producing knowledge that is relevant and useful for abolitionist political campaigns and for people directly impacted by policing. The members of our group have different and shifting relationships to the identities of "scholar," "activist," and "organizer," but we all agree with Adia Harvey Wingfield that politically relevant and directly impactful research is more urgent than ever.[2]

Academia has long been entwined with political movements. Struggles for racial and gender justice in the 1960s and 1970s, for instance, transformed the production of knowledge in the humanities and social sciences and led to the creation of new academic units and interdisciplinary fields, including Black studies, critical race and ethnic studies, gender and women's studies, disability studies, and Indigenous studies.[3] These fields, in turn, have nurtured innovative methodologies that are grounded in the standpoints of marginalized people, carried out through engagement and dialogue, and geared toward advancing social justice.[4] These methodologies provide the foundation for our work.

When we began planning for what would become the PCRG, we wanted to find a "road map" for carrying out collective activist research within the neoliberal academy. We eventually concluded that there can be no road map—no universal, step-by-step, how-to guidelines—for political activist scholarship. Instead, through conversations with radical antiracist, feminist, anticapitalist, and decolonial scholar-activists, we established a research methodology that values collectivity, multiplicity, and engagement. This praxis, which we call countersurveillant abolitionist research, has allowed us to navigate the challenges of collective activist research while providing effective research support for abolitionist movements and individuals targeted by state violence.

In this methodological appendix, we discuss countersurveillant abolitionist research and the methodological praxis that supports it. To be clear, we do not intend to position the PCRG as a model to be replicated; instead, we hope that a discussion of our praxis will help others navigate some of the tensions and challenges they face. We begin by discussing countersurveillant abolitionist research. We then describe our methodological praxis and explain how collectivity, multiplicity, and engagement facilitated our work. Finally, we close with some offerings for those interested in similar types of research.

COUNTERSURVEILLANT ABOLITIONIST RESEARCH

Our methodology is informed by a particular understanding of the relationship between knowledge production and social change. First, we center the knowledge of the most marginalized.[5] Our work is grounded in recognizing that oppressed people develop sophisticated and insightful (inciteful!) critiques of social and political power. For instance, young people of color develop a critical awareness of racialized surveillance through their everyday encounters with police. Our analysis builds on this subjugated knowledge, which Simone Browne calls "dark sousveillance."[6] Social movements are among the most important incubators of new knowledge. They raise pressing questions about domination and exploitation, produce new visions of liberation, and develop innovative frameworks for understanding social relations. Much of this takes place through dialogue and active engagement with more formal centers of knowledge production, including the work of scholar-activists. As Paulo Freire argues, such dialogue can provide a powerful source of critical new knowledge.[7] In the words of Robin D. G. Kelley, "the most radical ideas often grow out of a concrete intellectual engagement with the problems of aggrieved populations confronting systems of oppression."[8]

Second, we recognize that knowledge is a crucial resource for political organizing. Freire, bell hooks, and Bill Ayers highlight the dialectical relationship between developing a critical consciousness and understanding possibilities for change.[9] Grassroots organizations regularly engage with the work of radical scholars and conduct their own research as they conceptualize, design, and implement campaigns,[10] and confrontations help uncover hidden dimensions of power.[11] Direct action, for instance, can reveal a lot about tactics of repression. Similarly, confrontational meetings and court cases can shed light on discourses, strategies, mechanisms, and relations of power. In short, most organizers understand the importance of knowledge production, and many movements dedicate time and resources to identifying and addressing their research needs.

Yet social movements do not always have the capacity to fully address these needs. This is where collaborations between academics and organizers can be most effective. With access to training, funding, and dedicated time, academics can bring resources, knowledge, and unique skill sets to movement campaigns. Our labor time itself is an important resource. Much of the PCRG's research is work that our partners can and do carry out on their own, including Freedom of Information Act (FOIA) requests and analyses of publicly available policy documents. But our labor provides organizers with time to focus on other aspects of campaign building. Other aspects of academic research are more specialized, including archival research, interviews with public officials, quantitative analysis of large data sets, and engagement with political and social theory.

To be clear, this is not work that organizers are incapable of performing, but academic training enables scholar-activists to perform skilled labor on behalf of movements. While using these skills to support the work of our partners, the PCRG has also worked to democratize these skills and enhance our partners' research capacity through training workshops and participatory action research projects.

Finally, we understand that knowledge alone does not bring about change; social change is the product of organizing and struggle.[12] The most effective way to produce knowledge that can contribute to social transformation, therefore, is in dialogue with the ongoing campaigns of grassroots organizations. At its core, the PCRG approach to activist scholarship involves studying power in dialogue with social movements. Dialogue is the foundation of our commitment to making our research relevant and meaningful.[13] It helps ensure that our work remains aligned with the shifting research needs of communities in struggle. And these struggles are the motors of social transformation.

Countersurveillant abolitionist research involves movement-led, ethically grounded studies of imperial policing in support of struggles for abolition and liberation. Rather than studying movements and oppressed communities, we turn our research gaze upward to analyze and expose the structures and practices of power. Taking direction from organizers and people targeted by police—and inspired by the history of Copwatch and Police Watch movements—we uncover the practices, strategies, and frameworks that enable surveillance, policing, criminalization, incarceration, injury, and death.

We study power from two directions: top down and bottom up. From one angle, we conduct interviews with police officials, collect documents published by law enforcement agencies, and use FOIA requests to access public records. These data provide insight into the structures of policing and the mechanisms of coordination between agencies. From another angle, we engage with community members, organizers, and young people targeted by police. This allows us to take seriously subjugated, dark sousveillant knowledge that sheds light on practices of power that police officials are hesitant to discuss or simply do not understand.

The work of the PCRG is grounded in an abolitionist perspective. Our methodology is based on a commitment to studying the empire state and abolishing a world in which policing, criminalization, and empire are acceptable. These political and ethical commitments include an emphasis on relationships, partnerships, and coalition building.[14] "Political quilting" describes the work of building connections between movements and bringing together organizers, lawyers, researchers, journalists, and others, because it takes a coalition of actors occupying a range of different positions to do the work of abolition.[15] Abolitionist research, therefore, requires being in relationship with one another, sharing resources, creating space, showing up, and doing the work together. Through dialogue, we ensure that our research is aligned with the goals, needs, and interests of existing grassroots movements and community members directly impacted by state violence, with the ultimate goal of abolishing, not reforming, the violent structures and institutions.

THE METHODOLOGICAL PRAXIS OF COUNTERSURVEILLANT ABOLITIONIST RESEARCH

Arguing for the urgency of public sociology, Adia Harvey Wingfield asks, "what tactics and strategies allow sociologists to speak to and engage with publics who have historically been disenfranchised and excluded from actively participating in influencing policy?"[16] In response to Wingfield's question, the PCRG offers a methodological praxis that describes our imperfect, always-in-process approach to activist research. Rather than a model that can be replicated, we outline a methodological praxis that we regularly reassess and aim to improve.

Freire defines praxis as "reflection and action upon the world in order to transform it."[17] It is an iterative process by which action leads to reflection, reflection generates theory, and theory transforms action. As opposed to a standardized and dispassionate research process, praxis is both flexible and grounded in a commitment to transforming material conditions. For Freire, a transformative praxis can exist only through collective dialogue and engagement with those directly impacted by structural violence. Moreover, it is not enough merely to understand the world; action must accompany theory. As bell hooks states, "[the struggle to unite theory and practice] has been undermined . . . by elitist academics who believe their 'ideas' need not have any connection to real life."[18] Drawing on the work of Freire and hooks, we conceptualize our methodological praxis as valuing collectivity, multiplicity, and engagement. It has helped us remain grounded in shared theoretical, political, and ethical commitments while adapting and expanding our work in multiple directions through active engagement with our movement partners.

Collectivity

Research groups are often organized hierarchically, with power centralized in the hands of the principal investigator, who makes major decisions, assigns tasks for the research assistants to carry out, and becomes the main beneficiary of the research. The PCRG pushes back against this structure by insisting on the importance of collectivity. We developed the PCRG as a collective, horizontally organized research group, because producing knowledge that is relevant and useful to ongoing struggles against racist policing requires that decision-making power be shared among research team members and community partners.

In our praxis, collectivity is a description of *how* we do research. What we study, how we conduct research, how we share our findings, and who represents us are subject to collective discussions, consent, and approval. PCRG meetings are opportunities for collective dialogue about these and other issues. Each meeting offers time for people to check in, raise concerns, debate next steps, and make decisions. We seek to maintain a culture of open communication and collective decision-making. And we attempt to hold ourselves accountable and address tensions along the way.

Having a collective structure has allowed us to take our work in directions that no individual member working alone could have conceived. At various points in our work, different members have stepped up to represent the PCRG and share our findings at press conferences, local government meetings, community teach-ins and workshops, organization meetings, and conferences. And each member is able to use their networks, skills, and knowledge to make our work useful for communities targeted by police.

More than simply bringing together various individuals, collectivity must be built. After all, we are not exempt from social and academic hierarchies. Andy Clarno is a white, male, tenured professor leading a research collective composed of current and former graduate students who are also people of color, women, and/or immigrants. Andy is in a far less economically and politically precarious position than the rest of the group.

To address this imbalance, we attempt to center the voices and perspectives of students with marginalized subjectivities. Our meetings are spaces where students challenge Andy and one another. As Sudbury and Okazawa-Rey point out, "although radical scholars from subordinated social groups experience particular vulnerabilities arising from race, gender, and other systems of dominance, they also tap into genealogies of resistance and transformation."[19] PCRG meetings include reflective and generative dialogue about our project goals, priorities, and directions. They also provide a space for the research team to have honest (and sometimes difficult) conversations about problems, tensions, concerns, contradictions, and critiques of our work. These dialogues have been important for revealing internal disagreements and moments in which our practices have not lived up to our stated commitments.

We developed a shared theoretical orientation/lexicon by reading feminist, antiracist, and decolonial scholarship together. We also engage in open dialogues about ethics, theory, and practice. Among other important topics, we discuss the bridges and barriers between academic research and activist organizing, address tensions and contradictions that we encounter while doing research, explore innovative ways to collect data and communicate findings, and plan future steps for the PCRG.

Through this work, we have developed a set of shared political and ethical commitments. First, we are committed to supporting abolitionist movements that are working to end policing, incarceration, border securitization/militarization, and the military–industrial complex while building systems that actually produce safety and justice for our communities. The PCRG is also collectively committed to producing research that prioritizes the needs and goals of social movements and communities above the needs of academics. Researchers have a long history of extracting labor and knowledge from marginalized communities without contributing anything back. The PCRG works against extractive research practices by conducting research in support of campaigns organized by movements led by marginalized communities. These shared commitments provide a foundation on which we make decisions, build partnerships, and conduct our research.

Multiplicity

The PCRG began by conducting two simultaneous research projects—on Chicago Police Department gang databases and fusion centers—in response to the research needs of our community partners. Since that time, our work has expanded in multiple directions, including predictive algorithms, regional gang databases, entanglements between police and community organizations, interagency data-sharing agreements, and suspicious activity reports. We have facilitated youth-led participatory action research projects and cohosted a series of briefings on police surveillance in Chicago. And we now support numerous mobilizations against data-based policing and racialized surveillance. In short, our praxis is defined by multiplicity.

Our research involves multiple projects and methodologies simultaneously. This multiplicity is driven by our community partners, because political mobilizations develop more quickly than academic research, requiring us to remain flexible and responsive to shifting research needs. And the rapid expansion of social movements challenging racialized surveillance in Chicago has opened multiple opportunities for us to develop new partnerships and support new campaigns.

Moreover, the members of the PCRG not only bring unique knowledge and perspectives to the project; they also take our projects in new directions based on their subjectivities, political views, and relationships. For example, Haley insisted that the PCRG engage more with young people directly impacted by policing. On the basis of her relationships and experience, she challenged the initial framing of the PCRG as focusing solely on organizers and social movements. She asked how the PCRG's work would benefit young people who confront police surveillance, harassment, and arrest on a daily basis. Haley's interventions pushed the PCRG to develop youth-led participatory action research projects with Circles & Ciphers and the Arab American Action Network's Youth Organizing Program. As a result, our work has expanded in various directions and become a site where multiple, intersecting research projects, all focused on policing, exist simultaneously.

To say that the PCRG is multiple does not mean that we are simply a collection of individuals doing their own thing. Andy's coordination and the strength of our collective political and ethical commitments hold everything together. We continue to meet to share our research, provide feedback and critiques, and collectively produce knowledge.

Members working on one project often benefit from another project's findings and research methods. For example, findings about the function of fusion centers clarified the ways that gang databases circulate between law enforcement agencies. And our youth-led participatory action research projects impacted and were impacted by our findings on gang databases and fusion centers. As a result, we are now able to draw clear connections between various aspects of data-based policing, as we demonstrate in this book.

As a group, we encourage multiplicity by challenging archetypes of the ideal scholar-activist. We recognize that race, gender, sexuality, class, immigration status, parenting status, health, ability, and social networks, among other things, shape how individuals engage in activist research. As a result, the PCRG has become a space from which members can determine which skills, resources, and privileges they have and how they can leverage them to the benefit of our partner organizations. We also reject the problematic dichotomies between university–community and scholar–activist that have produced a taxing feeling of in-betweenness for many PCRG members. Instead of trying to resolve this liminality, our praxis lets us sit in this space, examine it, and develop third options outside of the two dominant choices. We reject "either–or" thinking and embrace "both–and" understandings of the PCRG and ourselves. Rather than choosing one side of the binary, we find it productive to critically examine the assumptions that ground dichotomies and highlight their failure to encapsulate and nourish our work.

We struggled with tensions but ultimately embraced messiness rather than purity and perfection. As Angela Davis, Gina Dent, Erica Meiners, and Beth Richie explain, an abolitionist feminist praxis "proclaims that we can and must do multiple things at the same time."[20] Working without a road map, allowing our work to expand in multiple directions, challenging dominant dichotomies, and embracing the process of research without a predetermined and fully conceptualized plan made it certain that our work would be imperfect and messy. We collected data and conducted analyses that could not address our partners' needs. Sometimes we employed new research methods inefficiently and analyzed data incorrectly. We have hit dead ends, paused projects, and changed directions. We have failed to attract funding. And we have let down our partners. But these missteps have proven generative. Over time, we abandoned the preoccupation with flawless, controlled research and allowed our collective work always to be in process. Mistakes are inevitable, and research is not linear. Our methodological praxis helps us embrace the possibilities of messiness and imperfection. This has fundamentally shaped us as researchers and members of movements.

Engagement

Above all, our methodology involves active engagement with our partners and with the shifting political context. Drawing inspiration from radical scholars, especially feminists of color, we set out to build strong, supportive research partnerships with our community collaborators. Through ongoing dialogues, we engage with these organizations as partners in the knowledge production process. They shape our research questions, inform our priorities and our timeline, envision innovative research methods, and develop original analysis of the data.

While we embrace the radical potential of political activist scholarship, we also take seriously feminist warnings about extractive forms of "engagement." As Judith Stacey and Linda Tuhiwai Smith point out, academics have a long history of building successful careers on the basis of knowledge extracted from oppressed and exploited communities while doing little to transform their conditions of existence.[21] The PCRG has attempted to remain accountable to our partners by building on our long-standing relationships and relying on open dialogue, reflective self-criticism, and a prioritization of our partners' research needs.

Rather than allowing hegemonic academic–community divisions to derail our work, our engagement helps us to navigate and disrupt these divisions. We have done this in several ways. First, we have ensured that there are organizers on the research team. The long-standing and ongoing involvement of members of the research team in social movement and transformative justice organizations helps challenge simple distinctions between researchers and organizers. Second, we have worked with two of our partners to facilitate youth-led research projects on surveillance. By sharing skills and supporting youth-led research, these projects respond to Tuhiwai Smith's call to develop the capacity of communities to conduct research for themselves.[22] Above all, the PCRG has attempted to confront divisions between academics, organizers, and community members by building accountable relationships grounded in trust, respect, and solidarity. Dialogue that is rooted in a shared commitment to the abolition of policing, prisons, incarceration, deportation, and militarism has been key to those relationships and to ensuring that our research is accountable and responsive to their needs.

Research team members participate in meetings, speak at events, and show up at demonstrations to support struggles for social justice. Although we could certainly do more, being present with our partners has been critical for building real relationships. During a series of program assessments, our community partners shared reflections on the PCRG. They emphasized the importance of having organizers on the research team, our commitment to following the lead of movement organizers, our ability to add research capacity to their campaigns, our regular report-backs at community meetings, and our presence and participation in campaign events as key to building trust and maintaining accountability.[23] Moreover, we share our findings with organizers and community members to give them additional resources on which to draw when they speak as experts. To be sure, our partners have deep knowledge and expertise grounded in their everyday experiences. But organizers suggest that officials often take their concerns more seriously when they share statistics or cite reports by university-based researchers. At teach-ins on the gang database or meetings with elected officials, therefore, community members and organizers regularly share personal knowledge alongside data from our reports. In effect, our methodology, grounded in engagement, helps to democratize expertise.

CLOSING OFFERINGS

To the extent that the PCRG has been successful, it is due to the collective efforts of three groups. First, a network of radical scholar-activists created space for this work at UIC and facilitated connections with organizers across the city. Second, members of the research team have contributed knowledge, labor, and connections to the project. Finally, our community partners' organizing makes our research relevant and impactful. A network of support, a dedicated research team, and effective community partners are essential foundations for a project like this.

Yet these foundations do not ensure success. The development of our project depended on the timing of our practicum, the composition of the research team, interpersonal relationships, and political dynamics in Chicago and nationwide. There is no guarantee that we could replicate this project under different circumstances.

Nevertheless, we can identify several principles that ground our approach to building a research collective and maintaining accountable partnerships with community organizations. First, open communication and ongoing dialogue are key to building trust within the research group and with community partners. Second, recognizing limitations and working through tensions are more productive than seeking purity and perfection. Third, it is important that the research remains rigorous yet flexible, because activist research is subject to intense scrutiny and has no blueprint and, often, little institutional support. Finally, remain humble, listen to your partners, and remember that the needs of the community come first.

Rather than promoting the PCRG as a model to be replicated, we share our experiences and our methodological praxis to provoke conversations about activist scholarship and community engagement. We hope this offers academics interested in this type of work an opening to critically reflect on how they might create, maintain, and navigate nonexploitative and accountable partnerships in solidarity with social movement organizations. We close this appendix with suggestions for scholars who want to engage in work similar to ours or to create space for activist scholarship in universities.

Above all, activist scholarship requires a fundamental reassessment of our approach to research. Relationships with movements and commitment to their goals supplant beliefs about the intrinsic value of research and scholarly knowledge. The members of our team have relationships and commitments to movements that exist before, beyond, and independently of the PCRG. The work (community building) begins before the work (research) is even conceptualized. We therefore warn against "parachuting researchers" who enter into relationships with communities and movements primarily for the purpose of conducting research.

We also encourage scholars to shift from a deficit lens to one of abundance. With the decreasing support for, and open attacks on, the social sciences and the humanities, many scholars understandably focus on competition for dwindling resources. However, the PCRG has pushed us to take inventory of the resources and power that scholars often take for granted and can leverage in service of movements. Our credentials and institutional affiliations provide us with space, time, skills, and money—as little as it may be—to which many movements do not have access but from which they would greatly benefit. We encourage scholars to find creative and strategic ways to make do with, distribute, and share these often-limited resources with movements as part of their research.

Possibly the most difficult suggestion is that scholars embrace uncertainty, conflict, and imperfection. Years of academic training discipline scholars to (over)emphasize certainty, strive for linearity, fear disruption and conflict, and seek perfection. On the basis of our experience, the best description for this kind of work is "messy." This is not necessarily a bad thing. We urge scholars to find messiness productive rather than disruptive. It helps us remain accountable to our partners and ourselves.

Scholar-activists also need space within universities where they can engage in this type of work. We urge administrators to fund activist scholarship. Lack of financial resources is one of the biggest obstacles we have faced. We have few resources to compensate our partners and research team members for their time and labor. This limits our capacity for data collection and analysis. With more funding, we could also address our partners' other research needs.

Furthermore, we encourage academic departments to provide more flexibility in their graduate and undergraduate training. Structured programs can create obstacles to this type of work. Flexibility in curriculum and program benchmarks can open space for courses on activist scholarship and for students—especially graduate students—to engage in activist research. Activist scholarship does not abide by traditional academic timelines. And neither do the outcomes.

In addition, universities must expand how they value scholarly contributions. The contributions that our partners found most valuable were not articles in academic journals; public reports, workshops, teach-ins, press conferences, meetings, and testimonies were far more beneficial to their needs. None of these would significantly benefit a grad student's job prospects or a junior scholar's case for tenure and promotion. That should change.

Last, and most important, we urge academics to rethink and challenge the university–community dichotomy. Far too often, "community engagement" positions the community as distinct from the university and situates the university as the only space where valid knowledge and intellectual labor exist. The PCRG highlights the problems with this dichotomy. Scholars can be community members, and community members can be scholars. Movement spaces are spaces of knowledge production and sophisticated intellectual dialogue. As a result, creating space for activist scholarship means seeing already existing community spaces as valuable intellectual sites.

We share our experiences and methodological praxis with the hope that they will help other scholar-activists produce impactful research for social movements in ways that exceed what we have been able to do. Ultimately, we want to support the emergence of politically engaged, transformative scholarship that can bring about liberation for oppressed communities.

Acknowledgments

The work that informed this book involved countless contributions by loving and generous people who truly believed in the ethos of the project. The book is a manifestation of collective labor over seven years by the Policing in Chicago Research Group. We have learned from each other and our collectivity. We have struggled together and alongside our movement families through challenging political realities. We have grown together, knowing that we still have a long way to go.

We are grateful for everyone who contributed research to this project. In 2017, our colleagues in Sociology 501 and 509 at the University of Illinois at Chicago dedicated important labor to helping get this project off the ground. They wrote Freedom of Information Act requests, collected archival materials, observed protests, and interviewed law enforcement officials and people directly impacted by imperial policing. We give an extra-special shout-out to the young people from the Arab American Action Network and Circles & Ciphers who participated in YPAR projects, blessing us with their brilliance, their courage, and their precious time. We are also grateful for Sage Kim, who provided invaluable quantitative support for this project and was part of our book journey for several years.

This work would not have been possible without the leadership, trust, generosity, and camaraderie of our partners from Black Youth Project 100, Organized Communities Against Deportations, the Arab American Action Network, Circles & Ciphers, Mijente, and the entire Erase the Database Coalition. Their valor and integrity in the struggle for liberation, their generosity in sharing space, and their knowledge and strength in organizing inspired and informed our research, analysis, and writing. We are especially grateful for the young people who fiercely and unapologetically led the way and shared their lives, struggles, and journeys with us in deep vulnerability. We hope this book is a reflection of our commitment and a reciprocal offering in support of the struggle toward freedom for everyone. We also want to thank colleagues at ACRE, the Invisible Institute, and the Lucy Parsons Labs for collaborations throughout the journey. Extra-special thanks go to Nadine Naber, Barbara Ransby, and Amalia Pallares for facilitating connections with key organizers early in the project.

Much gratitude goes to the centers and institutes at the University of Chicago Illinois that trusted our vision and funded our research: the Institute for Research on Race and Public Policy, particularly Amanda Lewis, Iván Arenas, and Deana Lewis; the Institute for Policy and Civic Engagement, especially Joseph Hoereth and Norma Ramos; and the Institute for the Humanities, led by Mark Canuel and Linda Vavra. We also received valuable seed grant funding from the Humanities without Walls consortium.

Thanks to Nicole Marroquin, Sarah-Ji Rhee, Monica Trinidad, Isaac Silver, Antonio Gutierrez, Miguel Lopez, Alec Dunn, and Edvetté Wilson Jones for the beautiful, powerful images that are part of this work. And much appreciation to Tim Johnson and Derek Gottlieb for stepping in at the last minute to help with the index.

We are ever grateful to colleagues at UIC and around the country who read early drafts and helped us workshop the manuscript. Deep gratitude to David Stovall, who was involved in initial discussions and has provided continued support throughout. Our analysis benefited from Northwestern University's CREA program with feedback from Nitasha Sharma and Geraldo Cadava, along with critical engagement from Nadine Naber and Robert Vargas. Many thanks to Joey Mogul, Beth Richie, Susila Gurusami, Anna Kornbluh, Yann Robert, Jeff Sklansky, and Beate Geissler, who provided important feedback at a workshop organized by the UIC Institute for the Humanities. Infinite gratitude goes to friends, colleagues, and costrugglers Claire Decoteau, Dylan Rodriguez, Michael Rodriguez-Muñiz, Rey Wences, Alyx Goodwin, Damon Williams, Muhammad Sankari, Moon Kie Jung, Tanya Golash Boza, Louise Cainkar, A. Naomi Paik, Sarah Brayne, and Ruth Gomberg Muñoz for reading the manuscript and providing deep and meaningful suggestions, challenges, and feedback. Without each of you, we could not have achieved the analytical clarity or political insight that we offer in this book. We deeply appreciate your willingness to keep it real and your trust in our ability to learn and do better.

In addition to the gifts bestowed on our collectivity by everyone named herein (and many more unnamed), we have deep and lasting gratitude to friends, family, comrades, and loved ones who nurtured each of us and allowed us to work on this project over the years.

Andy: Infinite thanks to my favorite people in the world: Felix and Claire. You inspire and sustain me, you keep me grounded, you push me forward, and you fill my life with love, happiness, water slides, and Jedi knights. I offer my respect and appreciation to the entire PCRG for your brilliance, your inspiration, and your perseverance.

Enrique: *Mil gracias* to Wilmer Catalan-Ramirez and Celene Adame, who opened the doors to their lives and taught me the meaning of critical hope and the fight for justice, and to OCAD, especially Rodrigo Anzures for his trust, leadership, and activism to contest state violence and create a better world for immigrants in Chicago. My participation in this book is in many ways a result of a journey started in Manaus, Brazil, and then continued in Santiago, Chile, a decade ago. Deep gratitude goes to Iran Lamego, Delza Lopes, Marcia Silva, Roberto Porto, Margareth Soares, Guillermo Cardona, Roberto Jaramillo, Rafael Alvear, Patricio Miranda, Rodrigo Garcia, Mike Van Treek, Oscar Alvear, and other friends and chosen family who have taught me an inspiring combination of love, solidarity, and struggle for justice. Finally, a special thank-you to Yesenia Vargas and Pascale Alvear-Vargas, with infinite love and respect for being with me unconditionally. Living with you is so much better.

Janaé: Many thanks to my BYP100 comrades, OCAD, and the entire Erase the Database Coalition in Chicago—you all are freedom fighters who continue to teach me how to fight. A special shout-out goes to Tania Unzueta Corrasco, whose leadership has taken our movements so far; it's been an honor to build, struggle, and co-conspire with you. I also thank my chosen Chicago family, Alexis Pegues-Wilson, for always showing up for me and reminding me of how I am when I inevitably forget. Finally, endless gratitude goes to my biggest sources of joy, Leldon and

Kofi Blue Bonsu-Love, for being everything I didn't know I needed. I love you to infinity and beyond.

Lydia: Thanks go to many. To my mentors over the years—Shawn Christian, Paula Krebs, Renée T. White, Jo Trigilio, Jyoti Puri, and Saher Selod—for leading me to this work, feeding my mind with authors, sharpening my critique, nurturing my spirit, and modeling values by which to work, protest, and live. To my family of origin—particularly my parents, Helen Hadley and Richard Dana—for deeply caring for and sustaining my physical body through the health battles that hung over multiple years of this work. To my partner, Ro White, for countless coconspirator huddles, hugs, and living room dances. To my chosen family of Chicago—notably Cal Lee Garrett, Meaghan L. Tomasiewicz, Haley Volpintesta, Enrique Alvear Moreno, Yesenia Rosario Vargas, and Allison Ng Leonard—for unconditional love and radical care.

Michael: I owe the beginning of my abolitionist journey to Owen Daniel-McCarter. Since then, so many members of my community have shaped my thinking and praxis in immeasurable ways. I am eternally grateful for the constant support of so many friends, colleagues, and family.

Ilā: Thanks to my dearest chosen human and nonhuman family, Savneet Talwar, Tiffany SanJose, Mellow Dorai (RIP), and Iris Kutty, for always showing up and being my personal hype-beings. Unending gratitude goes to my friends Mariame Kaba, Deana Lewis, and Rachel Caïdor for continuously politicizing me and for their humor; to my mentor and sister-friend Nadine Naber for always being available to teach, explore, and grow with me; to my spiritual family Radha Modi and JJ Uenten for always getting me unstuck; and to my entire human and nonhuman movement, spiritual, and queer village for being messy, angry, joyful, nurturing, and imaginative with me. Thanks to Nesreen Hasan, Jenine Wehbeh, Stacey Krueger, Muhammad Sankari, and Hatem Abudayyeh for their work, support with this research, random texts, laughter, and friendship. I have deep respect for my Amma, my Appa, and P&T Thatha for unconditional love and for giving me the freedom to travel toward my political work and fight for justice. All of you help me believe that we will win!

Haley: Thanks to my children—Elijah, Noah, Korah, and Micah—who have given me countless reasons to demand a better world, and to my thought-partner, Emmanuel, who patiently and lovingly supported me and this work. Thanks to Andrea for taking care of my children when I couldn't; her friendship and care sustained us, particularly when the grief was too hard to bear. My deepest gratitude goes to Circles & Ciphers for the years of trust and for co-creating spaces for radical imagination. Thanks to Wayne, Tati, Brianna, and Reef for their trust and leadership and to all of the young people whose experiences, insights, and analyses transformed this project; without them, we would have written a very different book. Endless love to Marquise, Jaquan, Devell, Taivon, Derrick, and Deshawn—rest in peace.

Abbreviations

AAAN	Arab American Action Network
ACRE	Action Center on Race and the Economy
ADL	Anti-Defamation League
ALPR	automated license plate reader
ATC	area technology center
ATF	U.S. Bureau of Alcohol, Tobacco, Firearms, and Explosives
BAH	Booz Allen Hamilton
BIPOC	Black, Indigenous, and people of color
BYP100	Black Youth Project 100
CANS	Community Alliance for Neighborhood Safety
CAP	Criminal Alien Program
CAPS	Chicago Alternative Policing Strategy
CBT	cognitive behavioral therapy
CCCT	U.S. Cabinet Committee to Combat Terrorism
CCSO	Cook County Sheriff's Office
CEIS	CPD Criminal Enterprise Information System
CIA	Central Intelligence Agency
CLEAR	CPD Citizen and Law Enforcement Analysis and Reporting data system
COINTELPRO	FBI Counter-Intelligence Program
CP4P	Communities Partnering for Peace
CPD	Chicago Police Department
CPIC	CPD Crime Prevention and Information Center
CRED	Creating Real Economic Destiny
CRO	Community Restoration Ordinance
CVE	Countering Violent Extremism
DEA	U.S. Drug Enforcement Agency

DHS	U.S. Department of Homeland Security
DOC	CPD Deployment Operations Center
DOJ	U.S. Department of Justice
FBI	Federal Bureau of Investigation
FOIA	Freedom of Information Act
FRSO	Freedom Road Socialist Organization
FTO	foreign terrorist organization
GKMC	Good Kids, Mad City
GVRS	CPD Gang Violence Reduction Strategy
HIDTA	High Intensity Drug Trafficking Area
IACP	International Association of Chiefs of Police
ICE	U.S. Immigration and Customs Enforcement
IIT	Illinois Institute of Technology
INS	U.S. Immigration and Naturalization Service
INV	Institute for Nonviolence Chicago
IPR	Northwestern University Institute for Policy Research
ISP	Illinois State Police
ISR	CPD investigatory stop report
JTTF	Joint Terrorism Task Force
MLAT	Mutual Legal Assistance Treaty
NNSC	National Network for Safe Cities
OCAD	Organized Communities Against Deportations
OCS	Operation Community Shield
OEMC	Office of Emergence Management and Communications
OIG	City of Chicago Office of Inspector General
OIIG	Cook County Office of the Independent Inspector General
OVB	Operation Vulgar Betrayal
OVS	Operation Virtual Shield
PATF	Chicago Police Accountability Task Force
PCRG	Policing in Chicago Research Group
PEP	Priority Enforcement Program
PFLP	Popular Front for the Liberation of Palestine
PLO	Palestine Liberation Organization
POD	police observation device
PSN	Project Safe Neighborhoods

PSPC	Partnership for Safe and Peaceful Communities
READI	Rapid Employment and Development Initiative
RGID	Regional Gang Intelligence Database
RICO	Racketeering Influenced and Corrupt Organizations (Act)
SAR	suspicious activity report
SDSC	CPD Strategic Decision Support Center
SSL	CPD Strategic Subjects List
STIC	ISP Statewide Terrorism Intelligence Center
UIC	University of Illinois at Chicago
USCIS	U.S. Citizenship and Immigration Services
WCO	Welcoming City Ordinance
YPAR	youth-led participatory action research

Glossary of Key Terms and Concepts

abolition A political vision that aims to dismantle structures of organized violence (i.e., imprisonment, policing, deportation, and surveillance) while building substitutive projects, institutions, and conceptions for collectively regulating our social lives and redressing shared problems through a collective commitment to the well-being of all peoples.

carceral liberalism Disciplinary projects grounded in the logics of individual responsibility and carceral expansion. They offer services and support to people who make "good" choices, while expanding the power to punish people who make "bad" choices.

countersurveillant abolitionist research A methodology for movement-led, ethically grounded studies of policing that support struggles for abolition. The analysis focuses on exposing and critiquing structures and practices that enable organized violence. The methodological praxis values collectivity, multiplicity, and engagement.

criminal archetypes Recurring representations that evoke powerful emotional responses and shape how a person's appearance or behavior will be interpreted, despite individual circumstances or realities. The gang member, the terrorist, and the criminal alien are racialized criminal archetypes that reduce people to dangerous figures who deserve arrest, deportation, or elimination.

dark sousveillance A term developed by Simone Browne to describe a critical awareness of and strategies for navigating racialized surveillance, including tactics to render people and communities invisible, to co-opt or resist the tools of surveillance, and to turn a countersurveillant lens on systems of power.

data-based policing Use of advanced technology to generate data, which police store in massive databases, analyze to determine deployments, and share with other agencies. This process transforms racialized surveillance and criminal archetypes into supposedly objective "facts" about individuals and communities.

dif/fusion Highlights the proliferation of state and private sector carceral agencies (diffusion) as well as the mechanisms that enable coordination within the multiscalar networks of imperial policing (fusion).

disavowed collusion A mechanism of interagency coordination based on the circulation of data when the agencies deny that they are cooperating.

empire Transnational political formations that exercise power over racially devalued populations through territorial conquest, political domination, cultural imposition, labor exploitation, and resource extraction.

fetishism (of data) The term *fetish* signifies the popular belief that certain objects have mysterious properties, including the magical ability to erase the social conditions of their production. The claim that policing strategies are "data driven" activates popular assumptions about scientific objectivity, enabling people to accept police data as "facts" while erasing the conditions and relations through which police data are produced.

focused deterrence A concept coined by the National Network for Safe Cities to describe programs that seek to identify and intervene with "high-risk" individuals to prevent gun violence.

fusion centers High-tech rooms located in police headquarters that are designed to facilitate data sharing between local, state, tribal, and federal agencies. In big cities, they are also used by police to monitor surveillance equipment, analyze police data, and shape deployments.

imperial policing The extensive, multiscalar network of repressive agencies that collectively work to police the racialized poor, enforce order, and suppress struggles for social justice. Three interconnected police wars constitute the pillars of imperial policing in Chicago: the War on Crime, the War on Terror, and the War on Immigrants.

liberalism A set of ideas grounded in individual rights and liberties. Liberalism holds individuals responsible for making good "choices" without considering the structural conditions that shape their lives. Infused with racial logics that deny the full humanity of subject people, liberalism has been used to justify slavery, colonialism, and empire.

neoliberalism A capitalist ideology that prioritizes "free market" competition, extends business logics to all spheres of life, and holds individuals responsible for their own well-being. It finds expression in corporate-friendly policies, cuts to social spending, and a reliance on repression to contain crises and enforce social order.

nonprofit–industrial complex A network of academics, philanthropists, and nonprofits that work together to expand social controls, depoliticize grassroots movements, and roll back state spending on social welfare.

organized abandonment The process of governing populations through austerity and purposeful neglect, framing many humans and other life-forms as surplus to the contemporary political-economic order.

organized violence The ways that states dispossess and control the already impoverished and marginalized through criminalization, policing, prisons, detention, and deportation.

police wars Imperial strategies to contain crises, enforce order, and protect the powerful. They are grounded in repressive violence and racialized criminal archetypes but may also incorporate carceral liberal strategies.

political quilting The work of building connections between movements and bringing together organizers, lawyers, researchers, journalists, and others because it takes a coalition of actors occupying a range of different positions to do the work of abolition.

punitive exceptions Explicit denials of sanctuary protection that create a formal mechanism for cooperation between local police and Immigration and Customs Enforcement.

racial capitalism Highlights the connections between capital accumulation and racialized forms of dispossession, exploitation, and exclusion. Capitalism cannot be understood without attention to processes of racial formation that define categories of difference, assign differential value to human lives and labor, and create unequal vulnerability to premature death.

respectability narratives Representations of marginalized individuals that depict them as sharing traits, values, and morals that align with the dominant definition of "respectability." Respectability politics utilizes these narratives as the basis for enacting social, political, and legal change.

sanctuary The policy and/or practice of offering refuge or protection for targeted peoples (e.g., immigrants under deportation orders).

Liberal sanctuary describes sanctuary cities that offer rights and protections for "law-abiding" immigrants while denying these rights to noncitizens classified as "criminals."

Abolitionist sanctuary is a radical alternative to liberal sanctuary. It combines the logic of providing safety and protection for all members of targeted communities (sanctuary) with the goal of undoing the structures and conditions through which people become vulnerable in the first place (abolition).

settler colonialism The processes and structures through which settler populations establish and institutionalize their domination over Indigenous land and people through dispossession, elimination, and subjugation.

War on Crime Primarily an effort to contain or eliminate the Black poor rendered disposable by neoliberal restructuring. In Chicago, the front line of the War on Crime is known as the War on Gangs.

War on Immigrants An imperial project to control the flow and regulate the behavior of migrants from the Global South displaced by war, repression, and capitalism.

War on Terror An imperial project to support U.S. hegemony in the greater Middle East, corporate access to inexpensive oil, and Israeli settler colonialism in Palestine.

weaponized data The deployment of data as a weapon of policing. It involves producing data through racialized deployments and criminal archetypes (production), transforming those data into supposedly objective "facts" (cleansing), and sharing the data throughout the carceral webs of empire to further criminalize targeted communities (circulation).

white supremacy The dominant racial project behind modern racial formations, including efforts to exploit, assimilate, exclude, and eliminate Black people, Indigenous people, and other people of color.

Notes

INTRODUCTION

1   E.g., Geib 2015. Although popularized by Saskia Sassen's (2001) critical scholarship on the neoliberal restructuring of corporate and state power, the term *global city* has become a marketing tool for elites.

2   Darren Bailey, the 2022 Republican candidate for Illinois governor, repeatedly used the term *hellhole* to describe Chicago. See Bauer 2022.

3   Ackerman and Stafford 2015; Ackerman 2015b.

4   Personal communication from Damon Williams, May 2023.

5   Wolfe 2006; Coulthard 2014; Simpson 2017; Estes 2019.

6   Robinson (1983) 2000; Melamed 2011; Kelley 2017; Kundnani 2023; Gilmore 2022; Bhattacharyya 2018; Clarno and Vally 2023.

7   Mills 1997; Bonilla-Silva 2001; Jung, Costa Vargas, and Bonilla-Silva 2011; Jung 2015; Maher 2021; Rodriguez 2021.

8   Lenin (1916) 1963; Harvey 2003; Steinmetz 2005; Go 2008, 2023.

9   Cohen 1997; Mohanty 2003; Ferguson 2004; Spade 2015.

10 Black Hawk (1833) 2008.

11 Jung (2015) argues that the relative strength of white domination determined why some conquered territories were "incorporated" into the United States, while others remained "unincorporated."

12 For an analysis of the Irish as a target of transnational racialized police repression, see Go 2023.

13 Mitrani 2013.

14 Mitrani 2013. Before the creation of the CPD, Chicago elites relied on a county sheriff, constables connected to the municipal court, and a night watch. See also Flinn 1887.

15 Mitrani 2013, 194.

16 Mitrani 2013; Balto 2019.

17 Drake and Cayton 2015; Ingatiev 1995; Roediger 2022.

18 Muhammad 2010; Shabazz 2015.

19 Balto 2019, 2.

20 Mitrani 2013.

21 Goodman 2020, 62–71.
22 Haas 2010; Lebrón 2017.
23 Taylor 2019; Ralph 2019.
24 Balto 2019. See also chapter 3.
25 See chapter 1.
26 Institute for Research on Race and Public Policy 2017, 2018, 2019, 2020, 2023.
27 There are also pockets of multiracial poverty on the North Side, as well as middle-class Black and Latinx spaces on the South and West Sides.
28 Brodkin 1998.
29 Wilson 1996; Fernandez 2012; Estes 2019.
30 Balto 2019.
31 Balto 2019.
32 Haas 2010; Balto 2019; Sonnie and Tracy 2011; Losier 2018.
33 Haas 2010.
34 Skidmore, Owings, and Merrill 1973.
35 Clarno 2017.
36 This list, which includes both current and recent headquarters, is not stable because neoliberal competition for corporate investment incentivizes cities to lure corporations with tax breaks and business-friendly policies. See Harvey 1989.
37 Weber 2015; Tresser 2018; Poulos 2022.
38 Hong 2015; Ferguson 2004; Lorde 1984.
39 Walia 2021.
40 Theodore 2003, 2021.
41 There are exceptions to this trend, particularly in transportation, sanitation, education, and the postal service, where unions have helped protect the jobs of Black workers.
42 Venkatesh 2009; Theodore 2021.
43 Betancur 2011.
44 Smith 1996; Gordon 2022.
45 Smith 2013; Robinson 2021.
46 Kozol 2005.
47 Lipman 2007, 2011.
48 Richie 2012; Allard 2006.
49 Davis 2006; Walia 2021; Caldeira 2000.
50 Naber 2014.
51 Clarno 2017; Walia 2021; Dillon 2018; Peck 2010; Wacquant 2009; Lebrón 2019.
52 Dillon 2018.
53 Gilmore 2015.
54 Ritchie 2017; Nguyen 2019; Schenwar and Law 2020; Ben-Moshe 2020.
55 Through a close reading of U.S. Supreme Court cases, Moon-Kie Jung documents two key features that distinguish an empire state from a nation-state. First, the lands over which an empire state claims sovereignty are ruled differentially on

the basis of race. Second, empire states subject different populations to distinct but interrelated forms of racial rule. In short, Jung (2015, 71–72) argues, "the racial subjection of one [group] was related to the racial subjection of the other, evidencing a common field of white supremacy." Inspired by the work of Stuart Hall, Jung describes the overall structure of racial rule in an empire state as a "unified but differentiated field" (80).

56 Jung 2015.

57 McCoy 2009; Loyd, Mitchelson, and Burridge 2012; Khalili 2013; Camp and Heatherton 2016; Lebrón 2017; Seigel 2018; Schrader 2019; Go 2020, 2023; Balko 2021; Elliot-Cooper 2021.

58 Naber 2014.

59 Parenti 2003; Browne 2015; Zuboff 2019; Brayne 2021.

60 Du Bois (1935) 1998; Hall et al. 1978.

61 Hall 1980.

62 Seigel 2018; Schrader 2019.

63 See chapter 5.

64 McQuade 2019.

65 Brayne 2017; Eubanks 2017; Ferguson 2016; Zuboff 2019.

66 To be clear, these are not the only police wars. Police also criminalize sex and wage war on people who are unhoused, gender nonconforming, nonheteronormative, confronting mental illness, and more.

67 President Lyndon Johnson declared the War on Crime in 1965, Mayor Daley launched the War on Gangs in 1969, and President Richard Nixon announced the War on Drugs in 1971. We use the term *War on Crime* broadly to encompass all three of these overlapping police wars.

68 Cohen 1997; Ferguson 2004; Richie 2012; Hong 2015; Spade 2015; Ritchie 2017.

69 Rios 2011.

70 Lovato 2020; Elliot-Cooper 2021; Villela 2021; Muñiz 2022.

71 The War on Terror has transimperial dimensions as well. For instance, Russia has pursued its own version of the "War on Terror," from Afghanistan in the 1980s to Chechnya in the 1990s to Syria in the 2010s. At some points, the United States and Russia have coordinated efforts in pursuit of their "Wars on Terror," but competing imperial interests often override these convergences.

72 Naber 2014.

73 Macías-Rojas 2016; Lovato 2020; Paik 2016; Hernandez 2010; Nevins 2002; Rosas 2012.

74 Armenta 2017; Muñiz 2022.

75 Legomsky 2007; Stumpf 2006, 2013; Chacón 2007; Bosworth and Kaufman 2011; Loyd, Mitchelson, and Burridge 2012; Miller 2005; Varsanyi 2010; Provine et al. 2016.

76 Golash-Boza 2015.

77 Ackerman and Stafford 2015; Ackerman 2015a.

78 CBS Chicago 2020.

79 Balko 2021.

80 Alexander 2010, 2.

81 Mogul, Ritchie, and Whitlock 2011. Bringing a focus on sexuality into studies of criminalization, Mogul, Ritchie, and Whitlock analyze queer criminal archetypes, such as the "queer killer," "disease spreader," and "sexual predator."

82 Fanon (1952) 2008; Said 1978.

83 Cacho 2012.

84 Note that immigration is a *civil* rather than a *criminal* offense—but crimmigration studies have documented the increasing overlap between the two fields.

85 Paik 2016.

86 Russell-Brown 2008.

87 Muhammad 2010.

88 Hall et al. (1978) demonstrate that racial archetypes also circulate transnationally. They argue that the figure of the "black mugger"—imported from the United States—was instrumental for criminalizing the Black British proletariat and containing a crisis of racial capitalism in the United Kingdom during the 1970s.

89 Muhammad 2010. John Bardes (2020) and Singh (2019) argue that Blackness was criminalized even during slavery.

90 Rodriguez 2021, 181.

91 Jung 2022.

92 Said 1978; Shaheen 1984; Alsultany 2012; Kumar 2012; Naber 2012; Kundnani 2014.

93 Naber 2012.

94 Bosniak 2008; Nevins 2002; Chavez 2013.

95 Nevins 2002; Macías-Rojas 2016.

96 Macías-Rojas 2016, 59, 75.

97 Armenta 2017.

98 Cacho 2012.

99 Cacho 2012, 31.

100 Singh 2019, 55–56. Neocleous (2021) insists that police power and war power have been entangled from their inception.

101 Singh 2019; Schrader 2019; Rodriguez 2021; Williams 2022.

102 Foucault (1975) 1995; Seigel 2018; Rodriguez 2019.

103 We are not the first to use this concept. See Macías-Rojas 2021; Tillman 2022; Pillai 2023.

104 As Go (2020) explains, "professionalization" reforms have historically intensified the militarization of policing.

105 Davis et al. 2022; Kaba 2021; INCITE! 2006; Richie 2012; Ransby 2018; Gilmore 2022.

106 Gilmore, forthcoming.

107 Kaba 2020.

108 Rodriguez 2019.

109 Moten and Harney 2013, 42.

110   Critical Resistance and INCITE! 2006, 226.
111   Rodriguez 2019, 1611.
112   Rodriguez 2021.
113   Ferguson 2004, 65.
114   Richie 2012; Mogul, Ritchie, and Whitlock 2011.
115   https://m4bl.org/policy-platforms/the-preamble/.
116   Kaba and Hayes 2018.
117   Gilmore 2020. See also Berger, Kaba, and Stein 2017.
118   Rodriguez 2019, 1578.
119   Haas 2010; Sonnie and Tracy 2011.
120   Rosa, Trinidad, and May 2016.
121   Mogul 2015.
122   Kaba 2016; Taylor 2018.
123   Ransby 2018.
124   Collins 1990, 2013; hooks 2003; Kelley 2002; Smith (1999) 2012; Stacey 1988; Sudbury and Okazawa-Rey 2009.

1. WEAPONIZED DATA

Andy Clarno is the lead researcher and author of this chapter.

1   Careless 2007.
2   Pastore 2004; Skogan et al. 2005.
3   https://chicagopolicesurveillance.com/.
4   Chicago Police Department 2020a.
5   Hollywood et al. 2019.
6   Spielman 2020.
7   Brayne 2021, 138.
8   Brayne 2021, 101.
9   Browne 2015, 10.
10   Browne 2015; Parenti 2003.
11   Browne 2015, 79.
12   Browne 2015, 42.
13   Benjamin 2019, 82.
14   Eubanks 2017, 4–5.
15   Eubanks 2017, 178, 182. Brayne (2021, 6) uses the term *techwashing* to refer to the same process. *Mathwashing* or *techwashing* refers to the use of algorithms and other tools of data analysis to conceal structural inequality. It is similar to concepts like *greenwashing* (using environmental language to conceal destructive practices) and *pinkwashing* (using support for LGBTQ rights to conceal settler-colonial or imperial practices). Our analysis of the "cleansing" of data builds on these frameworks.

16   Benjamin 2019.
17   Browne 2015, 21.
18   Espeland and Stevens 2008; Hansen 2015; Brayne and Christin 2021.
19   Chicago Police Department 2018.
20   U.S. Department of Justice 2017; Police Accountability Task Force 2016; State of Illinois v. City of Chicago, case 17-cv-6260 (N.D. Ill. Aug. 16, 2018).
21   Go 2020, 2023.
22   Zuboff 2019.
23   Murakawa 2014; Hinton 2016; Camp 2016; Balto 2019; Rodriguez 2021.
24   https://vault.fbi.gov/cointel-pro.
25   Chicago Alliance for Neighborhood Safety, n.d.
26   Schrader 2019. Demonstrating the circulation of imperial policing, Vollmer infused local policing with knowledge gained through his experience conducting counterinsurgency operations in the Philippines with the U.S. military. See Go 2020.
27   Buslik and Maltz 1998; Pastore 2004; Jefferson 2020.
28   Balto 2019. While emphasizing technology, Wilson also promoted community engagement to increase public trust and expand surveillance. He established "Officer Friendly" programs and "Police–Community Workshops" in each district. Although never high on the department's lists of priorities, these programs provided positive press coverage and added legitimacy to Wilson's broader package of reforms. See Detzer 1966.
29   Hinton 2016.
30   Hinton 2016; Seigel 2018; Jefferson 2020.
31   Maltz et al. 1989; Buslik and Maltz 1998.
32   Jefferson 2020, 64.
33   Maltz et al. 1989; Maltz 1993.
34   Block and Green 1994; Block and Block 1995.
35   Skogan and Hartnett 1997.
36   Booz Allen Hamilton 1992a, 1992b. Not incidentally, BAH also does privatized intelligence work for the DHS and the National Security Agency (NSA). The contractor gained notoriety when its employee Edward Snowden released a trove of documents on NSA surveillance operations.
37   Skogan and Hartnett 1997, 60.
38   Chicago Police Department 1993, 3. The CPD explained that the new strategy was a response to contradictions generated by Wilson's reforms. "The very technology that O. W. Wilson and others introduced to help professionalize law enforcement—squad cars, radios, 911 systems, and the like—ended up isolating officers from the citizens they were sworn to serve and protect. Ironically, this isolation from the community cut police off from a critical source of information and support they needed to succeed under the traditional model." Chicago Police Department 1993, 8.
39   We Charge Genocide, n.d., 3–4. See also Yan 2021.

40 Skogan and Hartnett 1997.

41 An early use of the term *data fusion* appears in a 1998 article on CAPS by CPD commander Marc Buslik and UIC professor Mike Maltz (1998, 122).

42 Buslik and Maltz 1998.

43 Chicago Police Department 1993, 17.

44 Rich 1996. ICAM was built with funding from the Illinois Motor Vehicle Theft Prevention Council, which was established by the insurance industry, based on an assessment that computerized mapping could reduce the number of auto thefts in Chicago, thereby saving the insurance industry millions of dollars each year.

45 U.S. Department of Justice 2017, 14.

46 Police Accountability Task Force 2016, 14; U.S. Department of Justice 2017, 14.

47 Wexler, Wycoff, and Fischer 2007; Skogan et al. 2003; Skogan et al. 2005; Jefferson 2020. Before creating CLEAR, the CPD and Oracle developed the Criminal History Records Information System, a data system that police rejected as more burdensome than helpful.

48 Wexler, Wycoff, and Fischer 2007, 41.

49 Calculations by the PCRG based on a review of contracts between the CPD and Oracle.

50 In 2007, there were already 182 data columns; see DuBois et al. 2007. Although more recent data are difficult to confirm because the CPD refuses Freedom of Information Act requests for information on the structure of CLEAR, in 2017, commander Jonathan Lewin explained that CLEAR has approximately seven hundred columns (interview with Jonathan Lewin, July 2017).

51 Pastore 2004.

52 Skogan et al. 2005, i.

53 Skogan et al. 2005, 51.

54 Skogan et al. 2005, 50; Jefferson 2020, 109–10.

55 Pastore 2004.

56 Skogan et al. 2005, 40.

57 Skogan et al. 2005, 22–23.

58 U.S. Department of Justice 2017.

59 Skogan et al. 2003, 70.

60 Office of Inspector General 2019, 47.

61 Skogan et al. 2003, foreword.

62 Pastore 2004.

63 Bureau of Justice Assistance 2005, 18.

64 Marx (1867) 1906, 81–87.

65 Rodriguez-Muñiz 2021, 7.

66 Hall et al. 1978, 13.

67 Alonso and Starr 1987; Curtis 2001.

68 Espeland and Stevens 2008; Berman and Hirschman 2018.

69 Rodriguez-Muñiz 2021.

70 American Civil Liberties Union of Illinois 2015.

71 Jefferson 2020, 154–55.

72 Nguyen 2019.

73 Macías-Rojas 2016.

74 Benjamin 2019.

75 In addition, as Ricarda Hammer and Tina Park (2021) explain, advanced technology relies on globalized racial and colonial relations to extract raw material, perform digital labor, and test new technology.

76 Office of Inspector General 2019, 33.

77 https://chicagopolicesurveillance.com/.

78 Schwartz 2013.

79 https://www.chicago.gov/city/en/depts/oem/provdrs/tech/svcs/link_your_cameras.html. See also Ward 2021.

80 Demonstrating the rapid expansion of video surveillance in Chicago, various estimates suggest that the city had access to ten thousand cameras in 2011, twenty-seven thousand by 2016, thirty-five thousand in 2019, and fifty thousand by 2022.

81 Jefferson 2020, 179.

82 https://chicagopolicesurveillance.com/; https://www.eff.org/sls/tech/automated-license-plate-readers/faq.

83 https://chicagopolicesurveillance.com/.

84 https://endpolicesurveillance.com/.

85 Winston 2015.

86 https://chicagopolicesurveillance.com/; https://www.eff.org/pages/cell-site-simulatorsimsi-catchers.

87 https://chicagopolicesurveillance.com/.

88 Greenwald 2015; Snowden 2020.

89 See Snyder 2020 on the use of spy planes for surveillance and countersurveillance in Baltimore.

90 Schuba and Main 2021.

91 Brayne 2021; Jefferson 2020.

92 Ruppenthal 2019. Chicago Public Schools also uses social media monitoring software; see Liebowitz 2019.

93 Hvistendahl 2021; PathAR, n.d.

94 Chicago Police Department 2020b.

95 Hvistendahl 2022.

96 Bauer 2020. See also Pratt and Gorner 2020.

97 Zuboff 2019.

98 Patton et al. 2018; King 2019.

99 Schuba 2020b.

100 Schuba 2020a.

101 https://chicagopolicesurveillance.com/.

102 Schuba 2020b.

103 Browne 2015.

104 Ravichandran 2022.

105 Chief Jonathan Lewin, quoted in Genetec, n.d.

106 The SDSC initiative was developed in cooperation with Sean Malinowski, famous for shaping the predictive policing strategy of the Los Angeles Police Department. The ATCs were funded by a $10 million grant from billionaire hedge fund manager Ken Griffin. See Gorner 2018; Main 2018.

107 Fourcade 2016; Krippner and Hirschman 2020.

108 Office of Inspector General 2019.

109 Arab American Action Network and Policing in Chicago Research Group 2022.

110 Cacho 2012.

111 Lageson 2020.

112 Miller 2021, 228.

113 Pager 2009.

114 Alexander 2010.

115 Fassin 2013.

116 Arab American Action Network and Policing in Chicago Research Group 2022.

117 Office of Inspector General 2019.

118 Hatch 2022.

119 Hall et al. 1978.

120 Office of Inspector General 2021, 26.

121 Hansen 2015; Brayne 2021; Cruz 2022; Ferguson 2016; Hong 2015.

122 Interview by the PCRG with Commander Marc Buslik, June 2017.

123 Alderden et al. 2012.

124 Skogan et al. 2005.

125 Interview by the PCRG with CPD official, August 2017.

126 Interview by PCRG with Chief Jonathan Lewin, July 2017.

127 Alderden et al. 2012.

128 Pastore 2004.

129 Perry et al. 2013; Kennedy 2015.

130 In the 1980s, Wernick conducted research for the U.S. military on predictive algorithms that could distinguish targets from other objects, especially using night-vision technology; see Wernick 1991; Wernick and Morris 1986.

131 See Fourcade 2016.

132 Interview by the PCRG with Commander Marc Buslik, June 2017.

133 Saunders, Hunt, and Hollywood 2016.

134 Interview by the PCRG with Commander Mac Buslik, June 2017.

135 See chapter 3.

136 Brian Jefferson (2020, 123) argues that individualized predictive policing has "no practical significance" because it merely reproduces the focus on people living in areas targeted through hot spot policing.

137 Office of Inspector General 2020. Earlier that year, the CPD renamed the SSL the "Crime Victimization Risk Model." See Chicago Police Department n.d.-a and -b.

138 Eubanks 2017, 178, 182.

139 Rodriguez-Muñiz 2021.

140 Balto 2019, 199.

141 Gilmore 2007; Wilson 2009; Neely and Samura 2011; Delaney 2010; Herbert and Brown 2006; Jefferson 2018; Brayne 2017; Van Cleve and Mayes 2015; Benjamin 2019.

142 Ferguson 2018; Anselin 1995; Jefferson 2018.

143 Wang 2018, 42.

144 Sweeney and Fry 2018.

145 The image is inspired by Harvey's (2017) analysis of the "madness" of capitalist reason.

146 Benjamin 2019, 83.

147 Rodriguez-Muñiz 2021; Chavez 2013.

148 Hall et al. 1978.

149 Farnia 2022. Jefferson (2020, 130) traces these data-sharing processes to slave patrols and frontier wars.

150 Bureau of Justice Assistance 2005, 3.

151 Kean and Hamilton 2004, 418.

152 Bureau of Justice Assistance 2005.

153 McQuade 2019, 15.

154 Skogan et al. 2005.

155 Office of Inspector General 2019, 27.

156 Now the Indiana HIDTA.

157 See chapter 6.

158 McQuade 2019, 65–77.

159 U.S. Department of Homeland Security 2018.

160 Chicago Police Department 2020a.

161 Price 2013.

162 Chicago Police Department 2011.

163 Armenta 2017.

164 Muñiz 2022.

165 See https://www.state.gov/wp-content/uploads/2019/02/12925-Israel-Law-Enforcement-MLAT-1.26.1998.pdf.

166 Brayne 2017; Ritchie 2017; Schenwar and Law 2020.

167 Ferguson 2016; Zuboff 2019.

168 American Civil Liberties Union 2022.

169 Espeland and Stevens 2008; Hansen 2015.

170 McQuade 2019.

171 Interview with Commander Marc Buslik, June 2017. On the other hand, the CPD does not currently provide detailed crime data to the FBI's National Incident Based Reporting System, preferring only to provide summary statistics through the Uniform Crime Reporting system.

172 Chicago Police Department 2018.

173 State of Illinois v. City of Chicago, case 17-cv-6260 (N.D. Ill. Aug. 16, 2018).
174 See Balto 2019; Brayne 2017.

2. FOCUSED DETERRENCE

Lydia Dana and Andy Clarno are the lead researchers and authors of this chapter.

1 City of Chicago 2020.
2 City of Chicago 2020, 3.
3 The "public health" approach has informed the work of street outreach organizations in Chicago for more than twenty years, most notably through CeaseFire/
   Cure Violence. Although it claims to address "root causes" of violence, most
   interventions informed by this approach concentrate on interrupting the spread
   of violence through social networks.
4 City of Chicago 2020, 22, 26.
5 Chicago Police Department 2018.
6 City of Chicago 2020, 26.
7 Kennedy 2019a.
8 O'Donnell and Aviles 2017.
9 The report treats this as an expansive category, including not only active participation but also a "reputation" for involvement or a "family history" of gang
   activity.
10 City of Chicago 2020, 102.
11 City of Chicago 2020, 26.
12 City of Chicago 2020, 22, 65.
13 City of Chicago 2020, 72.
14 City of Chicago 2020, 70.
15 Kennedy 2019a.
16 del Pozo et al. 2022.
17 Lanfear et al. 2023.
18 INCITE! 2007; Willse 2015; Spade 2016.
19 Rodriguez 2007, 2021; Bhungalia 2024.
20 Stuart 2016, 6.
21 Haney 2010; Rios 2011; Miller 2014; Nguyen 2019; Schenwar and Law 2020;
    Dana 2023; Fong 2023.
22 Mills 1997; Murakawa 2014; Camp 2016; Rodriguez 2021.
23 Fassin 2011; Khalili 2013; Esmeir 2014; Weizman 2017.
24 Gilmore 2017, 235.
25 Macías-Rojas 2016; Tillman 2022; Pillai 2023. We learned of Tillman's and
    Pillai's work just days before our book went to press. We are excited to enter into
    dialogue with these radical scholars of color to develop this important concept.
26 Tillman 2022, 3.

27   Kennedy 2019a.
28   Kennedy 2011, 35.
29   Kennedy 2011.
30   Papachristos, Meares, and Fagan 2007; McGarrell et al. 2009.
31   Kennedy 2011, 221.
32   Papachristos, Meares, and Fagan 2007, 10–11.
33   Papachristos 2009, 2011; Papachristos, Hureau, and Braga 2013; Papachristos et al. 2015; Papachristos and Bastomski 2018.
34   Papachristos 2009, 75.
35   https://nnscommunities.org/.
36   Kennedy 2019a.
37   Kennedy 2019a.
38   Kennedy 2019a.
39   Interview by the authors with David Kennedy, November 2018.
40   Moore 1978; Hagedorn (1988) 1998, 2015; Conquergood and Siegel 1990; Venkatesh 1997; Vigil 2002; Brotherton and Barrios 2004; Durán 2013, 2018; Aspholm 2019; Stuart 2020.
41   Interview by the authors with David Kennedy, November 2018.
42   Kennedy 2011, 270.
43   Kennedy 2011, 43.
44   Interview by the authors with David Kennedy, November 2018.
45   Interview by the authors with David Kennedy, November 2018.
46   Kennedy 2015.
47   Kennedy 2015, 20. See also Kennedy 2019b, n.d.
48   Aspholm 2019, 146.
49   Kennedy 2019a.
50   Aspholm 2019, 147.
51   Aspholm 2019, 146–47.
52   See chapter 3.
53   Chicago Police Department 2019c.
54   Policing in Chicago Research Group 2018a; Office of Inspector General 2019.
55   Jobs for R-Users 2017.
56   See chapter 4.
57   Papachristos 2012.
58   Buntin 2013.
59   Chicago Police Department 2019d; Hollywood et al. 2019.
60   Interview by lead author with NNSC staff members, June 2019.
61   Interview by lead author with NNSC staff members, June 2019.
62   Interview by lead author with NNSC staff members, June 2019.
63   Crandall and Wong 2012.
64   Crandall and Wong 2012, 7. See also Kennedy 2011.
65   Interview by lead author with NNSC staff members, June 2019.
66   Interview by lead author with NNSC staff members, June 2019.

67 Rhee 2016.

68 Interview by lead author with NNSC staff members, June 2019.

69 Personal communication with PCRG member, December 2017.

70 Office of Inspector General 2021, 23.

71 Chicago Police Department 2015b.

72 Partnership for Safe and Peaceful Communities, n.d.

73 Interview by the authors with Teny Gross, May 2019.

74 Crown 2019.

75 Evans 2020.

76 WBBM Newsradio 2020.

77 Shepelavy 2020.

78 This book went to press soon after mayor Brandon Johnson's inauguration. We cannot speculate on what may have changed.

79 Chicago CRED 2020.

80 Shepelavy 2020.

81 Shepelavy 2020; Vargas 2020.

82 Chicago CRED, n.d.

83 Duncan 2020.

84 Crown 2019.

85 Interview by the authors with Teny Gross, May 2019.

86 Initially eighteen months but cut down in 2020–21 due to budget cuts.

87 Heartland Alliance, n.d.

88 Bynum and Moreno 2020.

89 Chicago CRED 2020.

90 Duncan 2020.

91 Interview by lead author with NNSC staff members, June 2019.

92 Kerr et al. 2003; Hardiman et al. 2004.

93 James 2011.

94 Crown 2019.

95 A large service provider, Metropolitan Family Services, serves as financial sponsor and convener of CP4P. MFS's government grants have grown from $30.7 million to $50.3 million from 2016 to 2020, while its private contributions have grown from $7 million to $17.2 million during that same time period (based on a review of MFS annual reports).

96 Metropolitan Family Services, n.d.

97 MacArthur Foundation 2019.

98 Miller 2021.

99 Interview by lead author with CP4P staff, August 2020.

100 Interview by lead author with CP4P staff, August 2020.

101 Interview by the authors with Teny Gross, May 2019.

102 Interview by the authors with community data manager, January 2019.

103 Interview by PCRG with Teny Gross, November 2017.

104 Interview by lead author with CP4P staff, August 2020.

105 Interview by PCRG with director of violence-reduction organization, November 2017.

106 Interview by lead author with CP4P staff, August 2020.

107 Interview by lead author with CP4P staff, August 2020.

108 Interview by the authors with violence-reduction practitioner, July 2020.

109 Interview by PCRG with director of violence-reduction organization, November 2017.

110 Interview by the authors with Teny Gross, May 2019.

111 Interview by the authors with violence-reduction practitioner, July 2020.

112 Interview by PCRG with director of violence-reduction organization, November 2017.

113 Interview by PCRG with director of violence-reduction organization, November 2017.

114 Interview by the authors with violence-reduction practitioner, July 2020.

115 Interview by lead author with NNSC staff members, June 2019.

116 Interview by lead author with CP4P staff, August 2020.

117 Interview by the authors with violence-reduction practitioner, July 2020.

118 Interview by the authors with Teny Gross, May 2019.

119 Interview by lead author with NNSC staff members, June 2019.

120 Kennedy 2019a.

121 Interview by lead author with NNSC staff members, June 2019.

122 Interview by the authors with Teny Gross, May 2019.

123 Personal communication with PCRG member, May 2017.

124 Chicago Justice Project 2021.

125 Crandall and Wong 2012, 29.

126 Crandall and Wong 2012, 29.

127 Interview by the authors with Teny Gross, May 2019. Joronen (2016) describes a similar legitimization strategy used by Israel: the military drops leaflets on Palestinian houses to inform residents that their homes will be imminently destroyed by shelling. See chapter 4 for further discussion of links between Israeli settler colonialism and U.S. imperial policing.

128 City of Chicago 2020, 3.

129 Some foundations already embrace this approach. For example, the Crossroads Fund and Woods Fund Chicago have provided grants to many of our community partner organizations.

3. STRATEGIC SUBJECTS

Haley Volpintesta and Andy Clarno are the lead researchers and authors of this chapter.

1 Interview with community member, November 2020. Unless otherwise noted, quotations in this chapter come from interviews with young people directly impacted by imperial policing.

2   Chicago Police Department 2019a.

3   Fraternal Order of Police 2019.

4   Chicago Police Department 2019b.

5   See the methodological appendix.

6   Browne 2015, 21.

7   We also conducted interviews with private defense attorneys, public defenders, and restorative justice practitioners. Our interviews with professionals and young adults were complemented by informal conversations and field observations.

8   The interview sample included eleven Black men, three Black women, two Latinas, one Latino, and one nonbinary Black young person, some of whom were first- or second-generation immigrants and/or Muslim. We deidentified our field notes and transcripts to protect the confidentiality of the research participants.

9   Wang 2018.

10 Bauer 2016.

11 Fraternal Order of Police 2019.

12 Interview with criminal defense attorney, May 2017.

13 Mogul, Ritchie, and Whitlock 2011.

14 Russell-Brown 2008.

15 Muhammad 2010; Rodriguez 2021.

16 Chicago Crime Commission 2018.

17 Chesney-Lind and Hagedorn 1999; Dorais and Corriveau 2009; Jones 2009; Miller 2000.

18 Haley 2019; Hartman 1997; Mogul, Ritchie, and Whitlock 2011; Richie 2012.

19 Thrasher 1927; Moore 1978; Hagedorn (1988) 1998, 2015; Conquergood and Siegel 1990; Venkatesh 1997; Vigil 2002; Brotherton and Barrios 2004; Durán 2013, 2018; Aspholm 2019; Stuart 2020.

20 Durán 2013, 52.

21 Chicago Crime Commission 2012, 6.

22 Chicago Crime Commission 2012, 3.

23 Chicago Crime Commission 2018, 5.

24 Office of Inspector General 2019, 49.

25 U.S. Department of Justice 2017, 146.

26 U.S. Department of Justice 2017, 146.

27 Khalili 2013; Lebrón 2017, 2019; Schrader 2019; Go 2020; Elliot-Cooper 2021.

28 Chicago Police Department 2013.

29 Office of Inspector General 2019.

30 Office of Inspector General 2021, 26.

31 Office of Inspector General 2019, 35.

32 Skogan 2022.

33 American Civil Liberties Union of Illinois 2015.

34 Chicago Police Department 2017a.

35 Based on our review of data released by the CPD in response to a FOIA request.

36 Office of Inspector General 2019, 18.

37 Chicago Police Department 2019c.
38 Interview with criminal defense attorney, May 2017.
39 Policing in Chicago Research Group 2018a.
40 Policing in Chicago Research Group 2018a.
41 Office of Inspector General 2020.
42 Chicago Police Department 2015a.
43 Interview with criminal defense attorney, May 2017.
44 Browne 2015, 16.
45 Dumke 2018.
46 Office of Inspector General 2019, 48–49.
47 Chicago Police Department 2019c. These criteria may change if the CPD adopts a proposed new gang database, the Criminal Enterprise Information System (CEIS).
48 Office of Inspector General 2019, 40.
49 This would also change under the CEIS.
50 Interview with criminal defense attorney, May 2017.
51 Before the introduction of ISRs, Chicago police handed out "contact cards" when they stopped but did not arrest a person.
52 Office of Inspector General 2019, 39.
53 Aspholm 2019; Hagedorn et al. 2019.
54 Kunichoff and Sier 2017.
55 Heeder and Hielscher 2017.
56 U.S. Department of Justice 2017, 145.
57 Meisner and Sweeney 2021.
58 Goudie, Horng, and Markoff 2020.
59 Spielman 2021b.
60 Stovall, forthcoming.
61 Stovall, forthcoming, citing Fanon.
62 Aspholm 2019.
63 Vargas 2016.
64 U.S. Department of Justice 2017, 148–49.
65 Balto 2019, 202.
66 Nolan and Kelly 2020.
67 See also Gurusami 2019.
68 Fong 2023.
69 Butler 2006.
70 Aspholm 2019, 90.
71 Stuart 2020.
72 Tepper 2019.
73 Office of Inspector General 2019, 38.
74 Serrato 2019.
75 Cacho 2012.
76 Fisher 2012.

77 BYP100 2020.
78 Nishida 2022; Piepzna-Samarasinha 2022.
79 Miller v. Alabama, 567 U.S. 460 (2012).
80 Freire 2014, 89.
81 As we finalize our edits to this chapter, two more young people associated with the project have been killed. Like the spiral of surveillance, the number of young people lost continues to grow.

4. MANUFACTURING TERRORISTS

Ilā Ravichandran and Andy Clarno are the lead researchers and authors of this chapter.

1   Arab Women's Committee 2018.
2   U.S. Attorney's Office 2013.
3   Bassiouni, ed. 1974; Pennock 2017; Cainkar 2018.
4   Pennock 2017; Kumar 2012.
5   Said 1978; Shaheen 1984; Alsultany 2012.
6   Fanon (1952) 2008; Said 1979, 1996.
7   Cainkar 2018, 37.
8   After the Iranian revolution, the archetype of the terrorist began to expand through a process that conflated Arabs, Muslims, and "Middle Easterners"; see Naber 2000, 2008, 2014.
9   Stork and Theberge 1973.
10 The Zionist movement emerged in response to European anti-Semitism, offering a nationalist solution to European racism by creating a Jewish settler-colonial state in Palestine. Backed first by the British and then by the U.S. empire, the Zionist movement established Israel as a Jewish state and has steadily expanded the area of Jewish-only settlements through the systematic colonization of Palestinian land and the forced displacement of Palestinian people.
11 Bassiouni, ed. 1974; Akram 2002; Kumar 2012; Pennock 2017.
12 Abowd 1995; Naji v. Nelson, 113 F.R.D. 548 (N.D. Ill. 1986). Odeh was Rasmea's cousin and a cofounder of the Arab Community Center, precursor to the AAAN.
13 Farnia 2022; Abdulhadi 2004.
14 Naughtie 1981.
15 The ADL is a nonprofit organization that brands itself as progressive while enacting policies that target struggles for social justice, including Palestinian rights, and while partnering with right-wing organizations and law enforcement agencies to support Israeli apartheid and settler colonialism. For more information, see DropTheADL 2021.
16 As Bazian (2012) argues, the ADL remains a private communication hub that collects and assembles data on Palestinians and other social justice organizers.

17   Arab American Anti-Discrimination Committee 2022; Sheen 2020.

18   Cainkar 2018, 40.

19   Naber 2000; Li 2020.

20   Human Rights Watch 2014; Said 2015.

21   During the 1980s, Bridgeview had become an important center of Palestinian and Muslim life in the Chicago area. See Lybarger (2020).

22   Information in the following paragraphs is based in part on an interview by the authors with Salah's attorney, Michael Deutsch, March 2019.

23   Deutsch and Thompson 2008a.

24   U.S. Department of State, n.d.

25   See https://www.state.gov/wp-content/uploads/2019/02/12925-Israel-Law-Enforcement-MLAT-1.26.1998.pdf.

26   Deutsch and Thompson 2008b.

27   Boundaoui 2018.

28   Ahmed-Ullah et al. 2004.

29   Naber 2008; Naber and Rana 2019; Nguyen 2019; Selod 2018; Kumar 2012.

30   Kundnani 2014; Hagopian 2004.

31   Cainkar 2009.

32   Ahmed-Ullah et al. 2004.

33   Deutsch and Thompson 2008b.

34   See chapter 4.

35   Deutsch and Thompson 2008b. Deutsch and Thompson argue that "the tentacles of almost every known Hamas-related investigation or prosecution in the United States, including against the Holy Land Foundation (the largest Muslim charity in the United States), lead back to Salah's forced confession" (52).

36   Kean and Hamilton 2004, 416–17.

37   Kean and Hamilton 2004, 418.

38   Said 2015, 75.

39   Federal Bureau of Investigation, n.d.

40   Nguyen 2019.

41   Deutsch and Thompson 2008b.

42   Khalili 2010.

43   Information in this section is based in part on interviews by the authors with Joe Iosbaker (March 2019), Hatem Abudayyeh (February 2019), and two organizers from the Arab American Action Network (December 2018, March 2019).

44   Committee to Stop FBI Repression 2010; *Fight Back! News* 2011.

45   Grimm and Dizikes 2010.

46   U.S. District Court for the District of Minneapolis 2010.

47   U.S. District Court for the District of Minneapolis 2010; Khoury 2004.

48   Harris 2012.

49   Using grand juries to repress activists is a well-known strategy of the U.S. government. Activists such as Bernardine Dohrn, from the antiwar committee, and Salah's codefendant, Abdelhaleem Ashqar, have been charged with civil and

criminal contempt for refusing to appear before a grand jury. See Dohrn 2010.

50 See https://www.state.gov/wp-content/uploads/2019/02/12925-Israel-Law
-Enforcement-MLAT-1.26.1998.pdf.

51 U.S. Court of Appeals for the Sixth Court, n.d.

52 In ruling on the admissibility of this evidence, judge J. Rogers explained, "Odeh
argues that the district court should have first determined the truth or validity
of the documents, and the legality or fairness of the system that produced them.
The terms of the MLAT do not require or permit this type of inquiry." See U.S.
Court of Appeals for the Sixth Circuit 2015, 13.

53 U.S. Court of Appeals for the Sixth Circuit 2015. See also Hajjar 2005; Abdo,
n.d., 2014.

54 Hajjar 2005; War on Want 2021.

55 Field notes, October 2015, April 2017, and August 2017.

56 Khoury 2004.

57 Abdulhadi 1998; Darraj 2005; Naber, Desouky, and Baroudi 2011.

58 Abdo 1991.

59 Yuval-Davis 1993; Abdo 1991.

60 Hong 2020.

61 McQuade 2019.

62 Nguyen 2019.

63 U.S. Department of Homeland Security 2018.

64 McQuade 2019, 34.

65 Chicago Police Department 2020a.

66 For more information, see Arab American Action Network and Policing in
Chicago Research Group 2022.

67 U.S. Department of Homeland Security, n.d.

68 Questions on the SAR form ask officers to identify the "race" and "race subtype"
of a suspect. Fusion center staff often leave the race and subtype questions blank,
and other times this information is redacted. But there is also a "narrative" section
of the report, where officers regularly include indicators of racial, ethnic, national,
or religious identity. The findings herein are based on our analysis of racial, ethnic,
national, and religious markers included in response to the "race" and "racial
subtype" questions on the SAR form and in the "narrative" section of the report.

69 Some of the SARs that included racial, ethnic, national, or religious descriptors
also identified the suspects by name. Interestingly, when the suspect was *not*
identified by name, even higher percentages of people were described as "Arab,"
"Middle Eastern," "Muslim," or "olive skinned" (68 percent among CPIC SARs
and 60 percent among STIC SARs) and people of color (84 percent at CPIC, 75
percent at STIC). In other words, if law enforcement agencies already knew a
suspect's name, they did not need to include racial descriptors in the SAR. But
they depended on racial markers for identification purposes in cases when they
could not confirm the suspect's name.

70 On these forms, "Middle Eastern/Persian" is listed as a "subtype" of white. Latinx

people are also generally classified as white. Documents from STIC indicate that people born in Arab countries are equally likely to be classified as "white" (with no subtype), "white" (with subtype "Middle Eastern"), or "unknown."

71 According to federal guidelines, only SARs with a "potential nexus to terrorism" should be uploaded to the FBI's eGuardian database. Yet our investigation shows that STIC and CPIC shared SARs with the FBI even when the analysts determined that there was no "potential nexus to terrorism." Most of the SARs that we reviewed had been redacted to conceal the section where analysts indicate whether there was a "potential nexus to terrorism." That section was left unredacted in eleven CPIC reports and twenty-two STIC reports. Among these, only two of the eleven CPIC reports (18 percent) and five of the twenty-two STIC reports (23 percent) indicated a "potential nexus to terrorism." The rest indicated that their investigation was "inconclusive" or "undetermined" or that there was no "potential nexus to terrorism." Yet all of these reports were uploaded to the FBI eGuardian database. This suggests that anything even remotely concerning is considered worth sending to the FBI, even when it directly violates federal guidelines.

72 Price 2013, 23.

73 Arab American Action Network and Policing in Chicago Research Group 2022; Assad and Hickey 2022.

74 Hickey 2022.

5. WELCOMING CITY?

Enrique Alvear Moreno and Andy Clarno are the lead researchers and authors of this chapter.

1 City of Chicago 2012.

2 Emanuel and Mendoza 2012, 30043.

3 Emanuel and Mendoza 2012, 33044. As we explain later, the WCO was amended in 2021 to remove these exceptions.

4 City of Chicago 2012.

5 City of Chicago 2012.

6 U.S. Department of Homeland Security 2021a.

7 Walia 2021.

8 Tanfani 2017.

9 Paik 2017, 2020; Roy 2019; Alvear Moreno, forthcoming.

10 Macías-Rojas 2016.

11 Armenta 2017, 24.

12 Provine et al. 2016.

13 Wells 2004; Varsanyi 2010; Varsanyi et al. 2012; Coleman 2012; Armenta 2017; Armenta and Alvarez 2017.

14 Armenta 2017; Ridgley 2008; Wells 2004.

15 Ridgley 2008; Colbern 2017; Villazor and Gulasekaram 2018; Colbern, Amoroso-Pohl, and Gutiérrez 2019.

16 Darling and Squire 2012; Bagelman 2013; Walia 2014; Bauer 2016; Houston and Lawrence-Weilmann 2016; Scherr and Hofmann 2016; Paik 2017, 2020; Roy 2019; Gomberg-Muñoz and Wences 2020.

17 Paik 2017, 2020; Roy 2019.

18 Macías-Rojas 2016, 23–24.

19 Macías-Rojas 2016, 112.

20 Kanstroom 2000.

21 De Genova 2005, 8. Cecilia Menjívar and Leisy Abrego (2012) describe this as a racialized regime of legal violence.

22 Armenta 2017.

23 Macías-Rojas (2016, 2021) demonstrates that federal immigration authorities also support local crime control efforts in the Arizona/Sonora border region.

24 Unless otherwise noted, quotations and stories in this chapter are based on a long interview with Wilmer Catalan-Ramirez and Celene Adame in November 2018.

25 Paik 2020.

26 Roy 2019; Macías-Rojas 2021; Alvear, forthcoming.

27 For more on punitive exceptionalism, see Alvear Moreno, forthcoming.

28 Daley 1989.

29 Washington 1985, 164.

30 Washington 1985, 165.

31 Davis 1992.

32 Rumore 2023.

33 Davis 1992, emphasis added.

34 Daley 2006, 74329.

35 Emanuel and Mendoza 2012, 33044.

36 Jacobs 2017.

37 Golash-Boza 2015; Escobar 2016.

38 Ridgley 2008, 2012; Armenta 2017; Wells 2004.

39 Bauer 2016; Bagelman 2013; Darling and Squire 2012; Scherr and Hofmann 2016; Houston and Lawrence-Weilmann 2016; Walia 2014; Gomberg-Muñoz and Wences 2020.

40 De Genova and Peutz 2010; Vigil 2003; Cacho 2012.

41 Rios 2011.

42 Information in this paragraph is based on the "contact card" filed by Chicago police on June 16, 2015.

43 One of the officers has a documented history of using force against residents of the neighborhood where Wilmer lives, and both officers were charged with "false arrest" for an incident that took place the day before they stopped Wilmer and his friend. Information was obtained from the Invisible Institute's Citizen Police Data Project at https://cpdp.co/.

44 This officer also has a documented history of using force against residents of the

neighborhood where Wilmer lives. Information was obtained from the Invisible Institute's Citizen Police Data Project at https://cpdp.co/.

45 Armenta 2017.

46 Information in this paragraph is based on the gang arrest card filed by Chicago police on November 21, 2016.

47 Office of Inspector General 2019, 40.

48 Based on information contained on the gang arrest card filed by Chicago police on November 21, 2016, and maps published in Chicago Crime Commission 2018.

49 While in detention, Wilmer met three other people who were wrongfully identified as gang members. He told us about one of the cases: "There was a case of two brothers where one was a gang member and the other one was just studying, and the police caught and arrested both of them. As if like the fact of being a brother of a gang member, makes you a member of a gang too! As soon as you are related. It's like my case. The police were saying that I'm gang related but I'm not actually affiliated to a gang. However, *I am related*."

50 Wacquant 2011.

51 Chacón 2007.

52 U.S. Immigration and Customs Enforcement 2017.

53 Winston 2016.

54 Muñiz 2022.

55 Office of Inspector General 2019, 27.

56 U.S. Immigration and Customs Enforcement 2017.

57 Bauer and Nitkin 2017.

58 Catalan-Ramirez v. Wong et al., case 1:17-cv-03258, second amended complaint (N.D. Ill. Sep. 6, 2017).

59 Hing 2017.

60 *Catalan-Ramirez*, EARM case summary: Catalan-Ramirez, Wilmer.

61 *Catalan-Ramirez*, DHS document submission.

62 See chapter 3 for more on *The Gang Book*.

63 Interview with a lawyer from the Northwestern University MacArthur Justice Center, November 2018.

64 Organized Communities Against Deportations 2020.

65 Chicago Police Department 2017b.

66 Interview with a lawyer from the Northwestern University MacArthur Justice Center, November 2018.

67 Serrato 2018.

68 Office of Inspector General 2019, 39.

69 Office of Inspector General 2019, 27.

70 Organized Communities Against Deportations 2020.

71 Quoted in Goodwin 2017.

72 Just Futures Law et al. 2021.

73 U.S. Department of Homeland Security 2021b.

74 U.S. Department of Homeland Security 2021a.
75 U.S. Department of Homeland Security 2021a.
76 Rios 2011.
77 Gomberg-Muñoz and Wences 2020, 2.

6. EXPAND SANCTUARY! ERASE THE DATABASE!

Janaé Bonsu-Love, Tania Unzueta Carrasco, and Andy Clarno are the lead authors of this chapter. Tania Unzueta Carrasco is the policy director for Mijente, a national Latinx political organization. She ran the campaign against the Chicago Gang Database for three years. She is also a longtime, nationally known immigrant rights organizer, particularly for her work with undocumented immigrants in Chicago and around the country.

1   Critical Resistance, n.d.
2   Paik 2020.
3   Unzueta 2017.
4   See chapter 5.
5   Ransby 2018.
6   Assata's Daughters 2016.
7   Mijente 2017. See also Franco 2017.
8   Strasser 2016.
9   The limits of the dominant understanding were evident in the invisibility of Black immigrants' vulnerability. Because Black communities are overpoliced and criminalized, Black immigrants face not only harassment and arrest but also high rates of detention and deportation. In fact, among all immigrants, Black immigrants are nearly three times more likely to be detained and deported as a result of an alleged criminal offense. See Golash-Boza 2015; Morgan-Trostle, Zheng, and Lipscombe 2016.
10 Bonsu 2017.
11 Neil 2018.
12 Muñiz-Pagan 2019.
13 See chapter 5 for a deeper discussion of Chicago's liberal sanctuary policies.
14 There was also an effort led by Asian Americans Advancing Justice (AAAJ)-Chicago to prohibit police officers from using anti-immigrant or racial slurs. In 2015, AAAJ-Chicago joined the Chicago Immigration Working Group, and the two efforts moved forward together. In October 2016, the Chicago City Council passed an amendment to the Welcoming City Ordinance addressing the amendments put forward based on the Klyzek incident, but not removing the carve-outs.
15 City of Chicago v. Jefferson Beauregard Sessions III, Case No. 17 C 5720 (N.D. Ill. Oct. 13, 2017), 8.

16 Spielman 2021a.
17 See chapter 5.
18 Lyons 2020.
19 Just Futures Law 2021.
20 Campos 2022.
21 Dumke and Joravsky 2011.
22 Unzueta-Carrasco is a founder of both organizations.
23 Chabria and Miller 2020.
24 Grench 2021.
25 Policing in Chicago Research Group 2018b.
26 Office of Inspector General 2019.
27 Chicagoans for an End to the Gang Database et al. v. City of Chicago et al., case 18-CV-4242 (N.D. Ill. June 19, 2018).
28 Organizational plaintiffs included Black Youth Project 100 Chicago chapter, Blocks Together, Brighton Park Neighborhood Council, Latino Union, Mijente, and Organized Communities Against Deportations.
29 ABC7 Chicago 2020; Office of Inspector General 2021.
30 Quig 2019.
31 For details, see Policing in Chicago Research Group 2019.
32 MOCIC is part of the Regional Information Sharing Systems (RISS) network, a federal data-sharing initiative that maintains the nationwide RISSGang database.
33 Dumke 2019.
34 Black Lives Matter–Chicago 2020.
35 Del Vecchio 2020; Good Kids, Mad City 2021.
36 Cherone and Blumberg 2023.
37 Davis et al. 2022, 33–34.

CONCLUSION

1   Benjamin 2019; Brayne 2017; Ferguson 2016.
2   https://cpdp.co/.
3   Ferguson 2016.
4   Benjamin 2019.
5   Chicago Alliance for Neighborhood Safety, n.d.
6   Benjamin 2019.
7   Spade 2013, 1050.
8   Interrupting Criminalization 2021, 33.
9   Critical Resistance and INCITE! 2006; Rodriguez 2019; Kaba 2020.
10 Just Futures Law et al. 2021.
11 Gilmore 2007, 242.
12 Critical Resistance, n.d.; Spade 2016.
13 Davis et al. 2022.

14 Kaba 2021; Davis et al. 2022.
15 Movement for Black Lives, n.d.
16 Bonsu 2018, 192.
17 Spade 2015, 115.
18 Interrupting Criminalization 2021.
19 BYP100 2020.
20 Dixon 2016, 162.
21 hooks 2000; Thom 2019.
22 Rodriguez 2019, 1589.
23 Cacho 2012.
24 Hong 2015.
25 Davis et al. 2022, 66.
26 Naber and Rojas 2021.
27 Davis et al. 2022, 22–23.
28 Naber and Rojas 2021.
29 Ransby 2018.
30 See the methodological appendix.
31 Kaba 2021, 178.

METHODOLOGICAL APPENDIX

Michael De Anda Muñiz and Andy Clarno are the lead authors of this appendix.

1 Burawoy 2005; Lewis and Embrick 2016; Wingfield 2016.
2 Wingfield 2016.
3 Ferguson 2012.
4 As Ferguson (2012) notes, university administrators agreed to establish these interdisciplinary units in an effort to contain movements from below. He calls on us to defend their radical potential by producing forms of knowledge that are *in* but not *of* the university.
5 Moraga and Anzaldúa 1981; Smith 1987; Collins 1990; Smith (1999) 2012; Davis 2013.
6 Browne 2015.
7 Freire 2014.
8 Kelley 2002, 8.
9 Freire 2014; hooks 1994; Ayers et al. 2016.
10 Lipsitz 2008. The Student Non-violent Coordinating Committee Research Department, for example, collected newspaper archives, conducted legal research, provided political analysis, and supplied information for campaigns and public speakers. Similarly, the Palestine Research Center conducted and published groundbreaking research on Zionism, racism, and settler colonialism in support of the Palestinian struggle for liberation, until Israel destroyed the center

and confiscated its materials during the siege of Beirut in 1982. Closer to home, Chicago-based movements, such as We Charge Genocide, the Collaborative for Community Wellness, the Arab American Action Network, and No Cop Academy—as well as national movements like Mijente and Black Youth Project 100—maintain active research agendas in support of political campaigns.

11 Smith 2006.
12 Kelley 2002; Calhoun 2008; Smith 2006.
13 hooks 2003; Burawoy 1998; Collins 2013.
14 Davis et al. 2022.
15 Ransby 2018.
16 Wingfield 2016, 3.
17 Freire 2014, 51.
18 hooks 1984, 112.
19 Sudbury and Okazawa-Rey 2009, 4.
20 Davis et al. 2022, 4.
21 Stacey 1988; Smith (1999) 2012.
22 Smith (1999) 2012.
23 Muñiz et al. 2020, 145–48.

Bibliography

ABC7 Chicago. 2020. "CPD to Overhaul Gang-Related Database, Announces New 'Criminal Enterprise Information System.'" February 27. https://abc7chicago.com/chicago-police-department-criminal-enterprise-information-system-cpd-gang-database-violence/5970975/.

Abdo, Nahla. 1991. "Women of the Intifada: Gender, Class and National Liberation." *Race and Class* 32, no. 4: 19–34.

Abdo, Nahla. 2014. *Captive Revolution: Palestinian Women's Anti-colonial Struggle within the Israeli Prison System.* London: Pluto Press.

Abdo, Nahla. n.d. "Criminalising the Victim: The Life Story of Rasmea Odeh." *Pluto Books Blog.* https://www.plutobooks.com/blog/criminalizing-the-victim-the-life-story-of-rasmea-odeh/.

Abdulhadi, Rabab. 1998. "The Palestinian Women's Autonomous Movement: Emergence, Dynamics, and Challenges." *Gender and Society* 12, no. 6: 649–73.

Abdulhadi, Rabab. 2004. "Activism and Exile: Palestinianness and the Politics of Solidarity." In *Local Actions,* edited by Melissa Checker and Maggie Fishman, 231–54. New York: Columbia University Press.

Abowd, Mary. 1995. "In Memoriam: Samir Odeh, 1951–1994." *Washington Report on Middle East Affairs,* January/February, 35, 88.

Ackerman, Spencer. 2015a. "Bad Lieutenant: American Police Brutality, Exported from Chicago to Guantánamo." *The Guardian,* February 18.

Ackerman, Spencer. 2015b. "The Disappeared: Chicago Police Detain Americans at Abuse-Laden 'Black Site.'" *The Guardian,* February 24.

Ackerman, Spencer, and Zach Stafford. 2015. "Chicago Police Detained Thousands of Black Americans at Interrogation Facility." *The Guardian,* August 5.

Ahmed-Ullah, Noreen S., Kim Barker, Laurie Cohen, Stephen Franklin, and Sam Roe. 2004. "Hard Liners Won Battle for Bridgeview Mosque." *Chicago Tribune,* February 8.

Akram, Susan M. 2002. "The Aftermath of September 11, 2001: The Targeting of Arabs and Muslims in America." *Arab Studies Quarterly* 24, no. 2/3: 61–118.

Alderden, Megan, Amie Schuck, Cody Stephens, Timothy Lavery, Rachel Johnston, and Dennis Rosenbaum. 2012. "Gang Hot Spots Policing in Chicago: An Evaluation

of the Deployment Operations Center Process." https://www.ojp.gov/pdffiles1
/nij/grants/239207.pdf.

Alexander, Michelle. 2010. *The New Jim Crow: Mass Incarceration in the Age of Color-blindness*. New York: New Press.

Allard, Patricia. 2006. "Crime, Punishment, and Economic Violence." In *Color of Violence*, edited by INCITE!, 157–63. Cambridge, Mass.: South End Press.

Alonso, William, and Paul Starr. 1987. Introduction to *The Politics of Numbers*, edited by William Alonso and Paul Starr. New York: Russell Sage Foundation.

Alsultany, Evelyn. 2012. *The Arabs and Muslims in the Media: Race and Representation after 9/11*. New York: New York University Press.

Alvear Moreno, Enrique. Forthcoming. "The Paradox of Sanctuary: How Punitive Exceptions Converge to Criminalize and Punish Latinos/as." *Law and Social Inquiry*.

American Civil Liberties Union. 2022. "New Records Detail DHS Purchase and Use of Vast Quantities of Cell Phone Location Data." July 18. https://www.aclu.org/news/privacy-technology/new-records-detail-dhs-purchase-and-use-of-vast-quantities-of-cell-phone-location-data.

American Civil Liberties Union of Illinois. 2015. *Stop and Frisk in Chicago*. Chicago: ACLU. https://www.aclu-il.org/sites/default/files/wp-content/uploads/2015/03/ACLU_StopandFrisk_6.pdf.

Anselin, Luc. 1995. "Local Indicators of Spatial Association—Lisa." *Geographical Analysis* 27, no. 2: 93–115.

Arab American Action Network and Policing in Chicago Research Group. 2022. *Suspicious Activity Reports and the Surveillance State: The Suppression of Dissent and the Criminalization of Arabs and Muslims in Illinois*. Chicago: Arab American Action Network.

Arab American Anti-Discrimination Committee. 2022. "Alex Odeh; 37 Years and Still No Justice for a Civil Rights Hero." Washington, D.C.: Arab-American Anti-Discrimination Committee. https://adc.org/alex-odeh-37-years-and-still-no-justice-for-a-civil-rights-hero/.

Arab Women's Committee. 2018. *Towards the Sun/نحو الشمس*. Washington, D.C.: Tadween.

Armenta, Amada. 2017. *Protect, Serve, and Deport: The Rise of Policing as Immigration Enforcement*. Berkeley: University of California Press.

Armenta, Amada, and Isabela Alvarez. 2017. "Policing Immigrants or Policing Immigration? Understanding Local Law Enforcement Participation in Immigration Control." *Sociology Compass* 11, no. 2: 1–10.

Aspholm, Roberto R. 2019. *Views from the Streets: The Transformation of Gangs and Violence on Chicago's South Side*. New York: Columbia University Press.

Assad, Samah, and Meghan Hickey. 2022. "When 'If You See Something, Say Something' Goes Wrong: Unfounded Reports of Suspicious Activity Overwhelmingly Target Arabs, Muslims Doing Routine Activities, New Report Shows." CBS Chicago, July 1. https://www.cbsnews.com/chicago/news/unfounded-reports-of-suspicious-activity-overwhelmingly-target-arabs-muslims-doing-routine-activities-new-report-shows/.

Assata's Daughters. 2016. "Breaking: Chicagoans Halt Loop Traffic with 'Defund Police, Dismantle ICE' Blockade—Assata's Daughters Statement." February 16. https://www.assatasdaughters.org/statements#not1more.

Ayers, William, Kevin Kumashiro, Erica Meiners, Therese Quinn, and David Stovall. 2016. *Teaching toward Democracy: Educators as Agents of Change.* 2nd ed. London: Routledge.

Bagelman, Jennifer. 2013. "Sanctuary: A Politics of Ease?" *Alternatives* 38, no. 1: 49–62.

Balko, Radley. 2021. *Rise of the Warrior Cop: The Militarization of America's Police Forces.* New York: Hachette.

Balto, Simon. 2019. *Occupied Territory: Policing Black Chicago from Red Summer to Black Power.* Chapel Hill: University of North Carolina Press.

Bardes, John. 2020. "Mass Incarceration in the Age of Slavery and Emancipation: Fugitive Slaves, Poor Whites, and Prison Development in Louisiana, 1805–1898." PhD diss., Tulane University.

Bassiouni, M. Cherif, ed. 1974. *The Civil Rights of Arab-Americans: The Special Measures.* North Dartmouth, Mass.: Arab-American University Graduates.

Bauer, Kelly. 2016. "Read Rahm Emanuel's Speech on Chicago Violence Here (TRANSCRIPT)." *DNA Info,* September 22. https://www.dnainfo.com/chicago/20160922/downtown/rahm-emanuel-chicago-violence-speech-four-ps-parenting.

Bauer, Kelly. 2020. "City Says It's Going All-Out to Stop Looting: Social Media Surveillance, Raised Bridges, CTA Shutdowns." *Block Club Chicago,* August 14. https://blockclubchicago.org/2020/08/14/social-media-surveillance-raised-bridges-cta-shutdowns-city-says-its-going-all-out-to-stop-looting/.

Bauer, Kelly. 2022. "Darren Bailey Calls Chicago a 'Hellhole' Again—and Chicagoans Respond: 'This Should Work Out Well for Him.'" *Block Club Chicago,* August 19. https://blockclubchicago.org/2022/08/19/darren-bailey-calls-chicago-a-hellhole-again-and-chicagoans-respond-with-jokes-this-should-work-out-well-for-him/.

Bauer, Kelly, and Alex Nitkin. 2017. "ICE Agents 'Pointed Pistols in Our Faces . . . Shot My Dad,' Daughter Says." *DNA Info,* March 27. https://www.dnainfo.com/chicago/20170327/belmont-cragin/police-shoot-wound-person-belmont-cragin/.

Bazian, Hatem. 2012. "Muslims—Enemies of the State: The New Counter-Intelligence Program (COINTELPRO)." *Islamophobia Studies Journal* 1, no. 1: 163–206.

Benjamin, Ruha. 2019. *Race after Technology: Abolitionist Tools for the New Jim Code.* Cambridge, Mass.: Polity Press.

Ben-Moshe, Liat. 2020. *Decarcerating Disability: Deinstitutionalization and Prison Abolition.* Minneapolis: University of Minnesota Press.

Berger, Dan, Mariame Kaba, and David Stein. 2017. "What Abolitionists Do." *Jacobin,* August 24. https://jacobin.com/2017/08/prison-abolition-reform-mass-incarceration.

Berman, Elizabeth Popp, and Daniel Hirschman. 2018. "The Sociology of Quantification: Where Are We Now?" *Contemporary Sociology* 47, no. 3: 257–66.

Betancur, John. 2011. "Gentrification and Community Fabric in Chicago." *Urban Studies* 48, no. 2: 383–406.

Bhattacharyya, Gargi. 2018. *Rethinking Racial Capitalism: Questions of Reproduction and Survival*. London: Rowman and Littlefield.

Bhungalia, Lisa. 2024. *Elastic Empire: Refashioning War through Aid in Palestine*. Stanford, Calif.: Stanford University Press.

Black Hawk. (1833) 2008. *Life of Black Hawk, or Mà-ka-tai-me-she-kià-kiàk, Dictated by Himself*. New York: Penguin Books.

Black Lives Matter–Chicago. 2020. "BAN Defund CPD Demands." August 24. https://www.blacklivesmatterchicago.com/ban-defund-cpd-demands/.

Block, Richard L., and Carolyn Rebecca Block. 1995. "Space, Place and Crime: Hot Spot Areas and Hot Places of Liquor-Related Crime." *Crime and Place* 4, no. 2: 145–84.

Block, Richard, and L. A. Green. 1994. *The GeoArchive Handbook: A Guide for Developing a Geographic Database as an Information Foundation for Community Policing*. Washington, D.C.: Bureau of Justice Statistics.

Bonilla-Silva, Eduardo. 2001. *White Supremacy and Racism in the Post–Civil Rights Era*. Boulder, Colo.: Lynne Rienner.

Bonsu, Janaé E. 2017. "Black People Need Sanctuary Cities, Too." *Essence*, March 10. https://www.essence.com/news/politics/sanctuary-cities-black-families-immigrants/.

Bonsu, Janaé E. 2018. "Fund Black Futures as an Abolitionist Demand." In *The Long Term: Resisting Life Sentences, Working toward Freedom*, edited by A. Kim, E. Meiners, A. Petty, J. Petty, B. Richie, and S. Ross, 192–94. Chicago: Haymarket Books.

Booz Allen Hamilton. 1992a. *Improving Police Service: Vol. 1. Patrol Operations and Strategy*. McLean, Va.: Booze Allen Hamilton.

Booz Allen Hamilton. 1992b. *Improving Police Service: Vol. 2. Neighborhood Based Strategy*. McLean, Va.: Booze Allen Hamilton.

Bosniak, Linda. 2008. *The Citizen and the Alien: Dilemmas of Contemporary Membership*. Princeton, N.J.: Princeton University Press.

Bosworth, Mary, and Emma Kaufman. 2011. "Foreigners in a Carceral Age: Immigration and Imprisonment in the United States." *Stanford Law and Policy Review* 22, no. 2: 429–54.

Boundaoui, Assia, dir. 2018. *The Feeling of Being Watched*. Film. Women Make Movies.

Brayne, Sarah. 2017. "Big Data Surveillance: The Case of Policing." *American Sociological Review* 82, no. 5: 1–32.

Brayne, Sarah. 2021. *Predict and Surveil: Data, Discretion, and the Future of Policing*. New York: Oxford University Press.

Brayne, Sarah, and Angèle Christin. 2021. "Technologies of Crime Prediction: The Reception of Algorithms in Policing and Criminal Courts." *Social Problems* 68: 608–24.

Brodkin, Karen. 1998. *How Jews Became White Folks*. New Brunswick, N.J.: Rutgers University Press.

Brotherton, David C., and Luis Barrios. 2004. *The Almighty Latin King and Queen*

Nation: Street Politics and the Transformation of a New York City Gang. New York: Columbia University Press.

Browne, Simone. 2015. *Dark Matters: On the Surveillance of Blackness.* Durham, N.C.: Duke University Press.

Buntin, John. 2013. "Social Media Transforms the Way Chicago Fights Violence." Governing the Future of States and Localities, September 26. https://www .governing.com/archive/gov-social-media-transforms-chicago-policing.html.

Burawoy, Michael. 1998. "The Extended Case Method." *Sociological Theory* 16, no. 1: 4–33.

Burawoy, Michael. 2005. "For Public Sociology." *American Sociological Review* 70, no. 1: 4–28.

Bureau of Justice Assistance. 2005. *The National Criminal Intelligence Sharing Plan, CD.* Washington, D.C.: U.S. Department of Justice. https://bja.ojp.gov/sites/g /files/xyckuh186/files/media/document/national_criminal_intelligence_sharing _plan.pdf.

Buslik, Marc, and Michael Maltz. 1998. "Power to the People: Mapping and Information Sharing in the Chicago Police Department." *Crime Prevention Studies* 8: 113–30.

Butler, Judith. 2006. *Precarious Life: The Powers of Mourning and Violence.* London: Verso.

Bynum, Steve, and Nereida Moreno. 2020. "Budget Shortfall Could Shutter One of Chicago's Largest Anti-Violence Programs." WBEZ Chicago, September 28. https://www.wbez.org/stories/budget-shortfall-could-shutter-one-of-chicagos -largest-anti-violence-programs/777dd36c-cbb0-4430-97a7-e986b0b69b2f.

BYP100. 2020. "Black Queer Feminist Curriculum Toolkit." https://drive.google.com /file/d/1e9clSyQdl4H1KGdFRlzQuSqIZFwcWqBy/view.

Cacho, Lisa. 2012. *Social Death: Racialized Rightlessness and the Criminalization of the Unprotected.* New York: New York University Press.

Cainkar, Louise. 2009. *Homeland Insecurity: The Arab American and Muslim American Experience after 9/11.* New York: Russell Sage Foundation.

Cainkar, Louise. 2018. "Fluid Terror Threat: A Genealogy of the Racialization of Arab, Muslim, and South Asian Americans." *Amerasia Journal* 44: 27–59.

Caldeira, Teresa. 2000. *City of Walls: Crime, Segregation, and Citizenship in São Paulo.* Berkeley: University of California Press.

Calhoun, Craig. 2008. Foreword to *Engaging Contradictions: Theory, Politics, and Methods of Activist Scholarship,* edited by Charles Hale, viii–xxvi. Berkeley: University of California Press.

Camp, Jordan T. 2016. *Incarcerating the Crisis: Freedom Struggles and the Rise of the Neoliberal State.* Berkeley: University of California Press.

Camp, Jordan, and Christina Heatherton, eds. 2016. *Policing the Planet: Why the Policing Crisis Led to Black Lives Matter.* London: Verso.

Campos, Alma. 2022. "Cook County Investigates ICE Purchasing of Data Software to Target Undocumented Immigrants." *South Side Weekly,* August 5.

Careless, James. 2007. "Chicago's OEMC: A Unified Approach to First Response."

EMSWorld, May. https://www.emsworld.com/article/10321909/chicagos-oemc -unified-approach-first-response.

CBS Chicago. 2020. "Chicago Police Superintendent Apologizes for 'Operation Surge.'" April 24. https://www.cbsnews.com/chicago/news/chicago-police-superintendent -apologizes-for-operation-surge/.

Chabria, Anita, and Leila Miller. 2020. "Reformers Want California Police to Stop Using a Gang Database Seen as Racially Biased." *Los Angeles Times,* June 24.

Chacón, Jennifer M. 2007. "Whose Community Shield: Examining the Removal of the Criminal Street Gang Member." *University of Chicago Legal Forum* 2007: Article 11.

Chavez, Leo. 2013. *The Latino Threat: Constructing Immigrants, Citizens, and the Nation.* Stanford, Calif.: Stanford University Press.

Cherone, Heather, and Nick Blumberg. 2023. "Police Oversight Board Votes to Permanently Scrap New Chicago Gang Database." WTTW News, September 7. https://news.wttw.com/2023/09/07/police-oversight-board-votes-permanently -scrap-new-chicago-gang-database.

Chesney-Lind, Meda, and John Hagedorn. 1999. *Female Gangs in America: Essays on Girls, Gangs, and Gender.* Chicago: Lake View Press.

Chicago Alliance for Neighborhood Safety. n.d. "Chicago's Secret Police on Trial." University of Illinois Chicago Library archives, Box 1, File 14.

Chicago CRED. 2020. *Reimagining Public Safety: A Preliminary Report on Community Partner Focus Groups.* Chicago: CRED. https://cred.app.box.com/s/6k4tblknx3 ot9954t7p7w6wsokgt57wb.

Chicago CRED. n.d. "The Workforce of the Future." https://chicagocred.org/workforce -development.

Chicago Crime Commission. 2012. *The Gang Book.* Chicago: Chicago Crime Commission.

Chicago Crime Commission. 2018. *The Gang Book.* Chicago: Chicago Crime Commission.

Chicago Justice Project. 2021. "Chicago Justice Show: Achieving Gun Violence Reduction." February 10. https://www.youtube.com/watch?v=ZfYZBhdN4LI&ab _channel=ChicagoJusticeProject.

Chicago Police Department. 1993. *Together We Can.* Chicago: Chicago Police Department.

Chicago Police Department. 2011. "Chicago Police Department's Crime Prevention Information Center: Privacy, Civil Rights, and Civil Liberties Protection Policy." March.

Chicago Police Department. 2013. "Chicago Police Department General Order G10-01-01: Gang Audit." October 16.

Chicago Police Department. 2015a. "Chicago Police Department Special Order S10-06: Targeted Repeat-Offender Apprehension and Prosecution (T.R.A.P.) Program." July 20.

Chicago Police Department. 2015b. "Chicago Police Department Special Order S10-05: Custom Notifications in Chicago." October 6.

Chicago Police Department. 2017a. "Investigatory Stop Report CPD-11.910 (Rev 7/17)."

Chicago Police Department. 2017b. "Letter to USCIS." December 1.

Chicago Police Department. 2018. *Next Steps for Reform*. Chicago: Chicago Police Department. https://home.chicagopolice.org/wp-content/uploads/2020/06/Chicago-Police-Department-2018-Next-Steps-for-Reform.pdf.

Chicago Police Department. 2019a. Case Supplementary Report JC298208. June 9.

Chicago Police Department. 2019b. "Chicago Police Department General Order G03-03-01: Emergency Vehicle Operations—Eluding and Pursuing." April 9.

Chicago Police Department. 2019c. "Chicago Police Department General Order G10-01: Gang Violence Reduction Strategy." February 8.

Chicago Police Department. 2019d. "Chicago Police Department Special Order S03-19: Strategic Decision Support Centers." January 2.

Chicago Police Department. 2020a. "Chicago Police Department Special Order S03-04-04: Crime Prevention and Information Center." August 10.

Chicago Police Department. 2020b. "Chicago Police Department General Order G09-01-06: Use of Social Media Outlets." October 22.

Chicago Police Department. n.d.-a. "Factsheet: Crime and Victimization Risk Model." https://home.chicagopolice.org/wp-content/uploads/2019/01/FACT-SHEET-Crime-and-Victimization-Risk-Model-1.pdf.

Chicago Police Department. n.d.-b. "Violence Reduction Strategy." https://home.chicagopolice.org/information/violence-reduction-strategy-vrs/.

City of Chicago. 2012. "Mayor Emanual Introduces Welcoming City Ordinance." July 10. https://www.chicago.gov/city/en/depts/mayor/press_room/press_releases/2012/july_2012/mayor_emanuel_introduceswelcomingcityordinance.html.

City of Chicago. 2020. "Our City, Our Safety: A Comprehensive Plan to Reduce Violence in Chicago." https://www.chicago.gov/content/dam/city/sites/public-safety-and-violenc-reduction/pdfs/OurCityOurSafety.pdf.

Clarno, Andy. 2017. *Neoliberal Apartheid: Palestine/Israel and South Africa after 1994*. Chicago: University of Chicago Press.

Clarno, Andy, and Salim Vally. 2023. "The Context of Struggle: Racial Capitalism and Political Praxis in South Africa." *Ethnic and Racial Studies* 46, no. 16: 3425–47.

Cohen, Cathy. 1997. "Punks, Bulldaggers, and Welfare Queens: The Radical Potential of Queer Politics?" *GLQ: A Journal of Lesbian and Gay Studies* 3, no. 4: 437–65.

Colbern, Allan. 2017. "Today's Runaway Slaves: Unauthorized Immigrants in a Federalist Framework." PhD diss., University of California Riverside. https://escholarship.org/uc/item/4pbowosq.

Colbern, Allan, Melanie Amoroso-Pohl, and Courtney Gutiérrez. 2019. "Contextualizing Sanctuary Policy Development in the United States: Conceptual and Constitutional Underpinnings, 1979 to 2018." *Fordham Urban Law Journal* 46, no. 3: 489–547.

Coleman, Matthew. 2012. "The 'Local' Migration State: The Site-Specific Devolution of Immigration Enforcement in the US South." *Law and Policy* 34, no. 2: 159–90.

Collins, Patricia Hill. 1990. *Black Feminist Thought: Knowledge, Consciousness, and the Politics of Empowerment.* London: Routledge.

Collins, Patricia Hill. 2013. "Truth-Telling and Intellectual Activism." *Contexts* 12, no. 1: 36–39.

Committee to Stop FBI Repression. 2010. "Timeline of Events." https://stopfbi.org /news/timeline-of-events/.

Conquergood, Dwight, and Taggart Siegel, dirs. 1990. *The Heart Broken in Half.* Film. Filmmakers Library.

Coulthard, Glen S. 2014. *Red Skin, White Masks: Rejecting the Colonial Politics of Recognition.* Minneapolis: University of Minnesota Press.

Crandall, Vaughn, and Sue-Lin Wong. 2012. *Practice Brief: Call-In Preparation and Execution.* New York: National Network for Safe Communities.

Critical Resistance. n.d. "Reformist Reforms vs. Abolitionist Steps in Policing." https://criticalresistance.org/wp-content/uploads/2021/08/CR_abolitioniststeps _antiexpansion_2021_eng.pdf.

Critical Resistance and INCITE! 2006. "Statement on Gender Violence and the Prison Industrial Complex." In *Color of Violence,* edited by INCITE!, 223–26. Cambridge, Mass.: South End Press.

Crown, Judith. 2019. "Foundations Step Up on Gun Violence." *Crain's Chicago Business* 42: 17.

Cruz, Taylor M. 2022. "The Social Life of Biomedical Data: Capturing, Obscuring, and Envisioning Care in the Digital Safety-Net." *Social Science and Medicine* 294: 114670.

Curtis, Bruce. 2001. *The Politics of Population: State Formation, Statistics, and the Census of Canada, 1840–1975.* Toronto: University of Toronto Press.

Daley, Richard M. 1989. Executive Order 89-6. Office of the Mayor, City of Chicago. http://www.chicityclerk.com/legislation-records/journals-and-reports /executive-orders.

Daley, Richard M. 2006. "Amendment of Title 2 of Municipal Code of Chicago by Creation of New Chapter 173 to Disallow Disclosure of and Conditioning Benefits and Services on Individual's Citizenship and Residency Status." https://chicityclerk.s3.amazonaws.com/s3fs-public/document_uploads/journals -proceedings/2006/032906VII.pdf.

Dana, Lydia. 2023. "Serv/eillance: Cops, Queers, and Clinics in Segregated Chicago." *Social Problems.* https://doi.org/10.1093/socpro/spado52.

Darling, Jonathan, and Vicki Squire. 2012. "Everyday Enactments of Sanctuary." In *Sanctuary Practices in International Perspectives: Migration, Citizenship, and Social Movements,* edited by Randy Lippert and Sean Rehaag, 191–204. New York: Routledge.

Darraj, Susan Muaddi. 2005. "Personal and Political: The Dynamics of Arab-American Feminism." *MIT Electronic Journal of Middle East Studies* 5: 158–68.

Davis, Angela, Gina Dent, Erica Meiners, and Beth Richie. 2022. *Abolition. Feminism. Now.* Chicago: Haymarket Books.

Davis, Dána-Ain. 2013. "Border Crossing: Intimacy and Feminist Activist Ethnography in the Age of Neoliberalism." In *Feminist Activist Ethnography: Counterpoints to Neoliberalism in North America,* edited by Christa Craven and Dána-Ain Davis, 23–38. Boulder, Colo.: Lexington Books.

Davis, Mike. 2006. *Planet of Slums.* London: Verso.

Davis, Robert. 1992. "Immigrant Policy Is Defended." *Chicago Tribune,* June 5. https://www.chicagotribune.com/news/ct-xpm-1992-06-05-9202200012-story.html.

Decoteau, Claire Laurier. 2024. *Emergency: COVID-19 and the Uneven Valuation of Life.* Chicago: University of Chicago Press.

De Genova, Nicholas. 2005. *Working the Boundaries: Race, Space, and "Illegality" in Mexican Chicago.* Durham, N.C.: Duke University Press.

De Genova, Nicholas, and Nathalie Peutz. 2010. *The Deportation Regime: Sovereignty, Space, and the Freedom of Movement.* Durham, N.C.: Duke University Press.

Delaney, David. 2010. "The Space That Race Makes." *Professional Geographer* 54, no. 1: 6–14.

del Pozo, Brandon, Alex Knorre, Michael J. Mello, and Aaron Chalfin. 2022. "Comparing Risks of Firearm-Related Death and Injury among Young Adult Males in Selected US Cities with Wartime Service in Iraq and Afghanistan." *Journal of the American Medical Association* 5, no. 12: e2248132.

Del Vecchio, Grace. 2020. "4 Actual Proposals for Cutting Chicago's Police Budget Right Now." *Injustice Watch,* November 23. https://www.injusticewatch.org/news/police-and-prosecutors/2020/proposals-cuts-chicago-police-budget/.

Detzer, Karl. 1966. "Crime-Stop Stops Crime." *Chicago Sunday Tribune Magazine,* September 4.

Deutsch, Michael, and Erica Thompson. 2008a. "Secrets and Lies: The Persecution of Muhammad Salah (Part I)." *Journal of Palestine Studies* 37, no. 4: 38–58.

Deutsch, Michael, and Erica Thompson. 2008b. "Secrets and Lies: The Persecution of Muhammad Salah (Part II)." *Journal of Palestine Studies* 38, no. 1: 25–53.

Dillon, Stephen. 2018. *Fugitive Life: The Queer Politics of the Prison State.* Durham, N.C.: Duke University Press.

Dixon, Ejeris. 2016. "Building Community Safety: Practical Steps toward Liberatory Transformation." In *Who Do You Serve, Who Do You Protect? Police Violence and Resilience in the United States,* edited by Maya Shanwar, Joe Marare, and Alana Price, 161–70. Chicago: Haymarket Books.

Dohrn, Bernardine. 2010. "The Curious, Mysterious, Obsolete, and Dangerous Federal Grand Jury." *Fight Back! News,* October 11. http://www.fightbacknews.org/2010/10/11/curious-mysterious-obsolete-and-dangerous-federal-grand-jury.

Dorais, Michel, and Patrice Corriveau. 2009. *Gangs and Girls: Understanding Juvenile Prostitution.* Montreal: McGill-Queen's University Press.

Drake, St. Claire, and Horace Cayton. 2015. *Black Metropolis: A Study of Negro Life in a Northern City.* Chicago: University of Chicago Press.

DropTheADL. 2021. "The ADL Is NOT an Ally: Why Communities Say NO to the

Anti-Defamation League in Our Schools, Coalitions, and Movements." https:// droptheadl.files.wordpress.com/2021/04/adl-primer-april-2021.pdf.

DuBois, Jill, Wesley G. Skogan, Susan M. Hartnett, Natalie Bump, and Danielle Morris. 2007. *CLEAR and I-CLEAR: A Report on New Information Technology in Chicago and Illinois.* Chicago: Chicago Community Policing Evaluation Consortium.

Du Bois, W. E. B. (1935) 1998. *Black Reconstruction in America.* New York: Free Press.

Dumke, Mick. 2018. "Chicago's Gang Database Is Full of Errors—and Records We Have Prove It." *ProPublica,* April 19. https://www.propublica.org/article/politic -il-insider-chicago-gang-database.

Dumke, Mick. 2019. "Cook County Takes Steps to Erase Its Regional Gang Database." *ProPublica,* February 20. https://www.propublica.org/article/cook-county-sheriffs -office-database-new-ban-law.

Dumke, Mick, and Ben Joravsky. 2011. "The Grass Gap." *Chicago Reader,* July 7. https://chicagoreader.com/news-politics/the-grass-gap/.

Duncan, Arne. 2020. "Reimagining Public Safety." Speech to the City Club of Chicago. September 23. https://www.youtube.com/watch?v=JnATTDlGSL8&ab _channel=CityClubofChicago.

Durán, Robert J. 2013. *Gang Life in Two Cities: An Insider's Journey.* New York: Columbia University Press.

Durán, Robert J. 2018. *The Gang Paradox: Inequalities and Miracles on the U.S.–Mexico Border.* New York: Columbia University Press.

Elliot-Cooper, Adam. 2021. *Black Resistance to British Policing.* Manchester, U.K.: Manchester University Press.

Emanuel, Rahm, and Susana A. Mendoza 2012. "Amendment and Renaming of Chapter 2-173 of Municipal Code as 'Welcoming City Ordinance' Regarding Immigration Status and Enforcement of Federal Civil Immigration Laws." *Journal of the Proceedings of the City Council of the City of Chicago, Illinois* 2. https://chicityclerk.s3.amazonaws.com/s3fs-public/document_uploads/journals -proceedings/2012/091212VII.pdf.

Escobar, Martha D. 2016. *Captivity beyond Prisons: Criminalization Experiences of Latina (Im)migrants.* Austin: University of Texas Press.

Esmeir, Samera. 2014. *Juridical Humanity: A Colonial History.* Stanford, Calif.: Stanford University Press.

Espeland, Wendy, and Mitchell Stevens. 2008. "A Sociology of Quantification." *European Journal of Sociology* 49, no. 3: 401–36.

Estes, Nick. 2019. *Our History Is the Future: Standing Rock versus the Dakota Access Pipeline and the Long Tradition of Indigenous Resistance.* London: Verso.

Eubanks, Virginia. 2017. *Automating Inequality: How High-Tech Tools Profile, Police, and Punish the Poor.* New York: St. Martin's Press.

Evans, Maxwell. 2020. "If City Wants Gun Violence to Drop 20%, It Must Invest in Prevention Programs, Activists Say." *Block Club Chicago,* January 28. https://block clubchicago.org/2020/01/28/activists-civic-leaders-want-to-decrease-chicagos -gun-violence-by-20-percent-in-2020/.

Fanon, Frantz. (1952) 2008. *Black Skin, White Masks.* New York: Grove Press.

Farnia, Nina. 2022. "Imperialism in the Making of U.S. Law." *St. John's Law Review* 96, no. 1: 131–85.

Fassin, Didier. 2011. *Humanitarian Reason: A Moral History of the Present.* Berkeley: University of California Press.

Fassin, Didier. 2013. *Enforcing Order: An Ethnography of Urban Policing.* Cambridge, Mass.: Polity Press.

Federal Bureau of Investigation. n.d. "Joint Terrorism Task Forces." https://www.fbi .gov/investigate/terrorism/joint-terrorism-task-forces.

Ferguson, Andrew Guthrie. 2016. *The Rise of Big Data Policing: Surveillance, Race, and the Future of Law Enforcement.* New York: New York University Press.

Ferguson, Andrew Guthrie. 2018. "Illuminating Black Data Policing." *Ohio State Journal of Criminal Law* 15: 503–25.

Ferguson, Roderick A. 2004. *Aberrations in Black: Toward a Queer of Color Critique.* Minneapolis: University of Minnesota Press.

Ferguson, Roderick A. 2012. *The Reorder of Things: The University and Its Pedagogies of Minority Difference.* Minneapolis: University of Minnesota Press.

Fernandez, Lilia. 2012. *Brown in the Windy City: Mexicans and Puerto Ricans in Postwar Chicago.* Chicago: University of Chicago Press.

Fight Back! News. 2011. "FBI Infiltration of Anti-War Movement Uncovered in Minneapolis." January 12. http://www.fightbacknews.org/2011/1/12/fbi-infiltration -anti-war-movement-uncovered-minneapolis.

Fisher, Jennifer. 2012. "Opinion: Do We Dare Love the Shooter?" *Patch,* October 12. https://patch.com/illinois/evanston/opinion-do-we-dare-love-the-shooter.

Flinn, John J. 1887. *History of the Chicago Police: From the Settlement of the Community to the Present Time.* Chicago: Police Book Fund.

Fong, Kelley. 2023. *Investigating Families: Motherhood in the Shadow of Child Protective Services.* Princeton, N.J.: Princeton University Press.

Foucault, Michel. (1975) 1995. *Discipline and Punish: The Birth of the Prison.* New York: Vintage.

Fourcade, Marion. 2016. "Ordinalization: Lewis A. Coser Memorial Award for Theoretical Agenda Setting 2014." *Sociological Theory* 34, no. 3: 175–95.

Franco, Marissa. 2017. "A Radical Expansion of Sanctuary: Steps in Defiance of Trump's Executive Order." *Truthout,* January 25. https://truthout.org/articles/a -radical-expansion-of-sanctuary-steps-in-defiance-of-trump-s-executive-order/.

Fraternal Order of Police. 2019. "Foxx Strikes Again: Mayhem Follows Release of Once Charged Men." *Lodge 7 Blog,* September 26. https://fop7blog.org/news/2019/9/26 /foxx-strikes-again-mayhem-follows-release-of-once-charged-men.

Freire, Paulo. 2014. *Pedagogy of the Oppressed.* New York: Bloomsbury.

Geib, Phil. 2015. "Chicago's Place among Global Cities." *Chicago Tribune,* May 19. https://www.chicagotribune.com/news/ct-nw-global-cities-gfc-htmlstory.html.

Genetec. n.d. "Strategic Decision Support Centers." https://info.genetec.com/strategic -decision-support-centers.html.

Gilmore, Ruth Wilson. 2007. *Golden Gulag: Prisons, Surplus, Crisis, and Opposition in Globalizing California.* Berkeley: University of California Press.

Gilmore, Ruth Wilson. 2015. "Organized Abandonment and Organized Violence: Devolution and the Police." Speech delivered at University of California, Santa Cruz.

Gilmore, Ruth Wilson. 2017. "Abolition Geography and the Problem of Innocence." In *Futures of Black Radicalism,* edited by Gaye Theresa Johnson and Alex Lubin, 225–40. London: Verso.

Gilmore, Ruth Wilson. 2020. "COVID-19, Decarceration, and Abolition." April 16. https://www.youtube.com/watch?v=lyTOspzD1ZQ&ab_channel=Haymarket Books.

Gilmore, Ruth Wilson. 2022. *Abolition Geography: Essays toward Liberation.* London: Verso.

Gilmore, Ruth Wilson. Forthcoming. *Change Everything: Racial Capitalism and the Case for Abolition.* Chicago: Haymarket Books.

Go, Julian. 2008. *American Empire and the Politics of Meaning: Elite Political Cultures in the Philippines and Puerto Rico during U.S. Colonialism.* Durham, N.C.: Duke University Press.

Go, Julian. 2020. "The Imperial Origins of American Policing: Militarization and Imperial Feedback in the Early 20th Century." *American Journal of Sociology* 125, no. 5: 1193–254.

Go, Julian. 2023. *Policing Empires: Militarization, Race, and the Imperial Boomerang in Britain and the US.* Oxford: Oxford University Press.

Golash-Boza, Tanya. 2015. *Deported: Immigrant Policing, Disposable Labor, and Global Capitalism.* New York: New York University Press.

Gomberg-Muñoz, Ruth, and Reyna Wences. 2020. "Fight for the City: Policing, Sanctuary, and Resistance in Chicago." *Geographical Review* 111, no. 2: 252–68.

Good Kids, Mad City. 2021. "An Ordinance to Create a Peace Book." https://drive .google.com/file/d/1gncHpxyxWpiTJIW8hsIq3shVpFtHcHRp/view.

Goodman, Adam. 2020. *The Deportation Machine: America's Long History of Expelling Immigrants.* Princeton, N.J.: Princeton University Press.

Goodwin, Alyxandra. 2017. "What You Need to Know about Chicago's 'Gang Database' and a Lawsuit from Local Activists." *Truthout,* May 10. https://truthout .org/articles/what-you-need-to-know-about-chicago-s-gang-database-and-a -lawsuit-from-local-activists/.

Gordon, Daanika. 2022. *Policing the Racial Divide: Urban Growth Politics and the Remaking of Segregation.* New York: New York University Press.

Gorner, Jeremy. 2018. "Crime-Fighting Technology in Chicago Gets $10 Million Boost from Billionaire Ken Griffin." *Chicago Tribune,* April 11. https://www .chicagotribune.com/news/breaking/ct-met-griffin-donation-chicago-police -20180411-story.html.

Goudie, Chuck, Eric Horng, and Barb Markoff. 2020. "President Trump Sending 'Hundreds' of Federal Agents to Chicago as Part of Anti-violence Effort; Mayor Lightfoot Says Focus Will Not Be on Protesters." ABC 7 Eyewitness News, July 22.

https://abc7chicago.com/chicago-violence-crime-federal-agents-president-don
ald-trump/6328585/.

Greenwald, Glenn. 2015. *No Place to Hide: Edward Snowden, the NSA, and the US Surveillance State*. New York: Picador Press.

Grench, Eileen. 2021. "Department of Investigation Confirms Probe of NYPD Gang Database after Advocates Rally." *The City*, July 27. https://www.thecity.nyc/2021/7/27/22597212/department-of-investigation-probes-nypd-gang-database.

Grimm, Andy, and Cynthia Dizikes. 2010. "FBI Raids Anti-war Activists' Homes." *Chicago Tribune*, September 24. https://www.chicagotribune.com/nation-world/ct-xpm-2010-09-24-ct-met-fbi-terrorism-investigation-20100924-story.html.

Gurusami, Susila. 2019. "Motherwork under the State: The Maternal Labor of Formerly Incarcerated Black Women." *Social Problems* 66, no. 1: 128–43.

Haas, Jeffrey. 2010. *The Assassination of Fred Hampton: How the FBI and the Chicago Police Murdered a Black Panther*. Chicago: Haymarket Books.

Hagedorn, John. (1988) 1998. *People and Folks: Gangs, Crime, and the Underclass in a Rustbelt City*. Chicago: Lakeview Press.

Hagedorn, John. 2015. *The Insane Chicago Way: The Daring Plan by Chicago Gangs to Create a Spanish Mafia*. Chicago: University of Chicago Press.

Hagedorn, John, Roberto Aspholm, Teresa Córdova, Andrew Papachristos, and Lance Williams. 2019. *The Fracturing of Gangs and Violence in Chicago: A Research-Based Reorientation of Violence Prevention and Intervention Policy*. Chicago: University of Illinois at Chicago Great Cities Institute.

Hagopian, Elaine C. 2004. *Civil Rights in Peril: The Targeting of Arabs and Muslims*. London: Pluto Press.

Hajjar, Lisa. 2005. *Courting Conflict: The Israeli Military Court System in the West Bank and Gaza*. Berkeley: University of California Press.

Haley, Sarah. 2019. *No Mercy Here: Gender, Punishment, and the Making of Jim Crow Modernity*. Chapel Hill: University of North Carolina Press.

Hall, Stuart. 1980. "Race, Articulation, and Societies Structured in Domination." In *Sociological Theories: Race and Colonialism*, edited by UNESCO, 305–45. Paris: UNESCO.

Hall, Stuart, Chas Critcher, Tony Jefferson, John Clarke, and Brian Roberts. 1978. *Policing the Crisis: Mugging, the State, and Law and Order*. London: Macmillan.

Hammer, Ricarda, and Tina Park. 2021. "The Ghost in the Algorithm: Racial Colonial Capitalism and the Digital Age." *Political Power and Social Theory* 38: 221–49.

Haney, Lynne. 2010. *Offending Women: Power, Punishment, and the Regulation of Desire*. Berkeley: University of California Press.

Hansen, Hans Krause. 2015. "Numerical Operations, Transparency Illusions, and the Datafication of Governance." *European Journal of Social Theory* 18, no. 2: 203–20.

Hardiman, Tio, Norman L. Kerr, Elena D. Quintana, Tim Metzger, Cody D. Stephens, and Gary Slutkin. 2004. "CeaseFire: Reducing Neighborhood Shootings via a Public Health Approach." Presentation at the 132nd annual meeting of the American Public Health Association, Washington, D.C., November 6–10.

Harris, Paul. 2012. "Carlos Montes: Political Activist Faces 22 Years in Jail over Thrown Soda Can." *The Guardian,* May 30. https://www.theguardian.com/world/2012/may/30/carlos-montes-faces-22-years-jail.

Hartman, Saidiya V. 1997. *Scenes of Subjection: Terror, Slavery, and Self-Making in Nineteenth-Century America.* Oxford: Oxford University Press.

Harvey, David. 1989. "From Managerialism to Entrepreneurialism: The Transformation of Urban Governance in Late Capitalism." *Geografiska Annaler, Series B* 71, no. 1: 3–17.

Harvey, David. 2003. *The New Imperialism.* New York: Oxford University Press.

Harvey, David. 2017. *Marx, Capital, and the Madness of Economic Reason.* Oxford: Oxford University Press.

Hatch, Anthony Ryan. 2022. "The Data Will Not Save Us: Afropessimism and Racial Antimatter in the Covid-19 Pandemic." *Big Data and Society* 9, no. 1: 1–13.

Heartland Alliance. n.d. "READI Chicago." https://www.heartlandalliance.org/readi/program/.

Heeder, Matthias, and Monika Hielscher, dirs. 2017. *Pre-crime.* Film. Floos.

Hendershot, Steve. 2022. "The Inequality of Safety." *Crain's Chicago Business,* October 24.

Herbert, Steve, and Elizabeth Brown. 2006. "Conceptions of Space and Crime in the Punitive Neoliberal City." *Antipode* 38, no. 4: 755–77.

Hernandez, Kelly Lytle. 2010. *Migra! A History of the U.S. Border Patrol.* Berkeley: University of California Press.

Hickey, Meghan. 2022. "Chicago's Arab American Community Launches Campaign to End Racial Profiling after Report Documenting Unfounded Accusations of Suspicious Activity." CBS Chicago, July 1. https://www.cbsnews.com/chicago/news/chicago-arab-american-community-campaign-to-end-racial-profiling-unfounded-accusations-suspicious-activity/.

Hing, Julianne. 2017. "ICE Admits Gang Operations Are Designed to Lock Up Immigrants: The Gang Database Is a Weapon That Allows ICE Agents to Indiscriminately Round Up Immigrants of Color." *The Nation,* November 20. https://www.thenation.com/article/archive/ice-admits-gang-operations-are-designed-to-lock-up-immigrants/.

Hinton, Elizabeth. 2016. *From the War on Poverty to the War on Crime: The Making of Mass Incarceration in America.* Cambridge, Mass.: Harvard University Press.

Hollywood, John S., Kenneth McKay, Dulani Woods, and Denis Agniel. 2019. *Real Time Crime Centers in Chicago: Evaluation of the Chicago Police Department's Strategic Decision Support Centers.* Santa Monica, Calif.: RAND Corporation.

Hong, Grace Kyungwong. 2015. *Death beyond Disavowal: The Impossible Politics of Difference.* Minneapolis: University of Minnesota Press.

Hong, Sun-ha. 2020. *Technologies of Speculation: The Limits of Knowledge in a Data-Driven Society.* New York: New York University Press.

hooks, bell. 1984. *Feminist Theory: From Margin to Center.* Boston: South End Press.

hooks, bell. 1994. *Teaching to Transgress: Education as the Practice of Freedom.* New York: Routledge.

hooks, bell. 2000. *All about Love: New Visions.* New York: William Morrow.

hooks, bell. 2003. *Teaching Community: A Pedagogy of Hope.* New York: Routledge.

Houston, Serin, and Olivia Lawrence-Weilmann. 2016. "The Model Migrant and Multiculturalism: Analyzing Neoliberal Logics in US Sanctuary Legislation." In *Migration Policy and Practice: Interventions and Solutions,* edited by Harald Bauder and Christian Matheis, 101–26. New York: Springer.

Human Rights Watch. 2014. "Illusions of Justice: Human Rights Abuses in US Terrorism Prosecutions." https://www.hrw.org/report/2014/07/21/illusion-justice /human-rights-abuses-us-terrorism-prosecutions.

Hvistendahl, Mara. 2021. "Oracle Boasted That Its Software Was Used against US Protesters. Then It Took the Tech to China." *The Intercept,* May 25. https:// theintercept.com/2021/05/25/oracle-social-media-surveillance-protests-endeca/.

Hvistendahl, Mara. 2022. "FBI Provides Chicago Police with Fake Identities for 'Social Media Exploitation' Team." *The Intercept,* May 20. https://theintercept. com/2022/05/20/chicago-police-fbi-social-media-surveillance-fake/.

INCITE!, ed. 2006. *The Color of Violence.* Cambridge, Mass.: South End Press.

INCITE!, ed. 2007. *The Revolution Will Not Be Funded: Beyond the Non-profit Industrial Complex.* Cambridge, Mass.: South End Press.

Ingatiev, Noel. 1995. *How the Irish Became White.* London: Routledge.

Institute for Research on Race and Public Policy. 2017. *A Tale of Three Cities: The State of Racial Justice in Chicago Report.* Chicago: University of Illinois at Chicago.

Institute for Research on Race and Public Policy. 2018. *A Tale of Diversity, Disparity, and Discrimination: The State of Racial Justice for Asian American Chicagoans.* Chicago: University of Illinois at Chicago.

Institute for Research on Race and Public Policy. 2019. *Adversity and Resiliency for Chicago's First: The State of Racial Justice for American Indian Chicagoans.* Chicago: University of Illinois at Chicago.

Institute for Research on Race and Public Policy. 2020. *Between the Great Migration and Growing Exodus: The Future of Black Chicago?* Chicago: University of Illinois at Chicago.

Institute for Research on Race and Public Policy. 2023. *Beyond Erasure and Profiling: Cultivating Strong and Vibrant Arab American Communities in Chicagoland.* Chicago: University of Illinois at Chicago.

2020. https://static1.squarespace.com/static/5ee39ec764dbd7179cf1243c/t/608068 39979abc1b93aa8695/1619028044655/%23DefundThePolice%2BUpdate.pdf.

Jacobs, Julia. 2017. "Chicago Sues Trump Administration over Sanctuary City Plan." *Reuters,* August 7. https://www.reuters.com/article/usa-immigration-sanctuary /chicago-sues-trump-administration-over-sanctuary-city-plan-idUSL1N1K T09R.

James, Steve, dir. 2011. *The Interrupters.* Film. Kartemquin Films.

Jefferson, Brian Jordan. 2018. "Predictable Policing: Predictive Crime Mapping and Geographies of Policing and Race." *Annals of the American Association of Geographers* 108, no. 1: 1–16.

Jefferson, Brian Jordan. 2020. *Digitize and Punish: Racial Criminalization in the Digital Age.* Minneapolis: University of Minnesota Press.

Jobs for R-Users. 2017. "Data Analyst, Chicago Violence Reduction Strategy." May 5. https://www.r-users.com/jobs/data-analyst-chicago-violence-reduction-strategy/.

Jones, Nikki. 2009. *Between Good and Ghetto: African American Girls and Inner-City Violence.* New Brunswick, N.J.: Rutgers University Press.

Joronen, Mikko. 2016. "'Death Comes Knocking on the Roof': Thanatopolitics of Ethical Killing during Operation Protective Edge in Gaza." *Antipode* 48, no. 2: 336–54.

Jung, Moon-Ho. 2022. *Menace to Empire: Anticolonial Solidarities and the Transpacific Origins of the U.S. Security State.* Berkeley: University of California Press.

Jung, Moon-Kie. 2015. *Beneath the Surface of White Supremacy: Denaturalizing U.S. Racisms Past and Present.* Stanford, Calif.: Stanford University Press.

Jung, Moon-Kie, Joao H. Costa Vargas, and Eduardo Bonilla-Silva. 2011. *The State of White Supremacy: Racism, Governance, and the United States.* Stanford, Calif.: Stanford University Press.

Just Futures Law, Mijente, Organized Communities Against Deportations, and the University of Chicago Law School. 2021. "The Digital Deportation Machine: How Surveillance Technology Undermines Chicago's Welcoming City Policy." https://www.flipsnack.com/justfutures/the-digital-deportation-machine/full-view.html.

Kaba, Mariame. 2016. "Four Years since a Chicago Police Officer Killed Rekia Boyd, Justice Still Hasn't Been Served." *In These Times*, March 21.

Kaba, Mariame. 2020. "Yes, We Mean Literally Abolish the Police." *New York Times*, June 13. https://www.nytimes.com/2020/06/12/opinion/sunday/floyd-abolish-defund-police.html.

Kaba, Mariame. 2021. *We Do This 'til We Free Us.* Chicago: Haymarket Books.

Kaba, Mariame, and Kelly Hayes. 2018. "A Jailbreak of the Imagination: Seeing Prisons for What They Are and Demanding Transformation." *Truthout*, May 3. https://truthout.org/articles/a-jailbreak-of-the-imagination-seeing-prisons-for-what-they-are-and-demanding-transformation/.

Kanstroom, Daniel. 2000. "Deportation, Social Control, and Punishment: Some Thoughts about Why Hard Laws Make Bad Cases." *Harvard Law Review* 113, no. 8: 1890–935.

Kean, Thomas, and Lee Hamilton. 2004. *The 9/11 Commission Report: Final Report of the National Commission on Terrorist Attacks upon the United States.* Vol. 3. Washington, D.C.: U.S. Government Printing Office.

Kelley, Robin D. G. 2002. *Freedom Dreams: The Black Radical Imagination.* Boston: Beacon Press.

Kelley, Robin D. G. 2017. Introduction to *Race, Capitalism, Justice*, 5–8. Boston: Boston Review.

Kennedy, David. 2011. *Don't Shoot: One Man, a Street Fellowship, and the End of Violence in Inner-City America.* New York: Bloomsbury.

Kennedy, David. 2015. "Hot People, Hot Places: Two Frameworks for Modern Strategic Crime Control." Presentation at the National Organization of Black Law Enforcement Executives, Hollywood, Fla., February 12.

Kennedy, David. 2019a. "Group Violence Intervention." Presentation to the Virginia Crime Commission, New York, August 19.

Kennedy, David. 2019b. "Keynote Remarks: Toward a Science and Practice of Violence Prevention." National Network of Safe Communities 10th Anniversary Conference, New York, June 18. https://youtu.be/ybWtEtNwmwU.

Kennedy, David. n.d. "Deterrence and Crime Prevention." Presentation to the Illinois Governor's Commission on Criminal Justice and Sentencing Reform.

Kerr, Norman L., Elena D. Quintana, Cody D. Stephens, Tio Hardiman, and Gary Slutkin. 2003. "CeaseFire: Reducing Neighborhood Shootings via a Public Health Approach." Presentation at the 131st annual meeting of the American Public Health Association, Washington, D.C., November 6–10.

Khalili, Laleh. 2010. "The Location of Palestine in Global Counterinsurgencies." *International Journal of Middle East Studies* 42, no. 3: 413–23.

Khalili, Laleh. 2013. *Time in the Shadows: Confinement in Counterinsurgencies.* Stanford, Calif.: Stanford University Press.

Khoury, Buthaina Canaan, dir. 2004. *Women in Struggle.* Film. Women Make Movies.

King, Elizabeth. 2019. "Chicago Cops Use Social Media to Track Grieving Families of Gunshot Victims." *OneZero,* December 4. https://onezero.medium.com/chicago-cops-use-social-media-to-track-grieving-families-of-gunshot-victims-e68e5a6dc40c.

Kozol, Jonathan. 2005. *The Shame of the Nation: The Restoration of Apartheid Schooling in America.* New York: Crown.

Krippner, Greta, and Daniel Hirschman. 2020. "The Person and the Category: The Pricing of Risk and the Politics of Classification in Insurance and Credit." *Theory and Society* 51: 685–727.

Kumar, Deepa. 2012. *Islamophobia and the Politics of Empire.* Chicago: Haymarket Books.

Kundnani, Arun. 2014. *The Muslims Are Coming! Islamophobia, Extremism, and the Domestic War on Terror.* London: Verso.

Kundnani, Arun. 2023. *What Is Antiracism? And Why It Means Anticapitalism.* London: Verso.

Kunichoff, Yana, and Patrick Sier. 2017. "The Contradictions of Chicago Police's Secretive List." *Chicago Magazine,* August 21.

Lageson, Sareh Esther. 2020. *Digital Punishment: Privacy, Stigma, and the Harms of Data-Driven Criminal Justice.* Oxford: Oxford University Press.

Lanfear, Charles C., Rebecca Bucci, David S. Kirk, and Robert J. Sampson. 2023. "Inequalities in Exposure to Firearm Violence by Race, Sex and Birth Cohort from Childhood to Age 40 Years, 1995–2021." *Journal of the American Medical Association* 6, no. 5: e2312465.

Lebrón, Marisol. 2017. "Puerto Rico and the Colonial Circuits of Policing." *NACLA Report on the Americas* 49, no. 3: 328–34.

Lebrón, Marisol. 2019. *Policing Life and Death: Race, Violence, and Resistance in Puerto Rico.* Berkeley: University of California Press.

Legomsky, Stephen H. 2007. "The New Path of Immigration Law: Asymmetric Incorporation of Criminal Justice Norms." *Washington and Lee Law Review* 64: 469–527.

Lenin, Vladimir Ilyich. (1916) 1963. *Imperialism, the Highest Stage of Capitalism.* Moscow: Progress.

#LetUsBreathe Collective. 2022. "Imagining a World." https://www.letusbreathe collective.com/freedomsquare.

Lewis, Amanda E., and David G. Embrick. 2016. "Working at the Intersection of Race and Public Policy: The Promise (and Perils) of Putting Research to Work for Societal Transformation." *Sociology of Race and Ethnicity* 2, no. 3: 253–62.

Li, Darryl. 2020. *The Universal Enemy: Jihad, Empire, and the Challenge of Solidarity.* Stanford, Calif.: Stanford University Press.

Liebowitz, Aaron. 2019. "Chicago Public Schools Monitored Social Media for Signs of Violence, Gang Membership." *ProPublica,* February 11. https://www.propublica .org/article/chicago-public-schools-social-media-monitoring-violence -gangs.

Lipman, Pauline. 2007. "Renaissance 2010: The Reassertion of Ruling Class Power through Neoliberal Policies in Chicago." *Policy Futures in Education* 5, no. 2: 160–78.

Lipman, Pauline. 2011. "Contesting the City: Neoliberal Urbanism and the Cultural Politics of Education Reform in Chicago." *Discourse: Studies in the Cultural Politics of Education* 32, no. 2: 217–34.

Lipsitz, George. 2008. "Breaking the Chains and Steering the Ship: How Activism Can Help Change Teaching and Scholarship." In *Engaging Contradictions: Theory, Politics, and Methods of Activist Scholarship,* edited by Charles R. Hale, 88–111. Berkeley: University of California Press.

Lorde, Audre. 1984. *Sister Outsider.* Berkeley: Crossing Press.

Losier, Toussaint. 2018. "The Rise and Fall of the 1969 Chicago Jobs Campaign: Street Gangs, Coalition Politics, and the Origins of Mass Incarceration." *University of Memphis Law Review* 49: 101–36.

Lovato, Roberto. 2020. *Unforgetting: A Memoir of Family, Migration, Gangs, and Revolution in the Americas.* New York: HarperCollins.

Loyd, Jenna, Matt Mitchelson, and Andrew Burridge, eds. 2012. *Beyond Walls and Cages: Prisons, Borders, and Global Crisis.* Athens: University of Georgia Press.

Lybarger, Loren D. 2020. *Palestinian Chicago.* Berkeley: University of California Press.

Lyons, Kim. 2020. "Thomson Reuters Faces Pressure over ICE Contracts." *The Verge,* May 21. https://www.theverge.com/2020/5/21/21266431/thomson-reuters-ice -clear-software.

MacArthur Foundation. 2019. "Professionalizing Street Outreach." August 27. https:// www.macfound.org/press/grantee-stories/professionalizing-street-outreach.

Macías-Rojas, Patrisia. 2016. *From Deportation to Prison: The Politics of Immigration Enforcement in Post–Civil Rights America.* New York: New York University Press.

Macías-Rojas, Patrisia. 2021. "Liberal Policies, Punitive Effects: The Politics of Enforcement Discretion on the U.S.–Mexico Border." *Law and Social Inquiry* 46, no. 1: 69–91.

Maher, Geo. 2021. *A World without Police: How Strong Communities Make Cops Obsolete.* London: Verso.

Main, Frank. 2018. "Los Angeles–Style Policing Driving Down Chicago Shootings, City's Experts Say." *Chicago Sun-Times,* February 9. https://chicago.suntimes.com/2018/2/9/18372071/los-angeles-style-policing-driving-down-chicago-shootings-city-s-experts-say.

Maltz, Michael D. 1993. "Crime Mapping and the Drug Market Analysis Program (DMAP)." In *Workshop on Crime Analysis through Computer Mapping Proceedings,* 271–77. Chicago: Illinois Criminal Justice Information Authority.

Maltz, Michael D., Andrew C. Gordon, and Warren Friedman. 1989. *Mapping Crime in Its Community Setting: A Study of Event Geography Analysis.* Washington, D.C.: National Institute of Justice.

Marx, Karl. (1867) 1906. *Capital: A Critique of Political Economy, Volume 1.* New York: Modern Library.

McCoy, Alfred. 2009. *Policing America's Empire: The United States, the Philippines, and the Rise of the Surveillance State.* Madison: University of Wisconsin Press.

McGarrell, Edmund, Natalie Hipple, Nicholas Coraro, Timothy Bynum, Heather Perez, Carol Zimmerman, and Melissa Carmo. 2009. *Project Safe Neighborhoods—A National Program to Reduce Gun Crime: Final Project Report.* Washington, D.C.: National Institutes of Justice.

McQuade, Brendan. 2019. *Pacifying the Homeland: Intelligence Fusion and Mass Supervision.* Berkeley: University of California Press.

Meisner, Jason, and Annie Sweeney. 2021. "54 Slayings, More Than 80 Charged: As Chicago's Gangs Have Changed, So Have Federal RICO Prosecutions." *Chicago Tribune,* November 19.

Melamed, Jodi. 2011. *Represent and Destroy: Rationalizing Violence in the New Racial Capitalism.* Minneapolis: University of Minnesota Press.

Menjívar, Cecilia, and Leisy Abrego. 2012. "Legal Violence: Immigration Law and the Lives of Central American Immigrants." *American Journal of Sociology* 117, no. 5: 1380–421.

Metropolitan Family Services. n.d. "Communities Partnering 4 Peace." https://www.metrofamily.org/cp4p/cp4p-info/.

Mijente. 2017. "Mijente Concept Plan for Resisting and Building in 2017." January 20. https://mijente.net/2017/01/conceptplan/.

Miller, Jody. 2000. *One of the Guys: Girls, Gangs, and Gender.* Oxford: Oxford University Press.

Miller, Reuben Jonathan. 2014. "Devolving the Carceral State: Race, Prisoner Reentry, and the Micro-Politics of Urban Poverty Management." *Punishment and Society* 3, no. 16: 305–35.

Miller, Rueben Jonathan. 2021. *Halfway Home: Race, Punishment, and the Afterlife of Mass Incarceration.* New York: Hachette.

Miller, Teresa A. 2005. "Blurring the Boundaries between Immigration and Crime Control after September 11th." *Boston College Third World Law Journal* 25: 81–123.

Mills, Charles M. 1997. *The Racial Contract.* Ithaca, N.Y.: Cornell University Press.

Minnis, Jack, Walter Tillow, Rick Manning, Jerry Tecklin, Barbara Brandt, Bruce Palmer, John Perdew, Jerry DuMuth, and Joe Teller. 1965. "At Last!! The Paper You All Have Been Waiting For!! What Is the SNCC Research Department . . ." Lucile Montgomery Papers, 1963–1967. Wisconsin Historical Society Library, micro 44, reel 3, segment 48.

Mitrani, Sam. 2013. *The Rise of the Chicago Police Department: Class and Conflict, 1850–1894.* Chicago: University of Illinois Press.

Mogul, Joey. 2015. "The Struggle for Reparations in the Burge Torture Cases: The Grassroots Struggle that Could." *Public Interest Law Reporter* 17: 209–25.

Mogul, Joey, Andrea Ritchie, and Kay Whitlock. 2011. *Queer (In)justice: The Criminalization of LGBT People in the United States.* Boston: Beacon Press.

Mohanty, Chandra Talpade. 2003. *Feminism without Borders: Decolonizing Theory, Practicing Solidarity.* Durham, N.C.: Duke University Press.

Moore, Joan. 1978. *Homeboys: Gangs, Drugs, and Prison in the Barrios of Los Angeles.* Philadelphia: Temple University Press.

Moraga, Cherríe, and Gloria Anzaldúa. 1981. *This Bridge Called My Back: Writings by Radical Women of Color.* Bath, U.K.: Persephone Books.

Morgan-Trostle, Juliana, Kexin Zheng, and Carl Lipscombe. 2016. "The State of Black Immigrants, Pt 2: Black Immigrants in the Mass Criminalization System." https://www.sccgov.org/sites/oir/Documents/sobi-deprt-blk-immig-crim-sys.pdf.

Moten, Fred, and Stefano Harney. 2013. *The Undercommons: Fugitive Planning and Black Study.* New York: Autonomedia.

Movement for Black Lives. n.d. "Policy Platforms." https://m4bl.org/policy-platforms/.

Muhammad, Khalil Gibran. 2010. *The Condemnation of Blackness: Race, Crime, and the Making of Modern Urban America.* Cambridge, Mass.: Harvard University Press.

Muñiz, Ana. 2022. *Borderland Circuitry: Immigration Surveillance in the United States and Beyond.* Berkeley: University of California Press.

Muñiz, Michael De Anda, Janaé Bonsu, Lydia Dana, Sangeetha Ravichandran, Haley Volpintesta, and Andy Clarno, with Reyna Wences, Rodrigo Anzures, Rosi Carrasco, and Tania Unzueta. 2020. "From Graduate Practicum to Activist Research Collective: A Roundtable with Members of the Policing in Chicago Research Group and Our Community Partners." *Radical History Review* 137: 141–56.

Muñiz-Pagan, Karina. 2019. "Expanding Sanctuary." *Race, Poverty, and the Environment* 22, no. 1. https://www.reimaginerpe.org/22/muniz.

Murakawa, Naomi. 2014. *The First Civil Right: How Liberals Built Prison America.* Oxford: Oxford University Press.

Naber, Nadine. 2000. "Ambiguous Insiders: An Investigation of Arab American Invis-ibility." *Ethnic and Racial Studies* 23: 37–61.

Naber, Nadine. 2008. "Introduction: Arab Americans and U.S. Racial Formations." In *Race and Arab Americans before and after 9/11: From Invisible Citizens to Visible Subjects*, edited by A. Jamal and N. Naber, 1–45. Syracuse, N.Y.: Syracuse University Press.

Naber, Nadine. 2012. *Arab America: Gender, Cultural Politics, and Activism*. New York: New York University Press.

Naber, Nadine. 2014. "Imperial Whiteness and the Diasporas of Empire." *American Quarterly* 66, no. 4: 1107–15.

Naber, Nadine, Eman Desouky, and Lina Baroudi. 2011. "The Forgotten -Ism." In *Color of Violence*, edited by INCITE!, 97–112. Cambridge, Mass.: South End Press.

Naber, Nadine, and Junaid Rana. 2019. "The 21st Century Problem of Anti-Muslim Racism." *Jadaliyya*, July 25. https://www.jadaliyya.com/Details/39830.

Naber, Nadine, and Clarissa Rojas. 2021. "To Abolish Prisons and Militarism, We Need Anti-Imperialist Abolition Feminism." *Truthout*, July 16. https://truthout.org/articles/to-abolish-prisons-and-militarism-we-need-anti-imperialist-abolition-feminism/.

Naughtie, James. 1981. "Palestinian, Jailed in Chicago, Fighting Extradition to Israel." *Washington Post*, July 24. https://www.washingtonpost.com/archive/politics/1981/07/24/palestinian-jailed-in-chicago-fighting-extradition-to-israel/9811 20d1-27bb-4d4c-8deb-8bfd0ba0b936/.

Neely, Brooke, and Michelle Samura. 2011. "Social Geographies of Race: Connecting Race and Space." *Ethnic and Racial Studies* 34, no. 11: 1933–52.

Neil, Emily. 2018. "PARS Has Ended, but Work Continues for Immigrant Rights Activists." *Al Día*, September 4. https://aldianews.com/articles/politics/pars-has-ended-work-continues-immigrant-rights-activists/53781.

Neocleous, Mark. 2021. *A Critical Theory of Police Power: The Fabrication of Social Order*. London: Verso.

Nevins, Joseph. 2002. *Operation Gatekeeper: The Rise of the "Illegal Alien" and the Making of the U.S.–Mexico Boundary*. London: Routledge.

Nguyen, Nicole. 2019. *Suspect Communities: Anti-Muslim Racism and the Domestic War on Terror*. Minneapolis: University of Minnesota Press.

Nishida, Akemi. 2022. *Just Care: Messy Entanglements of Disability, Dependency, and Desire*. Philadelphia: Temple University Press.

Nolan, Jermaine, and Sam Kelly. 2020. "Death of Cook County Jail Detainee Found Dead in His Cell Ruled a Homicide." *Chicago Sun-Times*, February 2.

O'Donnell, Maggie, and Louisa Aviles. 2017. *Group Violence Intervention: A Guide for Project Managers*. Washington, D.C.: Bureau of Justice Assistance.

Office of Inspector General. 2019. *Review of the Chicago Police Department's "Gang Database."* Chicago: Office of Inspector General. https://igchicago.org/wp-content/uploads/2019/04/OIG-CPD-Gang-Database-Review.pdf.

Office of Inspector General. 2020. *Advisory Concerning the Chicago Police Department's*

Predictive Risk Models. Chicago: Office of Inspector General. https://igchicago
.org/wp-content/uploads/2020/01/OIG-Advisory-Concerning-CPDs-Predictive
-Risk-Models-.pdf.

Office of Inspector General. 2021. *Follow-Up Inquiry on the Chicago Police Department's "Gang Database."* Chicago: Office of Inspector General.

Organized Communities Against Deportations. 2020. "Wilmer's Victory." *OCAD Blog,*
March 3. https://www.organizedcommunities.org/blog-posts/wilmers-victory.

Pager, Devah. 2009. *Marked: Race, Crime, and Finding Work in an Era of Mass Incarceration.* Chicago: University of Chicago Press.

Paik, A. Naomi. 2016. *Rightlessness: Testimony and Redress in U.S. Prison Camps since
World War II.* Chapel Hill: University of North Carolina Press.

Paik, A. Naomi. 2017. "Abolitionist Futures and the US Sanctuary Movement." *Race
and Class* 59, no. 2: 3–25.

Paik, A. Naomi. 2020. *Bans, Walls, Raids, Sanctuary: Understanding U.S. Immigration
for the Twenty-First Century.* Berkeley: University of California Press.

Pallares, Amalia, and Nilda Flores-Gonzales, eds. 2010. *Marcha! Latino Chicago and
the Immigrant Rights Movement.* Urbana: University of Illinois Press.

Papachristos, Andrew. 2009. "Murder by Structure: Dominance Relations and the
Social Structure of Gang Homicide." *American Journal of Sociology* 115, no. 1:
74–128.

Papachristos, Andrew. 2011. "Too Big to Fail: The Science and Politics of Violence
Prevention." *Criminology and Public Policy* 10, no. 4: 1053–62.

Papachristos, Andrew. 2012. "What Is a 'Gang Audit'?" *Huffington Post—the Blog,* July 5.
https://www.huffpost.com/entry/what-is-a-gang-audit_b_1651386.

Papachristos, Andrew, and Sara Bastomski. 2018. "Connected in Crime: The Enduring Effect of Neighborhood Networks on the Spatial Patterning of Violence."
American Journal of Sociology 124, no. 2: 517–68.

Papachristos, Andrew, Anthony Braga, Eric Piza, and Leigh Grossman. 2015. "The
Company You Keep? The Spillover Effects of Gang Membership on Individual
Gunshot Victimization in a Co-offending Network." *Criminology* 53, no. 4:
624–49.

Papachristos, Andrew, David Hureau, and Anthony Braga. 2013. "The Corner and
the Crew: The Influence of Geography and Social Networks on Gang Violence."
American Sociological Review 78, no. 3: 417–47.

Papachristos, Andrew, T. L. Meares, and J. Fagan. 2007. "Attention Felons: Evaluat-
ing Project Safe Neighborhoods in Chicago." *Journal of Empirical Legal Studies*
4: 223–72.

Parenti, Christian. 2003. *The Soft Cage: Surveillance in America from Slavery to the
War on Terror.* New York: Basic Books.

Partnership for Safe and Peaceful Communities. n.d. "About Us." https://safeand
peaceful.org/about-us/.

Pastore, Richard. 2004. "Chicago Police Department Uses IT to Fight Crime, Wins
Grand CIO Enterprise Value Award 2004." *CIO,* February 15. https://www.cio

.com/article/272672/it-organization-chicago-police-department-uses-it-to-fight
-crime-wins-grand-cio-enterprise-value-aw.html.

PathAR. n.d. "Social Media Intelligence." Internal document.

Patton, Desmond U., Owen Rambow, Johathan Auerbach, Kevin Li, and William Frey.
2018. "Expressions of Loss Predict Aggressive Comments on Twitter among
Gang-Involved Youth in Chicago." *npj Digital Medicine* 1: Article 11.

Peck, Jamie. 2010. "Zombie Neoliberalism and the Ambidextrous State." *Theoretical
Criminology* 14, no. 1: 104–10.

Pennock, Pamela E. 2017. *The Rise of the Arab American Left: Activists, Allies, and
Their Fight against Imperialism and Racism, 1960s–1980s.* Durham: University
of North Carolina Press.

Perry, Walter, Brian McInnis, Carter Price, Susan Smith, and John Hollywood. 2013.
Predictive Policing: The Role of Crime Forecasting in Law Enforcement Operations.
Santa Monica, Calif.: RAND Corporation.

Piepzna-Samarasinha, Leah Lakshmi. 2022. *The Future Is Disabled: Prophecies, Love
Notes, and Mourning Songs.* Vancouver, B.C.: Arsenal Pulp Press.

Pillai, Shreerekha, ed. 2023. *Carceral Liberalism: Feminist Voices against State Violence.*
Urbana: University of Illinois Press.

Police Accountability Task Force. 2016. *Recommendations for Reform: Restoring Trust
between the Chicago Police and the Communities They Serve.* Chicago: Police
Accountability Task Force.

Policing in Chicago Research Group. 2018a. *Expansive and Focused Surveillance: New
Findings on Chicago's Gang Database.* Chicago: Policing in Chicago Research
Group.

Policing in Chicago Research Group. 2018b. *Tracked and Targeted: Early Findings on
Chicago's Gang Database.* Chicago: Policing in Chicago Research Group.

Policing in Chicago Research Group. 2019. *Accountability after Abolition: The Regional
Gang Intelligence Database.* Chicago: Policing in Chicago Research Group.

Poulos, Chris D. 2022. "Permanent Austerity Public Finance: A 40 Year Case Study
of Public Finance Policy in Chicago, IL." PhD diss., University of Illinois at
Chicago.

Pratt, Gregory, and Jeremy Gorner. 2020. "Mayor Lori Lightfoot Announces Beefed-
Up Chicago Police Plan to Track, Prevent Future Looting throughout the City."
Chicago Tribune, August 14. https://www.chicagotribune.com/politics/ct-lori
-lightfoot-public-safety-plan-news-conference-20200814-uw36wzrezjeu7h4wjj
ccbvvupy-story.html.

Price, Michael. 2013. "National Security and Local Police." Brennan Center for Justice,
December 10. https://www.brennancenter.org/our-work/research-reports/national
-security-and-local-police.

Provine, Doris Marie, Monica W. Varsanyi, Paul G. Lewis, and Scott H. Decker, eds.
2016. *Policing Immigrants: Local Law Enforcement on the Front Lines.* Chicago:
University of Chicago Press.

Quig, A. D. 2019. "County Database May Be Gone, but Activists Want to Know How to Help Those Whose Lives Were Already 'Destroyed' by It." *Block Club Chicago,* January 25. https://blockclubchicago.org/2019/01/25/after-dart-decommissions -gang-database-county-board-commissioner-and-activists-demand-answers/.

Ralph, Lawrence. 2019. *The Torture Letters: Reckoning with Police Violence.* Chicago: University of Chicago Press.

Ransby, Barbara. 2018. *Making All Black Lives Matter: Reimagining Freedom in the 21st Century.* Oakland: University of California Press.

Ravichandran, Sangeetha. 2022. "'A Little Right of Center': Carceral Feminism and the Expansion of Biosurveillance." *Feminist Formations* 34, no. 2: 43–68.

Rhee, Nissa. 2016. "Can Police Big Data Stop Chicago's Spike in Crime?" *Christian Science Monitor,* June 2. https://www.csmonitor.com/USA/Justice/2016/0602 /Can-police-big-data-stop-Chicago-s-spike-in-crime.

Rich, Thomas F. 1996. *The Chicago Police Department's Information Collection for Automated Mapping (ICAM) Program.* Washington, D.C.: U.S. Department of Justice, Office of Justice Programs, National Institute of Justice.

Richie, Beth. 2012. *Arrested Justice: Black Women, Violence, and America's Prison Nation.* New York: New York University Press.

Ridgley, Jennifer. 2008. "Cities of Refuge: Immigration Enforcement, Police, and the Insurgent Genealogies of Citizenship in U.S. Sanctuary Cities." *Urban Geography* 29, no. 1: 53–77.

Ridgley, Jennifer. 2012. "The City as a Sanctuary in the United States." In *Sanctuary Practices in International Perspectives: Migration, Citizenship, and Social Movements,* edited by Randy Lippert and Sean Rehaag, 237–49. New York: Routledge.

Rios, Victor. 2011. *Punished: Policing the Lives of Black and Latino Boys.* New York: New York University Press.

Ritchie, Andrea. 2017. *Invisible No More: Police Violence against Black Women and Women of Color.* Boston: Beacon Press.

Robinson, Cedric. (1983) 2000. *Black Marxism: The Making of the Black Radical Tradition.* Chapel Hill: University of North Carolina Press.

Robinson, John N., III. 2021. "Surviving Capitalism: Affordability as a Racial 'Wage' in Contemporary Housing Markets." *Social Problems* 68, no. 2: 321–39.

Rodriguez, Dylan. 2007. "The Political Logic of the Non-Profit Industrial Complex." In *The Revolution Will Not Be Funded: Beyond the Non-Profit Industrial Complex,* edited by INCITE!, 21–40. Cambridge, Mass.: South End Press.

Rodriguez, Dylan. 2019. "Abolition as Praxis of Being Human: An Afterword." *Harvard Law Review* 132: 1575–612.

Rodriguez, Dylan. 2021. *White Reconstruction: Domestic Warfare and the Logics of Genocide.* New York: Fordham University Press.

Rodriguez-Muñiz, Michael. 2021. *Figures of the Future: Latino Civil Rights and the Politics of Demographic Change.* Princeton, N.J.: Princeton University Press.

Roediger, David. 2022. *The Wages of Whiteness: Race and the Making of the American Working Class.* London: Verso.

Rosa, Asha, Monica Trinidad, and Page May. 2016. "We Charge Genocide: The Emergence of a Movement." In *Who Do You Serve, Who Do You Protect? Police*

Violence and Resilience in the United States, edited by Maya Shanwar, Joe Marare, and Alana Price, 119–23. Chicago: Haymarket Books.

Rosas, Gilberto. 2012. *Barrio Libre: Criminalizing States and Delinquent Refusals of the New Frontier.* Durham, N.C.: Duke University Press.

Roy, Ananya. 2019. "The City in the Age of Trumpism: From Sanctuary to Abolition." *Environment and Planning D: Society and Space* 37, no. 5: 761–78.

Rumore, Kori. 2023. "Timeline: Chicago's More Than 40-Year History as a Sanctuary City." *Chicago Tribune,* May 26. https://www.chicagotribune.com/news /ct-chicago-sanctuary-history-htmlstory.html.

Ruppenthal, Alex. 2019. "Records: CPD Used CIA-Backed Software to Monitor Social Media Accounts." WTTW News, February 28. https://news.wttw.com/2019/02/28 /records-cpd-used-cia-backed-software-monitor-social-media-accounts.

Russell-Brown, Katheryn. 2008. *The Color of Crime: Racial Hoaxes, White Fear, Black Protectionism, Police Harassment, and Other Macroaggressions.* 2nd ed. New York: New York University Press.

Said, Edward. 1978. *Orientalism.* New York: Vintage Books.

Said, Edward. 1979. *The Question of Palestine.* New York: Times Books.

Said, Edward. 1996. *Peace and Its Discontents: Essays on Palestine in the Middle East Peace Process.* New York: Vintage.

Said, Wadie. 2015. *Crimes of Terror: The Legal and Political Implications of Federal Terrorism Prosecutions.* Oxford: Oxford University Press.

Sassen, Saskia. 2001. *The Global City: New York, London, Tokyo.* Princeton, N.J.: Princeton University Press.

Saunders, Jessica, Priscilla Hunt, and John Hollywood. 2016. "Predictions Put into Practice: A Quasi-experimental Evaluation of Chicago's Predictive Policing Pilot." *Journal of Experimental Criminology* 12: 347–71.

Schenwar, Maya, and Victoria Law. 2020. *Prison by Any Other Name: The Harmful Consequences of Popular Reforms.* New York: New Press.

Scherr, Albert, and Rebecca Hofmann. 2016. "Sanctuary Cities: Eine Perspektive für deutsche Kommunalpolitik?" *Kritische Justiz* 49, no. 1: 86–97.

Schrader, Stuart. 2019. *Badges without Borders: How Global Counterinsurgency Transformed American Policing.* Berkeley: University of California Press.

Schuba, Tom. 2020a. "CPD No Longer Using Clearview AI Facial Recognition Software, Department Says after ACLU Sues Controversial Firm." *Chicago Sun-Times,* May 28. https://chicago.suntimes.com/2020/5/28/21273248/aclu-sues-clearview-ai -facial-recognition-technology-chicago-police-department.

Schuba, Tom. 2020b. "CPD Using Controversial Facial Recognition Program That Scans Billions of Photos from Facebook, Other Sites." *Chicago Sun-Times,* January 29. https://chicago.suntimes.com/crime/2020/1/29/21080729/clearview-ai-facial -recognition-chicago-police-cpd.

Schuba, Tom, and Frank Main. 2021. "CPD Launched Secret Drone Program with Off-the-Books Cash." *Chicago Sun-Times,* May 12. https://chicago.suntimes .com/city-hall/2021/5/11/22425299/cpd-chicago-police-drone-secret-emails -hack-lori-lightfoot-dodsecrets-city-hall.

Schwartz, Adam. 2013. "Chicago's Video Surveillance Cameras: A Pervasive and Poorly Regulated Threat to Our Privacy." *Northwestern Journal of Technology and Intellectual Property* 11, no. 2: 47–60.

Seigel, Micol. 2018. *Violence Work: State Power and the Limits of Police.* Durham, N.C.: Duke University Press.

Selod, Saher. 2018. *Forever Suspect: Racialized Surveillance of Muslim Americans in the War on Terror.* New Brunswick, N.J.: Rutgers University Press.

Serrato, Jacqueline. 2018. "Chicago Gang Database under Review by Oversight Agency." *Chicago Tribune,* April 13. https://www.chicagotribune.com/voice-it /ct-chicago-gang-database-under-review-by-oversight-agency-20180413-story .html.

Serrato, Jacqueline. 2019. "Coalition Calls for an Investigation of the Cook County Gang Database." *Chicago Tribune,* January 25. https://www.chicagotribune .com/voice-it/ct-coalition-calls-for-an-investigation-of-the-cook-county-gang -database-20190125-story.html.

Shabazz, Rashad. 2015. *Spatializing Blackness: Architectures of Confinement and Black Masculinity in Chicago.* Urbana: University of Illinois Press.

Shaheen, Jack. 1984. *The TV Arab.* Bowling Green, Ohio: Bowling Green State Press.

Sheen, David. 2020. "Decades after a Palestinian American Activist Was Assassinated in California, Two Suspects in His Killing Are Living Openly in Israel." *The Intercept,* February 6. https://theintercept.com/2020/02/06/alex-odeh-bombing -israel/.

Shepelavy, Roxanne Patel. 2020. "The Transformative Power of Replacing Guns with Jobs." *Reasons to Be Cheerful* (blog), December 9. https://reasonstobecheerful .world/the-transformative-power-of-replacing-guns-with-jobs/.

Simpson, Leanne Betasamosake. 2017. *As We Have Always Done: Indigenous Freedom through Radical Resurgence.* Minneapolis: University of Minnesota Press.

Singh, Nikhil Pal. 2019. *Race and America's Long War.* Berkeley: University of California Press.

Skidmore, Owings, and Merrill. 1973. *Chicago 21: Plan for the Central Area Communities.* Chicago: Skidmore, Owings, and Merrill.

Skogan, Wesley. 2022. *Stop and Frisk and the Politics of Crime Control in Chicago.* Oxford: Oxford University Press.

Skogan, Wesley, and Susan Hartnett. 1997. *Community Policing, Chicago Style.* Oxford: Oxford University Press.

Skogan, Wesley, Susan Hartnett, Jill DuBois, Jason Bennis, and So Young Kim. 2003. *Policing Smarter through IT: Learning from Chicago's Citizen and Law Enforcement Analysis and Reporting (CLEAR) System.* Washington, D.C.: U.S. Department of Justice, Office of Community Oriented Policing Services.

Skogan, Wesley G., Dennis P. Rosenbaum, Susan M. Hartnett, Jill DuBois, Lisa Graziano, and Cody Stephens. 2005. *CLEAR and I-CLEAR: A Status Report on New Information Technology and Its Impact on Management, the Organization and Crime-Fighting Strategies.* Chicago: Chicago Community Policing Evaluation Consortium.

Smith, Dorothy E. 1987. *The Everyday World as Problematic: A Feminist Sociology.* Boston: Northeastern University Press.

Smith, George. 2006. "Political Activist as Ethnographer." In *Sociology for Changing the World: Social Movements/Social Research,* edited by Caelie Frampton, Gary Kinsman, A. K. Thompson, and Kate Tilleczek, 44–70. Halifax, N.S.: Fernwood.

Smith, Janet. 2013. "The End of U.S. Public Housing as We Knew It." *Urban Research and Practice* 6, no. 3: 276–96.

Smith, Linda Tuhiwai. (1999) 2012. *Decolonizing Methodologies: Research and Indigenous Peoples.* London: Zed Books.

Smith, Neil. 1996. *The New Urban Frontier: Gentrification and the Revanchist City.* London: Routledge.

Snowden, Edward. 2020. *Permanent Record.* New York: Picador.

Snyder, Benjamin. 2020. "'Big Brother's Bigger Brother': The Visual Politics of (Counter) Surveillance in Baltimore." *Sociological Forum* 35, no. 4: 1315–36.

Sonnie, Amy, and James Tracy. 2011. *Hillbilly Nationalists, Urban Race Rebels, and Black Power: Community Organizing in Radical Times.* Brooklyn, N.Y.: Melville House.

Spade, Dean. 2013. "Intersectional Resistance and Law Reform." *Signs* 38, no. 4: 1031–55.

Spade, Dean. 2015. *Normal Life: Administrative Violence, Critical Trans Politics, and the Limits of Law.* Durham, N.C.: Duke University Press.

Spade, Dean. 2016. "When We Win, We Lose: Mainstreaming and the Redistribution of Respectability." Kessler Award Lecture, Center for LGBT Studies, City University of New York Graduate Center, New York, December 9. https://www.youtube.com/watch?v=VNKTX6RqTlM&ab_channel=DeanSpade.

Spielman, Fran. 2020. "Chicago's 911 Emergency Center to Get a $75 Million Upgrade." *Chicago Sun-Times,* January 22. https://chicago.suntimes.com/city-hall/2020/1/22/21077637/chicagos-911-emergency-center-75-million-upgrade.

Spielman, Fran. 2021a. "City Council Eliminates Carve-Outs to Strengthen Welcoming City Ordinance." *Chicago Sun-Times,* January 27. https://chicago.suntimes.com/2021/1/27/22252689/immigration-chicago-city-council-eliminates-carve-outs-welcoming-city-ordinance-ice-undocumented.

Spielman, Fran. 2021b. "City Council Passes Mayor's 2022 Budget in Record Time." *Chicago Sun-Times,* October 27. https://chicago.suntimes.com/city-hall/2021/10/27/22748658/chicago-city-council-budget-vote-approval-lightfoot-federal-relief-funds-coronavirus-property-taxes.

Stacey, Judith. 1988. "Can There Be a Feminist Ethnography?" *Women's Studies International Forum* 11, no. 1: 21–27.

Steinmetz, George. 2005. "Return to Empire: The New U.S. Imperialism in Comparative Historical Perspective." *Sociological Theory* 23, no. 4: 339–67.

Stork, Joe, and Rene Theberge. 1973. "Any Arab or Others of a Suspicious Nature . . ." *MERIP Reports* 14: 3–13.

Stovall, David. Forthcoming. *Engineered Conflict: School Closings, Public Housing, Law Enforcement, and the Future of Black Life.* Chicago: Haymarket Books.

Strasser, Franz. 2016. "Sanctuary Cities under Threat by Donald Trump." BBC

News, December 22. https://www.bbc.com/news/av/world-us-canada-38370634.

Stuart, Forrest. 2016. *Down, Out, and Under Arrest: Policing and Everyday Life in Skid Row.* Chicago: University of Chicago Press.

Stuart, Forrest. 2020. *Ballad of the Bullet: Gangs, Drill Music, and the Power of Online Infamy.* Princeton, N.J.: Princeton University Press.

Stumpf, Juliet. 2006. "The Crimmigration Crisis: Immigrants, Crime, and Sovereign Power." *American University Law Review* 56: 367–419.

Stumpf, Juliet. 2013. "The Process Is the Punishment in Crimmigration Law." In *The Borders of Punishment: Migration, Citizenship, and Social Exclusion,* edited by Katja Franko Aas and Mary Bosworth, 58–75. Oxford: Oxford University Press.

Sudbury, Julia, and Margo Okazawa-Rey. 2009. "Introduction: Activist Scholarship and the Neoliberal University after 9/11." In *Activist Scholarship: Antiracism, Feminism, and Social Change,* edited by Julia Sudbury and Margo Okazawa-Rey, 1–16. Boulder, Colo.: Paradigm.

Sweeney, Annie, and Paige Fry. 2018. "Nearly 33,000 Juveniles Arrested over Last Two Decades Labelled as Gang Members by Chicago Police." *Chicago Tribune,* August 9. https://www.chicagotribune.com/news/breaking/ct-met-chicago-police-gang -database-juveniles-20180725-story.html.

Tanfani, Joseph. 2017. "Justice Department Rules Intensify Crackdown on Sanctuary Cities Like Chicago." *Chicago Tribune,* July 26. http://www.chicagotribune.com /news/nationworld/politics/ct-crackdown-sanctuary-cities-20170725-story.html.

Taylor, Flint. 2018. "The Power of Public Outrage: Laquan McDonald's Place in History." *Truthout,* October 10. https://truthout.org/articles/the-power-of-public -outrage-laquan-mcdonalds-place-in-history/.

Taylor, Flint. 2019. *The Torture Machine: Racism and Police Violence in Chicago.* Chicago: Haymarket Books.

Taylor, Keeanga-Yamahtta. 2016. *From #BlackLivesMatter to Black Liberation.* Chicago: Haymarket Books.

Tepper, Nona. 2019. "'Rowdy Funeral' Taskforce Comes to an End." *Wednesday Journal,* June 25. https://www.oakpark.com/2019/06/25/rowdy-funeral-taskforce -comes-to-an-end/.

Theodore, Nik. 2003. "Political Economies of Day Labour: Regulation and Restructuring of Chicago's Contingent Labour Markets." *Urban Studies* 40, no. 9: 1811–28.

Theodore, Nik. 2021. *Survival Economies: Black Informality in Chicago.* Chicago: Equity and Transformation. https://acrobat.adobe.com/link/track?uri=urn%3Aaaid%3A Ascds%3AUS%3Aab88350e-6838-4c09-b409-03dabf61f600.

Thom, Kai Chang. 2019. *I Hope We Choose Love: A Trans Girl's Notes from the End of the World.* Vancouver, B.C.: Arsenal Pulp Press.

Thrasher, Frederick. 1927. *The Gang: A Study of 1313 Gangs in Chicago.* Chicago: University of Chicago Press.

Tillman, Korey. 2022. "Carceral Liberalism: The Coloniality and Antiblackness of Coercive Benevolence." *Social Problems* 70, no. 3: 635–49.

Tresser, Tom, ed. 2018. *Chicago Is Not Broke: Funding the City We Deserve.* Chicago: CivicLab.

Unzueta, Tania A. 2017. *Expanding Sanctuary: What Makes a City a Sanctuary Now?* Phoenix, Ariz.: Mijente.

U.S. Attorney's Office, Eastern District of Michigan. 2013. "Naturalized U.S. Citizen Charged with Immigration Fraud for Failing to Disclose Terrorism Conviction." October 22. https://archives.fbi.gov/archives/detroit/press-releases/2013/naturalized-u.s.-citizen-charged-with-immigration-fraud-for-failing-to-disclose-terrorism-conviction.

U.S. Court of Appeals for the Sixth Circuit. 2015. "Defendant-Appellant's Brief on Appeal."

U.S. Court of Appeals for the Sixth Circuit. n.d. "Exhibit K to Motion of United States to Admit Foreign Evidence."

U.S. Department of Homeland Security. 2018. "If You See Something, Say Something." https://www.dhs.gov/publication/if-you-see-something-say-something-recognize-signs-infographic.

U.S. Department of Homeland Security. 2021a. "Guidelines for the Enforcement of Civil Immigration Law." September 30. https://www.ice.gov/doclib/news/guidelines-civilimmigrationlaw.pdf.

U.S. Department of Homeland Security. 2021b. "Interim Guidelines: Civil Immigration Enforcement and Removal Operations." February 18. https://www.ice.gov/doclib/news/releases/2021/021821_civil-immigration-enforcement_interim-guidance.pdf.

U.S. Department of Homeland Security. n.d. "Information Sharing Environment. Functional Standard. Suspicious Activity Reporting Version 1.5.5." https://www.dhs.gov/sites/default/files/publications/15_0223_NSI_ISE-Functional-Standard-SAR.pdf.

U.S. Department of Justice. 2017. *Investigation of the Chicago Police Department.* January 13. https://www.justice.gov/d9/chicago_police_department_findings.pdf.

U.S. Department of State. n.d. "Foreign Terrorist Organizations." https://www.state.gov/foreign-terrorist-organizations/.

U.S. District Court for the District of Minneapolis. 2010. "Search and Seizure Warrant: Case No. 10-MJ-00389." September 23.

U.S. Immigration and Customs Enforcement. 2017a. "ICE-Led Gang Surge Nets 1,378 Arrests Nationwide." May 11. https://www.ice.gov/news/releases/ice-led-gang-surge-nets-1378-arrests-nationwide.

Van Cleve, Nicole Gonzalez, and Lauren Mayes. 2015. "Criminal Justice through 'Colorblind' Lenses: A Call to Examine the Mutual Constitution of Race and Criminal Justice." *Law and Social Inquiry* 40, no. 2: 406–32.

Vargas, Robert. 2016. *Wounded City: Violent Turf Wars in a Chicago Barrio.* Oxford: Oxford University Press.

Vargas, Robert. 2020. "It's Time to Think Critically about the UChicago Crime Lab." *Chicago Maroon,* June 11.

Varsanyi, Monica. 2010 *Taking Local Control: Immigration Policy Activism in U.S. Cities and States.* Stanford, Calif.: Stanford University Press.

Varsanyi, Monica W., Paul G. Lewis, Doris Marie Provine, and Scott Decker. 2012. "A

Multilayered Jurisdictional Patchwork: Immigration Federalism in the United States." *Law and Policy* 34, no. 2: 138–58.

Venkatesh, Sudhir. 1997. "The Social Organization of Street Gang Activity in an Urban Ghetto." *American Journal of Sociology* 103, no. 1: 82–111.

Venkatesh, Sudhir. 2009. *Off the Books: The Underground Economy of the Urban Poor.* Cambridge, Mass.: Harvard University Press.

Vigil, James D. 2002. *A Rainbow of Gangs: Street Cultures in the Mega-City.* Austin: University of Texas Press.

Vigil, James D. 2003. "Urban Violence and Street Gangs." *Annual Review of Anthropology* 32, no. 1: 225–42.

Villazor, Rose Cuison, and Pratheepan Gulasekaram. 2018. "The New Sanctuary and Anti-sanctuary Movements Symposium: Immigration Law and Resistance: Ensuring a Nation of Immigrants." *University of California Davis Law Review* 52, no. 1: 549–70.

Villela, Priscila. 2021. "Transnational Policing Field: The Relations between the Drug Enforcement Administration and the Brazilian Federal Police." *Lua Nova* 114, no. 1: 105–36.

Vitale, Alex S. 2018. *The End of Policing.* London: Verso.

Wacquant, Loïc. 2009. *Punishing the Poor: The Neoliberal Government of Social Insecurity.* Durham, N.C.: Duke University Press.

Wacquant, Löic. 2011. "The Prison Is an Outlaw Institution." *Howard Journal of Criminal Justice* 51, no. 1: 1–15.

Walia, Harsha. 2014. "Sanctuary City from Below: Dismantling the City of Vancouver." *The Mainlander,* June 2. https://themainlander.com/2014/06/02/sanctuary-city -from-below-dismantling-the-city-of-vancouver/.

Walia, Harsha. 2021. *Border and Rule: Global Migration, Capitalism, and the Rise of Racist Nationalism.* Chicago: Haymarket Books.

Wang, Jackie. 2018. *Carceral Capitalism.* South Pasadena, Calif.: Semiotext(e).

Ward, Joe. 2021. "New 911 Service Allows Residents to Share Security Camera Footage with Police." *Block Club Chicago,* May 17. https://blockclubchicago .org/2021/05/17/new-911-service-allows-residents-to-share-security-camera -footage-with-police/.

War on Want. 2021. *Judge, Jury, and Occupier: Israel's Military Court System in the Occupied West Bank.* London: War on Want. https://waronwant.org/sites/default /files/2021-03/Judge_Jury_Occupier_report_War_on_Want.pdf.

Washington, Harold. 1985. Executive Order 85-1. Office of the Mayor, City of Chicago. http://www.chicityclerk.com/legislation-records/journals-and-reports /executive-orders.

WBBM Newsradio. 2020. "Arne Duncan's Idea: Another 'Defund the Police' Proposal, or Something Different?" September 23. https://www.audacy.com/wbbm780 /news/local/arne-duncan-suggests-variation-of-defund-police.

Weber, Rachel. 2015. *From Boom to Bubble: How Finance Built the New Chicago.* Chicago: University of Chicago Press.

We Charge Genocide. 2014. *Police Violence against Chicago's Youth of Color*. Chicago: We Charge Genocide.

We Charge Genocide. n.d. *Counter CAPS Report: The Community Engagement Arm of the Police State*. Chicago: We Charge Genocide.

Weizman, Eyal. 2017. *The Least of All Possible Evils: A Short History of Humanitarian Violence*. London: Verso.

Wells, Miriam J. 2004. "The Grassroots Reconfiguration of U.S. Immigration Policy." *International Migration Review* 38, no. 4: 1308–47.

Wernick, Miles N. 1991. "Pattern Classification by Convex Analysis." *Journal of the Optical Society of America A* 8: 1874–80.

Wernick, Miles N., and G. Michael Morris. 1986. "Image Classification at Low Light Levels." *Journal of the Optical Society of America A* 3: 2179–87.

Wexler, Chuck, Mary Ann Wycoff, and Craig Fischer. 2007. *"Good to Great" Policing: Application of Business Management Principles in the Public Sector*. Washington, D.C.: U.S. Department of Justice, Office of Community Oriented Policing Services.

Williams, Kristian. 2022. *Gang Politics: Revolution, Repression, and Crime*. Chico, Calif.: AK Press.

Willse, Craig. 2015. *The Value of Homelessness: Managing Surplus Life in the United States*. Minneapolis: University of Minnesota Press.

Wilson, David. 2009. "Introduction: Racialized Poverty in U.S. Cities: Toward a Refined Racial Economy Perspective." *Professional Geographer* 61, no. 2: 139–49.

Wilson, William J. 1996. *When Work Disappears: The World of the New Urban Poor*. New York: Alfred A. Knopf.

Wingfield, Adia Harvey. 2016. "Public Sociology When the 'Public' Is under Attack: Response to Hartmann." *Sociological Quarterly* 58, no. 1: 24–27.

Winston, Ali. 2015. "Chicago and Los Angeles Have Used 'Dirt Box' Surveillance for a Decade." *Reveal*, August 7. https://revealnews.org/article/chicago-and-los-angeles-have-used-dirt-box-surveillance-for-a-decade/.

Winston, Ali. 2016. "Marked for Life: US. Government Using Gang Databases to Deport Undocumented Immigrants." *The Intercept*, August 11.https://theintercept.com/2016/08/11/u-s-government-using-gang-databases-to-deport-undocumented-immigrants/.

Wolfe, Patrick. 2006. "Settler Colonialism and the Elimination of the Native." *Journal of Genocide Research* 8, no. 4: 387–409.

Yan, Jade. 2021. "Who Is the 'Community' in Community Policing?" *South Side Weekly*, March 31. https://southsideweekly.com/who-is-the-community-in-community-policing/.

Yuval-Davis, Nira. 1993. "Gender and Nation." *Ethnic and Racial Studies* 16, no. 4: 621–32.

Zuboff, Shoshana. 2019. *The Age of Surveillance Capitalism: The Fight for a Human Future at the New Frontier of Power*. New York: Hatchett Books.

Index

Andy Clarno is associate professor of sociology and Black studies and coordinator of the Policing in Chicago Research Group at the University of Illinois at Chicago. He is author of *Neoliberal Apartheid: Palestine/Israel and South Africa after 1994.*

Enrique Alvear Moreno is assistant professor of criminology and law studies at Marquette University.

Janaé Bonsu-Love is the director of research and advocacy at the National Black Women's Justice Institute.

Lydia Dana is a PhD candidate in sociology at the University of Illinois at Chicago.

Michael De Anda Muñiz is assistant professor in the Latina/Latino studies department at San Francisco State University.

Ilā Ravichandran is assistant professor in the area of legal studies at the University of Washington.

Haley Volpintesta is a PhD candidate in sociology at the University of Illinois at Chicago.

David Omotoso Stovall is professor of Black studies and criminology, law, and justice at the University of Illinois at Chicago. He is author of *Born Out of Struggle: Critical Race Theory, School Creation, and the Politics of Interruption.*

Tania Unzueta Carrasco is a recognized advocate in political and immigrant rights currently serving as national political director at Mijente.